THE
MEMORIAL
WAR BOOK

THE
MEMORIAL
WAR BOOK

As Drawn from Historical Records
and Personal Narratives
of the Men Who Served
in the Great Struggle

Major George F. Williams

ARNO PRESS
New York, 1979

Reprint edition 1979 by Arno Press Inc.

Manufactured in the United States of America

Library of Congress Cataloging in Publication Data

Williams, George Forrester, 1837-1920.
    The memorial war book.

    Reprint of the ed. published by Lovell Bros., New York.
    Includes index.
    1.   United States—History—Civil War, 1861-1865—
Pictorial works.   I.   Brady, Matthew B.,   1823 (ca.)-1896.
II.   Gardner, Alexander, 1821-1882.   III.   Title.
E468.7.W53   1979   973.7'022'2   79-13032
ISBN 0-405-12293-4

Reprinted from a copy in the
State Historical Society of Wisconsin Library.

THE
MEMORIAL
WAR BOOK

Copyright, 1866, by Frank B. Carpenter.

Abraham Lincoln

From Mrs. Lincoln.

Chicago, December 25, 1866.

Mr. Frank B. Carpenter.

My Dear Sir :—I write to you to-day to thank you
for the most perfect likeness of my beloved husband
that I have ever seen. . . . I have seen quite a
number of portraits of him, but none of them have
ever approached the truthfulness and perfection of
likeness of yours. , . . More we could not ask
or expect.

With sincere esteem,

MARY LINCOLN.

THE MEMORIAL
WAR BOOK

AS DRAWN FROM HISTORICAL RECORDS AND PERSONAL NARRATIVES OF THE MEN WHO SERVED IN THE GREAT STRUGGLE

BY

MAJOR GEORGE F. WILLIAMS

Author of " Bullet and Shell," " Lights and Shadows of Army Life," " Famous War Generals on Horseback," etc. Also Special War Correspondent with the Army of the Potomac, the Army of the James, the Army of the Shenandoah and the Army of the Cumberland ; also Correspondent in the Franco-Mexican War, the Guatemala-Nicaraguan War, and the Chili-Peruvian War, etc.

ILLUSTRATED BY

TWO THOUSAND MAGNIFICENT ENGRAVINGS

Reproduced largely from photographs taken by the

U. S. GOVERNMENT PHOTOGRAPHERS, M. B. BRADY AND ALEXANDER GARDNER,

Being the only original photographs taken during the war of the Rebellion ; making a

COMPLETE PANORAMA OF THIS GREATEST EVENT IN HISTORY

INCLUDING

PORTRAITS OF THE LEADERS AND COMMANDERS OF BOTH THE FEDERAL AND CONFEDERATE ARMIES AND NAVIES,

Giving, for the first time, a complete pictorial representation of the scenes, battles, and incidents, the whole forming a fitting memorial of the greatest event of the century, the most momentous of the ages.

NEW YORK

COPYRIGHT, 1894, BY

LOVELL BROTHERS COMPANY

A GROUP OF CONTRABANDS.

THE BRADY AND GARDNER PHOTOGRAPHS.

Most of the illustrations in this work are reproductions from the celebrated photographs made by M. B. Brady and Alexander Gardner, under authority of the U. S. Government.

These pictures are original photographs taken during the war of the Rebellion. It is more than a quarter of a century since the sun painted these real scenes of that great war, and the "negatives" have undergone chemical changes which makes it slow and difficult work to get "prints" from them. Of course no more "negatives" can be made, as the scenes represented by this series of war views have passed away forever. The great value of these pictures is, therefore, apparent.

Just how things looked "*at the front,*" during the great war, is, with the most of us, now, after the lapse of nearly thirty years, only a fading memory, cherished, it is true, and often called up from among the dim pictures of the past, but after all, only the vision of a dream. Artists have painted, and sketched, and engraved, with more or less fidelity to fact and detail, those "scenes of trial and danger," but all of their pictures are, in a greater or less degree, imaginary conceptions of the artist. Happily our Government authorized, during the war, skillful photographers to catch with their cameras the reflection, as in a mirror, of very many of those thrilling and interesting scenes.

These views vividly renew the memories of our war days. The camp, the march, the battle-fields, the forts and trenches, the wounded, the prisoners, the dead, the hurriedly made graves, and many other of these once familiar scenes are photographically portrayed and perpetuated. These are not sketches or imaginary scenes, but are the *original photographs* taken on the spot.

The wonderful progress in the art of photo-engraving enables the publishers of this work to place these inestimable records in permanent form, and thus preserve them for future generations for all time.

The original war views reproduced in this work are selected from more than 6,000 negatives taken by the Government Photographers, M. B. Brady and Alexander Gardner, during the years 1861, 1862, 1863, 1864 and 1865, by special arrangements with the owners, The War Photograph and Exhibition Company, of Hartford, Conn., from whom we have obtained their exclusive use.

CUB RUN, VA.

PREFACE

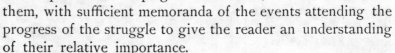

There are many good histories of the great American Civil War in existence, but they all dwell on a multitude of minor details, and devote much space to critical analysis of the military strategy displayed by the opposing commanders. The mind of the reader is therefore fatigued and confused, for he obtains only an imperfect conception of the precise scope of the various campaigns.

The actual scenes in the Civil War have not yet been described in a way to afford a realistic idea of their character, although participants have given, from time to time, abundant individual narratives of what they saw and did. The object of this MEMORIAL WAR BOOK is to present a series of pen pictures drawn from material that has never before been collected. It is not a history of the war, but a series of personal reminiscences of stirring adventures and lifelike descriptions of campaigns and battles, as the soldier saw them, with sufficient memoranda of the events attending the progress of the struggle to give the reader an understanding of their relative importance.

While the regular course of events will be closely followed, it has been the aim of the author to avoid all technicalities, and describe the heroic deeds of Federal and Confederate soldiers, just as the men, themselves, would do. But the greatest value of this work is the absolute fidelity of the illustrations. Many were taken during the progress of hostilities, and are now given to the public for the first time. These were not sketches, but actual photographs, and can never be reproduced, as the originals are rapidly fading. The reader is thus placed on the very ground where the historic scenes of the war occurred, and is carried back to a period of thirty years ago.

G. F. W.

MAJOR GEORGE F. WILLIAMS.

SLAVE PEN, ALEXANDRIA, VA.

Slave Pen, Alexandria, Va.   This is a view of one of the buildings known as Slave Pens, in which negroes were kept as chattels, while being bought and sold.   The building to the left was fitted up with iron cells, or cages, where the slaves were confined.

THE MEMORIAL WAR BOOK

HARPER'S FERRY.

CHAPTER I.

ORIGIN OF THE NATIONAL QUARREL

It is customary to speak of the war between the secession and loyal States of America as "The War of 1861-5," because men remember only the campaigns, battles and sieges which marked the period of actual hostilities. But the quarrel between the Northern and Southern sections of the country had been gathering force and bitterness, long before the battering of Fort Sumter by Confederate cannon finally broke the seal of peace, and lighted the torch that was to blaze with such dreadful fury for four long and weary years.

The American Civil War may be justly characterized as a national punishment for the sin of slavery committed by the Fathers of the Revolution, when they threw off England's yoke, and established a Free Republic. The very existence of negro slavery in one section of the country, while it was strictly forbidden in the other and larger part of the national territory, was calculated to create a feeling of antagonism which, though latent, must have, sooner or later, resulted in quarrels on public policy. The South believed that the

GENERAL WINFIELD SCOTT.

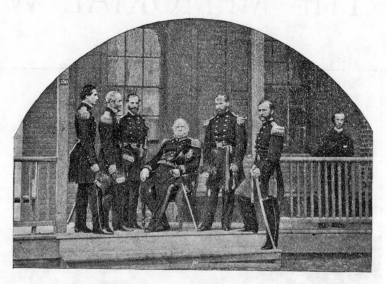

GENERAL WINFIELD SCOTT AND STAFF.—FROM AN OLD PHOTOGRAPH.

successful cultivation of cotton, tobacco and rice could only be profitably carried on by the perpetuation of slavery. The North, on the other hand, was receiving the best blood of Europe, for immigration had not then descended to its present low strata, and as this intelligent and educated labor came in search of personal, religious and political freedom, it set its face against the continuance of servile labor.

The historical student will, of course, find other causes of dispute. The South depended upon the products of the soil and demanded free trade, while the North, deriving its wealth from manufacturing interests, insisted on a protective tariff. There was also the divergent ideas, among great political leaders, concerning the bond that bound the States together. One class of statesmen held the belief that the Federal Union was a league, which could be terminated at will by any one of the States. Another class clung to the doctrine that the Federal Union meant a national government for the whole nation, and therefore no State could secede without the consent of all the others. This was a question that could only be settled by an appeal to arms. Meanwhile the tide of emigration flowed into the Territories and so rapidly developed them that the South sought to further extend the system of slavery. Thus the quarrel grew more and more bitter.

MONTGOMERY BLAIR, POSTMASTER GENERAL.

CHARLES A. DANA, ASSISTANT SECRETARY OF WAR.

HANNIBAL HAMLIN,
VICE-PRESIDENT.

1. SIMON CAMERON, SEC'Y OF WAR.
2. GIDEON WELLES, SEC'Y OF NAVY.
3. SALMON P. CHASE, SEC'Y OF TREASURY.

5. WILLIAM H. SEWARD, SEC'Y
   OF STATE.
6. CALEB B. SMITH, SEC'Y OF
   THE INTERIOR.
7. EDWARD BATES, ATTORNEY
   GENERAL.

VICE-PRESIDENT HAMLIN AND MR. LINCOLN'S FIRST CABINET.

FLAG OF THE CONFEDERACY.

Jefferson Davis

As is always the case among politicians, many expedients were resorted to, by both Northern and Southern statesmen, in hopes of bridging over the chasm that was hourly widening between the sections. The Missouri Compromise was the most famous of these futile efforts to cure a national disease by superficial treatment. When Louisiana was purchased from France in 1803, the present State of Missouri formed a part of the acquired territory. In 1820 Missouri sought admission into the Union as a State, when it was proposed by the North to prohibit slavery in the new State. After much angry and bitter discussion it was finally agreed that Missouri should have slavery, but the system was to be prohibited in all the United States territory north and west of the northern boundary of Arkansas. But this so-called compromise did not settle the question, it only postponed the final result. The South succeeded, in 1850, in having Congress pass the Fugitive Slave bill, by which owners were authorized to seize their slaves who might escape into a free State. Despite the latent anger of the Northern people, the South pursued its settled policy, and in 1854 secured the repeal of the Missouri Compromise. This repeal, or cancellation, was contained in the act organizing

RESIDENCE OF JEFFERSON DAVIS, MONTGOMERY, ALA.

territorial governments for Kansas and Nebraska, giving the people therein the sole right to decide for themselves the question of excluding or adopting slavery. By this unwise step Congress placed State Rights in the ascendant, and the South found itself at liberty to extend its peculiar and hateful institution all over the Southwest.

Seven years after, the civil war began.

In 1856, the young Republican party entered the field of national politics, with

ALABAMA RIVER AT MONTGOMERY, ALA.

Fremont as its standard bearer, while petty warfare was going on in Kansas, the "Border Ruffians" of Missouri, creating scenes of unparalleled violence. The election of Buchanan to the Presidency did not assist the South in its efforts to extend slavery. In 1857, Judge Taney decided that a slave owner might carry his slaves with him into any State of the Union. Dred Scott was a slave belonging to a surgeon in the army who took him to Fort Snelling, subsequently returning to Missouri. Suit being brought to secure Dred's freedom, Judge Taney affirmed that Congress could not forbid slavery in the Territories, and that "negroes have no rights which the white man is bound to respect." This decision, and the expression just quoted, was bitterly resented by several Northern States, which passed Personal Liberty Laws giving freedom to every slave entering within their borders. In 1859, John Brown's raid at Harper's Ferry gave the first outward sign that the blood of the people was growing hot with sectional passion and prejudice. From the day that Brown and his associates made their foolish and ill-timed demonstration, civil war, in all its horror and deformity, was

Alexander H. Stephens.

S.R.MALLORY.

L.P.WALKER.

J.H.REAGAN.

R.M.T.HUNTER.

R.TOOMBS.

J.P.BENJAMIN.

C.G.MEMMINGER.

PRESIDENT OF THE SENATE AND FIRST CONFEDERATE CABINET.

FOUNTAIN AND STREET IN MONTGOMERY, ALA.

only a question of time. John Brown had been for some time prominent in the guer-

CITY OF CHARLESTON, S. C., FROM TOP OF ORPHAN ASYLUM.

illa warfare of Kansas. He acquired the title of "Ossawattomie" from the desperate defence he had made at that place against a force ten times stronger than his own. Finally conceiving the idea that he was the destined liberator of the Southern slaves, he decided to strike a blow in their behalf. His theory was that the negroes

John A. Dix

were ripe for revolt, and only needed a leader, overlooking the fact that their servile habits and mental ignorance unfitted these slaves for the task he would set them at.

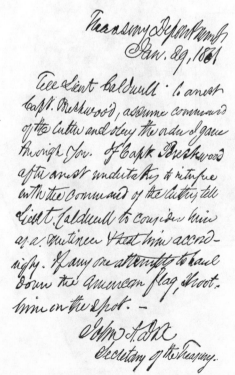

FACSIMILE OF GENERAL DIX'S FAMOUS DISPATCH.

CITY OF CHARLESTON, S. C., FROM TOP OF MILLS HOUSE.

The town of Harper's Ferry occupies the tip of a tongue of land formed by the junction of the Potomac and Shenandoah rivers. There is a break in the range of Blue Ridge mountains just there forming the pass through which the waters of these two rivers flow, the town nestling at its foot. On the one hand rises Bolivar Heights, on the other stands the beetling cliffs of the Maryland Heights, so that the town is completely shut in by the mountains which hold it in so close an embrace. The water power afforded

THE PALMETTO FLAG.

by the sudden fall in the current of the Shenandoah River, led General Washington, in 1794, to select it as the United States Armory for the manufacture of army muskets. The influx of so many skilled workmen made the town very prosperous for over half a century, but when the fierce tide of civil war surged through its steep streets, the place fell into wreck and decay, the historic memories associated with it now alone making it an object of interest to the tourist.

It was the presence of the Government armory at Harper's Ferry, that led John Brown to select it as the base of his ill-advised scheme of operations. Mustering together a force of twenty-one men, who he armed with pikes and muskets, he descended upon the town from Hall Town Heights. Seizing possession of the arsenal, he arrested the chief inhabitants of the town and held them as hostages. To his surprise, the slaves did not flock to his standard, while the State militia rapidly assembled, and the National Government proceeded to

CAPTAIN ABNER DOUBLEDAY.

LT. JEFF. C. DAVIS.
ASST. SURGEON S. W. CRAWFORD.

CAPT. J. G. FOSTER.
LT. TRUMAN SEYMOUR.

ANDERSON'S OFFICERS.

CASTLE PINCKNEY, CHARLESTON HARBOR.

take action. Two days after his seizure of the town, a body of United States marines attacked the arsenal in which Brown had entrenched himself. The conflict was brief, but bloody. Brown received six wounds, his two sons were killed, with eight of their companions. Being surrendered to the State authorities, Brown was tried for treason, convicted and hanged. From that day the South began its preparations for war.

The election of Abraham Lincoln to the Presidency solidified the slave States in their determination to secede and create a new Confederacy. The political campaign of 1860 was the bitterest that has ever been seen in this Republic. The Republican party nominated Lincoln and Hamlin on the platform that slavery should be prohibited in the Territories. The Constitutional party selected Bell and Everett, demanding the Union of the States and the enforcement of the laws. The Democratic party was split in two by the demands of the South. One section asserted that slavery should be extended by Congress into the Territories, and nominated Breckinridge and Lane. The other section held that the people of the Territories should decide the question of slavery for themselves, and selected Douglas and Johnson as their standard bearers.

As soon as it was known that Lincoln had carried the Electoral College, the South took action, the State of South Carolina leading the way by passing an ordinance of secession on December 20, 1860. The States of Mississippi, Florida, Ala-

MAJOR ROBERT ANDERSON.

"STAR OF THE WEST" ENTERING CHARLESTON HARBOR.

bama, Georgia, Louisiana and Texas followed in January and February, 1861. President Buchanan took the view that neither he nor Congress had the right to coerce a State, so no Federal action was taken against the revolting members of the sisterhood.

Despite the fact that it was known in the "Loyal" States that active preparations for war were going on in the South, the Northern people refused to believe that the men of the South seriously contemplated actual hostilities.

Even when "The Confederate States of America" entered into a formal compact at Montgomery, Ala., on February 4, 1861, and seized all Federal property within their borders, not a single step towards war was taken by the remaining States. At that moment the question of State rights stood on debatable ground. Many prominent Northern men believed in it, and prophesied that if fighting did ensue, it would not be along Mason and Dixon's line, but in the cities of the North. In the South it was believed that the people of the

North would submit to a disruption of the Union rather than face the horrors of war. There was a cloud in the minds of all men, but it was suddenly lifted by a cannon shot in Charleston harbor.

BOMBARDMENT OF FORT SUMTER FROM MORRIS ISLAND, CHARLESTON HARBOR, S. C.

CHAPTER II.

THE FIRST BLOW AND ITS CONSEQUENCES.

When the Confederate States formally organized its government by electing Jefferson Davis to be President and Alexander H. Stevens as Vice-President, nearly all the regular army and naval officers of Southern birth voluntarily surrendered their Federal commissions, and placed themselves at the command of their respective natal States. But while the military property in the hands of these officers also passed into the possession of the Confederacy, there were two strategic points which were retained by loyal officers. These were Fort Pickens, at Pensacola, Fla., and Fort Sumter, in Charleston Harbor. The former was saved to the North by its commander, Lieutenant Slemmer, the latter by Major Robert Anderson. Both officers recognized the importance of their positions, so fortified themselves and refused to surrender to the Secession powers.

Major Anderson gathered his eighty officers and men, and, leaving the comfortable quarters in Fort Moultrie, after spiking its guns, he removed the garrison to Fort Sumter. This structure had been erected on a rip-rap formation in the centre of the harbor, and being built of solid granite masonry, was deemed almost impregnable. Anderson, being isolated, soon found his food supplies running short, and it seemed only a question of time when he

FORT MOULTRIE AFTER BOMBARDMENT.

FORT MOULTRIE, SULLIVAN'S ISLAND, CHARLESTON HARBOR, S. C.

must surrender. Buchanan's Secretary of War, Floyd, asked the President's permission to withdraw Anderson's command from Charleston Harbor, and failing to obtain it, resigned and joined the Confederates.

For three long and weary months Anderson held possession of Sumter. Though he was treated as an enemy by Governor Pickens, of South Carolina, and could see the Secession batteries gathering shape on Morris Island, the Major refrained from firing a shot. The steamer Star of the West was sent to revictual Anderson and arrived at Charleston on the morning of January 9, 1861. As the steamer passed up the channel a masked battery on Morris Island opened fire, as did also the guns of Fort Moultrie. Captain John McGowan at once hoisted the American ensign, but it was not respected, and cannon balls continued to pass over and around the Star of the West, until she was compelled to put to sea again.

This was the first act of the Civil War that was to cost so much blood and treasure. It was hailed with delight by the people of the seceding States, while the people of the North were surprised at its audacity. Anderson rightly considering the act as one of war, sent a flag of truce to Governor Pickens, and demanded an apology and the right to receive supplies. The Governor refused to make the one or grant the other, so Anderson prepared for actual hostilities.

When Anderson hoisted the old Stars and Stripes over the battlements of Fort Sumter, the South Carolinians seized Castle Pinckney, Fort Moultrie and Fort Johnston. They found the guns all spiked, but contented

FORT JOHNSON, JAMES ISLAND, S. C.

This was in January, 1861. Lincoln's term would not begin for ten weeks yet. Secretary Dix did not hesitate, for in a moment of inspiration he sent a telegram ordering the arrest of Captain Breshwood as a mutineer, adding the memorable words: "If anyone attempts to haul down the American flag, shoot him on the spot." The telegraph being in the hands of the insurgents at both Mobile and New Orleans, the order was intercepted and did not reach the agent of the Treasury Department, and the cutters were both lost to the Government.

President Lincoln took his seat on March 4, 1861, and Vice-President Hamlin convened the United States Senate. Mr. Lincoln selected for his Cabinet William

INTERIOR VIEW, SHOWING HOW WALLS WERE STRENGTHENED.

themselves in hoisting over Castle Pinckney a Palmetto flag. It was the first Secession flag hoisted over a fortification belonging to the United States. Subsequently another ensign was designed.

The temper of the North at this critical juncture of affairs is clearly shown by the action of John A. Dix, who had become Secretary of the Treasury under Buchanan, whose cabinet was rapidly crumbling to pieces as the Confederate conspiracy grew to a head. When Dix went into office, the cutter Lewis Cass was at Mobile, and the Robert McClelland at New Orleans. He at once ordered their commanders to return with their vessels to New York. Both officers procrastinated, and Captain Breshwood finally and deliberately refused to obey.

INTERIOR VIEW ON PARAPET.

FORT SUMTER.—Interior Views.

H. Seward as Secretary of State; Simon Cameron, Secretary of War; Salmon P. Chase, Secretary of the Treasury; Gideon Welles, Secretary of the Navy; Caleb B. Smith, Secretary of the Interior; Montgomery Blair, Postmaster General and Edward Bates as Attorney General. Charles A. Dana was appointed Assistant Secretary of War; Caleb B. Smith was succeeded, in 1863, by John P. Usher as Attorney General, and Simon Cameron, in 1862, by Edwin M. Stanton, known afterwards as the great War Secretary.

FLAG OF SUMTER.

Jefferson Davis and Alexander H. Stephens had been inaugurated as President and Vice-President of the Confederate States, on the 18th of February, 1861, at a Convention held at Montgomery, Ala., assembled there on February 4th, 1861, the vote being declared by R. M. T. Hunter, President of the Senate, who subsequently succeeded Robert Toombs as Secretary of State. Mr. Davis selected for his Cabinet, Robert Toombs, Secretary of State; Leroy Pope Walker, Secretary of War; Stephen R. Mallory, Secretary of the Navy; Cristopher G. Memminger, Secretary of the Treasury; Judah P. Benjamin, Attorney General and John H. Reagan, Postmaster General. A per-

VIEW OF PARAPET, FORT SUMTER.

manent constitution was adopted March 11, 1861, and the Capitol removed to Richmond on the 18th of February, 1862, when the Provisional Congress expired and the new Constitution went into operation.

The excitement throughout the North and the South had now reached such a pitch that no man knew what the next day would bring forth. One of the first acts

SEA VIEW, FORT SUMTER.

of Lincoln was to take up the question of Fort Sumter. He was advised to tell Anderson to make terms with the enemy, but firmly refused, ordering instead an armed expedition for the relief of the beleagured garrison. This squadron consisted of the steamer Baltic, the sloops-of-war Pohowtan, Pawnee and Pocahontas, the cutter Harriet Lane and

some tugs. It started on April 9. On that day, four years after, General Lee and the Army of Northern Virginia surrendered at Appomattox Court House.

The Confederates were well informed regarding all movements of the Federal Government, and on April 11, General P. G. T. Beauregard sent a formal demand to Major Anderson to surrender with the honors of war. Ignorant of the fact that his Government had sent the relief squadron, Anderson agreed to do so by noon of the 15th, should he not receive contrary instructions before that time.   But while these negotiations were in progress, the Pawnee and the Harriet Lane arrived off Charleston harbor, the Confederates therefore, prepared to bombard Fort Sumter and resist the passage of the United States vessels.   Anderson was immediately notified that the Confederate batteries

would open fire in an hour, and the first shot flew through the air at twenty minutes past three o'clock on the morning of April 12, 1861.

A gun was fired on James Island as a signal, and a shell went whizzing through the darkness and exploded over the Fort.   Battery after battery opened fire, until nearly sixty heavy guns and mortars were in action.   For two hours the bombardment continued, the

Confederate gunners soon getting their range, the solid shot and loaded shells striking the granite walls of Fort Sumter with terrific force, some of the mortar shells falling inside the enclosure, and there exploded.

PRESIDENT LINCOLN AND GEN. MCCLELLAN IN MCCLELLAN'S TENT.

From Original Photo, by Brady and Gardner.

One December evening, during the siege of Petersburg, in 1864, the writer was sitting before the camp fire with Major-General Samuel W. Crawford, who then commanded the Pennsylvania Reserves, or *Third Division of the Fifth Corps, Army of the Potomac.* The

General was the surgeon in Anderson's command in Fort Sumter, and as we sat enjoying the pleasant warmth of our little fire, while listening to the rapid exchange of Meade's guns in Fort Hell, not many hundred yards distant, he gave me the following description of the scenes in Fort Sumter:

"When Major Anderson received the note telling him that we were about to be attacked, he summoned all of his officers, and announced that the Fort must be held at all hazards. Then the garrison flag was hoisted, the postern gate was closed, and the sentinels on the ramparts were withdrawn. Our men were instructed to not leave the bomb proofs unless ordered to do so. It was a strange scene as we stood round the

BURNING OF GOSPORT NAVY YARD, NORFOLK, VA., APRIL 21, 1861.

gallant old man, and listened to his brave words. We knew well enough that Bob would defend the Fort to the last, and every officer and man was with him in that determination.

"I shall never forget the sound of that first shell as it passed over our heads, because there had been so long a period of silence during the days we were waiting for orders from Washington. Both you and I have heard a good deal of cannonading since then, but it was really awful to hear those secession guns playing the devil's tattoo on our stone walls. We knew that Beauregard's men had been busy fortifying Morris Island and Fort Moultrie (they must have had a nice time of it cutting out the spikes we left in the guns when we abandoned them), but we had no idea that anything was being done on Sullivan's Island. The Confeds had cleverly masked their operations by pulling up brushwood and other stuff, so you may imagine our surprise when seventeen ten-inch mortars and nearly thirty columbiads opened from that point. The bombardment must have been going on over two hours, when we went to breakfast. We had as yet made no reply to the enemy's fire. One thing struck me at the time, and I often think of it, and that was the cool

REAR ADMIRAL H. PAULDING.

indifference displayed by our enlisted men. They sat down and ate their breakfast quietly and unconcernedly, though their ears were being deafened by the roar of the attacking guns and the detonations of the bursting shells.

"By the time breakfast was over it was broad daylight. Old Bob Anderson then divided the force into three reliefs. The first was commanded by General Doubleday, who was then a Captain; I was given the second relief, and Lieutenant Snyder, a splendid officer, took the third. We had plenty of gunpowder, but it was nearly all loose, so we had to put the off-reliefs to work preparing the cartridges. Doubleday fired his first gun a few minutes after seven o'clock, and I think he pulled the lanyard himself. At least, that is my impression. We soon had all of our guns at work, and kept them going until nearly noon. It would have delighted your heart to see how our men peppered Fort Moultrie, for we could see that our shot and shell were making gaps in the embrasures. But after all there was very little use in our replying to the enemy's fusilade, for they had heavier

HAMPTON, VIRGINIA.

metal, and were able to give a cross fire that battered us unmercifully. Still, you know, it's not in human nature to stand idle, while being pounded, so we went on banging away right merrily.

"We soon found that the enemy were trying to disable our barbette guns, and so well did they serve their pieces that not only were our barbette batteries silenced, but even a large section of the stone parapet was carried away by the huge solid shots that hit it. As you can readily understand, we had to abandon the ramparts and confine ourselves to the two lower tiers of guns, which were, of course, protected by casements. As I said before, Abner Doubleday's first gun was fired a little after seven o'clock, and our response to the furious storm of shot and shell that the Confederates had poured down on old Sumter, lasted until almost noon. You must remember that it was raining like everything, and there was a dense fog resting on the water of the harbor, and the

WILLIAM SPRAGUE, GOVERNOR OF RHODE ISLAND.

smoke from the opposing guns did not help matters much. Anderson wanted to know how things looked outside, so I offered to ascend the parapet and take an observation, as they say at sea. There has been a lot of foolish stuff written and printed about my doing this, but it was not so terrible a thing, and, of course, any other officer in

RUINS OF NORFOLK NAVY YARD.

the garrison would have done it. The fact that I was the "doctor," as surgeons are familiarly termed, made the boys say I was a trump. That was all there was to it.

"Well, I went to the parapet, and you may imagine my surprise and delight when I discovered, through the rolling fog and blinding rain, three vessels lying outside the bar. Though the confounded secession guns were still going, and I suppose some of their shells were falling pretty close to me, I know you will believe me when I say that I, for the moment, forgot all about the bombardment. As all of the vessels were flying the Stars and Stripes, I knew they must have come to our relief, so down I ran and told the Major. I can see his pale, worn face at this very moment. You know it had been a terrible strain for Bob Anderson. He is a Kentuckian and one of the few Southern regulars who remained true to the flag. Well, his eyes brightened, and he and Doubleday went up and satisfied themselves that I was not mistaken. As we afterwards learned, these vessels were the Pawnee, carrying ten guns, the saucy little Harriet Lane and her five guns, and the transport Baltic, carrying two hundred recruits. But they could not cross the bar, because Beauregard had removed all the buoys.

"I have heard that they signalled us, but we didn't know it at the time, and even if we had we could not have returned it, for our flag was all tangled up in the lanyards that had been cut by fragments of shell. During the afternoon the Confederate fire grew heavier, and some of the shot entered our embrasures, causing several slight casualties by flying splinters, so I had something to do in addition to my gunnery work. Our men behaved splendidly, though they were exhausted by fatigue, for, you know, eavy artillery practice is very

SCUDDING ALONG UNDER FULL SAIL OFF FORTRESS MONROE.

severe. The barracks got on fire from shells, brick and stone flew in all directions, smashing windows and making a tolerably good average of everything. We kept up our fire pretty well all day, but the supply of cartridges began running so low we were reduced to about six guns.

"At nightfall, the Major passed the order to stop firing and close port-holes. Then a guard was set, and the remainder took a rest. The rain storm continued all night, and so did the Confederate bombardment, though they contented themselves in sending us a shell every ten minutes or so. That was an awfully weary night, for very few of us got any sleep beyond a brief nap or two. The men were quite cheerful, though they knew that only one ration of rice remained. We knew relief was at hand, and supposed it would come after daylight.

"When the sun rose on the following morning it was in an unclouded sky, and Beauregard's guns opened on us with increased violence. He evidently hoped to blow us and old Sumter into the water together, for not only did the missiles fly faster and faster, they also sent us red-hot shot, which set all the woodwork on fire and filled the interior of

S. S. PENSACOLA, OFF ALEXANDRIA, VA.

the Fort with smoke. We had put the fire out four times the previous day, but now the entire barracks and officers' quarters were in a blaze and we had to let them burn, for you can't put out flames very well, when red-hot shot are flying round your heads. At least, we didn't try. Our only fear was about the magazine. If that had caught fire and exploded, I would not be here with a couple of silver stars on my shoulders. But the magazine escaped, though the main gate was burned, and the sally port could no longer be defended.

"As you may well suppose, our situation had then become desperate. There we were, penned up in a crumbling stone fort, no rations, no cartridges, and in the centre of a vortex of cannonading that was growing more and more severe. The intense heat and the smoke from the burning buildings was our worst trouble, while the crashing of the shells, the roaring of the flames, and the falling of masonry made one believe the end of all was soon coming. A little after the noon hour, our flag-staff was shot away, and down came the flag. As it fell, Lieutenant Hale caught it, else the grimy old banner might have been burned. Lieutenant Synder carried it to the ramparts, when that Police Sergeant Hart, who had come from the North with despatches for the Major, sprang on the sandbags. He and Mason Lyman fixed up the shattered staff, and the flag was again flying.

"While this was going on a curious thing happened. A man suddenly appeared at one of the lower embrasures (how he got there through the storm of shot and shell has always been a mystery to me), and he waved a white handkerchief that he had stuck on the point of a sword. He announced himself as Colonel or General Wigfall, I forget which it was, and asked for Major Anderson. Being admitted, for he seemed frightened to death, Captain Foster, Lieutenants Mead and Davis and myself met him. The man then said he was a messenger from General Beauregard, who wanted to stop any further bloodshed. This sounded funny to us, for no one man in the entire garrison had been seriously hurt, and, as you may

AQUEDUCT BRIDGE, POTOMAC RIVER.

AQUEDUCT BRIDGE, POTOMAC RIVER.

remember, there was only one man killed during the entire affair, and that was occasioned by the premature discharge of the fifteenth gun, while the details were saluting our flag before it was finally hauled down. 'Your flag is down,' said Wigfall, 'Sumter is in flames; let us stop this firing.' Captain Foster very coolly told the fellow that the flag had been shot down, but it was up again all right, and as to the firing, Fort Sumter wasn't doing much of it just then.

"Wigfall was terribly excited, and holding out his sword and handkerchief, asked Lieutenant Davis to hold them out of the embrasure. Forgetting the ridiculousness of expecting half a dozen batteries to stop firing at the wave of a small rag of a handkerchief, Davis indignantly refused. Wigfall then said he would wave it, and as we consented, he sprang into the next embrasure and waved

HEADQUARTERS OF GENERAL M'CLELLAN, ALSO USED BY GENERAL BEAUREGARD,
AT FAIRFAX COURT HOUSE, VA.

his absurd signal several times.   But the Confederate guns went on banging away, and one of the solid shot happened to come into the embrasure just at that moment.   If ever there was a man scared out of his seven senses, Wigfall was that individual.   He retreated in disorder, and Corporal Bringhurst picked up the fellow's sword and waved the handkerehief, but soon found he was making a fool of himself, so abandoned it. Captain Foster had gone to find the Major, and there we stood looking at the strange messenger, who seemed to have fallen from the clouds.   Wigfall then suggested that a white flag be hoisted on the ramparts, and Lieutenant Davis said it might be done if

GREAT FALLS ON POTOMAC RIVER.

Major Anderson so ordered.   Now it had not occurred to any of our party that if Beauregard had sent the messenger he would have first ceased firing.   But we were all excited, as you may well imagine, and did not stop to think.

"Major Anderson then appeared, when Wigfall again announced himself as one of Beauregard's aides.   He insisted that his General wanted to put an end to hostilities, and told the Major that, having defended his flag so nobly, he ought to be content and surrender.   'Come,' said Wigfall, 'let us stop this terrible work.   On what terms, sir, will you consent to evacuate?'   The Major eyed Wigfall curiously for a moment, and then said, 'General Beauregard knows my terms.   You may tell him that, instead of waiting for the 15th, I am ready to go now.'   Wigfall seemed delighted, and retired, saying that he would go and tell Beauregard.   After he had disappeared, the Major ordered a white flag to be hoisted over the ramparts, but the Confederate guns did not stop their infernal fusilade, which struck us as very odd.

"By-and-by three or four Confederate Colonels came over and asked the meaning of the white flag. Then it was learned that nobody knew of Wigfall's visit, and that he had no authority and had acted on his own responsibility. The old man—Major Anderson, I mean—was mad enough when he found that he had been fooled by a crazy madcap, and announced that the flag should come down immediately. A discussion then followed, and the Major finally decided that he would evacuate the Fort on the condition that his garrison be permitted to march out with its arms and company property, all private property and the privilege of saluting and retaining our flag. The gray-coated Colonels' Pryor, Chestnut, Lee and Miles, retired and the firing ceased; we put out the fire and got a little fresh air. But Beauregard didn't want to lose the glory of taking our flag, and there were discussions with the different deputations that came, still Bob was as firm as a rock, so he got all he demanded. The following morning was Sunday, and we marched out bag and baggage, and went on

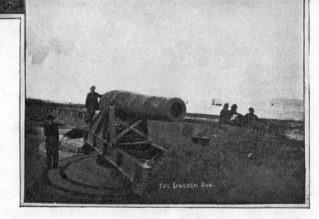

FORTRESS MONROE.

board the steamer Clinch. On Monday we were put on board the Baltic and sailed for New York. Despite our humiliation at being compelled to surrender a Government fort, there were some amusing incidents. After reserving sufficient gunpowder for the salute we were to pay our flag, in the morning our men very quietly rolled all the remaining barrels out of the magazine to the wharf and poured the contents into the waters of Charleston Harbor. The consequence was, that when the Confederates started in to salute their flag of secession, they found the magazine destitute of powder, and were compelled to send to one of their ports for a supply. By that means we escaped being in the presence of a Confederate salute.

Thus the first blow was struck, the veil had been rent, but the City of Charleston had to pay dearly for her share in precipitating the war. Those April days of glory and delight were to be atoned for in a way that her people will long remember. But when the secession flag rose on the walls of Sumter, none thought of the future, none dreamed that in exactly four years, the struggle would end in humiliation, defeat and ruin. The South was indeed terribly punished; but, thank God, that's all over now. As was natural, Beauregard received promotion, and was ordered to a more important command in the Confederate army, which had already begun to take visible shape and strength.

PANORAMA OF THE FORT.—FORTRESS MONROE.

CHAPTER III.

THE NORTH AND THE SOUTH RUSHING TO ARMS.

While the bombardment of Fort Sumter was in progress, the people in the North were kept fully advised, for the authorities of Charleston placed no restrictions on the telegraph wires, so special newspaper correspondents were kept busy.   When the first shot was fired, special editions were issued by newspapers in every Northern and Southern city.   In less than an hour, business was almost entirely suspended.   The busy wheel traffic of New York, Boston, Philadelphia and other Northern ports, disappeared almost by magic, while thousands of excited men filled the streets.

In the South, the news that Fort Sumter was being bombarded caused a tumult of joy, though there were men there who experienced a feeling of horror at the firing on the Stars and Stripes.

CITY OF RICHMOND, VA.

They were in the minority, however, and remained silent. To the Southern people, the surrender of Anderson and his garrison, though a perfectly honorable one, was taken as an indication that the "Yankee" President, as they already called Lincoln, would not fight. They discovered their error in that respect after a bitter experience.

The Northern people received the news with indignation and amazement. The cloud of doubt was removed, and as it rolled away, political party prejudice was swept aside by a gale of loyal passion. Men who had disputed on the question of Secession and State Rights the day before, now silently clasped hands, for the fact that the national ensign had been fired on, simplified the question. Before Beauregard's guns began bombarding a fort belonging to the United States, argument was all very well. But Confederate shot and shell now made it a matter of war.

MAJOR-GENERAL BENJAMIN F. BUTLER.

On that memorable Friday, Saturday and Sunday, the people of the two sections seemed possessed by a species of madness. The South believed that its independence had

RUINS OF ARSENAL, HARPER'S FERRY.

been already gained, but the North became fixed in its determination not to let the Seceding States go without a struggle. On Sunday, April 14, when news came to the

"Loyal" States that Fort Sumter had been evacuated, a torrent of anger swept through the hearts of the citizens. Preachers in the pulpits spoke of the nation's shame, and prayed for the safety of the Government. The streets of the cities, towns and villages were thronged, and a cry for vengeance was on every lip.

The course of public events now became rapid. President Lincoln issued his proclamation on April 15, calling upon the several States to furnish their quota of seventy-five thousand men, who were to serve for a period of two years. He also summoned Congress in extra session to decide on measures for pub-

THE PARADE GROUND.

THE SALLY PORT.

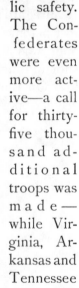

lic safety. The Confederates were even more active—a call for thirty-five thousand additional troops was made — while Virginia, Arkansas and Tennessee joined the Confederacy, thus widening the scope of the impending conflict. Inside of twenty-four hours after Lincoln's proclamation, the uniformed militia of New York, Connecticut, Massachusetts, Rhode Island, Pennsylvania and New Jersey were under arms, and some of them already on the march for Washington, while recruiting offices were opened throughout the North for

EXTERIOR OFFICERS QUARTERS.

FORTRESS MONROE.

LONG BRIDGE, WASHINGTON.

the formation of volunteer regiments. The youthful Governor of Rhode Island, William Sprague, not only ordered out his entire force of State militia, but marched at their head as commander-in-chief. The Northern War Governors, as they are called, were all very energetic men, but Sprague was the only one to leave his state on service. So eager was the response that the Government received three hundred thousand men. The volatile enthusiasm displayed by those volunteering on both sides of the sectional lines, was pathetic in its utter ignorance of the actual severity and cruelty of active military operations. As the new levies departed for the scene of war, tender-hearted women shed tears at seeing their loved ones go away in the garb of soldiers, but they did not then realize the extent of sorrow and suffering that was to be endured by them. As for the men, they looked upon the war as a sort of picnic, for neither side appreciated the fighting qualities of their opponents. Several ironclad railroad batteries were constructed for the protection of workmen employed in rebuilding the Baltimore and Ohio Railroad, but they were finally abandoned as useless. It was supposed that the war would last only a few weeks, and it took several months of hard campaigning before either Federals or Confederates understood the gigantic character which the struggle had assumed.

When the North began arming its troops, the National Government discovered that Buchanan's Secretary of War, Floyd, had denuded the armories and sent immense quantities of cannon, small arms and ammunition into the States that led the way to secession. Though somewhat crippled by this treasonable act, the armies were filled with extra workmen, and their productive capacity trebled, so that muskets were received by the troops a week after they had been finished and proved. The prompt arrival of troops in

Maryland and Delaware saved those two States for the Union, while Kentucky and Missouri were finally retained in the column of loyal States. General Benjamin F. Butler took possession of Baltimore with a few regiments of soldiers, a mob having attacked the Sixth Massachusetts militia on April 16, killing five or six men while the command was passing through the city *en route* for Washington. This important step was followed by another—Butler's seizure of Fortress Monroe at the mouths of the James and York Rivers, which form the Virginia Peninsula. He was accompanied by several volunteer regiments. The residents of Newport News and the village of Hampton fled, and their slaves flocked into the Federal lines, being declared by the Massachusetts lawyer-general to be contraband of war, thus giving them their freedom.

Lieutenant-General Winfield Scott was summoned to Washington by President Lincoln, to take command of the hastily-raised army. The old veteran of the war of 1812 and the hero of

E. E. Ellsworth

the Mexican War felt that the infirmities of age would prevent his assuming the fatigue of another series of active campaigns. He gave the President the benefit of his military knowledge and experience, but suggested the promotion of deserving regular and volunteer officers to the rank of Major-General. McDowell, McClellan, Patterson, Banks, Butler, Dix, and others, were immediately raised from the rank of Major and Captain, and placed in command of separate bodies of national troops.

Among the old regular officers selected for promotion was William Tecumseh Sherman. President Lincoln tendered him the position of Brigadier-General in the regular

MARSHALL HOUSE, ALEXANDRIA, VA.

army. He declined it and asked to be appointed to no higher place than Colonel —on the ground that in his opinion there were other men who were better fitted for the high command than he. His modesty was overruled and he lived to make the famous March to the Sea.

One of the official pets of General Scott was Colonel Robert E. Lee, his chief ofstaff. His name was presented to President Lincoln for a Major-General's commission, but he was a Virginian by birth and believed he owed allegiance to his State. Just at that juncture Virginia seceded from the Union, and Lee unhesitatingly cast his fortunes with the Confederacy. After acting for some time as

OLD CAPITAL PRISON, WASHINGTON.

military adviser to Jefferson Davis, he was made a Lieutenant-General, and will be known in history as the ablest commander the Confederacy possessed.

The fate of Fort Sumter had led the Northern people to almost forget Fort Pickens in Pensacola Bay. But, like Anderson, Lieutenant Adam J. Slemmer held his ground in the face of a gathering hostile force. He was in better shape, however, than Anderson had found himself, because Buchanan had so far overcome his timidity as to send Slemmer provisions and a small force of men. Having lost Fort Sumter by delay, the Government rescued Fort Pickens by starting a relief expedition from New York on April 7. The fleet carried four hundred and fifty soldiers, under command of Colonel Harvey Brown, who also had sixty-nine horses and a large supply of war ammunition and food supplies.

FOREST HALL PRISON, WASHINGTON

These were safely landed, as was an additional force which arrived while the first was going ashore. Lieutenant Slemmer was relieved of his command, and on his arrival in the North was promoted to the rank of Major and ultimately became a General.

It was soon perceived that the Confederates aimed at the capture of the City of Washington, for their troops were assembling under Beauregard at Warrenton, Va., in the shadow of the Blue Run Mountains. Every effort was, therefore, made to counteract this movement. Then the Confederates advanced to Manassas, only thirty miles from the Federal Capital. Despite the headlong eagerness of the South to precipitate the conflict, Lincoln hesitated to invade Virginia. But when he saw, from the windows of the White House, the light of the Confederate camp-fires, he gave the final order, and on May 23 the Federals advanced across the Potomac River, seizing possession of Arlington Heights and the town of Alexandria.

When the troops marched over the Long Bridge across the Potomac, the First New York Fire Zouaves entered Alexandria, Va. As Colonel Ephraim Ellsworth, who had raised the regiment by request of President Lincoln, passed up the main street, he saw a Confederate flag flying from the staff of the Marshall Hall. Ellsworth was a mere boy in years, but an ardent soldier. He came into prominence by organizing an independent corps of Zouaves in Chicago, which he drilled to such perfection that they created a furore throughout the Middle and New England States.

Forgetting in his youthfulness that it was not the business of a Colonel to go to a roof and capture an enemy's flag (a Corporal or Sergeant should have been sent), he left the head of his column and ascended the stairs. Getting possession of the hated flag, Ellsworth descended with it in his arms. James W. Jackson, the

BRIGADIER-GENERAL A. J. SLEMMER.

proprietor of the hotel, was an ardent secessionist, and resented the intrusion of the boy Colonel. Waiting deliberately in the lower hall with a loaded musket, he shot Ellsworth, who fell dead on the spot. The Fire Zouave Colonel had been accompanied by Corporal Francis E. Brownell, who at once levelled his own weapon and avenged his loved commander by killing Johnson.

The military operations of the opposing forces were now assuming definite shape. General Irwin McDowell was in command of the Federal army, confronting Beauregard, who stood at Manassas. General Patterson occupied Harper's Ferry with a strong body of United States volunteers, and faced General J. E. Johnson, who held possession of the Shenandoah Valley with a formidable Southern army. General George B. McClellan had crossed the Ohio River into West Virginia and taken up a strong position. General Benjamin F. Butler held Fortress Monroe and Hampton Roads. General John B. Magruder commanding the Confederate forces on the York River and protecting Yorktown. The hounds of war were in leash, waiting to be loosed and tear one another.

Meanwhile, many startling events had occurred. Gunpowder Bridge, between Baltimore and Philadelphia, had been burned by a mob, thus destroying the line of communication with Washington. Gosport Navy Yard, opposite Norfolk, Va., was destroyed on April 20. This was one of the largest and best appointed naval stations in the United States. It had cost over twelve millions of dollars. Commodore Charles S.

RELIEF OF FORT PICKENS, SANTA ROSA ISLAND, PENSACOLA BAY, FLA., BY U. S. FLEET, APRIL 17, 1861.

McCauley was in command, but was under the influence of his subordinate officers who were preparing to join the Confederacy. When Sumter fell, the Confederate Government began preparations for seizing the Gosport Yard, as it contained two thousand cannon and there were ten ships of war lying idle. It being evident that McCauley's procrastination would lead to the loss of the Yard, he was relieved by Captain Paulding, who with an extra force of marines, and Massachusetts Volunteers, was ordered to defend the Yard. Finding this to be impossible in face of the Confederate demonstrations, Paulding set fire to the ships and property, his command evacuating in the attending confusion. But the flames failed to do the work, and all the munitions of war fell into the hands of the Confederates, with one or two of the war vessels

J. E. Johnston

that were not distroyed. They also seized Fort Norwalk with three hundred thousand pounds of powder and immense quantities of loaded shells placed in its magazine by Secretary Floyd.

Those were busy April days. Fort Sumter fell on the 14th, and Harper's Ferry was abandoned by the United States troops on the 18th. The Governor of the State of Virginia decided to take possession of the Ferry and military stores in the arsenal. Lieutenant Jones had only a corporal's guard at his command, so when he learned that the Virginia militia were advancing on him, he set fire to the buildings and retreated across the bridge. The citizens followed the little party, but were halted by a threat from the Lieutenant that if they advanced he would give them a volley of musketry.

Jones and his party reached Hagerstown, in Maryland, the following morning after floundering all night through the canals, swamps and creeks which are abundant along the eastern shore of the Upper Potomac.

The war had now begun in dreadful earnest. Men stared at one another in mute amazement, for the recruiting drum was in every street, the martial tread of regiments had pushed aside the peaceful commerce of cities and towns. A few days

GRIGSLEY'S HOUSE, CENTREVILLE, USED AS HEADQUARTERS BY
GENERAL JOSEPH E. JOHNSTONE, C, S, A.

before it was the frothy talk of politicians that agitated the people, now the roar of cannons and the vengeful muttering of angry musketry must continue the argument to the bitter end. Brother stood against brother, the father against son. All knew that the contest must be a terrible one, but neither the people of the North or South shrank from the prospect. With the Con-

EXAMINING PASSES AT GEORGETOWN FERRY.

federate flag flying over the battered walls of Fort Sumter, Gosport Navy Yard in flames, and the arsenal at Harper's Ferry a mass of blackened and distorted ruins, the men and women on both sides of the sectional line saw that there could now be no definite peace until it was won at the point of the sword.

HARPER'S FERRY AFTER EVACUATION.

THE FIRST BATTLE OF THE WAR FOUGHT AT BIG BETHEL, JUNE 10, 1861.

CHAPTER IV.

HOW THE BATTLE OF BIG BETHEL WAS FOUGHT AND LOST.

The war between the North and the South will always be famous for the immense area of territory covered by its operations, but in the early part of 1861 it was believed, on both sides to the bitter quarrel, that a battle or two was all that would be necessary to decide the question whether the Union of the States was to stand, or be forever broken. This belief was another proof that the people of the two sections had entirely mistaken the character of their opponents, but under its influence the South devoted all its energies to the task of seizing the City of Washington, and consequently the scope of the Federal operations was confined to the East. All the Western States were responding nobly to the call for troops, but there seemed to be no present occasion for massing them in preparation for battle. They, however, held Kentucky and Missouri for the Union.

With Federal armies at Harper's Ferry, in West Virginia, at Fortress Monroe and at Fairfax Court House and Centerville, the people of the North became impatient, and demanded a forward movement which, to them, meant a total annihilation of the rebellious troops in the field. The stay-at-homes in the South also fretted, for they wanted the question settled, that planting might go on. It has always been very easy for men who have never donned the uniform to plan campaigns on paper with the certainty of victory at their close, but the task is vastly different when it comes to practice, not theory.

The first engagement between Northern and Southern soldiers occurred on June 3, 1861, at Philippi Junction, in Western Virginia. It was a very small affair, compared with

MULE TRAIN CROSSING BROOK.

THE FIGHT AT PHILIPPI, VA., JUNE 3, 1861.

subsequent battles, but it made a decided sensation at the time. Brigadier-General T. A. Morris, having ascertained that the Confederates, under Colonel Porterfield, had taken possession of the Junction, thus imperilling the Baltimore and Ohio and Northwestern Railroads, he sent two columns from Grafton, consisting of detachments from the First Virginia, the Sixth, Seventh and Ninth Indiana, Fourteenth and Sixteenth Ohio, with a section of Burnett's Ohio Battery. One column was under Colonel B. F. Kelley, of the First Virginia, and the other under Colonel E. Dumont, of Indiana. Dumont was the first to arrive, Kelly being misled by his guide, but the Federal movement was a complete surprise. A curious fact connected with this affair was that the first shot was fired by a woman, who discharged her revolver at Colonel F. W. Lander, of General McClellan's staff, as he rode past her house. The Confederates were driven from their camp by Burnett's guns, and Colonel Kelley, coming up just then, pursued them through the streets. Kelley was dangerously wounded by a bullet in his breast, and he was made a Brigadier-General. But, like all such preliminary affairs, it had no result, for both Confederates and Federals abandoned the Junction. Exactly one week after the Philippi skirmish, June 10,

COL. B. F. KELLEY.

General Butler ordered a movement on Big Bethel, but it ended in defeat for the Federals. The importance of the battle was greatly exaggerated, the South being highly elated, while the North was depressed, but it had no real influence on the final result. As the author carried a musket at Big Bethel, he intends to describe it as he and his comrades saw it, not as historians imagine it was like.

The Fifth New York Regiment had been in camp near Hampton Creek, behind Fortress Monroe, for over four weeks, and the boys were growing tired of so much drill. Colonel Abram Duryee had secured, as his second in command, Gouverneur K. Warren, a distinguished engineer officer of the Regular Army, who subsequently rose to the rank of Major-General and an important command. Duryee had been Colonel of the famous New

SIGNAL TOWER NEAR CAMP OF 14TH N. Y. INFANTRY.

York Seventh, he was a military student and a drill master. We were drilled by company every morning after breakfast, and before dinner time, and in the afternoon even at dress parade. It was hard work, but it strengthened our muscles and improved our health, but the boys did not like it all the same. They had come out to fight and everybody was anxious to see a battle. God knows, we saw enough of them before the war ended.

A rumor got into circulation about the 3d or 4th of June that something was going to happen. Old soldiers know how readily camp rumors are started, but in this case it was founded on fact. We knew that a Confederate force was entrenched on a creek on the York Road, some ten or fifteen miles from Fortress Monroe, and a few had seen the works. Captain Judson C. Kilpatrick, of our Company H, who subsequently became one of the famous cavalry generals of the war, had come out to our picket post one morning and selecting me and two other Zouaves, took us on a reconnaissance. I remember thinking it great fun at the time, and did "Kil.," but it was really a silly proceeding, as the General confessed one day when we talked about it a year or two after. We got

FAIRFAX COURT-HOUSE.

to about a mile from Little Bethel and saw a pile of freshly turned earth, and then we also turned and reached our lines as wise as when we started.

Sunday, the 9th of June, passed off quietly. There had been no drills, and the dress parade was a success. Then when the men were falling in for supper, the orderly sergeants announced that when bedtime came, every man was to sleep in his shoes and socks, and our belt boxes were filled to their full capacity with buck and ball cartridges.

"We are going to march in the early morning," said the Sergeant, "so get all the sleep you can, boys."

If our officers had intended to keep the men wide awake they could not have devised a better plan, for scarcely an eye was closed during the night. We conversed in whispers, while lying on our blankets in the tents, until we could stand it no longer. One by one we gathered around the company fires so that when orders came about eleven o'clock to get under arms they were quickly obeyed. There was very little ceremony in getting in line and we were soon moving up the road. There was no moon, but the stars gave sufficient light to keep us from tumbling over each other. Word was passed down the column to maintain silence, as the movement was intended to be a surprise. It turned out to be one, but we had it, not the enemy. The boys kept very mum for nearly half an hour as if they really believed that the Confederates could hear their voices at the distance

RAILROAD BATTERY FOR THE PROTECTION OF WORKMEN ON THE B. & O. RAILROAD.

of ten or twelve miles. But human nature could stand it no longer and we chatted among ourselves, but in subdued voices.

There was one thing connected with the war that was peculiar and it continued throughout its progress. The men in the ranks always had their own ideas how operations should be carried on, and criticised their commanders in the most fearless manner. The first thing we wanted to know was what other troops were going to help us, for while we naturally supposed that our regiment was, of course, to do the principal part of the fighting, we expected that there would be enough to go round. First the men asked the Sergeants, the latter pestered the Captains and they in turn pumped the Colonel. Then the news drifted back that the Albany regiment under Colonel Townsend, the New York Steuben Rifles under Colonel Bendix, and a part of the First Vermont and the Third Massachusetts had been ordered out. Where these commands were just then, no one knew. Somebody said they must be following us, others had heard that there were more troops on ahead.

We trotted along in high spirits, for we were all young and in splendid health, and now that a real battle was to be fought, the war would soon be over and there need be no more of those vexatious drills. Alas, one half of the fine fellows who were marching through the sand that warm Sunday night, laid down their lives on many a field during the next two years. I remember that I thought it was curious to see how hungry everybody about me had become, for scarcely a man in the ranks was not munching biscuits as he plodded along, encumbered by knapsack and musket.

As we subsequently ascertained, the movement was under the direction of Brigadier-General Pierce, of Massachusetts, and it had been planned that we Zouaves were to make a detour and being the first to start, finally reach the rear of the Confederate force. The

GENERAL JOHN MAGRUDER, C. S. A.

regiments under Colonels Bendix and Townsend were to act as reserves, while the Massachusetts and Vermont boys were to make the direct attack. No doubt it looked well on paper, but somehow it did not work quite as "old Contraband Butler," as we youngsters nicknamed him, thought it would. We had started at midnight and marched along until after two o'clock, yet saw no sign of either the front or the rear of the Confederate line, and it looked as though some mistake had been make in the road.

This idea seemed to be the correct one, for just then there was an awful crash of musketry in our rear. The order to halt was given and then there was another volley, so about face we went and on the double quick started for the supposed scene of battle. In about half an hour we were halted by a staff officer who said that the Albany regiment, while coming up on one road, had struck that occupied by the Steuben Rifles. The Dutchmen mistook Townsend's command for the Confederates and without waiting for orders, opened fire. Of course the Albany men were not going to be shot at for nothing, so they pitched into the Germans. By this time the Vermont and Massachusetts Volunteers had also fallen back and the entire force now lay massed in the main road.

There was no use expecting to make the movement a surprise, after the awful mistake that had cost nearly a dozen lives. I had forgotten all about being hungry by this time, and as we sat beside the road waiting for orders, I noticed that there seemed to be considerable confusion. Horsemen galloped to and fro; groups of officers consulted, yet nothing was done until almost daylight, when we were re-formed and set in motion. It was then announced that as General Pierce had come out for a fight he wasn't going back without having one. We all agreed that this was very good of the General, for it showed he had the right kind of stuff in him. None of the boys wanted to see camp without having had a brush with the enemy, for we longed to fire our muskets and kill somebody.

As the sun rose news ran along the column that Little Bethel had been abandoned by the advance line of the Confederates, which had fallen back on the main body at Big

Bethel. There was never a happier set of young fellows as were our Zouaves on learning this, for it showed that the enemy was afraid of us, and it would be all the more glorious to whip the whole force at once. But as it turned out we did nothing of the kind.

We made quite an imposing appearance by daylight and we were glad to find that artillery had been included in our offensive strength. All knew that Lieutenant Greble

W. T. Sherman

was a gallant officer, and it was certain he would do good service. As we reached the straggling village of Little Bethel, a line of skirmishers was thrown out, and the column pushed forward. There was no opposition, for the place was empty. For no good reason that I could see, orders were given to burn the village, and it was soon in flames. Our regiment had scarcely passed through the street, when dropping shots were heard in advance, and it was evident that we had at last struck General Magruder's forces. Then a sudden discharge of cannon broke the silence, and a shell flew over our heads. There was considerable bowing and scraping to the visitor, for we were not yet used to such things. As the skirmishers fell back and reported a masked battery, our line was formed. The German regiment, with the Vermont and Massachusetts men, filed off to the right of the road into a thick clump of woods, the Fifth and the Albany regiment were sent across some open fields into an apple orchard, while Greble and his battery occupied the road, to reply to the Confederate cannon that was now working rapidly. I noticed that at that time all their shells flew high, probably intended to worry our supports, though we had none. We were told that the Zouaves were to flank the enemy.

DEPARTURE FROM THE OLD HOMESTEAD.

The Confederates had taken up a position on the left bank of the Black River, and had thrown up earthworks guarding the road, and, as we found out to our cost, there was a line of intrenchments along the edge of a swamp which prevented our doing any flanking. They had some eighteen hundred men, while we had fully three thousand, but as they possessed twenty pieces of heavy ordinance

GROUP OF SOLDIERS, N. Y. 71ST.

and an entrenched position, the Confederates had decidedly the best of it. As we reached the outskirts of the swamp a volley of musketry burst from the banks of green boughs which concealed the enemy's breastworks and a few men fell. I could also hear volleys on our right, the Dutchmen having opened again without seeing anything to shoot at. Lieutenant Greble now began a rapid fire, and so well did his men serve their guns that the Confederates clung to their earthworks. While we were blazing away Lieutenant Colonel Warren came up and angrily stopped us, and we were ordered to lie down.

The cannonading by the opposing guns went on for nearly two hours, and we began wondering if there would be anything for the infantry to do. A change of position was then made, Colonel Townsend being sent to the right, and the first and second New York Regiments, who had come up unexpectedly, were sent somewhere out of sight. I afterwards learned that General Pierce wanted them to get to the rear of Magruder's position. Then orders were given to advance and charge. Away we went, pell mell, and forced our way close up to the breastworks, and I thought we were doing splendidly when orders came to fall back, which we did very unwillingly, though nearly all of our ammunition was gone. There was now a great deal of confusion, as Colonel Townsend had retreated before a part of his own command, mistaking it for the enemy. As we entered the road the Germans passed us, nearly every man swearing guttural oaths.

My company happened to be detached from the line, and as we struck "across lots" to join the regiment, we came to the spot where Lieutenant Greble's battery was standing. Nearly all the gunners were disabled and the Lieutenant lay dead in the dust, his head having been shattered by a cannon ball. We then discovered a party of Confederates creeping up, evidently hoping to capture the guns. We held them back with the few cartridges left in our pouches, and Greble's body was carried to the rear, while the Germans assisted in saving the guns. What struck me as very odd was that none of our boys seemed dazed or much excited, and from that day to this I

MAJOR THEODORE WINTHROP, KILLED AT BATTLE OF BIG BETHEL.

have been a firm believer in constant drilling in camp, for it keeps the men together while using their weapons in dead earnest.

Well, there is little more to tell, except an extraordinary act of reckless bravery which cost the perpetrator his life. While the several regiments were being mustered together in anticipation of falling back altogether, Major Theodore Winthrop, General Butler's military secretary, and an old member of the New York Seventh, coolly walked down the road, and, going beyond the battery position, took a look at the enemy's line.

CAPTAIN JUDSON C. KILPATRICK,

BRIG.-GENERAL EBENEZER W. PEIRCE,
COMMANDING THE FEDERAL TROOPS AT BIG BETHEL.

Several shots were fired, and he fell dead where he stood. An effort was made to get his body, but the men were called back, though it was subsequently sent in by General Magruder. When we reached camp, it was announced that sixteen men had been killed, fifty-three wounded and five were missing. Both General Butler and General Pierce were bitterly censured, but the soldiers were praised to the skies for bravery, though, as subsequent experience taught us, we had not done much to brag of. That was the end of the first pitched battle of the war, but it was soon forgotten in the presence of more stirring events.

Now that so many years have elapsed since these early battles were fought, it seems remarkable that the Americans, North and South, though inexperienced in the art of war,

COLONEL TOWNSEND.　　　　　LIEUT. JOHN TROUT GREBLE,　　　　COLONEL WARREN.
　　　　　　　　　　　　　　　(KILLED IN THE BATTLE AT BIG BETHEL.)

LIEUT.-COL. G. K. WARREN.　　　　　COLONEL BENDIX.　　　　　COLONEL ABRAM DURYEE.

rapidly learned how to conduct themselves in the field. It should be remembered that when the guns in Charleston Harbor woke the angry dogs of war, very few of the men who went to the front really knew just what army life was like. The merchant closed his ledger, and the lawyer threw aside his brief, to enter the ranks. The clerk exchanged his yardstick for a ramrod, the printer his shooting-stick for a musket. Men who had handled the rammer in foundries took it to the muzzle of a cannon, the carpenter gave up his saw and plane for the sabre of a cavalryman. The farmer boy threw away his pitchfork for a bayonet, and learned that shooting birds in the orchard was vastly different from being shot at by long lines of death-dealing muskets. Yet in the short space of three or four months these Northern and Southern Americans so quickly adapted themselves to a soldier's life, that they became the admiration of the entire civilized world.

BATTLE OF RICH MOUNTAIN, THE FEDERALS COMMANDED BY GEN. W. S. ROSECRANZ, THE CONFEDERATES BY GEN. JOHN PEGRAM.

CHAPTER V.

THE BATTLE OF BULL RUN AND SUBSEQUENT FEDERAL ROUT.

Nothing more was done for a month after the Big Bethel affair, greatly to the astonishment of the people on both sides of the conflict. Then General McClellan, with from fifteen to twenty thousand men, struck the enemy at Rich Mountain in West Virginia, having previously had two severe skirmishes at Bealington and Carrick's Ford, the latter occurring in a heavy rain storm. The battle between the forces of Garnett and McClellan was a hot one while it lasted. It occurred on July 10, and the Confederates were defeated with a loss of four hundred men, killed and wounded. They also lost all their cannons, ammunition, tents and camp equipage. General Pegram added to the disaster by surrendering to General Morris, on July 14, Garnett having been killed. General Cox, meanwhile, repulsed Wise's forces in the Kanawha Valley, and captured

MAJ.-GEN. JOHN PEGRAM, C. S. A.

MAJ.-GEN. W. S. ROSECRANZ.

Barboursville. The result was that the Confederates evacuated Harper's Ferry and the greater part of Western Virginia.

Then began the movement in the Virginia Valley. On July 15, General McDowell received instructions to attack the Confederates at Manassas Junction, while General Patterson, who commanded in the Shenandoah Valley, was ordered to prevent Joseph E. Johnston, the Confederate General, from reinforcing Beauregard. He failed to do this and the result was disastrous to the Federal arms.

PICKET POST, BULL RUN.

On the morning of July 16, McDowell's troops moved forward. A large portion of his command were ninety-day men and their time had almost expired, and this fact explains

GENERAL BEAUREGARD'S HEADQUARTERS.

part of what happened. The force under Beauregard was a little over twenty-five thousand, while McDowell had fully thirty thousand, the two largest armies in the field at that time. The Federals were in four divisions under Brigadier-General Tyler, Colonels Heintzelman, Runyon, Miles and Hunter. The Confederates fell back from Fairfax Court House, which elated the Federals. On July 18, there was a hot fight at Blackburn's Ford, which was brought about by Tyler trying to march straight to Manassas. The Confederates, however, had carefully laid their plans, and Tyler was met by a strong force which compelled him to retire with loss. McDowell then discovered that his long line

CONFEDERATE FORTIFICATIONS AT MANASSAS JUNCTION.

STONE HOUSE, WARRENTON PIKE, BULL RUN

of attack would not do, so fell back to Centreville, some of his troops, meanwhile, leaving him on the expiration of their term of service. On Sunday, July 21, McDowell began what is known in history, on the Federal side, as the Battle of Bull Run, the Confederates calling it Manassas. The list of leading officers on both sides was a remarkable one, for they all became famous in subsequent campaigns. There was Beauregard, Longstreet, Wheat, "Stonewall" Jackson and Johnston on the Confederate side, while McDowell, Sherman, Heintzelman, Miles, Burnside, Keyes, Ayres, Howard and Hunter were on the Federal lines. Here is a description of the movement and battle as given me in 1863, by a regular officer who participated in it, and subsequently rose to high rank:

GENERAL W. H. MORRIS.

"You must remember that when McDowell was getting ready, he was sadly hampered by the Washington people. Of course you know what I mean. The President knew about as much about real war as that contraband of mine who is rubbing down your horse. Lincoln is a great man and he has learned a

GENERAL R. S. GARNETT, C. S. A.
(KILLED AT THE BATTLE OF CARRICK'S FORD.)

great deal more about strategy since Bull Run than even some of us Generals are willing to give him credit for. He had dear old Scott at his elbow, who listened to a lot of young fellows not long out of West Point, and between them they sadly bothered McDowell. Besides that, we were all pretty green, for none of us had ever seen thirty thousand men under arms on a single field. Even Sherman himself, or Howard, or Ayres will tell you that we felt somewhat awed by the big army we belonged to.

"But you want me to tell you about Bull Run. Well, Tyler's division, with Ayres' and Carlisle's batteries, moved out along the Warrenton turnpike road. They were to get to the Stone Bridge by four o'clock and open a feint attack, while Hunter and Heintzelman were to make the direct assault, they being sent on a wide detour through a wood road to cross Cub Run and come out somewhere near Sudley Church, which would bring them in Beauregard's rear. Miles was left in reserve at Centreville, then our extreme left, while Keyes watched the Manassas road. It was a very pretty plan and would have succeeded, had not Johnston and "Stonewall" Jackson spoiled

MAJOR-GENERAL ROBERT PATTERSON.

our game. The death of the latter at Chancellorsville was a big loss to the Confederates.

"It is a curious fact that Beauregard contemplated taking the offensive on the same day, but we were ahead of him, If we had known that Johnston's advance column had already joined Beauregard, our hopes of success would not have run so high. Tyler began in time, and made so good an impression with his artillery, that the Confederates believed it was the main body of our troops, but they soon ascertained that McDowell intended mischief somewhere else, so there was a change of position. The divisions under Hunter and Heintzelman encountered unexpected difficulties and were delayed, so when they attacked, our line was not in good shape and it encountered a force greater than either Hunter or Heintzelman could present.

"It was McDowell's misfortune to be chosen for high command at the very beginning of the war. He is a brave and capable officer, but the people of the North demanded too much

THE BULL RUN.

when we first entered the field, so because Mac could not whip forty or fifty thousand men with less than twenty, he was turned down, and hasn't had much of a show since. We made a handsome appearance on starting out, and I never saw men in better spirits. As you may remember, the movement began at two o'clock in the morning. The men had not yet learned the necessity of caution, and the Volunteer officers did not see any harm in the boys building huge campfires before starting out. The sudden increase of light along our line about midnight, of course aroused the attention of the Confederates, and they were quite ready for us when we began. There was another fact that should be remembered. The South had been organizing and drilling for this war, long before you or I voted for Lincoln. Beauregard had been in command for months before our levies were raised, and he had under him the choicest blood of the South. No wonder that, being on their own ground, and in double our strength,

MAJOR-GENERAL J. MC DOWELL.

and better drilled in brigade and division movements, they won the day. It was a costly victory, though, as we now know, for it so intoxicated the South that the scope of these hostile operations was immediately spread over a vast area of country.

"I am not trying to give you a description of the battle of Bull Run, for like most soldiers, I saw only my own part, but now that we have seen so much service, and lost so many different commanding generals, I can perceive how and why the day was lost. It

HEADQUARTERS OF GENERAL J. MC DOWELL, ARLINGTON HOUSE.

was not for want of bravery. No men fought better than ours, until it was discovered that we were really fighting three times our strength. McDowell intended to turn the Confederate left and seize the Manassas Gap Railroad which lay in their rear. This was to prevent Johnston joining Beauregard. He had, of course, no idea that by Patterson's blunder the junction had already been made. The real fighting began when Burnside's brigade, which led Hunter's column, reached some open fields. Evans, who was opposing him, was well posted, and opened a sharp, destructive fire, cutting up the Second Rhode Island and killing Slocum, their Colonel. While Burnside was staggering in front of these fierce volleys, Colonel Edward Porter's brigade began forming, while Griffin's battery took position and he made his guns bark to some purpose. Evans was reinforced by

STONE BRIDGE, BULL RUN.

General Bee, who was killed during the day, which began turning the tide of battle. Then Sykes and his Regulars were hurried up and matters grew more even, the batteries of Captains Griffin and Ricketts doing most excellent service with shell and grape at short range, but the fighting was really of a desperate character, though the Confederate artillery having a better position cut us very badly. It was then that Slocum fell and Hunter was carried off the field wounded.

"I began to think that we were outnumbered, when Sherman's brigade came up, having forced its way across the Stone Bridge. Just then I was surprised to see the enemy breaking away. Sherman's men, the Thirteenth, Sixty-ninth and Seventy-ninth New York Militia, being fresh, were ordered to pursue the Confederates who were now falling back towards Sudley's Springs road. You must now understand that we had successfully carried out McDowell's plan by turning Beauregard's left. We had uncovered the Stone Bridge and pushed the enemy back for over a mile. But the worst was to come, for as the Confederates reached the plateau they found Jackson's brigade standing there, so quickly reformed, and met us with a blinding

GENERAL BARNARD E. BEE, C. S. A., KILLED AT BATTLE OF BULL RUN.

volley. We made several charges, the Fire Zouaves acting splendidly for they saved Griffin's and Rickett's batteries, but the enemy grew stronger instead of weakening and we had to fall back.

COL. MILES.   COL. HEINTZELMANN.   COL. HUNTER.

"You must remember that by these operations McDowell had got only thirteen thousand men into battle, none of the reserves having crossed Bull Run. That was his error, for while Beauregard and Johnston were bringing fresh men to the front,

STONE CHURCH, CENTREVILLE.

BVT. MAJ. GENERAL E. B. TYLER.

MILL AND HOTEL AT SUDLEY SPRINGS.

McDowell failed to see the necessity for sending in Miles, Burnside (who had been withdrawn), or Keyes. Had they come up, the result might have been different. Then came the final blow. We had been fighting for several hours when the Confederates pushed forward all their reserves and made a fierce attack on our right, finally turning our flank and getting into our rear. I shall not soon

BVT. MAJOR-GENERAL R. B. AYRES.

MAJOR-GENERAL E. D. KEYES.

forget the scene. Shells were coming in from all points of the compass and men were falling every moment. It was evident that we were outgeneraled, and our men became panic-stricken, there was a sudden break in the line and the next minute terrible confusion. Heintzelman was furious, and as he chanced to have a few Regular Cavalry near him, he bravely tried to make a stand, but it

BATTLE OF BULL RUN, JULY 21, 1861.

was no use, for the whole Federal army was retreating. Our retreat was most disorderly, even worse than that when we recrossed the Rappahannock after Chancellorsville. You can have no idea of the inextricable confusion. Brigades and regiments melted away, the wagon trains blocked the roads, and even the batteries lost their formation. Had the Confederates made a vigorous pursuit, God knows what the result might have been. But they were so elated by success that I suppose the idea of marching straight for Washington did not enter their minds until it was too late. They contented themselves by sending Early's brigade, but it was soon stopped by Porter and Blenker on the Warrenton road, and so we were not further molested. I

CAPTAIN, AFTERWARDS BVT. MAJ.-GEN. J. B. RICKETTS.

CAPTAIN, AFTERWARDS MAJ. GEN. CHARLES GRIFFIN.

remember seeing Sherman while we fell back. Tecumseh's face was pale with mortification and anger, as he tried to keep the men around him in some sort of order. But it was of no use, for the different commands had got so mingled and mixed up you could have got representatives of almost every regiment, at any point on the road. I was sent to Washington with dispatches, but found the news had gone ahead of me, so I got away again as quickly as I could, because it was not a pleasant place to be in."

In describing the rout at Bull Run, General William Tecumseh Sherman (who was then a Colonel in command of a brigade) says in his memoirs: "For two hours we continued to dash at the woods on our left front, which were full of rebels; but I was convinced their organization was broken, and that they had simply halted there and taken advantage of these woods as a cover, to reach which we had to

THORBURN'S HOUSE, BULL RUN.

pass over the intervening fields about the Henry House, which were clear, open, and gave them a decided advantage. After I had put in each of my regiments, and had them driven back to the cover of the road, I had no idea that we were beaten, but re-formed the regiments in line in their proper order, and only wanted a little rest, when I found that my brigade was almost alone, except Syke's regulars, who had formed square against cavalry, and were coming back. Many officers were reported dead or missing, and the wounded were making their way, with more or less assistance, to the buildings used as hospitals, on the ridge to the west. We succeeded in partially reforming the regiments, but it was manifest that they would not stand, and I

MATTHEW'S HOUSE, BULL RUN.

directed Colonel Corcoran to move along the ridge to the rear, near the position where we had first formed the brigade. General McDowell was there in person, and used all

SUDLEY'S FORD, BULL RUN.

possible efforts to reassure the men. By the active exertions of Colonel Corcoran, we formed an irregular square against the cavalry, which were then seen to issue from the position from which we had been driven, and we began our retreat toward the same ford of Bull Run by which we had approached the field of battle. There was no positive order to retreat, although for an hour it had been going on by the operation of the men themselves. About nine o'clock at night I received from General Tyler, in person, the order to continue the retreat to the Potomac. This retreat was by night and disorderly in the extreme. The men of different regiments mingled together, and some reached the river at Arlington, some at Long Bridge, and the greater part returned to their former camp, at or near Fort Corcoran. I reached this point at noon the next day, and found a miscellaneous crowd crossing over the aqueduct and ferries. Conceiving this to be demoralizing, I at once commanded the guard to be increased, and all persons attempting to pass over to be stopped. This soon produced its effect. Men sought their proper companies and regiments. Comparative order was restored, and all were posted to the best advantage."

The defeat at Bull Run was a severe blow to the pride of the Northern people, but the lessons of adversity have their usefulness, so the North sat down to repair the disaster with full determination to begin again, and more persistently. Another call for troops was made, McClellan replaced McDowell and set himself the task of forming the Army of the Potomac. In the South, an intoxication of vanity prevailed. Beauregard was promoted to the highest rank in the Confederate Service, cannon salutes were fired in Richmond, Charleston, New Orleans, and other Southern cities. Jefferson Davis made a speech from the balcony of the Spottswood House, declaring that the Confederate States had already secured their independence. But the war had really only begun, these few battles were simply the overture to a struggle which was to last for four long years, and make desolate a large area of territory, besides the sacrifice of thousands upon thousands of lives on both sides of the theatre of operations. At Bull Run the Federals lost four hundred and eighty-one killed and two thousand four hundred and seventy-one wounded and missing,

SUDLEY'S CHURCH, BULL RUN.

RUINS OF HENRY HOUSE, BULL RUN.

SOLDIERS' GRAVES, BULL RUN.

besides twenty-seven cannon, nine flags, and four thousand muskets. The Confederate loss was three hundred and seventy-eight killed, and fourteen hundred and eighty-nine wounded. The Federals became hardened and defiant, the Confederates were vain-glorious, boastful and over-confident. The victory at Bull Run was really a dear one, as all Southern Generals have since confessed, and so history records it.

DEDICATION OF MONUMENT ON BATTLEFIELD, BULL RUN.

RUINS OF BRIDGE NEAR POTOMAC.

CHAPTER VI.

THE SECTIONS GIRDING THEIR LOINS FOR MORTAL STRUGGLE.

President Lincoln's call for half a million more men, who were to serve three years, was met with the same alacrity as displayed at the initial call. While these new regiments were forming, the volcano of war began disturbing the Southwest. Several unimportant skirmishes occurred in Kentucky and Missouri, which prevented those States joining the Confederacy. The sudden increase in the Federal strength necessitated the appointment of a sufficient number of Brigadier-Generals and Major-Generals, and many of the men who were to stamp their names on the pages of history received commissions. Garnett, the Confederate General, having been killed at Rich Mountain ; Floyd, who, as Buchanan's War Secretary, had armed the Confederate troops, took his place. He attempted to drive the Federals out of Ohio, while General Lee, who then appeared on the scene for the first time, undertook to scatter Rosecranz's army in West Virginia. The plan of operations had been sketched out by Lee, but Floyd was too confident, and burned to distinguish himself. Wise failing to join Floyd, the latter was outnumbered, as Rosecranz hastened to Cox's relief. A battle took place at Powell Mountain, on August 10, and might have been a decided Federal victory had Rosecranz shown less caution. Lee also failed to carry out his part of the programme, so was sent to South Carolina. Neither the North or the South had any patience with unsuccessful generals.

GENERAL J. B. FLOYD, C. S. A.

Then there was another lull, though the Federals and Confederates faced each other in strong force along the course of the Potomac River, between Washington and Harper's Ferry. Both of these bodies of troops were dancing around, neither knowing much about what the other was doing. McClellan, besides being the commander of the new army of the Potomac, was understood to be also General-in-Chief, as Lieutenant-General Winfield Scott had retired from active service by permission of the President.

Up to this time military discipline in the Northern or Southern armies had not attained that degree of efficiency so necessary in actual war. When the Battle of Bull Run had been fought and apparently won, many of the men from North Carolina, Georgia and Virginia coolly dropped their muskets and walked home. They supposed that having whipped the "Yanks," as the Confederates styled the Northern troops all through the war, there was no further need

GENERAL WISE, C. S. A.

of their services. A more thoroughly astonished set of men never existed when they found themselves arrested, one by one, by provost guards and marched back to their regiments. The men of the North, being accustomed to the discipline of the bank, store or workshop, proved more amenable to the rigors of military command, but still desertion was not considered a very heinous offense, and, as General Sherman once said to me, some of the men who ran from Bull Run are probably running still. At all events the large number of men reported as "missing" at that engagement is due to this fact.

The writer was one of a recruiting party sent back to New York after the Battle of Big Bethel, and we were having a good time, posing as heroes, when the Bull Run disaster occurred. Three days after the battle I was going down Broadway with a squad of recruits, to have them sworn in, when a long, lanky individual, dressed in regulation soldier's uniform, met us.

GENERAL J. D. COX.

"I say, Corporal," he drawled, "whar do I get the train for Albany?"

"What are you going to Albany for?" I asked.

"Why, I'm going home of course."

"Home? are you sick or wounded?"

"Sick, that's what I am. I was at that thar Bull Run fight, and I'm sick enough, I tell ye."

"How did you get to New York?"

"Rode on the train, of course. I had to walk to Washington, and that was enough of that for me."

"But didn't they ask you for a pass on the train?" I demanded, for discipline had become pretty stiff with us at Fortress Monroe, where I had come from.

"Yes, a fellow with a sword kem aboard at Wilmington, and he says to me, says he, 'Hev ye a pass?' and I says to him, says I, 'Yes,' and he went on. But I didn't hev no pass, nuther."

SUDLEY'S SPRINGS, BULL RUN.

"Well, you come with me and we will fix you all right," said I and he obeyed quite cheerfully.

While my recruits were stripping in another room for their physical examination by the Regular Army surgeon, I took the man before Lieutenant-Colonel Ellis, the regular officer who was superintending the recruiting. On my explaining the situation to him, Colonel Ellis frowned, then laughed heartily. "What regiment do you belong to my man?" asked the Lieutenant-Colonel. "Second Varmount."

"And you were at Bull Run?"

"Yes, and a hell of a time, we had thar too."

"Do you know that you are a deserter?"

"Deserter? Do you mean that I hev run away?"

"I mean that, having left your regiment on the field of battle without leave, you have deserted your colors, broken your oath to faithfully serve the United States Government, and you can be shot to death for the crime. That's the rule in war."

"Now see here, Kurnel, I'm no deserter. The regiment deserted me. Leastways we all got kinder mixed up, and nobody knew nobody, and as one of the fellers sed the orders was to go to Washington, I jist went along with the rest. When we got thar, some of the boys sed as how we might as well go home for a spell, so I got on a train and here I am. When I've seen mother, and let her see I wasn't killed, I'm going back again."

"But that will not be right, or honest," said the Lieutenant-Colonel kindly, "Don't you see that if every man in your regiment had started for home, as you have done, there wouldn't be any Second Vermont left to fight the Rebs?"

"That's a fact. I didn't think of that. See here, I'm going back to Washington and jine the boys. Maybe they'll get into another battle before I get back, and I wouldn't like that, nohow."

"How many of the boys came with you on the train?"

"Guess thar whar a dozen or so."

"Do you know where they are?"

"Well, they sed they was agoing up the Hudson River Railroad, but we got scattered, and I got kinder lost."

"Now if this Corporal goes with you to the depot, will you tell the boys they have done wrong, and then

LIEUTENANT-COLONEL ELLIS.

you can all go back and join the regiment together? You know you can write to mother, and not be a deserter."

"So I can. I'm obleeged to you Kurnel, for telling me how things stand. When I volunteered up at Burlington, I wanted to do my duty, but yer see this soldering business is kinder new to me, and I haint exactly got the holt of it yet."

That afternoon the Vermonter and I had found ten of his comrades as ignorant as

T. J. Jackson

GENERAL T. J. (STONEWALL) JACKSON.

himself regarding military duty. When the matter was explained, they shouldered their muskets, for though each man had thrown away his knapsack, he had clung to his weapon. When the squad was paraded before Colonel Ellis, he talked kindly to them, and appointing our tall friend a Brevet-Corporal, gave them an order for transportation and rations, and sent them to Washington, unguarded.

"Oh, they'll go back safe enough," said Colonel Ellis, when a brother officer suggested a guard. "I would not hurt their feelings by so disgracing them. Those fellows will never skedaddle again. It was pure innocence on their part, rest assured."

But the officers on guard duty at Wilmington were curtly informed that passes must be shown by the soldiers, and no more such nonsense would be permitted. General Sherman, in his interesting personal memoirs, relates an anecdote of a similar character:—"One morning I found myself in a crowd of men crossing the drawbridge on their way to a barn close by, where they had their sinks; among them was an officer, who said: 'Colonel, I am going to New York to-day. What can I do for you?' I answered: 'How can you go to New York? I do not remember to have signed a leave for you.' He said,

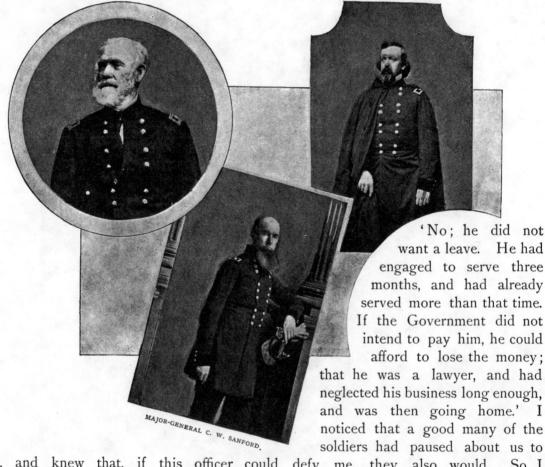

GENERAL W. S. HARNEY.   GENERAL C. P. STONE.

MAJOR-GENERAL C. W. SANFORD.

'No; he did not want a leave. He had engaged to serve three months, and had already served more than that time. If the Government did not intend to pay him, he could afford to lose the money; that he was a lawyer, and had neglected his business long enough, and was then going home.' I noticed that a good many of the soldiers had paused about us to listen, and knew that, if this officer could defy me, they also would. So I turned on him sharp, and said: 'Captain, this question of your term of service has been submitted to the rightful authority, and the decision has been published in orders. You are a soldier, and must submit to orders till you are properly discharged. If you attempt to leave without orders, it will be mutiny, and I will shoot you like a dog! Go into the fort *now*, instantly, and don't dare to leave without my consent.' I had on an overcoat, and may have had my hand about the breast, for he looked at me hard, paused a moment, and then turned back into the fort. The men scattered, and I returned to the house where I was quartered, close by. The same afternoon, President Lincoln went out to see the army, and the officer pushed through the throng of soldiers, and on reaching the President's carriage said: 'Mr. President I have a cause of grievance. This morning I went to speak to Colonel Sherman, and he threatened to shoot me.' Mr. Lincoln, who was still standing, said, 'Threatened to shoot you?' 'Yes, sir, he threatened to shoot me.'

Mr. Lincoln looked at him, then at me, and stooping his tall, spare form toward the officer, said to him in a loud stage-whisper, easily heard for some yards around: 'Well, if I were you, and he threatened to shoot, I would not trust him, for I believe he would do it.' The officer turned about and disappeared, and the men laughed at him. Soon the carriage drove on, and, as we descended the hill, I explained the facts to the President, who answered: 'Of course I didn't know anything about it, but I thought you knew your own business best.'"

While McClellan was organizing his army, it was announced in October

BATTLE OF BALL'S BLUFF AND DEATH OF COLONEL BAKER.

that the Confederates were massing at Leesburg, Va., so a reconnaissance was ordered. Generals Stone and McCall proceeded, with about three thousand men, as far as Balls' Bluff, Loudon County, where Colonel Devins disembarked with four companies of his Fifteenth Massachusetts from their flat boats on the Chesapeake and Ohio Canal. Devins found the enemy in strong force on October 21, and there was a sharp fight. The musketry hastened the movements of the First California Regiment, under Colonel Edward D. Baker, and the battle became a hot one. Baker, being the ranking officer, took command, and, supposing that McCall was coming up, he decided to make a stand. But McCall had been ordered back to camp, and the two Colonels had to fight it out against overwhelming odds. Baker fell dead, pierced by several bullets. A retreat followed and as the Federals had lost their best officers, they fell into disorder and were terribly cut up. To this day the exact number of their killed is not known, but official estimates place it at three hundred, with seven hundred wounded and missing. Half of the command with Colonels Coggswell and Lee, were made prisoners, Colonel Devins escaping by swimming his horse across the Potomac. Though a very small affair, compared to subsequent engagements, Ball's Bluff caused deep

COLONEL E. D. BAKER.

sorrow in the North, while the price of Gold rose ten points in unfeeling Wall Street. The gamble in Gold had already begun, the balance of the scale rising and falling as the Government forces won or lost battles.

John C. Fremont, who had run for the Presidency in 1856 on the Republican Party nomination, had been commissioned a Major-General, and placed in command of the Military Department of the West. His fame as a Rocky Mountain explorer gave the Northern people great hopes of his capacity, but he assumed to have political as well as military power, and as oil and water cannot mingle, Fremont proved a failure in in dependent command. The fact was, that like the citizen soldiery, even the high officers in the Federal army had to learn their precise duty in the exalted positions to which they were assigned. Sherman modestly thought a Colonelcy too much for him, but as he rose gradually in rank and studied the art of war in the field, he became only second in fame to Grant. The

J. C. Fremont.

trouble with Fremont was, that being placed in military command of debatable territory, he conceived the idea that he was really a Governor. This, of course, caused a friction between him and the civil authorities, which could only be removed by his transfer to another sphere of duty. Then this really distinguished citizen of the Republic fretted under his changed condition and his usefulness was impaired, greatly to the loss of the Government and the people.

General Nathaniel Lyon, at that time, occupied a position on the southern border of Missouri. He had less than

CAMP LILLIE, FREMONT'S HEADQUARTERS.

BATTLE OF WILSON'S CREEK.

six thousand men, while he was confronted by a Confederate force of nearly twice his strength. On August 1, he had a skirmish at Dug Springs which resulted in his favor, but it did not prevent a concentration of the Confederates. As retreat would be hazardous, Lyon decided to risk a battle at Wilson's Creek.

Colonel Franz Sigel was sent to make a wide detour with two regiments and a field battery, and get into the Confederate rear. Sigel performed his task most admirably, and, on August 10, was in the desired position. Lyon then advanced, and with the aid of Totten's battery drove in the opposing lines, the Confederates taking refuge on an elevated position. Both Sigel and Lyon followed, and for the first time in the war a hand-to-hand combat ensued. But the Federals were vastly outnumbered, and they were unmercifully handled.

General Lyon was personally a very brave man, and in his extremity exposed himself more than a General should. Each charge

COLONEL, AFTERWARDS BRIGADIER-GRNERAL, FRANZ SIGEL

saw him in the advance, and he was twice wounded before the battle had been an hour old, and his horse was killed under him. Colonel Mitchell, of the Second Kansas, seeing that the General had fallen, led his regiment on another charge. Scarcely had the Kansas men begun moving when their Colonel fell, pierced by bullets. His men shouted, "Who will lead us now?" "I will," exclaimed the wounded General, rising from the ground. "Come on boys." He had scarcely uttered the words when a bullet pierced his heart.

In the meantime Sigel and his brigade fell into difficulties owing to the superior force that faced him. At this juncture Dubois' battery sprang forward and opened a fierce discharge of grape and canister which shattered the Confederate line. Then their right wing fell into confusion and they hastily retreated to the convenient woods behind them. To add to their discomfort and dismay they lost a train of wagons which caught fire. By that time Major Sturgis and Colonel Sigel had joined forces, and the latter decided to retreat. Seizing a railroad train he went to Rolla, one hundred

N. Lyon

and twenty-five miles away from the scene of conflict. The Federals lost twelve hundred and thirty-six in killed, wounded and missing, while the Confedrates lost over one thousand.

Franz Sigel subsequently rose to the rank of Major-General and the command of a corps, mainly composed of German regiments, whose proudest boast was that they all "fought mit Sigel." When the will of General Lyon was read, it bequeathed $30,000 to the United States Government for the prosecution of the war. But his bequest was a mere drop in the bucket. The average cost of the war, per day, was one million dollars, consequently the General's money did not cover more than thirty minutes.

"HARD TACK."

BATTLE OF LEXINGTON, MO.

Having won the Battle of Wilson's Creek, General Sterling Price continued recruiting so rapidly, that he decided to go on a short invasion. Advancing on Lexington, Ky., he found the city fortified by Colonel James A. Mulligan, of the Twenty-third Illinois, who had only three thousand Federals to garrison and man his line of entrenchments. Price's command was fully twenty-four thousand strong, as he had been joined by Generals Harris, Rains, Pearce, and Parsons. Despite the fearful odds against him, Mulligan decided to make a stand, and when Price made a demand for his unconditional surrender, replied, "If you want us, come and take us." The siege of Lexington began on September 12, and continued for eight days. Mulligan's defence was a remarkable exhibition of bravery, for not only was he outnumbered, but his supply of ammunition was scanty, Price having captured the Federal supply steamer. He surrendered, with great honor, September 21, after a long parley, the principal officers on the Federal side being Colonels Mulligan, Marshall, Grover and Peabody. The Confederate losses were extraordinarily heavy, as over two thousand were either killed or wounded, for whenever they charged Mulligan's breastworks, he always exploded a mine, repeating the

COLONEL JAMES A. MULLIGAN.

GENERAL STERLING PRICE, C. S. A.

operation no less than six times. The Federal loss was four hundred and twenty killed and wounded. Colonel White was killed, while Colonels Marshall and Mulligan were wounded, the latter in the leg and arm. For his magnificent conduct, Colonel Mulligan received the thanks of Congress and the offer of a Brigadier-General's commission, which he modestly declined. His regiment was given the right to inscribe "Lexington" on its flag.

General Fremont ordered Sterling Price to be pursued, and Major Charles Zagonyi started on a raid with one hundred and fifty horsemen. On October 25, he struck the Confederates near Springfield, Missouri. Zagonyi was a man without fear, and though he was facing two thousand men, he did not hesitate for a moment. Quietly turning in his saddle, Zagonyi said to his men :—

"Follow me, and do like me ! Comrades, the hour of danger has come. Your first battle is before you. The enemy is two thousand strong, and we are but one hundred and fifty.

GEN. RAINS, C. S. A.   GEN. HARRIS, C. S. A.   GEN. PEARCE, C. S. A.
                              GEN. PARSONS, C. S. A.

CHARGE OF MAJOR ZAGONYI, OF GENERAL FREMONT'S BODY GUARD, UPON THE CONFEDERATES NEAR SPRINGFIELD, MO., OCT. 25, 1861.

It is possible no man will come back. If any of you would turn back, you can do so now!"

The only response made by his men was a hearty cheer, as they gathered in solid ranks. Delighted by the evident enthusiasm of his troopers, Zagonyi exclaimed: "I will lead you! Let the watchword be, '*The Union and Fremont!*' Draw sabres! By the right flank—quick trot—march!" Spurring forward, the Major dashed down a lane. Then the command galloped into some open fields, across a brook and over a fence. They were met by an outburst of musketry which emptied many saddles. Lieutenant Majthenyi then took thirty men to engage the Confederate cavalry, fully five times his own strength. The Major and Captain McNaughton continued with the remainder, and actually drove the Confederates through the streets of Springfield. This victory was a costly one, however, for out of Zagonyi's one hundred and fifty men, eighty-four were killed or wounded. It was a most brilliant affair, and caused unbounded enthusiasm in the North.

General Henry W. Halleck now superseded Fremont in command of the Missouri Department, and entered on a more vigorous military campaign. He found the city of St. Louis full of riotous soldiers who had strayed from their regiments, but with the aid of General Justus A. McKinstry, whom General Fremont had appointed as provost-martial, order was soon restored. General McKinstry became known to the North by the fearlessness he displayed in arresting Southern disturbers of the peace, when such action was attended with no small degree of danger.

Bishop Leonidas Polk, of the Episcopal Church, and Dr. Francis Vinton, then rector of Trinity Church, in New

MAJOR CHAS. ZAGONYI.

BRIG.-GENERAL JUSTUS A. MC KINSTRY.

York city, were both graduates of West Point before entering the ministry. Polk dropped his Bishop's gown for a Confederate General's coat, an example Vinton was anxious to follow. He was, however, persuaded to remain with his church. These incidents show how strong were personal convictions on both sides of the great quarrel. On September 4, Polk had invaded Kentucky on the West, and Zollicoffer entered on the East. Columbus was fortified with one hundred and twenty heavy guns, supported by twenty-five thousand men.

Major Anderson, having been raised to the rank of Major-General, was in command of the Army of the Cumberland, his second in command being Brigadier-General Sherman. Then Anderson fell ill, and Sherman, on taking command, told Secretary of War Cameron that two hundred thousand men would be necessary to expel the Confederates from Kentucky. This utterance, being repeated, led to a serious inquiry regarding Sherman's sanity. Writing on the subject in his memoirs, the General says : "In the general conversation which followed, I remembered taking a large map of the United States, and assuming the people of the whole South to be in rebellion, that our task was to subdue them, showed that McClellan was on the left, having a frontage of less than a hundred miles, and Fremont the right, about the same ; whereas I, the centre, had from the Big Sandy to Paducah, over three hundred miles of frontier ; that McClellan had a hundred thousand men, Fremont sixty thousand, whereas to me had only been allotted about eighteen thousand. I argued that, for the purpose of defense, we should have sixty thousand men at once, and for offense, we should need two hundred thousand, before we were done. Mr. Cameron threw up his hands and exclaimed, 'Great God ! where are they to come from ?' I asserted that there were plenty of men at the North, ready and willing to come, if he would only accept their services ; for it was notorious that regiments had been formed in all the Northwestern States, whose services had been refused by the War Department, on the ground that they would not be needed. My attention was subsequently drawn to the publication in all the Eastern papers, which was of course copied at the West, of the report that I was crazy, insane, and mad, that I had demanded two hundred thousand men for the defense of Kentucky ; and the authority given for this report was stated to be the Secretary of War, himself, Mr. Cameron, who never, to my knowledge, took pains

FIELD TELEGRAPH STATION.

to affirm or deny it. My position was, therefore, simply unbearable, and it is probable I resented the cruel insult with language of intense feeling."

Then the Northern people began hearing about a Federal Brigadier-General bearing the name of Ulysses S. Grant. He was in command at Cairo, Ill., which occupies the tongue of land formed by the Junction of the Ohio and Mississippi Rivers. Grant seems always to have had a will of his own from the start, and like Sherman, he had trouble with his superiors in authority. He took possession of Paducah, Ky., at the mouth of the Tennessee River; next he occupied Smith Bend, finally deciding to threaten Columbus by attacking Belmont, which was directly opposite, on the Missouri side of the Mississippi.

The battle of Belmont occurred on November 7. General Charles F. Smith moved from Paducah, while Generals

GENERAL LEONIDAS POLK, C. S. A.

Grant and McClernand started from Cairo. Among the Colonels was John A. Logan, who subsequently rose to the rank of Major-General, and achieved a high reputation as a corps commander. The fight lasted six hours, but the result was so much in doubt that the battle was claimed as a victory by both Federals and Confederates. General Cheatham, who commanded the Confederates, lost over six hundred men, Colonel John V. Wright and Major Butler being among his killed. The Federal loss was six hundred and seven.

General Grant was by nature a reticent, self-contained man. While preparing for a campaign, he seldom asked for advice from his corps of commanders, but pondered over his plans in solitude, until they shaped themselves into a feasible outline; then, and then only, he unfolded to his Generals his objective point, and explained how he proposed to reach it. But there was always something held back, for it was impossible for Grant to reveal all that was in his mind. It was this habit of reticence that made Grant respected by his officers, even by the few who did not consider him their superior in strategic skill, or military genius. During the first two years of the war, it was his fate to encounter bitter opposition, fierce denunciation and shameful calumny, but neither one or the other had any apparent effect upon him, nor swerved him from the line of conduct he had laid out for himself.

GENERAL B. F. CHEATHAM, C. S. A.

WEST POINT.
OLD ARTILLERY, WAR RELICS &c

WEST POINT,
VIEW NORTH, FROM UPPER ROAD.

As a soldier, he showed the possession of qualities that have marked every great military commander, but he never issued any glowing orders calculated to fire the blood of his troops, neither did he seek their applause. Unlike other Generals, he would ride past a

GENERAL ULYSSES SIMPSON GRANT.

BORN APRIL 27, 1822, AT POINT PLEASANT, OHIO. CADET AT WEST POINT, 1839-1843. SERVED IN MEXICAN WAR FROM
SPRING OF 1846 TO AUTUMN OF 1847. COLONEL 21ST ILLINOIS INFANTRY, JUNE 17, 1861. BRIGADIER-GENERAL,
AUGUST 7, 1861. MAJOR-GENERAL, FEBRUARY 25, 1862. LIEUTENANT-GENERAL, MARCH 1, 1864.
APPOMATTOX, APRIL 9, 1865. GENERAL OF THE ARMY, JULY 25, 1866. PRESIDENT OF THE
UNITED STATES, 1869-1877. DIED AT MT. MC GREGOR, N. Y., JULY 23, 1885.
ENTOMBED AT RIVERSIDE PARK, NEW YORK CITY, AUGUST 6, 1885.

moving column, or gallop through a corps at rest, apparently unconscious of the cheers that saluted him. When he reached the Army of the Potomac, after being raised to the rank of Lieutenant-General, and the several corps began crossing the Rapidan River, the men cheered as he rode by the marching columns, but Grant paid no heed, and the troops soon learned that silence was the only greeting he asked for.   Grant seldom passed over the roads occupied by his infantry.   This was because he always wanted to avoid the noisy cheers of the men, and because he wished to ride rapidly.   When he started from camp or bivouac, the General used to swing himself into the saddle, and dash off without a word, leaving his staff officers and the mounted escort to follow as best they could.

When the preconcerted place of rendezvous was reached, Grant would sit on a stump, or a fence, for hours, listening to the guns, and only betraying his suspense by slowly chewing the unlit cigar he habitually carried between his teeth while conducting a battle. Staff officer after staff officer would ride up, deliver messages and receive answers, as if they knew their cues and exits before hand.   "We have a stronger force before us than I imagined," would write a corps commander.   "Stay where you are, and I will reinforce

IN THE FIELD HOSPITAL.

you," would go back, and before the aide was out of sight, the General's staff would be scattered, rapidly changing the positions of other bodies of troops to meet the emergency. To those who were near him, Grant was kind and considerate, and the fact that his staff officers clung to him through all the grades he attained, while they could have earned higher rank by more direct duty in the line, is a proof of his really lovable disposition, a trait that was clearly shown after he had laid down the duties and cares of rank and public office.   Like most men who have made their mark in the history of the world, Grant did not fully appreciate the important part he had taken during the war until he came to write his memoirs in the presence of death.

He was from boyhood an ardent lover of good horses, and he always had a large number of exceedingly fine animals at his disposal.   His utter indifference regarding the uniform of his rank somewhat detracted from his appearance as a horseman.   He never wore a sword or a sash after the battle of Shiloh, even on parade days for review.   In his memoirs, Grant mentions his sword and sash for the first and only time, saying: "Suddenly a battery with musketry opened upon us from the edge of the woods on the other side of the clearing.   The shells and balls whistled about our ears very fast for about a minute. I do not think it took us longer than that to get out of range and out of sight.   In the sudden start we made, Major Hawkins lost his hat.   He did not stop to pick it up.   When we arrived at a perfectly safe position, we halted to take an account of damages, McPherson's horse was panting as if ready to drop.   On examination, it was found that a ball had struck him forward of the flank, just back of the saddle, and had gone entirely through.   In a few minutes the poor beast dropped dead ; he had given no sign of injury until we came to a stop.   A ball had struck the metal scabbard of my sword, just below the hilt, and broken it nearly off ; before the battle was over, it had broken off entirely.

BATTLE OF BELMONT, MO., NOVEMBER, 7, 1861.

There were three of us : one had lost a horse killed ; one a hat, and one a sword-scabbard. All were thankful that it was no worse."

I once saw Grant ride along a line of battle, while the troops were actively engaged. Then his horse was walking, while the rider sat upright and seemed for the moment transfigured.   His hat was pushed back from his brow, and his eye was bright and keen. Every movement going on before him was evidently noticed, and he avoided a wounded man by a touch of the bridle, yet the General's demeanor was as impassive as ever.   Those who have had intimate relations with Grant in the field, remember that he always seemed to see everything, yet appeared not to be looking at anything.   When the Army of the Potomac was pursuing Lee's forces, after the evacuation of Richmond and the Petersburg siege works, Grant wore out no less than six horses inside of three days.   So furiously did he ride from point to point, it frequently happened that all of his orderlies were left

PASSAGE DOWN THE OHIO OF GENERAL JAMES S. NEGLEY'S BRIGADE.

behind. Indeed, very few of the headquarter staff could keep up the pace, though the officers always tried to have good horses. Many a time I have met the General galloping to some point in a battle-field, and twenty minutes after encountered his aides pumping along, with their orderlies steaming away behind them.

Grant's operations were so well planned that they attracted attention at Washington and one day he was surprised by the appearance of six magnificent river steamboats, all lashed together, and loaded to their guards with troops, cannon, horses and all the paraphernalia of war. It was the famous Pennsylvania Brigade, under Brigadier-General James S. Negley a veteran of the Mexican War, where he served while yet in his teens. General Grant said afterwards, that General Negley's use of steamboats, for the transportation of his brigade from Pittsburg, had taught him a lesson that he never forgot. General Negley did splendid service during the war, as will be seen hereafter.

BRIG.-GENERAL JAMES S. NEGLEY.

AMMUNITION SCHOONERS IN HAMPTON ROADS.

CHAPTER VII.

SEA-COAST OPERATIONS AND THE FEDERAL BLOCKADE.

Affairs were now assuming a more definite shape. McClellan was in supreme command in the East, with the nominal rank of General-in-Chief, while Halleck directed all operations in the Southwest. It was understood that a comprehensive and co-operative movement of the various Federal armies was contemplated, which would soon bring the war to a close. That was the one absorbing desire. While the land forces were thus being strengthened and advantageously placed, the Government turned its attention to the naval arm of the service. River and ocean steamers, ferry boats and other crafts were transformed into war vessels, to act as a flotilla in blockading Confederate seaports, while on the Ohio and Upper Mississippi Rivers, some queer-looking gunboats were improvised out of the steamers plying in those waters. The sound of the workman's hammer was heard in all the navy yards and machine shops ; factories were established for the manufacture of all kinds of military equipment ; foundries turned out shot and shell, instead of cooking stoves and plow-

COMMODORE SILAS H. STRINGHAM.

VIEW OF GEORGETOWN, D. C.

shares; thousands of young women dropped their needles to learn how to make musket cartridge cases. Every armory was busy, night and day; instead of peaceful machinery, the lathes in all the large iron works turned out cannon; in fact the Government and the people strained every nerve to meet the sudden emergency.

MAJOR-GENERAL JOHN E. WOOL.

The public censure that fell upon General Butler for the Big Bethel affair, resulted in his being relieved of his command by Major-General John E. Wool, of the Regular Army, and a distinguished veteran of the Mexican War. Poor Butler found himself idle and without orders. Appreciating his predecessor's feelings, Wool gave Butler command of all the troops outside of Fortress Monroe. Being a man of indomitable energy, Butler soon cut out some work for himself. It was this trait that gave the Massachusetts Militia General so much prominence during the entire war. Commodore Silas H. Stringham was, at that time, one of the oldest officers in the Navy, being in his sixty-fifth year when the bombardment of Fort Sumter shook the Republic to its centre. Stringham had been fifty-two years in the service, entering as a midshipman, in 1809, at the age of thirteen, on board the frigate President. He was given

WHARVES AT AQUIA CREEK.

command of the United States fleet, then being gathered in Hampton Roads, and soon ascertained that the Confederates were receiving English supplies of arms, ammunition and clothing, carried by blockade-runners through Hatteras Inlet. The old sea dog told

Butler, and the latter at once wrote to President Lincoln, suggesting that a combined naval and land force be sent to capture the forts defending the inlet, and thus close the passage. "The Council of War," as it was sometimes styled by the soldiers at the front, approved of the suggestion. General Butler was to take nine hundred soldiers, and Commodore Stringham was to command the fighting squadron. The fleet consisted of the Cumberland, Minnesota, Monticello, Pawnee, Wabash and Harriet Lane. Butler put his men on the transports Adelaide and George Peabody, and the expedition sailed on August 27, 1861.

Arriving off Cape Hatteras on the afternoon of August 28, Stringham came to

PONTOON BOAT ON WHEELS.

BOMBARDMENT OF FORT HATTERAS BY COMMODORE STRINGHAM'S FLEET, THE CUMBERLAND, MINNESOTA, MONTICELLO, PAWNEE,
WABASH AND HARRIET LANE, AUGUST 29, 1861.

anchor, when preparations to land the troops began. The Confederate Forts, Clark and Hatteras, stood on the west end of Hatteras Island, and commanded the Inlet. It was, therefore, arranged that Butler should land his men a short distance up the beach, and attack these forts in their rear, while the vessels assailed them in front. Great difficulty was experienced by the infantry in landing, the dreaded Hatteras surf dashing the heavily laden boats on the sand with terrific violence, but not a single man was lost. The attack began about ten o'clock, and was continued for four hours, when the flags on both forts were hauled down, the Federals supposing that the Confederates intended to surrender. The Monticello and the Harriet Lane then advanced up the Inlet, but met a vigorous fire from Fort Hatteras, which was returned by the entire fleet until half-past six, when the vessels drew out of range. The Monticello ran aground, but floated off again without the loss of a spar or a man. To show how mistakes are often made in hostile movements, it is only necessary to relate the following incident :—At the time the Confederate forts pulled down their flags and ceased firing, as a trap for the vessels, Butler's men advanced, and discovered that Fort Clark had been abandoned. Taking possession, the boys hoisted their own flag, when the vessels opened fire upon them, under the supposition that the ensign was a Confederate one, so the victorious troops were compelled to evacuate the fort before Federal shells.

CHESTER A. ARTHUR.

GENERAL RUGGLES, C. S. A.

The bombardment was resumed early the following morning, it being spiritedly replied to by Fort Hatteras. The Federal fire, however, became so hot that the garrison, unable to endure the tremendous punishment, ran to their bomb-proofs. They had scarcely done so, when an eleven-inch shell slipped in among them, and exploded with terrible result. Then the white flag was raised,

COLONEL "BILLY" WILSON.

and firing ceased. After some parleying, the Confederates surrendered, and the Inlet was won. Although the discharge of shot, shell and bullet had been severe during the two days, not a single Federal soldier or sailor was killed or wounded, while the Confederate loss was but slight.

By this victory Butler regained the confidence of the North, and his reputation was established. Stringham was made an Admiral, but his age prevented his doing much active service thereafter. The Government unwisely neglected to reinforce the Federal troops, left by Butler at Hatteras Inlet, or send an experienced officer to take command. The consequence was that the Confederates controlled two other inlets, and the blockade remained unbroken. These seacoast operations were often marked by curious incidents. Fort Pickens, in Pensacola Bay, Fla., had been garrisoned by the Sixth New York,

BURNING OF THE AMERICAN MERCHANTMAN, "HARVEY BIRCH," OF NEW YORK IN THE BRITISH CHANNEL, BY THE CONFEDERATE STEAMER "NASHVILLE," NOVEMBER 17TH, 1861.

MAJOR-GENERAL HORATIO G. WRIGHT.

BVT. MAJOR-GENERAL T. W. SHERMAN.

commanded by Colonel "Billy" Wilson. This officer was a curious character, and he used to boast that every man in his regiment ought to be in Sing Sing Prison. This was, of course, an exaggeration, but the men were a set of dare-devils of no regular occupation, and it was believed that some of them were thieves. When the regiment was mustered in, they marched into old Tammany Hall, (now the Sun office) and listened to speeches from their officers. Then the men rose to their feet, and with uplifted arms, collectively took an awful oath to kill every rebel they could lay their hands on. So desperate was the character of the material in the Sixth, it was considered safest to throw them into Fort Pickens, where they would be out of mischief.

But Wilson's men were not to be balked, and they contrived to have lots of fun with the Confederates. On the night of September 2, Lieutenant Shepley took a small number of the Zouaves in a boat, and, crossing over to Warrenton, actually succeeded in burning the dry dock at the navy yard. A similar experiment was made ten days later, when a Confederate privateer was captured, and burned to the water's edge. These daring acts infuriated the Confederates, so fifteen hundred men, under Generals Anderson and Ruggles, em-

RUINS OF OLD CHURCH, HAMPTON, VA.

barked during the night of October 8, and landed at Deer Point, on Santa Rosa Island, four or five miles from Wilson's camp. The Zouaves were completely surprised, but as the Confederates shouted "Death to Wilson,—no quarter," these New York street boys saw it was to be a free fight, so they soon rallied, and stubbornly contested every inch of ground as they fell back to Fort Pickens. Here they were reinforced by Majors Vodges and Arnold, with four companies of infantry, when the combined force charged upon the enemy, who were enjoying themselves in rifling the Federal camp. Taken by surprise in their turn, the Confederates took to their boats, and escaped with a loss of one hundred and fifty men, while the Federals lost sixty-four, Major Vodges being taken prisoner.

In a letter to State Quarter-master-General Chester A. Arthur (who afterwards became President by the assassination of Garfield), Colonel Wilson wrote that he had heard the Confederates had intended to put him in a cage, and exhibit him as a wild specimen of the genus Yankee. In November following, the Hatteras Inlet Blockading Squadron destroyed the village of Warrenton and silenced Fort McRae.

The Government, having got a little stronger in improvised war vessels, it was next decided to enforce the Southern blockade more severely.

BRIGADIER-GENERAL ISAAC I. STEVENS.

Accordingly, fifteen thousand men were assembled at Annapolis, Md., and placed under the command of Brigadier-General Thomas W. Sherman (no relation to the hero of "The March to the Sea)." There were also provided fourteen gunboats, thirty-four steamers and twenty-six sailing vessels, under the command of Commodore Samuel F. Dupont, who had been in the service since 1815. The expedition was to descend on the coast of North Carolina, and do something, nobody seemed to know exactly what. In due time the fleet rendezvoused in Hampton

BRIGADIER-GENERAL ISAAC I STEVEN AND STAFF.

COLLISION BETWEEN THE TRANSPORTS "STAR OF THE SOUTH" AND "PEERLESS," IN THE GREAT STORM, NOVEMBER 2, 1861.

Roads, and proceeded to sea on October 29. General "Tom" Sherman's troops were in three brigades, under Brigadier-Generals Egbert L. Viele, Isaac I. Stevens and Horatio G.

COOSAW FERRY, PORT ROYAL.

Wright. During the first and second day after the starting of the fleet, the weather continued favorable, and there was a tolerably calm sea until after all of the vessels had passed the much-dreaded Cape Hatteras, when an unusually severe storm set in, and so completely scattered the vessels, that, on the morning of Saturday, the 2d of November, but one of them could be seen from the flagship. Four of the transports were lost; the Peerless, which sank after colliding with the Star of the South, sent to her assistance, and whose crew was saved by the gunboat Mohican; the Osceola and the Union, both of which went ashore, and had all on board made prisoners; and the Governor, whose three hundred and fifty marines, under Major John Reynolds, with the exception of a corporal and six men, were saved by the frigate Sabine.

FORT LINCOLN, WASHINGTON, D. C.

CHAPTER VIII.

THE PORT ROYAL AND HILTON HEAD EXPEDITION.

One of the finest harbors on the South Atlantic coast, from Cape Hatteras to Pensacola Bay, is the one formed by a network of islands lying at the mouth of the Broad River, South Carolina. The largest island in the group is Hilton Head, and being of great strategic importance, the Confederates lost no time in fortifying the various inlets. It was a desire to possess this part of the coast as a basis for future offensive operations, that led to the formation of what is usually known as the Port Royal Expedition. The sealed orders that had been given to the commander of each vessel, directed him to rendezvous off Port Royal Bar, and the fleet made its final start from Hampton Roads on October 29. At this period of the war, the Federal army and naval commanders laid great stress on the necessity for surprising the enemy whenever any important movement was undertaken. That these labored efforts at

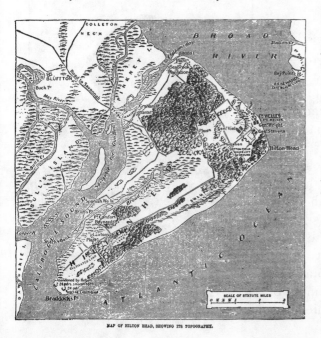

MAP OF HILTON HEAD, SHOWING ITS TOPOGRAPHY.

BOMBARDMENT OF FORT WALKER, HILTON HEAD, NOVEMBER 7, 1861.

concealment invariably failed, is not surprising, in view of the fact that the Southern States had many sympathizers in Northern cities, especially Washington, Baltimore, and New York. It was even said that spies lived in the White House. Under these circumstances, it naturally followed, therefore, that when any secrecy was observed, the fact only whetted the curiosity of these voluntary and paid agents, who never rested until they ascertained the positive or probable objective point of the contemplated movement. Had the weather continued favorable, the Sherman-Dupont flotilla might have reached its destination before the Confederate forces at Hilton Head could discover the fact, but the storm that delayed the expedition, gave them ample opportunity for defensive preparation.

Still, while Dupont's ships had been dispersed like a flock of frightened birds, the expedition was by no means ruined, for on Sunday, November 4, those vessels that had escaped the ravages of the storm, began arriving, one by one, off Port Royal, until twenty-five assembled. The rendezvous had been made with much difficulty, because the Confederates had long before extinguished every lighthouse, and removed every beacon and buoy on the Secession coast, for it must be confessed, by impartial writers, that the South began her warlike preparations in the most thorough manner. As more vessels hove in sight off the bar, careful soundings were made under the united direction of Mr. Boutelle, of the Coast Survey, and of Commander Charles H. Davis, fleet captain and and chief of the commodore's staff, and on November 5, a reconnaissance of the Confederate

COM. S. F. DUPONT, U. S. N.

works was made in force by Commander John Rogers and General Wright, with the gunboats Curlew, I. P. Smith, Ottawa and Seneca. These vessels had not proceeded far up the channel when they were met by four Confederate steamers, and a lively exchange of fire took place, the Confederates retreating as the Federal gunboats advanced toward the batteries on Hilton Head and at Bay Point opposite. When within range, the batteries opened on the Federals, as was naturally expected, and another engagement of nearly an hour ensued. The object of the reconnaisance having been accomplished, the gunboats hauled off and rejoined the fleet.

It was then decided that the forts should be attacked early on the following day, but a high wind having come up, this was found impossible, and it was not until the 7th that it could be properly made. The forced delay in beginning operations had enabled

the Confederates to strengthen their defenses. Earthworks had been erected wherever practicable, the largest of those being Fort Walker, which stood on Hilton Head, and had twenty-four cannon, of good calibre. The second largest earthwork was at Bay Point, on St. Phillip's Island, and had been named Fort Beauregard. It had twenty guns, while there were six or eight more guns in smaller sand batteries. These fortifications were manned by South Carolina troops and a company of Georgia Volunteers, there being also a small squadron of eight steamers made, under the command of Commodore Josiah Tatnall, a veteran of the war of 1812.

Agreeably to the formulated plan of operations the Federal fleet advanced in battle order soon after sunrise on Novem-

FORT BEAUREGARD, BAY POINT, S. C., NOV., 1861.

ber 7, the flagship Wabash at the head. Commodore Dupont's plan of attack was to pass up between Forts Beauregard and Walker, receiving and returning the fire of both; then to turn around, and, with a flanking squadron provided against an attack in the rear from Tatnall's steamers, to engage Fort Walker in front, after having enfiladed its waterfaces. This imposing programme was carried out to the letter, the firing beginning a little before ten o'clock, and continuing incessantly for three hours and a half, when it was discovered that both of the forts had been abandoned. Conflicts between shore and naval forces are always more picturesque than land battles, for they begin with a bombardment of the fortifications and the rapid movement of war vessels, each delivering its fire as the ship passes the object of attack. An engagement between two armies is usually fought out in a circumscribed space, amid woods, hills, creeks and farms. The smoke from cannon and

SCENES IN BEAUFORT, S. C., AND HILTON HEAD.

musket covers the earth like a hot mist, and the combatants are often hidden for hours from each other. It was not so at Hilton Head. As Dupont's ships performed their minuet between the two points of land, each checked her speed rather gracefully, and delivered a broadside, then passed on to repeat the dose on the opposite tack.

The bombardment during the last hour of its continuance had been at tolerably close quarters and evidences of its terrible effect were manifest when the forts were afterward taken possession of. Numbers of dead and dying lay in all directions, amidst dismounted and shattered guns, the hospital building at Fort Walker being shot through and through in many places. The Confederate forces, under General Drayton, had been obliged to abandon everything, and retreat hastily across an open space that lay for a distance of nearly a mile between the fort and some woods in the direction of Bluffton, whilst the men at

RHETTS HOUSE BEAUFORT, S.C.
FEB. 1862.

FULLER'S HOUSE, BEAUFORT, S.C.
FEB. 1862.

HEADQUARTERS OF GENERAL HUNTER
AT HILTON HEAD, S.C.

NATURAL ARCH AT SEABROOK POINT,
PORT ROYAL, S.C.

BOAT LANDING BEAUFORT, S.C.
1862.

FULLER'S HOUSE
. . . S.C.
FEB. 1862.

SIGNAL STATION AT BEAUFORT, S.C.
ONCE THE RESIDENCE OF J. G. BARNWELL
FEB. 1862.

RETREAT OF GARRISON FROM FORT WALKER.

Fort Beauregard had retreated to St. Helena, Cat and Port Royal Islands. The Federal loss was remarkably small, for so important an affair, there being only eight men killed and twenty-three wounded. The flagship was struck by thirty-four shells and solid shot, and she leaked very badly, but the remainder of the fleet escaped with little damages. As soon as practicable, General " Tom " Sherman's troops were landed, every officer and man fit for duty being on terra firma that same evening. The Federal soldiers at once began repairing and strengthening the captured fortifications at both Hilton Head and Bay Point, the former being named Fort Welles, in honor of the Secretary of the Navy and the latter received the name of Fort Seward, after the Secretary of State. While the land force was thus busily employed, Commodore Dupont organized several naval expeditions with the smallest of his vessels and ship launches. These cruised through all the inlets and among the islands, and made important captures. On November 9, two days after the fall of the Hilton Head and Bay Point Batteries, the City of Beaufort was seized and its arsenal subsequently destroyed by the crew of the Seneca. All of this work was done with-

DOCK AT HILTON HEAD BUILT BY SOLDIERS.

out meeting any resistance whatever, the only stand made, in fact, by the Confederates, being at Port Royal Ferry, when, as late as December 31, an expedition was organized to destroy their earthworks at that place.

Commander Rodgers was selected to conduct the affair, and right brilliantly did he acquit himself. He took with him the Ellen, Ottawa, Pembina, Seneca, one ferry-boat, and four of the large boats belonging to the Wabash, each carrying a twelve-pounder, and he was join-

COMMODORE JOHN RODGERS, U. S. N.

COMMANDER R. C. P. RODGERS, U. S. N.

ed by General Stevens, with the Forty-seventh; Forty-eighth and Seventy-ninth New York, the Eighth Michigan, and the Fifteenth and One Hundredth Pennsylvania

Sunken Hulks to Prevent Entrance of Vessels to Southern Harbors.

Regiments.   As the leading vessels ascended Broad River and entered Whale Creek, the land force was carried on the other side through the Coosaw River, meeting near the ferry, where, early the next morning, they attacked the enemy.   The Eighth Michigan being deployed as skirmishers, soon drew the fire of a masked battery, which was finally silenced by the shells from the gunboats.   The steady cannonading by the latter soon made the Confederate position untenable, so they were compelled to retire, being hastened in their movement by the howitzer practice of the Wabash's rowboats.   Without attempting any pursuit of the enemy, the abandoned works were at once taken possession of by the Federals, who returned to Beaufort, after having burned and demolished everything of any importance in the vicinity.   Such is the cruel necessity of war.   Destruction and sudden

SIEGE TRAIN, HILTON HEAD.

SMITHS PLANTATION, PORT ROYAL.

PREPARING COTTON FOR GIN.

SCENES AT HILTON HEAD AND PORT ROYAL, S. C.

death, desolation and despair, mark its awful path.   The torch finishes what shot and shell have shattered, and only those who have witnessed them can appreciate the savage and relentless character of battle, siege and skirmish.   Even the march of an army through friendly territory, leaves a seared footmark at almost every step it takes.   The re-occupation of South Carolina soil was cause for great rejoicing throughout the North, and celebrations were rendered the more extensive when, by a general order, thanking the commanders of the expedition, the Secretaries of the Army and the Navy directed that a salute be fired from each navy yard and Federal fort in honor of the event.   But the time was soon coming when the Government had something more important than salutes to think of, while the people began to exercise more patience regarding the progress of events on sea and land.

But Dupont had not yet finished his task, for it should be said that, though he did **not** entirely originate the Hilton Head Expedition, he so elaborated and embroidered it,

LANDING AFTER BOMBARDMENT OF FORT WALKER.

that it really became his own. Leaving the pretty little town of Beaufort, with its luxurious Summer houses, hidden by vine-covered verandahs and embosomed in orange and lemon groves, Dupont entered the Bay of St. Helena and Warsaw Sound, thus threatening command of the Savannah River and the Tybee. St. Helena Harbor is almost equal in size and security to that of Charleston. On November 25, Big Tybee Island also fell into the hands of the Federals, and the gallant Dupont was able to say in his despatches that the flag of the United States was again flying over the soil of Georgia. The final result of these operations was that all the coast, from Warsaw Sound, below the mouth of the Savannah River, northward as far as the entrance to the North Edisto River, was under control of the National Government. Forts Jackson and Pulaski alone remained in Confederate hands, and they effect-

COMMODORE JOSIAH TATNALL, C. S. N.

COMMODORE C H. DAVIS, U. S. N.

ually guarded the entrance of the Savannah River and protected the city bearing that name. Active and zealous as Dupont proved himself, he was well mated in General "Tom"

FORT PULASKI.

Sherman, who not only strengthened all the captured positions, but constructed an immense wharf at Hilton Head, erected large storehouses, and made it a depot for naval and army supplies. During all subsequent seacoast movements, such as the siege of Charleston, the attack in Mobile Bay, and the capture of New Orleans, the depots at Hilton Head and Port Royal Island performed an important part in receiving and forwarding food, rations, clothing, arms and ammunition. Thus ended the operations during the year 1861. The sword had been drawn for nearly eight months, yet the people of the North and the South

BUILDING PONTOON BRIDGE NEAR BEAUFORT, S. C.

had but barely crossed the threshold of their internecine and fratricidal struggle. The pause that ensued was an ominous one, for when hostilities were renewed in the Spring of 1862, they wrapped the entire Union in a cloud of flame from the banks of the Potomac to those of the Mississippi.

Among the Confederate offensive operations at this period of the war was the fitting out of armed privateers, which were to cruise over the Atlantic ocean and destroy Federal merchant shipping. The first of these privateers to attract notice was the Nashville, a sidewheeler of eleven hundred tons burden. She carried two rifled twelve-pounders, and was commanded by Captain Pegrim, who had as Lieutenants, Bennett and Fauntleroy. On November 17, 1861, the Nashville captured the merchantman Harvey Birch, in latitude 49 degrees, 6 minutes north, and longitude 9 degrees, 52 minutes, west (a part of the British Channel). Captain Nelson and his crew of twenty-nine men were made prisoners, and transferred to the Nashville. Captain Pegrim then removed all that was valuable in the merchantman's cargo, and setting fire to the ship, sailed for Southampton where the prisoners were released on British soil. This act caused intense excitement in the North.

Although General "Tom" Sherman and Commodore Dupont had achieved a great deal, they failed to secure control of the mouth of the Savannah River, consequently the blockade remained open at that point. The approaches to the Savannah were covered by Fort Pulaski and Fort Jackson, both formidable in structure and armament. Dupont had attempted several times to reach the city of Savannah by way of Warsaw Sound, but only succeeded in getting possession of Dawfuskie Island, where he stationed a few gunboats. It remained for General Quincy A. Gillmore, General Sherman's chief of staff and an eminent military engineer, to devise the proper method of

GENERAL DRAYTON, C. S. A.

EXTERIOR VIEW OF REAR.

EXTERIOR VIEW OF SIDE.

EXTERIOR VIEW OF FRONT.

FORT PULASKI.

reducing Fort Pulaski.   Gillmore placed batteries on Big Tybee Island, to the southeast of Cockspur, and at Venus Point, on Jones' Island, almost directly opposite.   It was

PONTOON BOAT READY FOR THE MARCH.

arduous work, but a secret artificial channel connecting the Savannah River with Calibogue Sound was discovered, it having been obstructed by the Confederates.   Through this

FORT PULASKI, DURING BOMBARDMENT, APRIL 11, 1862.

channel, and by way of Wilmington Narrows, St. Aug-
ustine's Creek and Warsaw Sound, a body of troops,
under General Viele, built a small fort on Venus Point,
and mounted several heavy guns. Other batteries were
erected on Long Island and at the mouth of Mud
River, which not only commanded the river entrance,
but cut off all communication between Fort Pulaski and
the City of Savannah.

By April 9, 1862, there were eleven batteries,
mounting thirty-six guns, and on the following day a
message was sent by General David Hunter, who had
three days before relieved Sherman of the chief command, to Colonel Charles H. Olmstead, calling on him
to surrender. The Confederate Colonel's reply was
characteristic and might have been expected. "I was
placed here to defend this fort," said he, "not to surrender before a shot has been fired."

There was therefore nothing for the Federals to do
but to open fire, and they proceeded to do so about eight
o'clock on April 10. Scarcely had the first shot gone

BRIG.-GENERAL QUINCY A. GILLMORE.

shrieking through the sunshine, when Olmstead, made a vigorous response. The exchange
of heavy metal was kept up all day, and at sunset the solid masonry of the fort showed the
effects of the terribly large rifle shells and solid bolts that had been hurled against it.
Finally the stone walls crumbled, as the missiles honeycombed it, each ten-inch shot
adding to the battering process. Five of Colonel Olmstead's guns were dismantled, and

FORT PULASKI.

his remaining pieces delivered a very feeble fire.   On the morning of April 11, the Federal batteries resumed their terrific bombardment, and as the sun gilded the awful scene, wide

SIGNAL TOWER.

MAJOR-GENERAL D. HUNTER.

gaps appeared in the Southern angle of Fort Pulaski.   Finding that the shots were penetrating to his magazine, the brave Colonel hoisted his token of surrender.   General Hunter thus came into possession of the fort, with its garrison of four hundred officers and

INTERIOR OF MORTAR BATTERY "STANTON," TYBEE ISLAND, S. C., DURING BOMBARDMENT OF FORT PULASKI, APRIL 10, 1862.

men, forty-seven pieces of cannon, an immense quantity of commissary supplies, and nearly fifty thousand pounds of powder.   Despite the severity of this heavy artillery duel, only one

FORT PULASKI.

Federal was killed, and three Confederates were wounded.   As Fort Pulaski gave the Federals control of the Savannah River, no effort was made to capture Fort Jackson, and it was subsequently voluntarily evacuated by the Confederate forces.

COMMODORE FOOTE'S FLOTILLA ON THE MISSISSIPPI.

CHAPTER IX.

CAPTURE OF FORT HENRY BY GENERAL GRANT AND COMMODORE FOOTE.

Great activity in the Southwest marked the beginning of the year 1862. At that time General Henry W. Halleck commanded the Federal Department of the Mississippi, and

MAJOR-GENERAL DON CARLOS BUELL.

General Don Carlos Buell controlled the Department of the Ohio. Confronting these leaders stood General Albert Sidney Johnston, who had a strong established defensive line. The Confederate left rested at Columbus, on the Mississippi River; Forts Henry and Donelson guarded the Tennessee and Cumberland Rivers, and an entrenched camp at Bowling Green protected the important network of railroads running Southward to Nashville. Johnston's right flank lay at Mill Spring, Kentucky. Stratgetically considered, this line was apparently perfect for defensive purposes, though it was not of much use in offensive operations. About January 10, a forward movement of the Federal forces began. General Grant was at Cairo, Illinois, his forces also occupying Paducah, Kentucky, while General George H. Thomas was threatening Mill Spring.

The Confederate force, under General Felix K. Zollicoffer, numbered about five thousand men, all Tennesseans, except one Mississippi and one

Alabama regiment. General Thomas had three thousand men from Ohio, Minnesota, Indiana, and Kentucky, having sent General Schoepf to Somerset, from which he was advanced. Zollicoffer decided to take the initiative and started to meet Thomas' column. The Confederàtes plodded through mud and mire, in a cold, drenching rain, during Saturday, January 18, finding the Fourth Kentucky and Tenth Indiana where the Somerset and Mill Spring Roads meet. The following morning, Zollicoffer advanced in

MAJOR-GENERAL HENRY WAGER HALLECK.

strong force, and drove the Federals from one position to another, until they had exhausted their ammunition and retired to the woods. Thomas then re-formed, and received another charge. So impetuous were the movements of the Confederates that they seemed to be carrying everything before them, but Colonel S. S. Fry, of the Fourth Kentucky, noticed Zollicoffer riding in advance of his line, and fired. The pistol shot was returned by one of Zollicoffer's aides, the bullet killing Fry's horse. The Federal Colonel disentangled himself, and again fired, the bullet entering Zollicoffer's heart, and killing him instantly.

General George B. Crittenden assumed command, but the Confederates were disheartened by Zollicoffer's death, and finally gave way before a magnificent Fede-

BRIGADIER, AFTERWARDS MAJOR-GENERAL, SCHUYLER HAMILTON.

BRIGADIER-GENERAL G. W. CULLUM.

ral charge led by the Ninth Ohio, under Colonel R. L. McCook.

General Sterling Price succeeded Zollicoffer in command of the Confederate forces in Missouri, and as he was being rapidly reinforced, Halleck sent General S. R. Curtis to Lebanon, with brigades under Sigel, Asboth, Carr, Davis and Prentiss.

Zollicoffer's death was disastrous to the Southern side, for his army was driven from its chosen position and compelled to retreat in wild confusion to its Winter camp. As the fruits of his victory, Thomas reported the capture of twelve pieces of field artillery, with their caissons and army forges, besides a large quantity of small arms and ammunition. In addition to these, there were twelve hundred horses and mules, nearly three hundred wagons, a vast quantity of commissary stores, tools and camp equipage.

General Thomas' success had an important influence on the subsequent operations in that part of the theatre of war. It elated the North, and depressed the South, for it shattered the Confederate line in Kentucky, and opened the door for the Federals to enter and redeem Tennessee. But Johnston's positions at Bowling Green and Columbus were still intact, so both armies

A FEDERAL GUNBOAT.

prepared for serious work. Halleck was fortunate in having under him several regular army officers who subsequently rose to high distinction. Besides Grant (who was ultimately to extinguish Halleck), and William T. Sherman, there were Buell and McCook, who had served in Mexico, and Mitchell, who graduated from West Point in the same class with Robert E. Lee and Joe Johnston. In Buell's army were T. L. Crittenden and William Nelson, both well experienced in the art of war. Among Buell's Colonels was James A. Garfield, who rode at the head of an Ohio regiment, and had shown remarkable capacity and courage. Garfield was made a Brigadier for gallantry at the Battle of Prestonburg, where, with fifteen hundred men, he defeated twenty-five hundred Confederates under Humphrey Marshall, on January 7, 1862. The Confederate General was never heard of afterwards. The page of history that was to speak of Garfield

MAJOR-GENERAL SAMUEL R. CURTIS.   MAJOR-GENERAL B. M. PRENTISS.   BVT. MAJOR-GENERAL JOSEPH B. CARR.

as sharing the martyred fate of Lincoln was then unwritten, but his remarkable career had begun.

General Halleck graduated from West Point in 1839, at the age of 24 years. He was assigned to the Engineer Corps, and became assistant professor of engineering at the Academy. Subsequently he served on the fortification board in New York harbor, when he was sent on a tour of examination of the public works in Europe. At the time of the Mexican War, he took an active part in the military and civil operations of the Government on the Pacific Coast, remaining there until the close of the year 1850. He was then made director-general of the New Almaden Quicksilver Mine, and, in 1854, resigned from the army, devoting himself mainly to the practice of law in San Francisco. In making up his staff, on being called into the service and given charge of a military department, Halleck selected Brigadier-General George W. Cullum as his chief of staff, and Schuyler Hamilton

GENERAL ALBERT SIDNEY JOHNSTON, C. S. A.

as assistant chief. Cullum, like Halleck, had had no experience in active operations. They were military students and professors. This fact explains why Grant found his practical ideas distasteful to headquarters.

To comprehend the importance of the movements about to be described, the reader should remember that Fort Henry stood on the east bank of the Tennessee River, while Fort Donelson occupied the west bank of the Cumberland. These two bastioned earthworks were about twelve miles apart, connected by an exceedingly well-constructed military road. There were also some Confederate redoubts on Island Number Ten. So elaborate was the network of forts and entrenchments, that the Confederates believed the City of Columbus to be impregnable, and they styled it "The Gibraltar of America." The garrisons in Forts Henry and Donelson consisted of twenty-four thousand men, who had some one hundred and twenty siege guns and field pieces. So evident was it that the two forts found the key to the Confederate line that they began independently to move upon it. General Buell suggested such a course to Halleck, while Grant, not knowing that his superior in rank had done so, also wrote to Halleck urging the same thing. These letters only confirmed the views of Sherman and Cullum who were with Halleck, and Grant at once received orders to go ahead.

General Grant had then at his disposal about seventeen thousand men, and it was decided to give him the assistance of the river gunboats under Commander Andrew H. Foote. While making his preparations for the movement, Grant ordered a reconnaisance which satisfied him that Fort Henry could easily be taken, if attacked promptly from the Tennessee River. On Monday, February 2, the combined Federal army and naval forces left Cairo for Paducah, where they arrived the same evening. The appearance of this formidable flotilla, as it moved up the Ohio River and through the Grand Chain, was a novel and picturesque one. The gunboats were flat-bottomed hulls on which mansard-shaped structures had been built of heavy planks, covered with two or three layers of railroad iron. The angles were so sharply deflected that a shot or shell would usually fly off at a tangent, instead of piercing the improvised armor. Foote had seven of these nondescript craft under his command, and he led the advance of the flotilla. Every sort of steam river craft had been pressed into the service as transports, so their number quite imposing. Grant's men were in high fettle, for nothing better pleases a foot soldier than to be carried to his fighting ground on a steamer, because he can loll at his ease and enjoy the scenery along the route, being quite indifferent to the fact that he may never see it again,

GENERAL THOMAS C. HINDMAN, C. S. A.

General Grant's attacking land force had been divided into two divisions, under command of Brigadiers John A. McClernand and Charles F. Smith, the entire command consisting of twenty Illinois regiments, two Iowa, two Missouri and one Indiana, besides a tolerably effective force of artillery and cavalry. The garrison in Fort Henry consisted of three thousand men, under Brigadier-General Lloyd Tilghman, and the batteries were armed with seventeen heavy guns. During the forenoon of Tuesday, February 3, Foote's gunboats advanced up the river to a point nine miles below Fort Henry, the troops having landed the previous day at Bailey's Ferry, going into camp on a high ridge near the river bank. Reconnaisances were made the next day, on both water and land, and everything was ready on Thursday, February 5, for the final attack. Grant and Foote had agreed that their advance should be made simultaneously on the 6th, in time for the engagement to begin about eleven o'clock. But during the night of the 5th, an unusually heavy rainstorm came up, so that while the rising river benefited the flotilla, the muddy roads and swollen streams they had to cross, proved a serious obstacle to the march of the troops, their artillery finding its progress to be both difficult and dangerous.

BRIGADIER-GENERAL JAMES A. GARFIELD.

The armored gunboats found no difficulty in passing the fire of the heavy guns in the fort, Foote taking advantage of the protection afforded by Panther Island, which stands in the Western channel of the Tennessee River. So well did the naval commander perform his part of the work, that he was able to open fire at a range of about six hundred yards, while Grant's force was laboriously advancing through the mud. General Smith's column was proceeding on the opposite bank of the river in the direction of Fort Hieman, while that of General McClernand staggered along through swamp and mire towards the Dover Road, between Forts Henry and Donelson. The Federal bombardment opened on time, and lasted for over three hours, the Confederates making a warm and vigorous response.

GENERAL HUMPHREY MARSHALL, C. S. A.

Long before the roar of cannon had died away, General Tilghman learned from his scouts of the advance of Grant's land forces, and as his position had already become untenable, he determined to save his command from capture by retreating to Fort Donelson. Acting on this determination, the unfortunate Confederate General saw his troops march away rather disorderly, leaving him with less than one hundred officers and men. By that time all but seven of the siege guns in the fort had been dismantled by the incessant and terrific shelling of the Federal fleet. One of these guns had burst during the engagement, killing several men, the entire Confederate loss being ten men killed and some thirty wounded. As soon as Tilghman made his signal of surrender, Commodore Foote sent Commander Stembel, of his flagship, with Lieutenant Phelps, to hoist the Federal flag over the captured fort, and it was soon flying there. When General Tilghman surrendered his position, the fort had been almost battered out of shape. The ramparts were ragged, the embrasures destroyed, and dismantled cannons added to the awful wreck. Grant's troops did not come up in time to join in the glory of the victory, though they felt consoled by the fact that while Foote's guns were smashing Fort Henry, it was their advance that finally led to its surrender. General Smith's force had meanwhile captured Fort Hieman, on the opposite bank of the Tennessee, which was not defended at all, though, by its more elevated position, it completely commanded Fort Henry. The strategy displayed by Grant on the Tennessee River was merely an example of what he was to do on more important campaigns. The Federal loss was only two killed and thirty-eight wounded, among the former being Lieutenant Brittan, who was struck on the head by a forty-two pound shot. The captured

MAJOR-GENERAL W. NELSON.

MAJOR-GENERAL T. L. CRITTENDON.   MAJOR-GENERAL ANSON G. MC COOK   MAJOR-GENERAL O. M. MITCHELL.

fort contained tents for eight thousand men, some fifteen serviceable cannon, a large quantity of small arms, ammunition, commissary stores and general equipments. Though General Grant had not been personally engaged in the affair, he received his full share of praise, while Foote was formally thanked in general naval orders for his gallantry.

This being General Grant's first independent movement, and the first great success in his wonderful career as a commander of large bodies of troops, he naturally writes at length concerning the capture of Fort Henry while dictating his memoirs. After telling how cavalierly Halleck treated him in St. Louis, and the ungracious consent given for the movement, Grant goes on to say : "The enemy at this time occupied a line running from the Mississippi River at Columbus, to Bowling Green and Mill Springs, Kentucky. Each of these positions was strongly fortified, as were also points on the Tennessee and Cumberland Rivers near the Tennessee state line. The works on the Tennessee were

Geo H Thomas

DEATH OF GENERAL ZOLLICOFFER, AT MILL SPRINGS.

called Fort Heiman and Fort Henry, and that on the Cumberland was Fort Donelson. At these points the two rivers approached within eleven miles of each other. The lines of rifle-pits at each place extended back from the water at least two miles, so that the garrisons were in reality only seven miles apart. These positions were of immense importance to the enemy; and, of course, correspondingly important for us to possess ourselves of. With Fort Henry in our hands we had a navigable stream open to us up to Muscle Shoals, in Alabama. The Memphis and Charleston Railroad strikes the Tennessee at Eastport, Mississippi, and follows close to the banks of the river up to the shoals. This road, of vast importance to the enemy, would cease to be of use to them for through traffic, the moment Fort

Henry became ours. Fort Donelson was the gate to Nashville—a place of great military and political importance—and to a rich country extending far east in Kentucky. These two points in our possession, the enemy would necessarily be thrown back to the Memphis and Charleston road, or to the boundary of the cotton states, and, as before stated, that road would be lost to them for through communication. In February, 1862, there were quite a good many steamers laid up at Cairo for want of employment, the Mississippi River being closed against navigation below that point. There were also many men in the town whose occupation had been following the river in various capacities, from captain down to deck hand. But there were not enough of either boats or men to move at one time the seventeen thousand men I proposed to take with me up the Tennessee. I loaded the boats with more than half the force, however, and sent General McClernand in command. I followed with one of the later boats and found McClernand had stopped, very properly, nine miles below Fort Henry. Seven

GENERAL ZOLLICOFFER, C. S. A.

BATTLE OF MILL SPRINGS, OR LOGAN CROSS ROADS. FEDERALS UNDER GENERAL THOMAS, CONFEDERATES UNDER GENERAL ZOLLICOFFER.

gunboats, under Flag-officer Foote, had accompanied the advance. The transports we had with us had to return to Paducah to bring up a division from there, with General C. F. Smith in command. When the landing was completed, I returned with the transports to Paducah, to hasten up the balance of the troops. I got back on the 5th with the advance, the remainder following as rapidly as the steamers could carry them. At ten oclock at night, on the 5th, the whole command was not yet up. Being anxious to commence operations as soon as possible, before the enemy could reinforce heavily, I issued my orders for an advance at 11 A. M. on the 6th. I felt sure that all the troops would be up by that time. Fort Henry occupies a bend in the river which gave the guns in the water battery a direct fire down the stream. The camp outside the fort was intrenched with riflepits and outworks, two miles back on the road to Donelson and Dover. The garrison of the fort and camp was about two thousand eight hundred, with strong reinforcements from Donelson halted some miles out. There were seventeen heavy guns in the fort. The river was very high, the banks being overflowed, except where the bluffs come to the water's edge. A portion of the ground on which Fort Henry stood was two feet deep in water. Below, the water extended into the wood, several hundred yards back from the bank on the east side. On the west bank, Fort Heiman stood on high ground, completely commanding Fort Henry. It also was captured. The distance from Fort Henry to Donelson is but eleven miles. Tilghman was captured

BRIGADIER-GENERAL I. LOYD TILGHMAN, C. S. A.

FOOTE'S GUNBOATS ADVANCING TO ATTACK FORT HENRY.

with his staff and ninety men, as well as the armament of the fort, the ammunition and whatever stores were there."

COMMODORE A. H. FOOTE.

The result of this movement completely changed the complexion of affairs, for it again proved that the Confederate line was not impregnable, as they had so fondly imagined. Every eye in the North was now fixed on Grant, for his star had risen above the horizon. The importance of this victory for the Federal cause was at once recognized by the Northern people, and as it was evident that this Western General intended to attack Fort Donelson, his next movement was awaited with interest. By his capture of Fort Henry, Grant had showed that he was a strategist of no mean order, and a man who when he started out to fight, actually did do something. The seizure of this little fort had a refreshing effect and was therefore hailed with enthusiasm and joy. It was a curious exhibition, for while Grant and Foote were active on the Tennessee River, the immense army intended for the capture of Richmond was idle on the Potomac.

INTERIOR OF WATER BATTERY, FORT DONELSON.

CHAPTER X.

THE FALL OF FORT DONELSON, ON THE CUMBERLAND RIVER.

The news that Fort Henry had fallen, and that the Federal forces were preparing to attack Fort Donelson, roused General Halleck, and he at once started reinforcements for Grant from St. Louis, Cincinnati and Kansas. It will be remembered that Fort Donelson was located at Dover, Tenn., twelve miles southeast of Fort Henry, on the west bank of the Cumberland River. The location of the fort was selected as a rear defense to Bowling Green, and also as a defense against the approach of the Federal troops on Nashville, by way of the Cumberland River. The Confederates believed that Fort Donelson would prove an effective barrier to the progress of the Federal forces into Tennessee. The railroad from Bowling Green to Memphis passed four miles south of it. So that the loss of these formidable fortifications meant to them the loss of all interior railroad communication. The characteristic energy of General Grant, as displayed by him in every movement undertaken, was never so distinctly shown as by his operations against Fort Donelson. Before sunset on the day that Tilghman surrendered Fort Henry, Grant ordered a reconnaissance up the Tennessee River. Lieutenant Phelps, who conducted it, soon returned and reported that the river was entirely free, consequently there could be no real hindrance to a southward movement by the Federal forces. General Grant and Commander Foote then held a council of war to decide the question whether they should make an immediate advance on Donelson, or wait for the reinforcements they knew were coming. Foote seems to have been as good a fighter as Grant, for the conference speedily resulted in the determination to take immediate action. Grant wisely inferred that the time he must lose in waiting for additional troops would be occupied by the Confederates in strengthening their position, and reinforcing the numerical strength of its garrison. But there was a slight delay, as Foote had to refit his gunboats, so it was not until February 12 that the combined movement began. Grant started from Fort Henry with fifteen thousand men. The day was warm and bright, the telegraph and Dover roads were in excellent condition, and the troops, being flushed with victory, were buoyant and hopeful.

An hour before sunset, the entire Federal force on land had arrived within striking distance of Fort Donelson, and Grant got his men into position before sunset. The entire night was occupied in throwing up entrenchments and posting the batteries. These Illinois, Missouri, Iowa, Kansas and Indiana Volunteers were already feeling that confidence in their leader, which it was Grant's exceeding good fortune to impart during all his subsequent campaigns. With his customary promptness, Grant had decided to begin the attack on the morn-

COLONEL, AFTERWARDS
MAJOR-GENERAL,
JOHN A. LOGAN.

COLONEL, AFTERWARDS MAJOR-GENERAL, R. J. OGLESBY.

ing of the 13th, but the gunboats, which were convoying some transports carrying a part of Lew Wallace's Division, did not arrive as expected, and, as he was unwilling to risk a general engagement without his full force, Grant waited. General Floyd, who had been driven out of West Virginia by Rosencranz, had meanwhile arrived in Fort Donelson, and being superior in rank to General Pillow, had assumed command. The Confederate force, including the escaping garrison of Fort Henry, was about twenty-three thousand strong, and they had no less than ninety-five field and siege cannon. Supposing that the Federals were before him in full strength, Floyd opened fire, which was responded to. There was also some sharp-shooting by picked marksmen, followed by a dash on what was known as the Middle Redoubt. Colonel Hahn led his troops most gallantly, but the Confederates were strongly posted, and delivered a galling fire which compelled the Federals to withdraw. A similar effort on the left, by part of Lanman's Brigade, was equally unsucessful, the losses of the Federals being heavy, a result which greatly disheartened Grant's men, for they found themselves back on the ground they had occupied in the morning. To add to their discomfort, it began to rain very heavily, the thermometer fell and the rain was followed by sleet and snow. At midnight a severe frost set in and the temperature dropped to ten degrees below zero. As the Federals were without tents, and fires were denied them in order to conceal their line of battle, the men suffered terribly. Food was scarce, and the wounded cried aloud in their agony. Thus the night was spent, the young Volunteers, learning for the first time that war is not altogether a matter of parade and review, but there is more horror and suffering than pageantry, attending the movements of large bodies of hostile troops.

Recognizing the necessity of having every available man on the ground, Grant had sent orders to Lew Wallace, who had been made a Brigadier only a few days before, to

BAYONET CHARGE OF 2D IOWA ON CONFEDERATE INTRENCHMENTS AT FORT DONELSON, FEBRUARY 15, 1862.

come up with his Fort Henry garrison. He reported at noon of February 14, finding the little army in splendid spirits, despite their night of suffering. Foote also arrived with the transports, and the remainder of Wallace's division landed. By the arrival of this force, Grant was able to entirely invest Fort Donelson and its outworks, a task of no small magnitude, as the Confederates had completely enclosed the town of Dover by their fortifications, the entire line having a length of over two and a half miles. The transports had also brought an abundance of commissary and ordnance supplies, and as the men satisfied their ravenous hunger, preparations for a general assault were completed. It should be understood that while Grant was never rash, once he began to fight he did not know when he was beaten. Anyone who has seen this remarkable man in the field, must remember the massive jaw, denoting strong will-power, while the sweet smile that often lingered on his bearded face, so softened its expression that you recognized how calm and deliberate was his mental character. Though Grant had now all of his men in hand, he did not act rashly, for, knowing that Donelson was powerfully mounted with artillery, he realized that an assault upon the Confederate intrenchments would be attended by an enormous loss of life. He therefore decided to give Foote and his gunboats an opportunity to repeat the service they had rendered on the Tennessee River.

Grant's forces were now in the positions assigned them. McClernand's division held

CAPTAIN, AFTERWARDS BVT. BRIG.-GENERAL W. S. HILLYER.

CAPTAIN, AFTERWARDS BVT. MAJOR-GEN. J. A. RAWLINS.

COLONEL, AFTERWARDS BVT. MAJOR--GENERAL J. D. WEBSTRR.

MEMBERS OF BRIGADIER-GENERAL U. S GRANT'S STAFF.

the right of the Federal line, with Smith's on the left, and Wallace occupied the centre. Instructing his three Division Commanders to preserve the line of investment intact, and stand ready to repel any attempt to break it, Grant sent word to Foote that he was to open the attack. The naval commander responded promptly, and at three o'clock in the afternoon, moved up the Cumberland River with four ironclads, two wooden armed vessels and the gunboat Carondelet, which had arrived a few days before. At the distance of a mile and a half, the ironclads opened fire, but no reply was made. The little fleet moved steadily forward, delivering a shower of shells, until it arrived within four or five hundred

ARMY WINTER QUARTERS.

yards of the batteries. Then the Confederates poured a plunging fire from twenty heavy guns that had been placed on the highest point of their fortified ground. Every shot told, but Foote pressed on until he silenced one of the upper batteries. The combat was, however, an unequal one, as the Louisville lost her rudder chains and drifted helplessly down the stream, the St. Louis, Foote's flagship, meeting a similar fate, the Commodore himself being wounded, and his pilot was killed.

The flotilla having withdrawn in a disabled con- dition, Grant discovered that he had underestimated the Confederate strength, and that the tactics he had adopted at Fort Henry would not be successful at Donelson. He therefore consented that Foote should proceed to Cairo, and return with a fleet of sufficient strength to cope with the heavier metal to be encoun tered. Meanwhile the land forces were to continue perfecting their investment, and thus effectually shut up the Confederates. In fact, it was to be a siege, and the experience that Grant gained at Donelson subsequently proved of immense value at Vicksburg on the Mississippi, and at Petersburg on the James. Speaking of his initial operations before Fort Donel- son, Grant says : "Fort Donelson is two miles north, or down the river, from Dover. The fort, as it stood in 1861, embraced about one hundred acres of land. On the east it fronted the Cumberland ; to the north it faced Hickman's Creek, a small stream

MAJOR-GENERAL J. A. McCLERNAND

which, at that time, was deep and wide, because of the back-water from the river ; on the south was another small stream or ravine, opening into the Cumberland. This also was filled with back-water from the river. The fort stood on high ground, some of it as much as a hundred feet above the Cumberland. Strong protection to the heavy guns in the water batteries had been obtained by cutting away places for them in the bluff. To the west there was a line of rifle-pits some two miles back from the river at the farthest point. This line ran generally along the crest of high ground, but in one place crossed a ravine which opens into the river between the village and the fort. The ground inside and outside of this intrenched line was very broken and generally wooded. The trees outside of the rifle-pits had been cut down for a considerable way out, and had been felled so that their tops lay outwards from the entrenchments. The limbs had been trimmed and pointed, and thus formed an abatis in front of the greater

GENERAL BUCKNER, U. S. A.

part of the line. I started from Fort Henry with fifteen thousand men, including eight batteries and part of a regiment of cavalry, and, meeting with no obstruction to detain us, the advance arrived in front of the enemy by noon. That afternoon and the next day were spent in taking up ground to make the investment as complete as possible. General Smith had been directed to leave a portion of his division behind to guard Forts Henry and Heiman. He left General Lew Wallace with twenty-five hundred men. With the remainder of his division he occupied our left, extending to Hickman Creek. McClernand was on the right, and covered the roads running south and southwest from Dover. His right extended to the back-water up the ravine opening into the Cumberland, south of the village. The troops were not intrenched, but the nature of the ground was such that they were just as well protected from the fire of the enemy as if rifle-pits had been thrown up. Our line was generally along the crest of ridges. The artillery was protected by being sunk in the ground. The men who were not serving the guns were perfectly covered from fire on

GENERAL G. I. PILLOW, C. S. A.

GENERAL BUSHROD JOHNSON, C. S. A.

taking position a little back from the crest. The greatest suffering was from want of shelter. It was midwinter and during the siege we had rain and snow, thawing and freezing alternately. It would not do to allow camp-fires except far down the hill out of sight of the enemy, and it would not do to allow many of the troops to remain there at the same time. In the march over from Fort Henry, numbers of the men had thrown away their blankets and overcoats. There was therefore much discomfort and absolute suffering."

MAJOR-GENERAL LEW WALLACE.

As often happens in war, while the Confederate soldiers were rejoicing over their brilliant and complete repulse of Foote's gunboat flotilla, their Generals were seriously debating how best they could escape from Fort Donelson. Grant says, in his memoirs, that he knew General Floyd was in command in the Fort, and contemptuously speaks of him as "no soldier," but while Floyd was not an educated soldier, he knew when he was whipped. Having been so thoroughly trounced by Rosencranz on the Upper Potomac, he had no stomach for a similar lesson at Grant's hands on the Cumberland. So at the very moment Grant, McClernand, Smith

CHARGE OF THE 8TH MISSOURI, AND 11TH INDIANA, LED BY GENERAL LEW WALLACE, AT FORT DONELSON.

and Wallace were gazing blankly at each other, Floyd was not at all elated by his apparent success. Both he and Pillow felt much like a couple of rats that have been caught in a trap. They had already discovered that Grant was rapidly hemming them in, which fact led Floyd to believe that the Federal strength was greater than it really was. Floyd, having been Buchanan's Secretary of War, knew better than any other officer in the Confederate service how great were the resources of the Federal forces. He may have been a poor soldier, but he was no fool, and realized that the entire available force of the United States western armies would soon be arrayed against him. So, while the gunboats were getting ready to go to Cairo, Floyd called a council of war, when it was unanimously decided to swallow the bitter pill, and face the people of the Confederacy by evacuating Fort Donelson. The military genius of Grant is revealed by his simple statement in his memoirs, that he thought fifteen thousand men could do more

THE SUTLER'S TENT.

SO WELL REMEMBERED BY ALL OLD SOLDIERS. "THE DEAREST PLACE ON EARTH."

with Fort Donelson in February than fifty thousand might accomplish in March. It was this faculty of rapid decision, and a willingness to take reasonable chances, that has given Grant his exalted position in American history.

Having resolved to get out of Fort Donelson, Floyd began to ponder on the best method of doing so. Acting on the advice of his subordinates, he determined to force a path around Grant's right, and so pass into the open country and march for Nashville. There were two roads suitable for this purpose, could he reach either of them, one was the Wynn's Ferry Road, leading from Dover through Charlotte, the other an undesirable route across the flats of the Cumberland. Owing to the sudden freshet, so frequent at that season of the year, the latter road was under water, so it was Hobson's choice, the Wynn's Ferry Road or none. A slight reconnaissance by a slender skirmish line revealed the presence of McClernand's troops. It was therefore decided that Pillow's division should make a strong attack upon McClernand's extreme right, while Buckner's division was to assault the Federal right centre and seize Wynn's Ferry Road. The Confederates hoped by this movement to force McClernand upon Wallace and eventually roll back the line upon Smith, thus opening the way for a successful retreat. Buckner even thought that they might possibly rout Grant's entire command and force it to embark on its transports. This daring plan was successful, so long as the original scheme was adhered to. On Saturday morning, February 15, Generals Gideon J. Pillow and Bushrod R. Johnston started with ten thousand men, Colonel Baldwin's brigade having the advance. So quietly was the movement executed, that Oglesby's brigade, of McClernand's division, were surprised, and had to give way after exhausting their ammunition. Then almost the entire right wing fell back until it reached the Thirty-first Illinois, under Colonel John A. Logan. But "Black Jack," as his men fondly called Logan, because of his coal-black hair and swarthy complexion, held his ground so firmly, that the threatened

MAJOR-GENERAL C. F. SMITH.

panic was averted. Then the Eleventh and Twentieth Illinois, of Wallace's division, came to Oglesby's support, followed by other regiments and some light batteries.

The fighting finally grew so severe, as brigade after brigade of Confederate troops moved forward, that the situation of McClernand became a desperate one. Pillow's men poured in fierce and continuous volleys of musketry, supplemented by well-directed discharges of artillery. One position after another was taken and re-taken, yet at eight o'clock no apparent advantage had been gained by either Federal or Confederate. McClernand on finding that his men were becoming physically exhausted, and also running out of ammunition, sent an urgent request to Wallace for immediate assistance. Now, Wallace had been a Brigadier scarcely a week, and as Grant had given him strict orders to hold the Federal centre at all hazards, he was in a quandary, especially as Grant was on a gunboat, in conference with Commodore Foote. The second message from McClernand announced that his flank had been turned. This decided Wallace's doubts, and he dispatched Cruft's brigade. Unfortunately, this slender reinforcement was guided beyond the Federal right and encountered a superior Confederate force. Nothing daunted, Cruft went into action, but was forced back, as were the commands under Oglesby, McArthur and W. H. L. Wallace. In this critical moment, Thayer's brigade arrived on the ground, with Lew Wallace at its head, and threw itself between the discomfited right wing and the victoriously advancing Confederate, a battery of light artillery, under Lieutenant Wood, doing splendid service in sweeping the road over which Pillow's columns were moving. As Wallace

MILITARY RAILROAD GUN.

deployed his forces and awaited attack, McClernand's men having refilled their cartridge pouches, fell in again and presented a firm front. The Confederates were, of course, ignorant of this, and ascended the crest held by the Federals with overconfidence. When they came within musket range, Pillow's and Buckner's men were astounded at meeting a well-directed withering series of volleys. So terrific, indeed, was this Federal musketry, that the Confederates staggered, then reeled, and finally broke in confusion. No one can ever accuse either the Northern or Southern soldiers of cowardice. So it was not surprising that the Confederates quickly re-formed and charged a second time. But their repulse was greater than before, and the men finally fled to the shelter of their entrenchments.

While all this was going on, Grant was hastening to join his army. He had heard the guns and was met by Captain Hillyer of his staff, who told him that everything seemed

THE CARONDELET PASSING CONFEDERATE BATTERIES AT ISLAND NUMBER TEN.

lost. The General arrived soon after the final repulse of the Confederates, and saw that whichever side next took the offensive had the best chance of winning. About three o'clock in the afternoon he directed McClernand to advance and retake the line he had lost in the morning, at the same time ordering the right wing, under Smith, to move forward and attack Floyd's right, while Wallace was to aid McClernand. The battle that ensued was hotly contested, but the Federals were animated by the presence of their Commanding General, and forced the Confederates inside their main line of forts. When darkness fell on the scene Wallace was almost inside the fortifications. Then ensued a night of horrible suffering, for the thermometer fell to twenty degrees below freezing point. Four thousand dead and wounded men lay scattered over the battle ground, many of the latter becoming frozen corpses before dawn. Grant had decided on making a general assault the following (Sunday) morning, but while he was sleeping in a negro's hut, Floyd held another council. Pillow and Buckner coincided with Floyd that nothing was left them but capitulation. Floyd's only thought was—how was he himself to escape, for he feared punishment as a traitor, if made a prisoner. Finally he threw up his command, and as Pillow declined to take it, the arrangement was made that Pillow should cross the river in a scow, while Floyd and his brigade embarked on board a steamboat, Buckner being left to endure the full humiliation of surrendering. General Forrest also escaped with ten thousand horsemen.

On Sunday morning, February 16, Buckner sent word to Grant that he would capitulate if allowed the honors of war. Grant's reply was a demand for unconditional and immediate surrender, adding that he proposed to move on the Confederate works at once. That settled it, and Grant not only captured Fort Donelson, but he received sixteen thousand men as prisoners, including Generals Buckner and Johnston, twenty thousand muskets, three thousand horses, seventeen heavy guns, forty-eight field-pieces, and a large

GALLANT CHARGE OF 17TH, 48TH AND 49TH ILLINOIS ON FORT DONELSON.

quantity of military stores. The Federals had lost four hundred and forty-six killed, one thousand seven hundred and forty-five wounded, and a few prisoners, who had already been taken across the Cumberland. The additional losses of the Confederates were two hundred and thirty-seven killed, and one thousand and seven wounded, thus swelling their total loss to seventeen thousand, two hundred and fifty-four. Generals Grant, McClernand and Wallace were each promoted to a Major-Generalship, and the fame of the future Lieutenant-General spread through the North. Grant's forces before Donelson numbered twenty-seven thousand men, and additional reinforcements arrived during the day of the capitulation. A curious fact in connection with the movement is revealed in Grant's memoirs, and it may be considered the foundation of the high regard and esteem which existed between Grant and Sherman during the remainder of their lives. Grant thus relates it : " During the seige, General Sherman had been sent to Smithland, at the mouth of the Cumberland River, to forward reinforcements and supplies to me. At that time he was my senior in rank, and there was no authority of law to assign a junior to command a

PONTOON BRIDGE BETWEEN GEORGETOWN AND ANALOSTA ISLAND.

senior of the same grade.   But every boat that came up with supplies or reinforcements brought a note of encouragement from Sherman, asking me to call upon him for any assistance he could render, and saying that if he could be of service at the front I might send for him and he would waive rank."

The capture of Fort Donelson had its natural effect on the people of both sections, the one was elated, the other depressed.   As is well known, Grant received no official recognition from Halleck, the seeds of jealousy being already sown in the breast of the older General, who could not forgive his subordinate for winning so signal a victory.   But Grant tasted of the delights of public praise, and he was content, as well he might be. Commodore Foote was promoted to Rear-Admiral, after the surrender of Island Number Ten.   He had, however, so neglected the wound he received at Fort Donelson that he died in June, 1863, much regretted by the nation he had so gallantly served.

DEAD LAID OUT FOR BURIAL.

The Confederate Iron-Plated Steamer Merrimac (or Virginia) running down the Federal Frigate Cumberland

CHAPTER XI.

THE COMBAT BETWEEN THE MONITOR AND THE MERRIMAC.

Among the war vessels burned by the Federals during the evacuation of Gosport Navy Yard, in April, 1861, was the steam frigate Merrimac, carrying forty guns. Having raised the hull, the Confederates constructed upon it a gigantic floating battery, thickly armored with railroad iron, the heavy guns being protected by the roof-shaped covering. The Merrimac had also been provided with a solid steel bow, or ram, and she carried eleven large guns, with an English Armstrong one-hundred-pound rifled gun at each end. When completed she was considered to be the most powerful vessel afloat. Rumors were afloat at Fortress Monroe that some sort of floating battery, of tremendous proportions, was being constructed, but it was not until March 8, 1862, that she appeared in Hampton Roads. Two small armed steamers accompanied the Merrimac, and at the same time two other Confederate gunboats came down the James River, from Richmond, and took position just above Newport News, then in Federal possession. The simultaneous appearance of all these vessels betokened a preconcerted plan, and every available point of observation was soon occupied by the Federal soldiers, anxious to see what was going to happen, while signal guns were fired by the United States ships of war, Congress and

J. Ericsson

Cumberland, as they lay off Newport News. The sound of these signals, given as a warning to the remainder of the Federal fleet, drew the attention of the Merrimac's commander, Franklin Buchanan, an ex-Federal naval officer, and he at once headed his vessel towards the Congress and the Cumberland. The latter ship swung across the channel and opened a rapid fire on the Merrimac, but the heavy eight and ten-inch solid shot from her guns glanced from the sloping iron-shod sides of the Merrimac, though their weight fairly stunned her. Then putting on steam, the Confederate vessel rushed upon the Cumberland, striking her amidship with its steel prow, tearing open the sloop's side, at the same time delivering a terrible fire from its forward batteries. The Cumberland immediately began sinking, when the Merrimac drew back and then rammed her antagonist a second time. Lieutenant George Morris, who commanded the Cumberland, saw that his vessel was doomed, so emptying all the guns above water, told his men to jump overboard and swim ashore. As they obeyed, being compelled to leave behind nearly one hundred sick and wounded shipmates, the Cumberland toppled over and sank in fifty-four feet of water, the tip of her topmast remaining above the surface of the water with the national ensign still flying. The shore batteries now opened on the strange craft without effect, for the Merrimac, after shelling the Federal camp, headed for the frigate Congress, then busily engaged with the gunboats. Pouring in a deadly broadside the Confederate vessel smashed the Federal frigate, killing her commander, Lieutenant Joseph B. Smith, and many of his crew. The fire from the Merrimac's batteries being repeated with like dreadful results, Lieutenant Pendergast was compelled to hoist a white flag, his ship having been set on fire.

To give the reader some idea of the stoical courage, and the stern professional character of the older officers of the United States Navy, in these trying and eventful days, it is only necessary to relate the following true incident. Lieutenant Smith's father, old Commodore Joseph Smith, was Chief of the Bureau of Yards and Docks, on duty in the Washington Navy Yard. On Sunday morning, March 9, one of the younger officers entered the

LT. JOHN L. WARDEN, COMMANDING THE "MONITOR."

ROANOKE. SEWALL'S POINT. FRENCH MAN-OF-WAR. JAMESTOWN. MONITOR. MERRIMAC. MINNESOTA. NEWPORT NEWS.

SCENE OF THE FIGHT OF THE IRONCLADS.

Commodore's room, and sorrowfully announced the sinking of the two Federal war ships by the Merrimac. Commodore Smith silently gazed into his informant's eyes for a moment, and then, with a smothered sigh, said: "Then Joe is dead?" "Oh, no," replied the young Lieutenant, "It is said that the officers of the Congress surrendered and are prisoners." "You don't know Joe," remarked the old veteran sadly, yet proudly. "If Joe's ship is sunk, he's dead, for he wouldn't surrender, no more than I would." Later intelligence confirmed the Commodore's belief in the stern courage of his gallant son, for young Joe Smith had indeed fought his last fight.

Despite the signal of surrender on board the Congress, Buchanan continued to batter the ship, as she lay too near shore to allow the use of the ram. By the time the survivors of the crew of the doomed ship had escaped, a red-hot shell from the Merrimac entered the

CREW ON DECK OF ORIGINAL "MONITOR."

LIEUT. COMMANDER W. M. JEFFRIES AND OFFICERS ON DECK OF THE "MONITOR."

service magazine of the Congress, causing it to blow up with a deafening detonation. The Federal loss during those eventful two hours, was nearly three hundred killed and drowned, for none of the wounded escaped. While the ship, having the appearance of a submerged house-top, was thus smashing and destroying everything in her path, the Federal frigate Minnesota was sent forward by Flag Officer Marston, his own ship, the Roanoke, being temporarily disabled in her machinery. The Minnesota got first within range of the battery at Sewall's Point, which crippled her mainmast, and then she ran hard aground about a mile and a half from Newport News. Down came the Merrimac, but being of heavier draught than the Minnesota she was unable to get within a mile of her. Both vessels exchanged a rapid fire without result, but as the smaller Confederate vessels crossed the shallows the Minnesota gave them a severe dose of solid shot. Then the Merrimac and her attendant gunboats passed out of sight around Sewall's Point, her

Engagement between the Merrimac (or Virginia) and Monitor, in Hampton Roads.

commander being wounded. There was consternation in Fortress Monroe and among the Federal fleet and transports, for it was evident that the strange naval monster would appear the next day and continue her ravages.

While every preparation was made for the events of the Sabbath morning, very few noticed a small vessel that arrived in the Roads about nine o'clock that night. Those who did see the visitor, were not particularly struck by her appearance, for she was apparently a small vessel, with a deck almost even with the surface of the water, with a circular iron box standing in the centre. Nevertheless, this warlike ship, the Monitor, was to revolutionize all previous methods of naval warfare. She was the invention of John Ericsson, a Swedish

FOUNDERING OF THE MONITOR IN STORM OFF CAPE HATTERAS, DECEMBER 30, 1862.

inventor, who had been a citizen of the United States since 1842, when he invented and built the first steam propeller in the world, she being the frigate Princeton. The appearance of the Monitor was "that of a cheese box on a raft" as was aptly said at the time she arrived in Hampton Roads. She had been built purely on trial, and she nearly foundered during a storm while on the way from New York harbor. It is now known that the Confederates were exceedingly well informed concerning the construction and possibilities of Ericsson's ship, for their secret agents were actually employed in the Greenpoint Yard where she was built. It was the knowledge that the new vessel was coming that led Captain Buchanan to anticipate her arrival. The delays and difficulties encountered by the inventor during her construction, prevented his turning the vessel over to the government for several weeks after the stipulated date. Then she was duly manned, and Lieutenant John L. Worden, her commander, was directed to proceed to Fortress Monroe "for official trial." On his arrival, Worden reported to Flag Officer Marston, and to General Wool, when he was told to proceed at once to Newport News, immediately on receiving an additional supply of ammunition. "My instructions, Worden, are to give your queer shaped craft a thorough and rigid trial,"

TURRET AND PART OF DECK OF ORIGINAL MONITOR, SHOWING DENTS MADE BY POINTED SHOT FROM THE GUNS OF THE "MERRIMAC."

remarked Commander Marston, very dryly, "and by the Lord Harry, you will have it, if Frank Buchanan brings that turtle-backed monster of his out here again." Worden smiled at the grim humor of his superior officer, for he alone knew the probable capacity of the vessel he commanded.

It will be difficult to portray the actual consternation that prevailed at Fortress Monroe, and in Washington, over the appearance of the Merrimac, and the destruction she had effected. Every steamer and sailing vessel under contract to the Government that happened to be waiting orders in Hampton Roads, lost no time in departing, while the officers and crews of the few remaining war vessels prepared for sharing the fate of their comrades of the Congress and the Cumberland. Inside the fortress, and in the camps, it was believed that the Merrimac would be able to batter down the frowning granite walls of the fort. General Wool telegraphed to Washington that he expected to be attacked the next day, and it was supposed in the capital that the Merrimac would eventually blockade the mouth of the Potomac River. The crew of the Monitor were exhausted by their labors during the storm they had just passed through, but they made every preparation for the anticipated "official trial." They took in the extra ammunition in the glare of the flames that were destroying all that was left of the Congress, and listened to the dull boom of her shotted cannon as they were discharged by the awful

OFFICERS ON DECK OF MONITOR.

COMMANDER FRANKLIN BUCHANAN, C. S. N., COMMANDING
THE "MERRIMAC."

heat. The gallant ship had been burning brightly for ten hours and at one o'clock in the morning there was another explosion, as her magazine caught fire, and the scene was left in darkness.

Never did day break more bright and clear, than on that eventful Sunday morning. No trace was left of the Congress, except a floating mass of charred timbers and the dead bodies of her brave crew, but the Cumberland's flag was still flying near the surface of the water. Long before the reveille hour, the sentries on the fortress and the war ships saw the dreaded Merrimac slowly rounding Sewall's Point. Then the sound of her drums beating to quarters floated on the air, and Lieutenant Worden at once got ready to meet her. The Confederate commander headed his armored ship towards the Minnesota, fully intending to capture her. When the stranger came within range of his guns, Captain Van Brunt opened fire with his heaviest metal, but the shot glanced harmlessly, for in addition to being armored, the Merrimac had been coated with tallow. Then the Monitor slipped out from behind the Minnesota. She was saluted by a broadside from the Confederate Ram, then her turret revolved and an eleven-inch solid shot struck the Merrimac, causing the vessel to tremble from prow to stern. To his astonishment, Catesby Jones, who was now in command, discovered that his heavy broadsides had not a particle of effect upon the low turret of Ericsson's ship, so he decided to "ram" her. This just suited Worden for he delivered a shot from each of his two enormous guns, in rapid succession, at the distance of only a few feet. Five times did the Merrimac try to sink the Monitor by running her down, but the latter avoided the encounter by steaming round her cumbrous antagonist, seeking the Merrimac's portholes. Finally a steel bolt from one of the Confederate's rifled guns struck the turret, but stuck there like a leaden bullet in a tree, while the

DESTRUCTION OF THE MERRIMAC.

THE MERRIMAC, OR VIRGINIA.

ponderous armor on the Merrimac was started in several places by the terrific punishment she had sustained. Then, like a bull in flytime, the Merrimac turned from her agile antagonist and attacked the Minnesota, but Van Brunt met her with a broadside and a ten-inch shot from his pivot gun. The discharge had no perceptible effect, though fully fifty solid masses of shots hit the iron mail, while the Minnesota was riddled by one of the huge Armstrong shells which tore open her internal economy in a most frightful way, and killed several men.

Worden's men had by this time got a brief breathing spell, and refreshed themselves with a little rum and water, so the Lieutenant resolved to renew the contest. As he approached, the Merrimac started for Norwalk, but the Monitor was not to be shaken off, and started in pursuit. Angered by what he deemed impudent pertinacity, Catesby Jones turned and resolved to run her down. His huge steel beak grated on the submerged deck of the Monitor and was wrenched out of position, leaving the smaller vessel entirely unharmed. Then ensued a scene never witnessed before in naval engagements. The two vessels were side by side, not ten feet apart, and discharging shot of the heaviest calibre. These immense masses of solid iron rattled on the opposing armor, yet neither vessel was injured. Armor had for the first time been in actual

LT. G. A. MORRIS,
COMMAND'G THE
"CUMBERLAND."

REAR ADMIRAL J. SMITH.

conflict, and a great leap had been made in naval warfare. Then the Monitor hauled off to hoist more shot into her turret, and Jones, supposing that Worden was silenced, again turned his attention to the shattered Minnesota, but before he could fire a shot the Monitor was back again. Then one of her shells cracked the armor of the Merrimac at the water line, causing a leak, while a second penetrated one of the boilers, scalding several men. Finding the vulnerable point to be along the water line Worden depressed his guns and with good effect. Jones now found that his vessel had at last met her equal, so he decided to go back to Norfolk. His last shot struck the Monitor's pilot house, and cutting the iron in two, severely wounded Worden and knocked him senseless on the floor. Both Lieutenant Green, who was in command of the guns, and Chief Engineer Steiners, who was working the turret, were also stunned, but they recovered in time to keep the gunners at work.

That was the end, for Worden's condition prevented the Monitor following the Merrimac and she reached Norfolk safely. Her defeat was a sad ending to the glorification of the citizens of that city during the previous evening, for it was evident that her career was ended. On the following 11th of May, she was blown up by the Confederates, and during the following Winter, the Monitor foundered in a gale Cape off Hatteras.

CAMP ALEXANDER. ARTILLERY CROSSING PONTOON BRIDGE.

When Worden recovered consciousness his first words were: "Did we save the Minnesota?" So severe were his injuries that he was completely blind for a time, and after his removal to Washington, his life was for a long time despaired of. Congress gave him a vote of thanks, and he subsequently passed through the various grades until he reached the rank of Rear-Admiral. It is related that President Lincoln called on Worden, a few days after his arrival in the National Capital, and handed the brave, blinded sailor his commission as Commander. The patient was lying in bed, attended by his faithful wife, with his eyes closely bandaged, and as Mr. Lincoln sat down beside Worden, the latter exclaimed: "Mr. President, you do me great honor!" To which Lincoln replied: "No, sir, no, sir; it is you who do me honor, and confer honor on the country."

The result of the Monitor's "official trial" caused the greatest rejoicing among the people of the Northern States, while it taught other nations that a new element had entered into naval construction. Ericsson was ordered to go on building Monitors to his heart's content, while he received the cordial thanks of the President and the Secretary of the Navy.

FEDERAL PICKET.—"ALL QUIET ON THE POTOMAC."

CHAPTER XII.

OPENING OF MCCLELLAN'S PENINSULAR CAMPAIGN.

During the combined army and naval movements on the seacoast, and on the Western rivers, which resulted in the capture of Hatteras Inlet, Hilton Head, and Forts Henry and Donelson, it was noticeable that the Army of the Potomac maintained an attitude of masterly inactivity. General McClellan showed by his work of reconstruction, that he had few equals as a military organizer, but he was like the mechanic, who can make a superb musical instrument, without the genius or power to show its full capacity for production of sweet and harmonious sounds. The defect in McClellan's military genius was that he was more of an engineer than a general. He succeeded in producing a magnificent army out of the rawest material, but having forged his weapon, he was loth to use it, and so mar its symmetry and beauty. Yet, no General was more loved by his men than George B. McClellan. Had he possessed a tithe of Grant's dogged pertinacity, there is no question that the war would have ended at least a year sooner than it did. By the end of October, 1861, McClellan had gathered one hundred and twenty thousand men. They were divided into grand divisions and brigades, each with its appropriate quota of artillery and cavalry, and they had received

GENERAL AND MRS. GEO. B. MCCLELLAN.

JOHN CABIN BRIDGE OVER THE POTOMAC RIVER.

RECONNOITERING BETWEEN ALEXANDRIA, VA., AND FAIRFAX COURT HOUSE.

the best description of arms then known to military science. He had announced that a general movement would take place before the close of November, and the people anxiously waited for it. But on October 31, General Scott formally resigned and retired from the fatigues of command, which his advancing infirmities rendered him unable to endure. By common consent, McClellan was selected for the position of commander-in-chief, and he no sooner became such, than he began planning campaigns for the simultaneous capture of Richmond and Nashville. He accordingly went to work increasing

HAMPTON, VA.

BATTLE OF DRAINESVILLE.

and solidifying the armies of the West, which caused more delay on his own, immediate front. The only serious engagement in the East, toward the close of 1861, was the Battle of Drainesville, in Virginia, on December 20. As the Confederates were very annoying along the Upper Potomac, General McCall decided to strike a blow. Brigadier-General E. O. C. Ord was ordered to march with his brigade direct for Drainesville, while two other brigades under Generals George G. Meade and J. F. Reynolds, were to ad-

BRIG.-GEN. G. A. MC CALL.

GENERAL J. E. B. STUART.

vance by way of Difficult Creek. Owing to the fact that Ord came up first, his command was the only one really engaged. Ord had five Pennsylvania regiments, the Sixth, Ninth,

Tenth, and Twelfth, and the Bucktail Rifles, a regiment that became famous for its cool bravery on many a subsequent battle field. There were also with the column Easton's battery and five squadrons of Pennsylvania Cavalry. The Confederate force was commanded by General J. E. B. Stewart, who lead the First Kentucky, Sixth South Carolina, Tenth Alabama and Eleventh Virginia Infantry, under Colonels Taylor, Secrest, Forney and Garland, Captain Cutt's battery and Major Gordon's North Carolina Cavalry.

THE SALLY PORT.

General Stuart had that very morning started from Drainesville with two hundred wagons to gather up supplies, and the Virginians and South Carolinians, who had the lead, were surprised to find the Federals already on the road. There was a change of position by the Confederates during which the Kentucky regiment mistook the South Carolinians for Federals, and delivered a heavy fire which being at very close range, did awful execution. This grievous mistake threw the Confederates into some confusion, and though Stuart made an effort to out-flank Ord, the movement was discovered in time to frustrate it. Then there occurred an incident that really ended the fight.

CHAIN BRIDGE, POTOMAC RIVER.

Colonel Thomas Taylor, commanding the First Kentucky, came across a line of troops, which he took for another Confederate regiment. Remembering his previous error, Taylor called out, "What regiment is this?" "The Ninth" was the reply. "What Ninth?" "The Ninth Pennsylvania," shouted the Federals as they poured in a volley which shattered the Kentucky line. General McCall reached the field after Stuart re-formed his men, and was emerging from a belt of woods on the Federal left. Colonel McCalmont immediately changed front, and Captain Easton opened with grape, which forced the Confederates to retire, an example followed by the rest of the line. The Federal loss was seven men killed and sixty wounded, while Stuart had forty-three killed and one hundred and thirty-six wounded. There was no pursuit as the movement had only been a reconnaisance in force.

EDWIN M. STANTON.

November and December rolled by without any movement, although the weather and the condition of the Virginia roads were unusually fine, and favorable for extensive military operations. Week after week, the Northern newspapers contained the stereotyped announcement, "All quiet on the Potomac," and to this day the phrase has grown to be a sort of proverb to denote inactivity. While McClellan was thus tempering the metal of his magnificent army, the Confederates were organizing its opponent, the Army of Northern Virginia. These two bodies of troops have become historic, for the endurance and dauntless courage displayed by them on many a hard-fought field. No wonder, therefore, that when they came in collision during the Summer of 1862, the struggle was a bloody one. It is pleasant for either the Federal or Confederate veterans, now that thirty years have softened the memories of those terrible campaigns, to meet with men who stood on the opposite side of the storm of shot and shell. The writer was on a Washington train, recently, and found himself seated in the smoking car beside a man who carried an empty

CONFEDERATES TRAPPING A BOAT'S CREW.

sleeve. We fell into conversation, and I soon discovered that he had fought on the Confederate side. "Who did you serve with?" I asked. "I was with Bob Lee, and served under Longstreet," he replied. "Were you at the battle of Gettysburg?" was my next question. "Yes. I left this arm there, where was you?" "At the Little Round Top, with the Fifth Corps. We drove you out of the Devil's Glen." "Yes, I remember.

That was a hot corner, wasn't it? Shake hands, old chap, them days is all over." So it is all the time, the men who fought during 1861-5 think more of one another than they do of those who did not fight.

On the 13th of January, a new character appeared on the stage of National events, for Edwin M. Stanton became Secretary of War, in place of Cameron, who was sent as Minister to Russia. The change was not intended to reflect on Secretary Cameron. On the contrary, it was his desire, as well as that of the other members of the administration, that the onerous and exacting position should be filled by some man, who, to more than ordinary intellectual ability and force of character, added great powers of physical and mental endurance. Of all the available men at that moment, Stanton was the man in whom those qualities seemed most united. He had already made himself conspicuous, during Buchanan's administra-

GENERAL GEORGE B. MC CLELLAN AND STAFF.

tion, by exposing and defeating the schemes of the conspirators who plotted for the seizure of Washington. Stanton's patience was completely exhausted by the inactivity of McClellan, and it was at his suggestion that the President issued an order that on February 22, a general forward movement of the land and naval forces of the United States should take place; that especially the army at or about Fortress Monroe, the Army of the Potomac, the Army of Western Virginia, the army near Mumfordsville, Kentucky, the army and flotilla near Cairo, and the naval force in the Gulf of Mexico, be ready to move on that day. This was supplemented by another order, issued January 31, that all the disposable force of the Army of the Potomac, after duly providing for the defense of Washington, be formed into an expedition for the immediate object of seizing upon the railroad southwestward of what was known as Manassas Junction. All the details

PUNISHMENT DRILL IN CAMP.

were to be in the discretion of the Commander-in-Chief, but the expedition was to "move before or on the 22d day of February next."

Grant obeyed, and Donelson fell, but McClellan did not set his columns in motion until the latter end of March. On the eighth of that month, the President again grew restive, for he issued a general order dividing the Army of the Potomac into four corps, under Major-Generals McDowell, Heintzelman, Sumner and Keyes. The divisions of Generals Banks and Shields were united and placed under the command of Banks. It was also ordered that the command of the Federal troops in the Mississippi Valley and westward be placed in the hands of General Halleck, while a Mountain Department, covering the area between McClellan and Halleck, was assigned to Fremont. Another slap at McClellan was the intimation that department commanders were to report direct to Secretary Stanton and not through the Commander-in-Chief, as had been the rule. There were subsequent orders tending to hurry up McClellan, but they need not be quoted here. Then General Joe Johnston evacuated Manassas, leaving McClellan the undisturbed possession of his earthworks and a lot of "Quaker" guns, made out of logs, so that when McClellan did move forward, his soldiers discovered that the enemy had stolen a march upon them. The President then relieved McClellan from command of all departments except that of the Potomac.

Roused by these reproofs, McClellan resolved on the Peninsula campaign, and his troops began moving to Fortress Monroe, as the future base of his operations. No man could be more energetic than George B. McClellan once he began, and it is therefore not surprising that he assembled on the Virginia Peninsula, one hundred and twenty thousand men of all arms, during the comparatively short period of five weeks. His army equipment consisted of two hundred and sixty-two pieces of artillery, twelve hundred wagons, one hundred ambulances, thirty thousand tents, fifteen thousand head of live

MISSISSIPPIANS PASSING IN REVIEW BEFORE GENERAL BEAUREGARD AND STAFF.

cattle to be slaughtered for food, seven million pounds of hard bread, and other commissary stores, besides an ample quantity of ammunition for all arms. Some seventy-three thousand men were left to guard the approaches to Washington. It is not the purpose of the writer to touch upon the correspondence between McClellan and Lincoln, touching the disposition of the latter force, as it is not necessary to lift that sad curtain. Suffice it to say, the army went to the Peninsula, and waited for the orders of its loved commander.

The scene in Hampton Roads, during the landing of the Army of the Potomac, was a magnificent and thrilling one. Passenger steamers from the Penobscot, in far off Maine, from the noble Hudson, from Baltimore, Philadelphia, New York, Boston, Providence, New Haven, Albany, the Long Island Sound and Portland, were constantly passing up and down the Potomac river, or the Chesapeake Bay, loaded down to their guards with enthusiastic Volunteer soldiers and Regulars. Week after week, day after day, hour after hour, these steamers drew up to the long wharf, in front of the Fortress, and from early dawn until late in the afternoon of each day, regiment after regiment disembarked and marched to the position allotted its brigade. The music of brass bands trembled on the crisp, bracing air of March, the roll of drums died away in the distance, and the shrill notes of many bugles rippled across the water to the ears of those soldiers who were impatiently awaiting their turn to go on shore. As the never-ending column of armed troops passed up the wharf and disappeared around the southern angle of the frowning fortress, the bright colors of the regimental and brigade ensigns fluttered in the frosty sunlight, adding color and beauty to the picture. Meanwhile the other side of the wharf was occupied by rapidly changing transports, engaged in the work of discharging tents and other camp equipage, powder, shot and shell for the field batteries, horses for cavalry and artillery, cattle for food, mules for the supply trains, commissary stores, ammunition for small arms, cannon, caissons and wagons, in fact all the complicated impedimenta of war. The wide

CUTTING OFF CONFEDERATE DESPATCH BOAT.

expanse of Hampton Roads was covered by a countless fleet of vessels. White sails were hoisted and lowered as the ships arrived or prepared to leave. Noisy tugs puffed hither and thither, towing transports to and from the wharf, or in search of business. The hoarse whistles of huge steamers added to the roar of confused sounds, each signal being rudely answered by others. In the distance lay trim ships of war, their black hulls glistening in the bright sunshine. In their midst lay the little Monitor, her round turret forming an object that attracted every eye. It was indeed a picture to be seen once in a lifetime, and never to be forgotten as long as memory lasts. To the spectator it was the realization of that pomp and circumstance of war, which in all ages has been the admiration of mankind. It was a scene to make the heart beat faster, and the cheek to glow with pride. Here was activity and apparent purpose, and as the sunset gun from the fortress boomed over Hampton Roads, each recurring evening the army took shape and increased power. The magnitude of this movement can be better appreciated, when it is said that the transportation of troops and

KILLING BULLOCKS IN FEDERAL CAMP.

supplies required the services of one hundred and twenty steamers, over two hundred sailing vessels and ninety barges, during a period of thirty days. Both soldiers and citizens looked forward with eager expectation for the result of the approaching campaign, for its full magnitude was better understood than it can be at this period of time with the softening influences caused by the lapse of over thirty years.

April 1, every man, horse and mule, every cannon and musket, had been landed and on the morning of April 3, the advance guard of McClellan's splendid-ly-appointed army marched forward, closely followed by a mighty column of enthusiastic troops. The Peninsula campaign that was to accomplish so much and end in the capture of Richmond, the Confederate Capital, had at last begun.

CONFEDERATE WATER BATTERY AT GLOUCESTER POINT.

City of Richmond, Va.

BATTERY No. 4 IN FRONT OF YORKTOWN.

CHAPTER XIII.

THE SIEGE AND FALL OF YORKTOWN.

The advance of McClellan's army from Newport News and Fortress Monroe, on April 3, 1862, was a grand and imposing one. One column under General Heintzelman marched up the old Yorktown Road, past Big Bethel, while the other, under General Keyes, moved over the Warwick road. Two days after, April 5, the head of the columns reached a line of fortifications in front of the town of Yorktown, the curtain extending from the banks of the York River to Warwick Creek. General John B. Magruder was still in command of the Confederate army of observation, his total force being at that time about eighteen thousand men. To maintain his line Magruder had placed garrisons on Mulberry Island, in the James River, and at Gloucester Point on the York, opposite the town. Viewed from in front, Magruder's earthworks had a formidable look, and as he had some heavy guns mounted on both sides of the York River, they commanded the channel. At that time McClellan had sixty thousand men assembled in front of Yorktown, with eighty thousand more rapidly following him, yet so wedded was he to routine, that scarcely a shot had been fired until April 16, when it was discovered that the Confederate were at work strengthening their entrenchments on Warwick Creek. Two batteries and one Vermont regiment advanced and opened fire without much result, though the

MAJOR-GENERAL GEO. B. McCLELLAN.

BATTERY MAGRUDER, (CONFEDERATE), YORKTOWN.

Vermonters did make a charge, the simple reason being that instead of a regiment, two or three brigades should have been sent forward. By the 20th of April, the Federal army numbered about one hundred thousand men, fully thirty thousand more arriving in front of Yorktown during the ensuing week. This enormous body of men was massed in one great camp, while their General amused himself in constructing a line of forts in which were mounted forty or fifty one-hundred-pound Parrott rifled guns, besides others of smaller calibre, and many large mortars. The appearance of the Army of the Potomac, as it lay in camp, was both formidable and impressive. As far as the eye could reach, symmetrical rows of snow-white tents covered the wide fields. To give them exercise, the soldiers were constantly drilled, but there were no cannon shots to be heard, and only the pickets heard the whistle of a bullet. The strange spectacle was thus presented of an army sitting down in comparative idleness, in front of a force about one third its own strength, for McClellan's procrastination had

CAPT CUSTER, U. S. A., AND LIEUT. WASHINGTON, A CONFEDERATE PRISONER.

BATTERY NO. 4 IN FRONT OF YORKTOWN.

enabled the Confederates to reinforce Magruder with thirty thousand additional troops. The headquarters staff of the Commanding General was a brilliant one, for it included many foreign officers who had come to see how Americans made war. Among these were the Prince de Joinville, the Duc de Chartres, and the Comte de Paris, while Germany, Italy, Russia and other nations were officially represented. McClellan had visited the Crimea a few years before and witnessed the closing scenes of the siege of Sebastopol, the capture of the Redan and the Malakoff. He saw the pomp and show of Louis Napoleon's army, and he aimed at imitating Canrobert and Pelissier, so it was not surprising that officers he had met in Europe gladly responded to his invitation to serve on his staff. General McClellan made a very handsome

NAVAL BATTERY IN FRONT OF YORKTOWN.

BATTERY NO. 1 IN FRONT OF YORKTOWN.

appearance on horseback, for he sat in the saddle with a grace and ease peculiarly his own. All his appointments were in the most correct taste, and his horses were full-blooded animals. Wearing highly polished riding boots coming up nearly to his hips, and wrinkled from the instep to the knee, he would go splashing over the roads until horse, rider, and boots were covered with Virginia mud, probably the stickiest substance in existence. His servant always had a clean pair of boots for the General on his return to headquarters, after which the poor man would spend a couple of hours cleaning the other pair. The soldiers at Yorktown used to say that "Little Mac" could collect more mud in an hour's time than any other General in the army. McClellan was passionately fond of horses, and preferred to have them coal black.

A Street in Yorktown During the War.

No other officer during the war possessed such magnetism over his troops as did McClellan. To see him ride by a moving column was a pleasant experience. "How is the road, boys?" he would ask, genially. And then the men would cheer, as if they had gone crazy. He was always looking out for cases of distress. After the battle of South Mountain, while the Army of the Potomac was advancing to Antietam, the General found a wounded man by the roadside. As the poor fellow could not walk, McClellan leaped from his saddle and assisted the soldier into it, sending an orderly with him to the field hospital. As McClellan mounted the orderly's horse, his chief of staff asked why he did not send the inferior animal, instead of his own. "Because," replied Little Mac, "a General's horse is not too good for a brave and wounded man." General McClellan always rode at a slapping pace, and saw that his staff were well mounted, for nothing more displeased him than their inability to keep up with him. He was very cool on the battlefield, and used to ride from point to point in the calmest manner. Selecting an

BATTERY No. 4 IN FRONT OF YORKTOWN.

HEADQUARTERS OF GENERAL MAGRUDER, YORKTOWN, VA.

advantageous position, he would survey the field of operations through his glass, the horse under him meanwhile champing and pawing until checked by a motion of the reins. Without attempting the cavalry seat or style, McClellan had at all times a perfect command over his charger.

The density of the camp at Yorktown, and the close proximity of an extensive swamp, soon caused disease, for soldiers are proverbially careless of sanitary arrangements, while it is difficult to keep clean and healthy on ground long occupied. The consequence was that instead of going up the Peninsula, thousands of men were carried to hospitals in Philadelphia, Baltimore and Washington, where a large percentage died, McClellan actually losing, in that way, more men than need have been sacrificed by a general assault on the Confederate works. General Johnston had meanwhile taken command at Yorktown, and waited patiently to see what his antagonist would do, having already decided on his own course should he be finally attacked in force. McClellan's men went on patiently digging long lines of earthworks that were never to be occupied, and mounting guns which were never loaded. The General did open fire once from a fort opposite Gloucester Point, and so destroyed a water battery. He also ordered a few empty Parrott shells thrown into Yorktown in order to show the Southern troops what they might expect. We subsequently found these empty shells standing on posts, in the dusty

RAVINE AT YORKTOWN, CONTAINING CONFEDERATE MAGAZINES.

CONFEDERATE FORTIFICATIONS AT YORKTOWN.

HEADQUARTERS ARMY OF POTOMAC, IN FRONT OF YORKTOWN.

streets of the town, with contemptuous inscriptions painted upon them. Joe Johnston, however, was not to be frightened by such absurd devices, but knowing through his spies, who were permitted to wander through the Federal camps in the guise of pedlars, that McClellan's siege guns were at last ready, the Confederate commander decided to evacuate Yorktown, and fall back to his selected line of defence, between the Pamunkey and James Rivers.

With the advent of May, McClellan had perfected his line of entrenchments, they containing fifteen batteries, mounting eighty heavy cannon and thirty huge mortars, enough metal to blow Johnston's army into the air. Malaria and fever had reduced the Army of the Potomac from one hundred and forty thousand men to about one hundred and twelve thousand, these twenty eight thousand disease-disabled soldiers not having fired a single shot. What a contrast to Fort Donelson ? The writer stood beside his huge Parrott gun, a few yards from the York River bank, on the evening of Saturday, May 3, looking across the fields at the line of works we were to bombard. The order had been given that the Sabbath was to be spent by the army in idleness, but on Monday morning all the guns along the line were to

COMTE DE PARIS.

Prince de Joinville, Duc de Chartres and Comte de Paris at Mess Table.

Prince de Joinville, Duc de Chartres, Comte de Paris and Foreign Officers and Staff at General McClellan's Headquarters.

open and the infantry were to form in mass ready to move at the proper moment. Our magazines had been crammed with shot and shell and we looked forward to the proposed bombardment with considerable satisfaction. I remember that I was wondering how long it would take our guns to demolish the Confederate entrenchments, when suddenly a cannon was fired right opposite me, and a shell flew over our heads. Then another and another columbiad had opened, followed by mortar shells.

Here was an unexpected programme, for instead of bombarding Yorktown, we were receiving the punishment. Our Colonel asked leave to reply, but he received strict orders to remain silent, as did all of the Federal batteries. From eight o'clock in the evening until almost dawn, the Yorktown batteries maintained a continuous, but

STAFF AND ENGLISH OFFICERS AND TOPOGRAPHICAL ENGINEERS AT GENERAL McCLELLAN'S HEADQUARTERS.

ineffectual fire. As the first streaks of daylight began darting athwart the Eastern sky, a negro timidly crept along the narrow path by the side of the river. The Federals had by this time grown accustomed to receiving fugitive slaves on their picket lines, so the man was permitted to approach. "Hullo, here's another contraband," exclaimed one of the men composing the little vidette, "Wonder how he got out of Yorktown?" "I'se jest kem ober to tell youse, dat dey be's all gone," said the negro. "Who's gone?" demanded the young Lieutenant. "Why dem Southern sodgers. Dey's bin a marching up country all dis blessed night, with all de cannon, and de muskets, and de wagons. De fac is, mister Ossifer, Marster Magruder he's just got up and gone clar 'way." "He must be lying," remarked a sergeant. "How could the Confederates serve their batteries if the army was in motion?" "I'se telling the gospel trufe," replied the contraband. "For I know'd dey was a going, and I jest hid and waited. De last of dem got away jest as de day was a breaking."

The contraband was sent to the rear under guard, his news soon spreading along the advanced Federal line. Then, as the sun rose above the horizon, we could see groups of citizens coolly walking along the Confederate parapets. "Yorktown is evacuated!" then ran along the line of entrenchments, and some general officers suddenly appeared near our battery. There was a great deal of galloping about by officers belonging to the headquarters staff, and by eight o'clock the head of a column of infantry came up, and pushed forward across the fields, disappearing soon after amid the defences of Yorktown. Then more troops marched through the gap that had been made in our fortifications for their passage, and by noon the entire army was in motion. The siege of Yorktown was over, and we had dug trenches, and mounted heavy cannon, only to leave them behind.

MAJ.-GEN. GEORGE STONEMAN, MAJ.-GEN. D. N. COUCH, MAJ.-GEN. W. F. SMITH, MAJ.-GEN. SILAS CASEY.

Our men, who belonged in the batteries, strolled into Yorktown by the river road, but were quickly recalled to take their places in the moving columns.

The Confederates abandoned fifty-three pieces of heavy artillery, and took up position at Williamsburg, twelve miles from Yorktown, where they were found by General George Stoneman, who had only cavalry and horse artillery. He was followed by the divisions of Generals Darius N. Couch, William F. Smith and Silas Casey, which took the Wynne's Mill Road, while the divisions of Generals Joseph Hooker and Phil Kearney, entered the Yorktown Road. The divisions of Generals Fitz John Porter, Israel B. Richardson, and John Sedgwick, remained in the immediate vicinity of Yorktown, where General McClellan began his arrangements for operations along the York River, and into the Pamunkey. Stoneman halted in front of the earthworks, as his cavalry were of little use. By five o'clock in the afternoon, General Smith's division arrived, followed closely by Sumner and Hooker. While these division commanders were forming line of battle a heavy rainstorm

STREET VIEW, YORKTOWN.

CORNWALLIS CAVE, YORKTOWN.

SALLY PORT.

CORNWALLIS CAVE. USED BY CONFEDERATES AS A MAGAZINE.

YORKTOWN LANDING.

COURT HOUSE, YORKTOWN.

WAGON PARK.

COURT HOUSE, YORKTOWN.

ARTILLERY PARK.

SCENES IN AND NEAR YORKTOWN.

Monitors and Gunboats on James River, Va.

began which drenched the men to the skin and extinguished their bivouac fires.   Despite the discomfort experienced during the night, Hooker's men were eager for a fight on Monday morning, so he sent in the First Massachusetts, and the Second New Hampshire, to attack Fort Magruder, the principal Confederate work on the Federal right.   The fort was soon silenced, and Hooker moved forward with his entire division, encountering a strong force under Longstreet.   Being of an impetuous nature, Hooker pressed on too ardently, and soon found himself all alone in front of a superior force, but he maintained his position during the day.   Phil Kearney's division did not arrive on the ground until near

MAJOR-GENERAL WINFIELD SCOTT HANCOCK.

five o'clock in the afternoon, two of Couch's brigade joining him in time to take position on his right.   General Winfield Scott Hancock had gone towards Queen's Creek, further to the right, but it was impossible to bring up more troops, owing to the terrible condition of the roads, they being knee deep in mud, caused by the heavy rain during the previou night.   Hooker had been fighting Longstreet, Pryor, Pickett and Gholson all day, his loss being seventeen hundred men and nearly all of Capt. Weber's battery.

General Hancock had better luck, for he was able to push forward to Cub Dam Creek and capture two redoubts.   This caused Johnston to despatch General Jubal Early to dislodge Hancock.   The latter fell back to the creek, and, forming in line, charged the

SCENES AND VIEWS IN YORKTOWN, IN 1862.

ORDERLIES AND SERVANTS, AND GROUP AT PHOTOGRAPHER'S TENT, YORKTOWN.

Confederates in most gallant style. Early had already been wounded, leaving Colonel McRae in command of his brigade, but the latter could not stand the shock, and finally

TABB'S HOUSE, YORKTOWN.

GENERAL JUBAL A. EARLY, C. S. A.

retired to Williamsburg in the darkness that soon fell on the scene. This part of the battle was noticeable for the courage displayed by both Federals and Confederates, and Hancock afterwards remarked that the Fifth North Carolina and Twenty-fourth Virginia deserved to have the word "Immortal" inscribed upon their banners. It was Hancock's headlong charge that decided the day, for by it he seized the key to the Confederate position. McClellan, arriving on the ground, then sent reinforcements to Hancock, who took possession of all the ground he had previously occupied. The night closed upon what proved to be a dear victory for the Federals, as they only gained it after sustaining a loss of over two thousand in killed and wounded, the Confederate loss being a little more than half that number. When daylight came, it was found that the Confederate army had fallen back to Hanover Court House, and McClellan began what he fondly imagined to be his triumphal march into Richmond. But he had no conception of the difficulties in his path or the military genius of the Confederate commanders who were to dispute his passage.

The evacuation of Yorktown brought President Lincoln to the Peninsula, with several members of his

GENERAL GEORGE E. PICKETT, C. S. A.

Cabinet. The President was not at all elated by the retreat of the Confederates, for, as he remarked in his quaint, homely way, it reminded him of a man in Illinois who got into a fight and came out with a bloody nose and a torn coat, but seemed satisfied because the other fellow had no coat to get torn. "General McClellan," said he, "has driven Johnston and Magruder out of Yorktown, but they took their own time about it. I had a client once who wanted to get rid of a tenant who would not pay his rent. He wanted me to begin legal proceedings for ejectment, and I made out the preliminary papers, telling him that the court would not open until the following month. Before court term came, the tenant found a house that suited him better than the one he was not paying for, so moved away. My client came to me next day, and gleefully announced that he had got rid of his tenant, so I might stop all proceedings,

GENERAL ROGER A. PRYOR, C. S. A.

BATTLE OF WILLIAMSBURG.

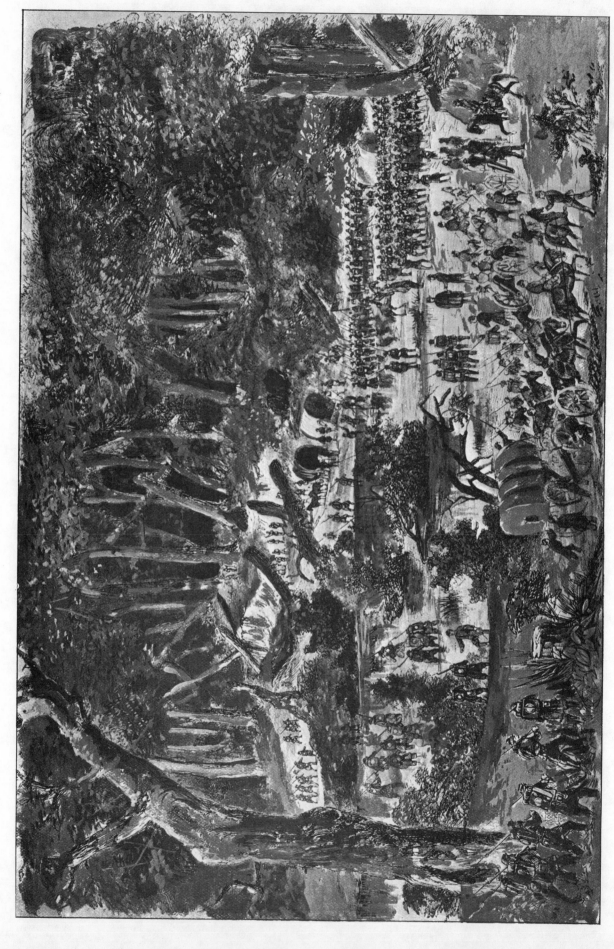

THE MARCH FROM WILLIAMSBURG.

EMBARKATION AT YORKTOWN FOR WHITE HOUSE LANDING.
GENERALS FRANKLIN, SLOCUM, BARRY, NEWTON AND STAFF OFFICERS.

GENERAL ANDREW PORTER AND STAFF.

at the same time paying me my fee.   I asked him how much the tenant owed him, when he replied that it was of no consequence, so long as he had got rid of him.   So you see General McClellan seems satisfied not to count the cost.   He only looks at results, and

we must be content, but it does seem to me that we have paid too much for our whistle." General Wool, who was still in command at Fortress Monroe, then spoke for the third time of the necessity for seizing the Norfolk (Gosport) Navy Yard, as it had always been a menace to the Federal lines.   He again asked for permission to use the army and navy resources at his command to attack Norfolk and destroy the Navy Yard. The President cast his eyes upon the floor, and, as everybody remained silent for a few seconds, he straightened his tall, uncouth figure, and said :—"General Wool, you know more about

CAMP AT GENERAL ANDREW PORTER'S, IN FRONT OF YORKTOWN.

BURNING OF NORFOLK NAVY YARD BY THE CONFEDERATES.

this matter than either Secretary Stanton, Secretary Welles, or myself. If you really think you can take the Navy Yard, I see no reason why you should not. At any rate you can't lose much."

Acting on this implied permission, General Wool began operations against Norfolk, and the result was that the Confederates evacuated, first destroying the Merrimac and all other military and naval property. This movement and the advance of McClellan's troops to the Chickahominy, forever removed the Confederates from control of that section of Virginia. The York and Pamunkey Rivers being opened, the base of operations for the Army of the Potomac was made at the White House, and McClellan began his confident preparations for capturing the Confederate capital. But he was facing generals who had no sentiment or fear, and they made moves on the board he never contemplated, and were thus able to cry "check" just when he thought the game of war was his own.

The same lavish expenditure of money and supplies, for which McClellan's movements were always noticeable, characterized his subsequent campaign. Enormous quantities of ordnance and commissary supplies were gathered at the White House, despite the fact that this base of operations was entirely untenable, and incapable of defense. Trusting to a few small gunboats to guard his food, ammunition, engineering tools, hospitals and reserve supplies, the enthusiastic young general plunged his army into the dreadful swamps of the Chickahominy, to do battle with a foe whose calibre he had not duly measured. The result of this

MAJOR-GENERAL JOHN E. WOOL.

PANORAMIC VIEWS OF CAMP NEAR CUMBERLAND LANDING, ARMY OF THE POTOMAC.

VIEW OF CAMP, ARMY OF THE POTOMAC, AT CUMBERLAND LANDING.

mad, headlong movement must be left to future chapters, for the important events of the war at that time were occurring elsewhere.

THE WHITE HOUSE, FORMER RESIDENCE OF MRS. CUSTER HARRISON.

BOMBARDMENT OF ISLAND NO. TEN. CONFEDERATE FORTIFICATIONS ON KENTUCKY SHORE.

CHAPTER XIV.

THE CAPTURE OF ISLAND NUMBER TEN, AND THE BATTLE OF PEA RIDGE.

By the capture of Forts Henry and Donelson, the Confederate line of defense from Columbus to Bowling Green was completely broken. The Federals gained possession of Kentucky and the greater part of Tennessee, with the State Capital. It must be admitted that Grant's magnificent success was mainly due to the incapacity of Albert Sidney Johnston in his disposition of the Confederate forces. When the fall of Fort Donelson was announced, the Southern troops promptly evacuated Bowling Green and marched South. Columbus and Nashville fell into the hands of the Federals, while desperate efforts were being made to hold the Mississippi River for the Confederacy by strongly fortifying Island Number Ten and New Madrid. To General Pope and Commander Foote was given the task of reducing these strongholds. Both places had been fortified in the most elaborate manner by General Beauregard, whose engineering genius grasped their importance. There is no question that Beauregard was really one of the most talented officers in the Confederate service. His training in the United States regular army made him a great tactician, and the experience gained by him as superintendent of

REAR-ADMIRAL A. H. FOOTE.

U. S. Transport, "W. B. Terry," Pushing Her Way Through the Swamps at Island Number Ten.

the West Point Academy, gave Beauregard such a grasp of military science that he was invaluable at the time hostilities began between the sections. This is shown by his fortification of the harbor of Charleston, and the way he handled his troops at Bull Run. But it was his misfortune to rise too rapidly at the outset, consequently when serious work began, he was thrust into positions which were untenable, and being lost, his reputation suffered. Both on the Federal and Confederate side it was the fate of those Generals who rose rapidly at the beginning of hostilities, to be more severely judged than those who attained high commands after the people of both sections had learned that two opposing armies cannot possibly win the same battle.

General Beauregard's record, as a military commander, stamps him as possessing genius, perseverance and fertility of resource, and had President Davis treated him more fairly, his career would have been more brilliant. The General made a very handsome appearance in the saddle and all his appointments were in the most correct taste. He was loved by his troops, for he was as ready to lead them as

MAJOR-GENERAL U. S. GRANT.

NIGHT EXPEDITION TO ISLAND No. TEN. SPIKING GUNS OF UPPER BATTERY.

order a charge. His French descent gave his features a foreign cast, so that Beauregard did not look like any of the Generals on the Confederate side.

Beauregard had been very active in the West, and was now at the head of the Confederate Department of the Mississippi. He placed a large force under General J. P. McGown, at New Madrid, while the garrison on Island Number Ten was under his own command.

On Washington's Birthday, in 1862, General Pope started from St. Louis with a

SIEGE OF ISLAND NO. TEN. NIGHT BOMBARDMENT BY MORTAR BOATS.

large force, arriving before New Madrid, seventy-six miles below Cairo, on March 3, finding a flotilla of Confederate gunboats, under Commodore Hollins, in addition to the land forces. Making an entrenched camp, Pope waited for siege guns, which, being placed in position, he began bombarding on March 13. The Confederate reply was vigorous, but the Federals silenced several guns in Fort Thompson, disabled most of the gunboats, and pushed back the line held by Generals J. M. Palmer and E. A. Paine. A terrific storm of

BOMBARDMENT OF ISLAND NO. TEN. GUN AND MORTAR BOATS.

rain, accompanied by thunder and lightning, was taken advantage of by McGown to evacuate New Madrid and Point Pleasant, the whole Confederate force being transferred to Island Number Ten. The following morning General Hamilton advanced and took possession of the forts, capturing thirty-three pieces of heavy artillery, six thousand muskets, and a vast amount of ammunition, supplies and camp equipage.

Commodore Foote was meanwhile coming from Cairo with a fleet of gunboats, consisting of the Benton (flagship), Lieutenant Phelps ; Cincinnati, Commander Stembel ; Carondelet, Commander Walke ; Conestoga, Lieutenant Blodgett ; Louisville, Commander Dove ; Mound City, Commander Kelley ; Pittsburg, Lieutenant Thompson ; and St. Louis, Lieutenant Paulding. He had also ten mortar boats, some small tugs and several transports carrying Colonel Heck's Fifteenth Wisconsin and Colonel Buford's Twenty-seventh Illinois. The Commodore took possession of the town of Hickman on March 15, tying up his fleet five miles above Island Number Ten, where two more transports arrived with two field batteries and the Sixteenth and Forty-Second Illinois Infantry.

On Sunday, March 16, the brave old Commodore notified General Pope that he was ready and the

COMMANDER WALKE.

bombardment began as soon as the crews and gunners had eaten their breakfasts, when the guns and mortars continued to vomit a fierce discharge of shells and bombs, until half-past-four in the afternoon. It was a strange and remarkable scene, for all of the queer, flat bottomed, box-shaped mortar boats had been pushed into the canebrake, as they were scattered along the edge of the winding and mighty river. As the gunners loaded and fired their large siege pieces, a tremendous roar rose from the brakes which concealed the boats, followed by the uncouth sound caused by the passage of the bomb, as it climbed into the air or fell with increased velocity on reaching the apex of its flight. Scarcely a minute passed throughout the day without one or more missiles being in the air, the deafening detonations being distinctly heard at the distance of twenty miles, the inhabitants of that war-torn region, listening to the uproar with bated breath. The Confederate guns made no reply whatever, and it was soon evident that the Federal fire had been ineffective. The engineering skill of Beauregard was shown by the way he had

NIGHT ATTACK ON ISLAND NO. TEN BY GUN BOATS AND MORTAR FLEET.

constructed his works, for they were in triple rows, wherever an assault was possible, and all of the seventy-five guns were of heavy calibre, besides an ironclad floating battery.

Finding that long range work was of no use, Foote sent the Second Illinois Battery to the Missouri bank of the river, where Lieutenant Keith opened at close quarters on the Confederate gunboats, and drove them away. On Monday, a thick fog settled down on river and land, so the firing did not begin until near noon. The Federals had meanwhile lashed the gunboats Cincinnati, St. Louis and Benton, together, and so made a battery. Pushing close to the Confederate forts, and supported by the remainder of the fleet, the Federals soon succeeded in silencing several of Beauregard's heaviest guns and smashed the earthworks. At seven o'clock the fleet withdrew, as it was too dark for the gunners.

Day after day the attack was renewed, but nothing was accomplished until late in the night of April 1, when a party of volunteers from the Forty-second Illinois under Colonel Roberts, started off in rowboats and muffled oars manned by picked crews. A violent storm was in progress at the time and the boats reached the battery on the upper end of the island without discovery until they were right on the bank. The Confederate sentinels

BATTLE OF PEA RIDGE, MARCH 6, 1862.

fired and retreated, the Federals contenting themselves in spiking every gun, and then rowing back to the fleet.

During the night of April 3, the gunboat Carondelet ran past Beauregard's batteries, encountering a terrific broadside from his guns, but Commander Walke had not a man hurt, neither was the gunboat injured. Then General Pope decided he must do something, and adopting General Hamilton's suggestion, a canal was cut across Donaldson's Point, between New Madrid and Island Number Eight, a distance of twelve miles, advantage being taken of swamps and bayous in its construction. Through this canal, which cost nearly a week's labor on the part of his entire army, some floating batteries, led by the steamboat W. B. Terry, passed through and opened a destructive fire on Island Number Ten, from a point not defended by earthworks. Troops were also landed at Tiptonville and Watson's Landing, General Paine moving up the river road while General Hamilton went round Reelfoot Lake. Commodore Foote then began a general bombardment from all of his vessels and batteries, while the Confederates were driven back at all points by the land forces. Seeing that his position was no longer tenable, Beauregard decided to evacuate Island Number Ten.

He sank several steamboats to blockade the channel. and, taking the larger part of his army, started for Corinth, leaving Generals Walker, Gantt and V. D. McCall to surrender with over seven thousand men. The Federals received, as the fruits of their victory, one hundred and twenty-six siege guns, field artillery and heavy mortars, over ten thousand muskets, several steamboats, a floating battery, nearly five hundred horses and mules, and an immense quantity of ammunition and military supplies of every description. The Federal loss was only eight killed and

BREVET MAJOR GENERAL A. ASHBOTH.

twenty-seven wounded.   The loss sustained by the Confederates was six men killed and nineteen wounded.   It may be thought remarkable that after so much heavy ammunition had been expended, there should be so few casualties, but throwing ten and fifteen-inch bombs a distance of two or three miles is vastly different from using grape and canister at four hundred yards range.   What the Federals sought was not so much the killing and wounding of men, as compelling the surrender of the forts and the possession of the river.

Simultaneous with this movement, General Samuel R. Curtis had followed Sterling Price from Missouri into Arkansas.   Going too rapidly, he struck Van Dorn, who by

GENERAL ASHBOTH AND STAFF AT BATTLE OF PEA RIDGE.

a skillful flank movement, compelled the Federals to change front.   Sigel joined Curtis, which increased the Federal force to nearly thirteen thousand men, with fifty pieces of artillery.   The Confederate General Van Dorn had over twenty thousand.   A great deal of manœuvering ensued, each commander seeking an advantageous position. Van Dorn finally succeeded in outflanking Curtis, who was compelled to change front. On March 7, he was ready for battle, and threw down the gauntlet.   General Carr's division was on Curtis' right, General Davis on the centre, while Generals Sigel and Ashboth held the left.   Both Van Dorn and Curtis made an error in lengthening their lines, for they extended from Elkhorn Tavern to Sugar Creek, a distance of nearly four miles. Van Dorn had placed Price on his right, McIntosh in the centre, and McCulloch on his left. Carr's division was forced back nearly a mile, when McCulloch swung round to join Price, who was moving on Sigel. The latter tried to intercept McCulloch by advancing part of a battery, supported by artillery, but the guns were seized, and Sigel found himself overwhelmed. General Davis wheeled to the left and Carr came up in time to add to his weight in the changing movement, and a most sanguinary struggle ensued. The debatable ground was held alternately several times by both armies, until finally Van Dorn's

GENERAL VAN DORN, C. S. A.

troops gave way, and fell back in great disorder. The desperate character of the fighting is shown by the fact that two out of the three Confederate Brigade-Generals—McIntosh and McCulloch—were mortally wounded. The Federal loss was

GENERAL MC INTOSH C. S. A., KILLED AT BATTLE OF PEA RIDGE.

over thirteen hundred men, the Confederates losing sixteen hundred.

This battle of Pea Ridge, as it is called, aided the Federals in their general movement on the Confederate defensive line, and while it was not of much importance, the bravery displayed by both the Federal and Confederate troops, lifted it into prominence at the time it occurred. The battle was also a lesson to the people of both sections, that the war would be of a desperate and sanguinary character, a fact neither side had yet realized.

GENERAL BEN MC CULLOCH, C. S. A. KILLED AT BATTLE OF PEA RIDGE.

FINAL STAND OF GENERAL GRANT'S ARMY, APRIL 6, 1862, AND REPULSE OF JOHNSTON'S ARMY.

CHAPTER XV.

THE BATTLE OF SHILOH CHURCH AND THE SIEGE OF CORINTH.

Grant having been placed in command of Western Tennessee, began preparations for opening a vigorous campaign. When he was ordered by Halleck to ascend the Tennessee River and establish himself somewhere near Corinth, on the line of the Memphis and Charleston Railroad, Grant obeyed, but made a personal trip up the Cumberland River to see General Buell, who had asked him to do so. It is now admitted that Halleck secretly feared Grant's popularity, and as human nature is the same all the world over, there were not wanting men who sought to fan this jealousy. Owing to the non-delivery of Grant's

GENERAL ULYSSES S. GRANT.

letters, the passage of his troops up the Tennessee was not known at headquarters, but Grant's presence in Nashville was speedily reported. Halleck immediately telegraphed to Grant, asking why his orders were not obeyed regarding a report on the effective strength of his army, and directing him to turn over the command of the Tennessee movement to General C. F. Smith, and remain at Fort Henry. Stung by this treatment, Grant asked to be relieved, but as Halleck soon discovered that he had gone too far, he restored Grant to his active command. That was the turning point in the career of the man who was eventually to rise to the command of all of the armies of the United States in the field.

General Sherman, having been ordered to join C. F. Smith, embarked his division of eight thousand men at Paducah. As he ascended the Tennessee, a Confederate fort at Pittsburg Landing opened fire on the Federal transports, and it was decided to capture the beyond the limits of my command without his authority, and that my army was more demoralized by victory than the army at Bull Run had been by defeat. General McClellan, on this information, ordered that I should be relieved from duty, and that an investigation should be made into any charges against me. He even authorized my arrest. Thus, in less than two weeks after the victory at Donelson, the two leading generals in the army were in correspondence as to what disposition should be made of me, and in less than three weeks I was virtually in arrest and without a command. On the 13th of March, I was restored to command, and on the 17th, Halleck sent me a copy of an order from the War Department, which stated that accounts of my misbehavior had reached Washington, and directed him to investigate and report the facts. He forwarded also a copy of a detailed dispatch from himself to Washington entirely exonerating me; but he did not inform me that it was his own reports that had created all the trouble. On the con-

SHILOH CHURCH WHERE BATTLE COMMENCED.

trary, he wrote to me 'Instead of relieving you, I wish you, as soon as your new army is in the field, to assume immediate command, and lead it to new victories.' In consequence, I felt very grateful to him, and supposed it was his interposition that had set me right with the Government."

Referring to this critical condition of affairs, Sherman makes the following comments in his own memoirs: "By the end of February, 1862, Major-General Halleck commanded all the armies in the valley of the Mississippi, from his headquarters in St. Louis. These were, the Army of the Ohio, Major-General Buell, in Kentucky; the Army of the Tennessee, Major-General Grant, at Forts Henry and Donelson; the Army of the Mississippi, Major-General Pope; and that of General S. R. Curtis, in Southwest Missouri. He posted his chief of staff, General Cullum, at Cairo, and me at Paducah, chiefly to expedite and facilitate the important operations then in progress up the Tennessee and Cumberland Rivers. On the 21st, General Grant sent General Smith with his division to beyond the limits of my command without his authority, and that my army was more demoralized by victory than the army at Bull Run had been by defeat. General McClellan, on this information, ordered that I should be relieved from duty, and that an investigation should be made into any charges against me. He even authorized my arrest. Thus, in less than two weeks after the victory at Donelson, the two leading generals in the army were in correspondence as to what disposition should be made of me, and in less than three weeks I was virtually in arrest and without a command. On the 13th of March, I was restored to command, and on the 17th, Halleck sent me a copy of an order from the War Department, which stated that accounts of my misbehavior had reached Washington, and directed him to investigate and report the facts. He forwarded also a copy of a detailed dispatch from himself to Washington entirely exonerating me; but he did not inform me that it was his own reports that had created all the trouble. On the con-

SHILOH CHURCH WHERE BATTLE COMMENCED.

trary, he wrote to me 'Instead of relieving you, I wish you, as soon as your new army is in the field, to assume immediate command, and lead it to new victories.' In consequence, I felt very grateful to him, and supposed it was his interposition that had set me right with the Government."

Referring to this critical condition of affairs, Sherman makes the following comments in his own memoirs: "By the end of February, 1862, Major-General Halleck commanded all the armies in the valley of the Mississippi, from his headquarters in St. Louis. These were, the Army of the Ohio, Major-General Buell, in Kentucky; the Army of the Tennessee, Major-General Grant, at Forts Henry and Donelson; the Army of the Mississippi, Major-General Pope; and that of General S. R. Curtis, in Southwest Missouri. He posted his chief of staff, General Cullum, at Cairo, and me at Paducah, chiefly to expedite and facilitate the important operations then in progress up the Tennessee and Cumberland Rivers. On the 21st, General Grant sent General Smith with his division to

Clarksville, fifty miles above Donelson, toward Nashville, and on the 27th went himself to Nashville to meet and confer with General Buell, but returned to Donelson the next day. Meantime, General Halleck, at St. Louis, must have felt that his armies were getting away from him, and began to send dispatches to me at Paducah, to be forwarded by boat or by a rickety telegraph line up to Fort Henry, which lay entirely in a hostile country, and was consequently always out of repair." After quoting the dispatch relieving Grant, which passed through Sherman's hands over the "rickety telegraph line," the old hero says, very quaintly : "Halleck was evidently working himself into a passion, but he was too far from the seat of war to make due allowance for the actual state of facts. General Grant had done so much, that General Halleck should have been patient. Meantime, at Paducah, I was busy sending boats in every direction—some under the orders of General Halleck, others of General Cullum ; others for General Grant, and still others for General Buell at Nashville."

MAJOR-GENERAL S. D. STURGIS.

MAJOR-GENERAL LOVELL H. ROUSSEAU.

On assuming command, Grant found no reason for changing the disposition of the Federal troops, even had he the time. Sherman was covering all the main roads leading to Pittsburg Landing, but there were dangerous gaps in his line, so Lew Wallace was sent to Crump's Landing, Hurlbut to the left of the Corinth road, McClernand and Prentiss being in the advance. Grant's entire force amounted to thirty-three thousand men, and as Buell, after repeated solicitations had received Halleck's permission to join Grant, the entire Army of the Ohio, forty thousand strong, was already marching from Nashville. Everything pointed to an important battle, for Beauregard was concentrating his troops at Corinth. Bragg came up from Pensacola, Polk from the Mississippi and Johnston brought his whole army from Murfreesboro, so that the Confederates had forty-five thousand men on the ground, with Van Dorn and Price, who had been driven out of Arkansas by Curtis and Sigel, coming up with thirty thousand more. Albert Sidney Johnston, being senior in rank, assumed command of the Confederate army, and there was a council of war, when it was decided not to wait for Price and Van Dorn, but attack Grant before Buell could join him. On April 4, both Wallace and Sherman found Confederate forces on their front, but none of the Federal Generals had any definite idea how many men Johnston had under him. There was a heavy rain during the night of the 5th, but the sun rose bright and clear the following (Sunday) morning. Spring had now so advanced in that region, that the woods wore a soft mantle of green, while the perfumes of field and forest filled the balmy air. Nature was in her calmest, sweetest mood, yet armed men were marshalling for deadly combat amidst these signs of the approaching season for tillage and sowing. There was indeed some deadly sowing to be done among these overflowing creeks, but Death was to be the grim harvester. Beauregard, who had planned the Confederate movement, was so confident of success that when the conference ended he shook his scabbarded sword with

RECAPTURE OF ARTILLERY AT BATTLE OF SHILOH BY 1ST OHIO UNDER GENERAL LOVELL H. ROUSSEAU.

one hand, as he pointed to the distant Federal camps with the other saying dramatically, "Gentlemen, we sleep in the enemy's camp to-morrow night." He got the camps but did not sleep. In the light of subsequent information there is but little doubt that had Beauregard been able to retain the chief command at the very beginning, the Battle of Shiloh would have had a different ending than the one history now gives it. The Confederate advance was extraordinarily swift and silent, for the soaked ground gave back no sound as the leading columns pushed through the woods. So sudden and unexpected was their descent that the Federal pickets were swept aside, and before Sherman knew what had happened Hardee was pounding him and Prentiss. Almost in an instant the battle had begun, there was no overture to the performance, for serious work was on hand from start to finish.   Grant had gone to Savannah to see Buell, who was expected, but when he heard the distant guns, Grant hastened back, reaching the field at eight o'clock. By that time the Confederates were moving round Sherman's rear, while Prentiss lost his camp. Seeing his danger, Sherman swung round, and taking new ground held it during the day, despite all efforts to dislodge him.   Sherman's troops were raw in the experience of war, but he managed to hold them together in the face of a most deadly series of musketry volleys, for the Confederates fought desperately.   It was a scene for a painter.   The sun shone hotly over fields and woods, the atmosphere was filled with dense volumes of smoke, which writhed and rolled under the constant concussion of thousands of muskets.   The awful yell of the Southerners pierced the ear, while shot and shell crashed among the trees amid which Sherman's troops had sought temporary shelter.   Still they held to their position,

CAPTURE OF MCCLERNAND'S HEADQUARTERS AT BATTLE OF SHILOH, APRIL 6, 1862.

although ammunition was running short.   "Can you hold your line?" wrote Grant to Sherman.   "Yes, I can, if you will send me powder and ball cartridge, and be damned quick about it," replied the impetuous brigade commander.   Grant took the hint, and as Sherman's men filled their pouches they gritted their teeth, and with blackened faces bit their cartridges and went to work in returning bullet for bullet.   Then ensued a fierce musketry duel, the air was filled with whistling missiles, and the Confederate advance was checked.   Sherman was twice wounded, in the hand and shoulder, and a third bullet passed through his hat.   He also had several horses shot from under him during the day. Again and again did the Confederates charge, but Sherman's line could not be shaken. The Thirteenth and Fortieth Missouri especially distinguishing themselves.   So the tide of battle ebbed and flowed, all of the other brigades finding it difficult to withstand the

ADVANCE OF FEDERAL TROOPS ON CORINTH, GENERAL HURLBURT'S DIVISION FORCING ITS WAY THROUGH THE MUD.

repeated rushes of the Confederates, who fought like demons. Cannon and musket, shell and bullet, did its deadly work, and the soddened earth was carpeted by dead and dying men, with the bright sun shining in full refulgence over the ghastly and repulsive scene.

Matters were now assuming a serious aspect for the Federals. By noon the Confederates had taken the ground occupied in the morning, and captured the camps of McClernand, Sherman, Prentiss and Stewart. In fact, three of the five Federal divisions had been completely routed, Hurlburt alone holding to his original position. General W. H. L. Wallace was killed, and the rear was thronged with fugitives from the raw regiments which had never before seen a battle of any kind. It was a moment of terrible suspense for Grant, for he found himself driven into a corner on the bank of the river, without any signs of Lew Wallace's five thousand men, who had been ordered up from Crump's Landing, neither had he heard from Buell. But the idomitable character of the man carried him through the emergency, and he fought on, the idea of surrendering never entering his mind. The success attained by the Confederates had, however, cost them dearly, for two of their Generals—Hindman and Gladdon—had been killed, while Johnston had left the field with a wound which subsequently proved fatal.

Beauregard, being now in command, decided to seize Pittsburg Landing, and all his energy was directed in that direction. But his men came to a deep ravine, at the mouth of which the gunboats Lexington and Tyler were posted, while on the opposite crest the Federals had hastily assembled twenty or thirty cannon. The Confederates bravely

MAJOR-GENERAL S. A. HURLBURT.

GENERAL BRAXTON BRAGG, C. S. A.

plunged into the ravine, led by such officers as Pond, Stuart, Ruggles, Chalmers, Stevens, Cheatham and Withers. But the soft earth had been soaked by the recent rains, and the men floundered in the deep mud. Colonel Webster, of Grant's staff, who had assembled the guns, then saw his opportunity, for he opened on the Confederate front with his hurriedly collected artillery, while the gunboats swept the ravine with eight-inch shells. Finding themselves in a trap, Beauregard's men here showed wonderful courage, for they charged the Federal batteries again and again, only to be cut down in broad swathes, for the Federal infantry was now rallying and delivering a deadly musketry fire. The scene at this point was a terrible one, the ground being thickly covered with dead, dying and wounded men, while the smoke from cannon and musket concealed the combatants from each other. Finally Beauregard decided to pause, thinking that he could finish Grant on the following morning with the greatest ease. As the Confederates fell back, Lew Wallace joined Grant, he having taken the wrong road, and Buell's advance under General Nelson was also on the field. Exhausted as were the Federals, these reinforcements gave them fresh hope and courage.

The sufferings of his troops during the night after the first day's battle is described by Grant in the following language :—" During the night rain fell in torrents, and our troops were exposed to the storm without shelter. I made my headquarters under a tree, a few hundred yards back from the river bank. My ankle was so much swollen from the fall of my horse, the Friday night preceding, and the bruise was so painful, that I could get no rest. The drenching rain would have precluded the possibility of sleep without this additional cause. Sometime after midnight, growing restive under the storm and the continuous pain, I moved back to the log house under the bank. This had been taken as a hospital, and all night wounded men were being brought in, their wounds dressed, a leg or an arm amputated as the case might require, and everything being done to save life or alleviate suffering. The sight was more unendurable than encountering the enemy's fire, and I returned to my tree in the rain."

During the night of April 6, twenty-seven thousand men were added to the strength of the Federal Army. Grant had personally superintended the disposition of his several divisions, and as Buell had brought up his own divisions under Nelson, McCook and Crittenden, he was assigned to the left and centre of the new line of battle. It had been arranged that the fresh troops were to begin, and Wallace's artillery opened at dawn as the Confederate left was attacked and driven back. Nelson and Crittenden were likewise engaged on Grant's left, finding the enemy in very strong force, because Beauregard had retained his purpose of capturing Pittsburg Landing. The fighting now grew desperate, for the entire line had become engaged, the Federal artillery fire proving too much for the Confederates to stand

BRIG.-GEN. W. H. L. WALLACE, KILLED AT BATTLE OF SHILOH.

before. Hazen's brigade had charged upon and captured one of Beauregard's batteries, turning the guns against him, while McCook's division came up with Terrill's battery, and pounded the Confederate centre with ten-pound shells and twelve-pound canister. Then came the turning event of the day. Mention has been made of the little log church which has given this battle its Federal name—for the Confederates only recognize the engagement as that of Pittsburg Landing. It was at the church that the final effort was made. Sherman had joined Wallace, and both Generals pressed steadily forward until they at length reached the ridge Sherman had occupied on the previous morning. Beauregard, finding his path to the Landing so stubbornly disputed, counter-marched and formed in front of Grant's right, finding himself again out-generaled. The fierce tide of battle now surged to and fro, as Beauregard, heroically endeavored to carry out his original plans, while Grant as stubbornly held to his own. Round the church the carnage was dreadful. Little did those humble Methodists imagine when they built their

A WAGON TRAIN IN PARK.
WAGON TRAINS WERE MASSED OR "PARKED" IN THIS MANNER, SO THEY COULD BE MORE EASILY AND SECURELY GUARDED.

log structure, that one day it would be the centre of a horrible battle, that its logs would be splintered by countless leaden bullets, and torn by solid shot, or exploding shell. They had used it for a place of prayer; these opposing armies now in deadly combat, held it as their common rallying point. The sound of song and praise to the Creator had given place to the roar of battle, the yells and cheers of advancing battalions, the agonized cries of shattered and wounded men, the deafening detonations of artillery, and the angry crash of musketry. Seldom has such a scene of carnage been enacted round the spot dedicated to divine worship. The church was taken and retaken a dozen times, each charge adding to the heap of dead or dying combatants. There was no opportunity for succoring those who had fallen, and many a Federal and Confederate soldier received a second and fatal wound, as he lay helpless on the bloody earth. The trees that surrounded the log church were riddled by leaden balls, and they, too, were added to the dead, for nearly all withered under the terrible force that tore them into splinters. The Demon of War swept over the gory field. With one despairing effort Beauregard gathered his force together and made a headlong, furious charge, but it was of no avail, the battle was ended, and the Confederates began retreating.   The cost of this victory for the Federals was, indeed, a heavy one, as there were no less than seventeen hundred men killed, seven thousand. four hundred and ninety-five wounded, and three thousand and twenty-two taken prisoners, an aggregate of twelve thousand two hundred and seventeen.   Buell lost over twenty-one hundred, Grant ten thousand and fifty.   Beauregard's loss was ten thousand, six hundred and ninety-nine. In writing about the battle in after years, Sherman says :—" Probably no single battle of the war gave rise to such wild and damaging reports.   It was publicly asserted at the North that our army was taken completely by surprise ; that the rebels caught us in our tents ; bayoneted the men in their beds ; that General Grant was drunk ; that Buell's opportune arrival saved the Army of the Tennessee from utter annihilation, etc.   These reports

THE HORRORS OF WAR.—GROUP OF UNION DEAD.

were in a measure sustained by the published opinions of Generals Buell, Nelson and others, who had reached the steamboat landing from the east, just before nightfall of the 6th, when there was a large crowd of frightened, stampeded men, who clamored and declared that our army was all destroyed and beaten."

General Halleck rose to the sublimity of the occasion, and forgetting his pique at being compelled to remain at St. Louis while his subordinates were winning laurels in the field, he issued an order thanking Generals Grant and Buell, their officers and men, for the bravery and endurance shown on April 6, and the heroic manner in which they had, on the following day, defeated and routed the Confederate army.   It may be mentioned here that Grant's detractors frequently brought the charge of drunkenness against him.   One day it was repeated to President Lincoln, who quietly inquired of the speaker, if he knew what brand of whisky Grant was in the habit of drinking.   Being answered in the negative, Lincoln expressed regret, saying it might be a good plan to serve the same brand to some of the other Federal Generals.

Beauregard retreated to Corinth in excellent order, under circumstances of great hardship. He had only one road, encumbered with wagons filled with wounded men, whose sufferings were increased by the heavy storms of wind and rain, hundreds dying *en route*. Being situated at the junction of the Memphis and Charleston Railroad and the Mobile and Ohio line, Beauregard decided that he must make a stand at Corinth, so began fortifying. In the meantime Brigadier-General Mitchell, acting under orders issued by Buell before he started to join Grant, had cut the Memphis and Charleston road at Huntsville, capturing an immense quantity of rolling stock. He also seized Decatur and Tuscumbia, thereby opening up another hundred miles of the Tennessee River, for which gallant service Congress rewarded him with a commission of Major-General. Sherman had also destroyed the railroad bridge at Bear Creek. These operations rendered Corinth of no value in a strategic sense, but Beauregard clung to it.

Halleck now made up his mind to have some share of the glory Grant was reaping,

GENERAL GRANT'S MILITARY RAILROAD.—THE DICTATOR.

so proceeded to Pittsburg Landing, arriving there April 12, when he assumed personal command of what was then called "The Grand Army of the Tennessee." Scarcely had Halleck appeared, than Grant had found himself nominally second in command, but in reality having no authority, or any real duty to perform. But Halleck, in St. Louis, calmly criticising battles as he sat in his office chair, and Halleck in the field, were two different persons. It should be remembered that this really talented man had no practical experience in the art of war. He had been a military professor, and a successful one, but, while he could detect mistakes when viewing a campaign at a distance, he was unable to grasp its salient points nearer at hand. Deciding to move on Corinth, Halleck proceeded so cautiously that the Confederates were able to gather up sixty-five thousand men. That the approaching engagement would be a heavy one was considered evident, as

Halleck had brought up Pope and some of Curtis' troops, his total strength being over one hundred thousand men. The Federal army was organized in three grand divisions, the old army that had fought so nobly under Grant, forming the right wing, under command of General George H. Thomas; the Army of the Ohio, under Buell, being the centre, while Pope's Army of the Mississippi occupied the left. Grant had a general supervision of the right wing.

Nine days after taking command, Halleck began his movement, but it was not until May 3 that Sherman, who had the advance, reached within six miles of Beauregard's advanced posts. Considerable fighting ensued, and on May 28 the Federals were only thirteen hundred yards from the Confederate breastworks, when heavy siege guns were placed in position and reconnaissances made on either flank. The following day, Pope and

EVACUATION OF CORINTH, MAY 30TH, 1862.

Sherman pushed forward more guns. Halleck now awaited results with calm confidence. He hoped for battle, and expected victory, and the capture of the greater part of Beauregard's army. Early the following morning, as the Federal skirmishers were seeking Confederate heads to shoot at, there was an awful and tremendous explosion, for Beauregard had departed, bag and baggage, during the night, leaving a few men to destroy the enormous quantity of ammunition he was compelled to leave behind. Thus ended the brief siege of Corinth, and Halleck reaped but a barren victory. It was now his turn to be criticised, and Halleck did not at all relish the experience. Few men do. Brave Beauregard also fell into trouble, for Jefferson Davis was wild with rage when he retired for a brief rest, and ordered Bragg to take permanent command, saying that Beauregard would never be trusted again. Some difference between Bull Run and Corinth. At the one Beauregard was a hero, the other brought him temporary disgrace.

BURNSIDE'S EXPEDITION OFF FORTRESS MONROE.

CHAPTER XVI.

BURNSIDE'S EXPEDITION TO ROANOKE ISLAND.

Following the leading events in the mighty struggle occurring between the National Government and the Revolted States, in their natural sequence, we now leave Halleck amid the smoking ruins of Corinth, and pass to the seacoast, where an important expedition is in progress. By this method the reader will gain a better conception of the relative importance of the various movements, as well as a clearer idea of their tremendous power and scope.

The success of the Hatteras and Port Royal expeditions led the Government to form a third, under command of General Ambrose E. Burnside. Its objective point was the coast of North Carolina, and it was organized at Annapolis, in December, 1861 and January 1862. The military force comprised sixteen regiments of infantry, one battery of field artillery, and a large number of artillerists, who were to mount and serve the siege guns that had been provided. This force of sixteen thousand men, was divided into three brigades, under Generals John G. Parke, Jesse L. Reno, and John G. Foster. When the fleet assembled in Hampton Roads, there were over one hundred vessels, steam and sail, divided in two columns, under the respective charge of Commanders Stephen H.

Rowan and Samuel G. Hazard, the chief naval command falling to Commodore Louis M. Goldsborough. The final departure of the expedition took place on the morning of Sunday, January 11, and it made the same imposing and picturesque appearance as did its predecessors. No difficulty was experienced in the movement until the fleet reached Cape Hatteras, when another terrible storm struck it with resistless fury, the consequence being that a gunboat, a floating battery and four transports were lost. Among these was the steamer City of New York, carrying fifteen hundred muskets, four hundred barrels of gunpowder, and other valuable ordnance supplies, but no lives were lost.

On Wednesday, January 14, Colonel J. W. Allen and Surgeon F. S. Waller, of the Ninth New Jersey, went ashore with a small reconnoitering party. On their return, the boat was capsized by the surf, and both officers were drowned. So boisterous did the

MAJ.-GENERAL JESSE L. RENO.   MAJ.-GENERAL JOHN G. PARKE.   MAJ.-GENERAL JOHN G. FOSTER.

weather continue, that the scattered fleet did not assemble in the peaceful waters of Pamlico Sound until February 7. The delay, though unavoidable, gave the Confederates ample time to discover the object of the expedition, and prepare for meeting it. Roanoke Island lies between Pamlico and Albermarle Sounds, and being exceedingly well fortified and garrisoned, was considered an effectual guard over the rear approaches to Portsmouth and Norfolk, Va. The garrison was at that time commanded by Colonel H. M. Shaw, of the Eighth North Carolina, owing to the illness of Brigadier-General Henry A. Wise. Besides the batteries, which commanded Pamlico and Croatan Sounds, there were some important fortifications on the mainland, covering the principal channels, while the water was filled with sunken vessels and other obstructions. To the defensive forces were added eight small gunboats, carrying eleven guns, and commanded by Lieutenant Lynch.

Heavy and threatening clouds obscured the sun on the morning of February 7, as Goldsborough's gunboats advanced up Croatan Sound, but at ten o'clock the clouds disappeared and bright, warm sunshine illumined the placid waters. Then Goldsborough hoisted his signal, "This day our country expects every man to do his duty," a paraphase of Nelson's famous annoucement to his fleet in Trafalgar Bay. At eleven o'clock the Federal gunboats opened on Fort Barton, at Pork Point, and in less than thirty minutes the engagement became general, the Confederate gunboats joining in the issue. But the

MAJOR-GENERAL AMBROSE E. BURNSIDE.

latter were soon driven beyond range, one receiving such punishment that it began to sink, and had to be beached. Fort Barton was so terribly pounded that the barracks were set on fire, and the entire work was shattered. General Burnside then began disembarking his troops on Roanoke Island, two miles from Fort Barton, finding a strong Confederate force concealed in the woods near by. The Federals were shelled by Lieutenant Lynch's flotilla, but Goldsborough's gunboats again drove him away, and also shelled the Confederate infantry position, so that by midnight nearly eight thousand Federals had

safely landed. But the movement was a fatiguing and perilous one, for the boats could not get within a quarter of a mile of the dry land, and the men had to wade ashore, frequently meeting small channels that were waist deep. The night grew cold, and a heavy rain storm added to the discomforts of the troops.

At daylight, the shivering columns were formed and began the advance. Foster's, brigade led, followed by those of Reno and Parke. The Confederate fire was drawn at eight o'clock, their position being admirably chosen, for there was a morass on either flank, leaving only a narrow strip of solid ground for the attack. Midshipman B. F. Porter accompanied Foster, with half a dozen boat howitzers, and he immediately opened fire. The Federal advance was necessarily slow and cautious, but the fighting was severe, as the Confederates held their position with characteristic stubbornness. For over two hours the battle raged fiercely, and Foster discovered that his men were running out of ammunition

COMMODORE LOUIS H. GOLDSBOROUGH.

SINKING OF THE CONFEDERATE FLEET.

LIEUT-.COL. G. F. BETTS.   COL. R. C. HAWKINS.   MAJOR E. A. KIMBALL.

'HAWKINS' ZOUAVES.

so he decided to use the bayonet. Major E. H. Kimball offered to lead the charge with part of Hawkins' Zouaves, and was told to go ahead. "Zouaves!" cried Kimball, "we are going to take that battery of guns; come along, boys." The men of the Ninth answered the Major with a cheer, and a away they dashed, closely followed by the Twenty-first Massachusetts and Fifty-first New York. So sudden and headlong was the charge that the Confederates had only time to fire one gun before abandoning the battery and retreating. The victors hoisted their regimental colors on the breastworks and then started in pursuit,

finally meeting a flag of truce asking for terms. "Unconditional surrender," was the reply, and two thousand men were made prisoners, including their commanding officer, Colonel Shaw.

Meanwhile General Reno had advanced toward Weir's Point, capturing Colonel Jordan and eight hundred men, and Colonel Hawkins seized the Shallowbag Bay battery and two hundred more men. Goldsborough's gunboats had in the interim been pounding Fort Barton, and when General Foster reached it, he found the place entirely empty, so hoisted the Stars and Stripes as a signal for the war vessels to cease firing. The damaged Confederate's gunboat, Curlew, was then blown up by her commander, the remainder of the flotilla retiring into Albemarle Sound. General Burnside found, on taking up his headquarters in Fort Barton, that he had possession of six forts, forty heavy siege guns, over three thousand stand of small arms and some thirty-three hundred prisoners. His loss was fifty killed,

COMMODORE ROWAN.

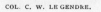

COL. C. W. LE GENDRE.

among them Colonel Charles S. Russell and Lieutenant-Colonel Vigeur de Monteuil, and two hundred and twenty-two wounded. With rare generosity Burnside gave all the credit in his dispatches to his brigade commanders. It was on Roanoke Island that Sir Walter Raleigh located his first American colony, in 1585. It therefore was historic ground.

Burnside's success only urged him on, his efforts being warmly supported by Goldsborough. It should be remembered that Elizabeth City, North Carolina, stands about thirty miles from the mouth of the Pasquotank River, which empties into Albemarle Sound. The city has also water communication with Norfolk, Virginia, via. the Dismal Swamp Canal. The Confederate gunboats having gone up the Pasquotank River, Commander Rowan started after them with fourteen vessels, and on February 10 found the object of his search. The fight lasted only forty minutes, the Confederate's gunboats were run ashore,

ATTACK ON ROANOKE ISLAND.—LANDING OF TROOPS BELOW NEWBERN.

the land batteries were silenced and the city fell into the hands of the Federals, who saved it from destruction by fire. A remarkable instance of personal bravery was shown during this brief engagement. One of the Confederate shells struck the gunboat Valley City, and set fire to the vessel. One of the gunners, John Davis, then deliberately sat upon and covered an open barrel of gunpowder, he had been using, thus protecting the inflammable material until the flames had been extinguished. For this act Davis was promoted, and Congress gave him a medal of honor. Similar smaller Federal successes followed all along the coast, and Burnside began operations against New Berne, Goldsborough returning to Hampton Roads, leaving Rowan, now a Commodore, in command of the naval force co-operating with Burnside.

New Berne is a town that had a population of six thousand, and access to its harbor is gained through Peracoke Inlet. On March 11, Burnside embarked fifteen thousand men from Roanoke Island, and started for the Neuse River. On the morning of the 13th the troops landed under cover of Rowan's saucy gunboats, and, marching forward a distance of twelve miles, bivouacked for the night within two miles of the Confederate lines. Burnside's men were enthusiastic, despite the difficulties they encountered, for heavy rain had fallen during the day, which made the roads next to impassable. In fact all movements of large bodies of troops is attended by rain, which they produce by filling the air with cannon and musket concussions; every important battle during the war being followed by drenching rains. So execrable, indeed, were the roads that the men had to

BATTLE OF ROANOKE ISLAND, FEBRUARY 8, 1862.

harness themselves to the artillery pieces with long ropes, and drag the guns forward by sheer strength, a feat the battery horses were unable to perform.

Striking the enemy's pickets early in the morning of the 14th, Burnside moved forward. The battle lasted for four hours and was quite severe, until finally Colonel Clarke, with his Twenty-first Massachusetts, charged and took the entrenchments. But the Confederates being reinforced, an awful hand-to-hand combat ensued, the Federals finally routing their antagonists, the Fifth Rhode Island, and the Eighth and Eleventh Connecticut, also distinguishing themselves. This ended the fight, Colonel Hartranft's Fifty-First Pennsylvania making a similar charge upon another battery, the Confederates retreated, leaving cannon, caissons, and horses behind them. On entering the town General Foster

THE TEN INCH MORTAR BATTERY IN ACTION AT FORT MACON.

was appointed Military Governor, while General Parke was sent to reduce Fort Macon, which defended the harbor of Beaufort, then used as a basis of operations for the blockade running steamships so abundantly supplied from English ports. Parke invested Fort Macon, which was commanded by Colonel Moses T. White, a nephew of Jefferson Davis, and General Burnside met the Confederate commander on April 24, under flag of truce. White declined to surrender, and the bombardment began the next morning. Both sides served their guns with obstinacy and precision, but, at four in the afternoon, a white flag

CAPTAIN MORRIS' BATTERY FIRING ON FORT MACON.

BOMBARDMENT OF FORT MACON.

SURRENDER OF FORT MACON.—LOWERING THE CONFEDERATE FLAG.

was hoisted over the fort and the Federals marched in. General Reno had also been as successful at South Mills, and Burnside's work was ended. Leaving General Foster in command of the department, "Rhody" sailed for Fortress Monroe, in July, with a part of his force, to join McClellan, who was then sadly in need of reinforcements.

SHELLING FORT MACON.—SIGHTING THE MORTAR.

This expedition had placed the Federals in possession of a considerable portion of the North Carolina coast, and drew the lines of the blockade still closer. It caused the Government to consider Burnside to be a really great commander, though he himself was aware he could not successfully handle more than a corps of nine or ten brigades. His subsequent career will be narrated hereafter. General Burnside was an imposing figure on a horse. His remarkable moustaches and whiskers, with the folded Burnside hat on his head, made him easy recognizable. He always wore full dress, even on the march, while a huge pair of snow-white gauntlets lent additional magnificence to his costume. As a rider, Burnside was easy and graceful, and he seemed to love being in the saddle. To see him as I did in 1864, at the head of the Ninth Corps, while on the march from Alexandria to the Rapidan River, was a remminiscence not to be forgotten, even after the

CONFEDERATE PRISONERS IN CAMP GEORGIA, ROANOKE ISLAND.

lapse of thirty years. The Ninth had come up to join the Army of the Potomac, in anticipation of Grant's overland campaign against Lee, and though the famous corps had been on the march since daylight, Burnside looked as clean at noon as if he had just stepped out of a bandbox. His sword hung gracefully, his broad orange sash was as carefully wrapped around his capacious waist as though he was on the line of review. There was a pleasant smile on his lips as he bowed to the men of the Fifth Corps. His own troops loved him, and though the Army of the Potomac had good reason to remember his disastrous campaign across the Rappahannock River, it respected him because he was a brave and gallant man.

MAJOR-GENERAL BUTLER AND STAFF.

CHAPTER XVII.

CAPTURE OF NEW ORLEANS BY FARRAGUT AND BUTLER.

When General Benjamin F. Butler returned from his Hatteras Inlet expedition, and reported to President Lincoln, the latter shook the General's hand saying : " You have a right to go home now, General, for a little rest; but study out another job for yourself." These few characteristic words were the foundation for the expedition of New Orleans. Butler went home to Boston, and traveled through the New England States for the purpose of pushing enlistments and the raising of new regiments, after which he was ordered to organize the military part of the New Orleans expedition. Then there was difficulty in getting off, because of the threatened war with England over the capture of Mason and Slidell, the Confederate commissioners to England and France, they having been taken from the English steamer Trent, by Capt. C. Wilkes, of the U. S. Frigate San Jacinto, on the high seas. The diplomacy of Secretary Seward in releasing the commissioners averted the difficulty, and established the precedent that no nation has a right to invade the deck of a vessel belonging to a friendly power.

On February 24, Butler took leave of the President. " Good bye, Mr. President," he said, " we shall take New Orleans, or you will never see me again." " The man that takes New Orleans is made a Lieutenant-General," said the Secretary of War. But New Orleans was taken by the navy, not the army, and the commander of the naval part of the expedition was raised to the rank of Vice-Admiral, equivalent to Lieutenant-General in the Army.

On February 25, 1862, Butler embarked his troops at Fortress Monroe, Commodore David G. Farragut, a veteran of the War 1812, and the Mexican War, having sailed February 2, to assume command of the Western Gulf Squadron. The acknowledged objective point of the expedition was Ship Island, while it was hinted that Mobile would possibly be attacked.   It is scarcely necessary here to call the reader's attention to the fact that the aim of the Federal Government was to finally take possession of all the Southern seaports and harbors, while its armies were to reduce the Northern and Western limits of the Confederate territory, the naval forces organized in the Mississippi and Ohio Rivers assisting.   When this was finally accomplished the war naturally ended.   Butler found Farragut at Ship Island, and preparations for ascending the Mississippi River were begun, but there were so many delays that it was not until April that the expedition reached the lower Passes.   On April 8, the Federal war fleet, consisting of six sloops, seventeen gunboats

MAJOR-GENERAL BENJAMIN F. BUTLER.

and twenty-one mortar schooners, entered the Southwest Pass.   General Butler remaining below, with his troops on transports.

The task set Farragut was an extremely hazardous one.   He had to pass between Fort St. Philip and Fort Jackson, on the north and south banks of the river, round a broad bend, thirty miles above the Pass.   These two forts had been armed with no less than one hundred and twenty-six guns of the heaviest calibre and largest range then known in warfare.   In addition to these, there was a huge chain stretched across the river on eight hulks, an obstruction somewhat similar to that used in the Hudson River during the Revolution.   The Confederates also had the Louisiana, a powerful ironclad battery, the steam ram Manassas, and thirteen gunboats, lying above the chain, with several fire ships and rafts in readiness below.   Other fortifications extended along the course of the river, and the effective land force defending New Orleans and its approaches was about twenty

D. G. Farragut

CAPTAIN, AFTERWARDS REAR-ADMIRAL CHARLES WILKES.

thousand men. It is rather a curious fact that the chief military command was held by General Mansfield Lovell, who had resigned his position in the New York City Government to join the Confederacy, while the river defences were in charge of General J. K. Duncan, another New York city office holder. On April 18, Farragut moved up the river, meeting a Confederate fire raft, which did no damage. It had been arranged that Captain David Porter was to creep up to the bend below the forts, with his mortar boats, and bombard. If this failed in reducing the forts, Farragut intended to run the gauntlet with his gunboats and sloops, and if he succeeded, Butler was to land in the rear of Fort St. Philip and carry it by assault.

Porter's bombardment was of the most terrific character. A mortar throws its missile high into the air, which then descends with tremendous force, the skill of the artillerists enabling them to so nicely calculate the line of flight, by elevating or depressing the mouth of their mortar, that shells can be placed anywhere within a radius of fifty yards. Scarcely had the mortars opened, when the barracks in Fort Jackson were set on fire and the guns were frequently silenced, the Confederate gunners being unable to serve their pieces in the presence of the bursting missiles. Then the fuses were not cut to give them full time to explode, and, as each of the twenty-inch globular masses fell inside the fort, they

SEIZURE OF MESSRS. MASON AND SLIDELL, ON BOARD THE BRITISH STEAMER TRENT, BY CAPTAIN WILKES, OF THE U. S STEAMER SAN JACINTO.

SHIP ISLAND.

penetrated the earth to the distance of several feet, and then exploding, threw the earth in all directions, creating havoc among the interior defences. During the first twenty-four hours, Porter's gunners flung no less than fifteen hundred bombs in and around the fort, the Confederates replying with equal energy. For six days and nights, or nearly one hundred and fifty hours, this awful iron rain continued. By daylight heavy banks of sulphurous smoke rolled down the Mississippi, and filled the dense woods sheltering the mortar boats. At night, the air was filled with fiery meteors, as the fuse lighted shells rose and fell. The roar of the contending artillery was deafening, being distinctly heard in the City of New Orleans. Trees were shattered, or torn up by the roots, great gaps were made in the fort, and the repeated detonations caused concussions that smashed windows thirty miles away, and killed millions of fish which

JAMES MURRAY MASON.

JOHN SLIDELL.

THE U. S. FLEET PASSING THE FORTS ON THE MISSISSIPPI, APRIL 19, 1862.

floated on the surface of the river as they followed the current. But despite this tremendous exchange of bursting iron, Fort Jackson was not reduced. The fact is, siege work is not so destructive of human life as are pitched battles, where the more deadly bullet comes in play. Once the troops become accustomed to huge shells and

PASSAGE OF THE 2D DIVISION OF THE FEDERAL-SQUADRON PAST FORTS JACKSON AND ST. PHILIP, APRIL 24, 1862

COMMANDER BELL, U. S. N.

CAPTAIN, AFTERWARDS REAR-ADMIRAL DAVID D. PORTER, U. S. N.

round shot falling in their midst, and have learned the use of the traverses or earthwork divisions which enable them to avoid the exploding fragments, they can cling to their works for almost an indefinite period. This was shown at Sebastopol during the Crimean War, and at Petersburg, where Lee stood Grant's pounding for over nine months. Farragut therefore decided to run the guantlet on the third night of the bombardment. Commander Bell with five gunboats, ran up to the boom about nine o'clock of the night of April 20, but the attempt to blow up one of the hulks failed, and revealed his presence.

FIRST DAY'S BOMBARDMENT OF FORTS JACKSON AND ST. PHILIP.

THE HARTFORD ON FIRE.

Fort Jackson opened a fierce fire on the Itaska, which had been lashed to a hulk, but her men worked away with saws, cold chisels and sledges until they had cut the chain. The Confederates then sent down more fire rafts, and the bombardment continued until twenty-

FIRE-RAFTS SENT FROM FORT JACKSON TO DESTROY THE FEDERAL FLEET.

Engagement Between U. S. Gunboat "Varuna" and Confederate Ram "Breckenridge" and Gunboat "Governor Moore."

six thousand shells had been expended on the Federal side, about one million and a half pounds of metal, equal to two hundred and fifty thousand six pound solid shot.

Just before daylight of April 24, the fleet weighed anchor and steamed up the river, safely passing through the broken chain, as the young moon was revealed above the tree tops. Then both forts opened furiously, as did a low water battery, the Federal gunboats making a vigorous response. The fog that had rested on the muddy waters of the Mississippi River now lifted, and the combat grew in its intensity. Porter's mortars pounded away, the forts and the fleet exchanged

COMMODORE T. BAILEY, U. S. N.

COMMANDER C. S. BOGGS, U. S. N.

FORT MASSACHUSETTS, SHIP ISLAND.

broadsides, and as these titanic forces struggled for the mastery, it seemed as if pandemonium reigned on earth. Farragut's ships finally got within half a mile of Fort Jackson, and poured in such rapid discharges of grape and canister that the Confederate gunners were swept from their barbette batteries. Then the Brooklyn became entangled in the chain, and the iron ram, Manassas, attempted to sink the Federal by firing a massive steel bolt from her huge bow gun, and by ramming. But the Brooklyn was protected by chain armor, and escaped. The Manassas next proceeded to push a fire raft against Farragut's flagship, the Hartford, which had run aground. The Hartford caught fire, but while one part of the crew extinguished the flames, the other section continued to work their guns. Finally the ship floated off, and the gallant Farragut found that his formidable and heroic task had been accomplished, for he had at last cleared the way to New Orleans. Commodore Bailey, with the second division, had quite as hard an experience. At one time he was in great peril, owing to the fact that his vessel, the Cayuga, had the greatest speed, which carried her ahead of her consorts. Down came the Louisiana and

THE FEDERAL FLEET BEFORE NEW ORLEANS.

Manassas to crush Bailey, accompanied by ten or twelve gunboats. The speed of the Cayuga, however, saved her, for it enabled Bailey to avoid the heavy ironclads, while he compelled three of the gunboats to surrender. Finding that his vessel had been struck by forty-two shells, and was partially disabled, Bailey retired from the fight, and pushed on up the river, leaving Captain Boggs with the Varuna to engage the

LAST BROADSIDE OF THE "VARUNA." COMMANDER BOGGS FIRES THREE BROADSIDES BEFORE SHE SINKS.

Confederate fleet. Boggs dashed forward, and used his guns so rapidly, with solid shot and grape, that he sank six of his antagonists. Then the ironclads used their rams and heavy guns, sending eight-inch shells through her unarmored stern, and the Varuna sank fifteen minutes later, her hull and rigging being in flames. General Butler, in his book, alludes to the advance of the Federal gunboats as a most gallant and inspiring one. Among other things, he says: "The moment Farragut's guns opened fire, the smoke settling down made it impossible to see anything one hundred yards away, except the bright flashes, or hear anything save the continuous roar of cannon of the heaviest calibre. It is vain to attempt to give a description of the appalling scene. The best one I ever heard was given by my staff-officer, Major Bell, in answer to a lady, who asked him to describe it. He said: ' Imagine all the earthquakes in the world, and all the thunder and lightning storms together, in a space of two miles, all going off at once ; that would be like it, madam.' "

Captain Boggs did not attempt to save his crew until the water rose to the trucks of the guns, but as the Varuna was tied to the trees on the river bank, he experienced no difficulty in getting all hands on shore, including his wounded. This extraordinary river battle only occupied ninety minutes of time, but in this comparatively brief period, the formidable forts had been successfully passed, and the Confederate Navy either destroyed or captured. Captain Porter describes the fate of the great ironclad,

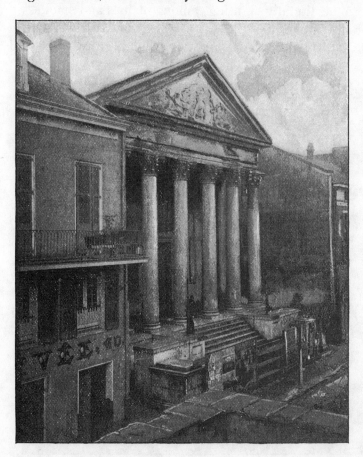

OLD CITY HALL, NEW ORLEANS, WHERE THE OFFICERS OF THE FLEET CAME TO DEMAND
THE SURRENDER OF THE CITY.

GENERAL BUTLER'S HEADQUARTERS, NEW ORLEANS.

Manassas, in the following graphic language: "It was reported to me that the celebrated ram, Manassas, was coming out to attack us, and sure enough, there she was, apparently steaming along shore, ready to pounce upon the defenceless mortar vessels; but I soon discovered that she could harm no one again. She was beginning to emit smoke from her port-holes; she was on fire and sinking. Her pipes were twisted and riddled with shot; her hull was cut up. She had evidently been used up by the squadron as she passed along. I tried to save her, as a curiosity, by getting a hawser around her and securing her to the bank; but just after doing so, she faintly exploded. Her only gun went off, and, emitting flames from her bow-port, like some huge animal, she gave a plunge and disappeared under the water. After the Manassas had gone down, there came a steamer on fire; after her two others, burning and floating down the stream. Fires seemed to be raging all along up the river, and we supposed that our squadron was burning and destroying the vessels as they passed along. The sight of this night attack was awfully grand. The river was lit up by rafts filled with pine knots; and the ships seemed to be literally fighting among flames and smoke."

As Captain Bailey sailed out of the smoke, he passed Farragut, and discovered the camp of the Chalmette regiment, which surrendered after receiving a shower of grape and

DESTRUCTION OF CONFEDERATE FLEET.

GENERAL MANSFIELD LOVELL.

canister. The Federal war ships that remained serviceable, now "took order," and proceeded up the Mississippi. As these nine gunboats approached the City of New Orleans, Farragut was surprised to meet steamers and flat boats adrift on the current, loaded with bales of cotton and all ablaze. Rounding the last bend of the river, the future Admiral found the entire levee one mass of flames, the Confederate troops having ruthlessly, but very naturally, applied the torch to all the remaining shipping. General Lovell had retired with his men, leaving the municipal authorities to settle their terms of surrender. Farragut took possession of the city during the afternoon of April 26, and General Butler arrived on May 1, when he assumed the military command. Troops having landed in rear of Fort St. Phillip, and intelligence reaching the garrisons that New Orleans had fallen, both the forts were surrendered. The commander of the ironclad battery, the Louisiana, set fire to his vessel after loading every gun, and it floated down stream, finally blowing up opposite the forts. This ended hostilities and the Lower Mississippi River was opened to Federal possession and control. To Farragut is due the entire credit, as was shown by the action of Congress, which created the rank of Admiral, and bestowed it upon him.

AN ENGLISH ARMSTRONG GUN.

A FIFTEEN INCH SMOOTH BORE GUN.

CHAPTER XVIII.

THE BATTLES OF HANOVER COURT HOUSE AND FAIR OAKS.

The engagement at Williamsburg, in Virginia, ending by Joe Johnston hastily falling back to his line of fortifications, beyond the Chickahominy River, McClellan established his new base of supplies at West Point, on the York River, the greater part of his reserve divisions passing up from Yorktown on transports. By May 15, the advance columns of the army reached White House, which marks the head of navigation on the tortuous stream known as the Pamunkey River, and three days after McClellan announced in a despatch to the President, that his headquarters were within nine miles of the City of Richmond. So far the Federal movement had every promise of ultimate success, despite its slowness, but McClellan was never certain that he had enough men, and invariably exaggerated the strength of his opponent. Consequently, no sooner did the Federal pickets get within sight of the church steeples of Richmond, than he asked for General McDowell's corps of forty thousand men. His request was so far granted

WHITE HOUSE LANDING.

FOLLER'S HOUSE.   CONTRABANDS AT FOLLER'S HOUSE.   CONWAY LANDING.

that McDowell proceeded down the Potomac to Acquia Creek, and marched to Fredericksburg, with the intention of joining McClellan's right. But Stonewall Jackson repeated his experiment of Bull Run, and made a rapid advance on Banks, who was occupying the Shenadoah and Virginia Valleys, a movement that so thoroughly alarmed the Washington authorities that they hastily recalled McDowell, though his cavalry videttes were in touch and communication with those of McClellan's command.

It is only just to the latter to say that this timidity at Washington destroyed what must be admitted was an excellent plan of operations, for with McDowell's fresh troops and a determined forward push by Banks, the Confederates would have been compelled to concentrate around Richmond. But Banks was ordered to fall back, and McDowell returned to Alexandria, leaving Stonewall Jackson to wheel and strike McClellan's right flank and double it up. For the purpose of opening a path for McDowell the Fifth Corps,

RUINS OF WHITE HOUSE.

Camp at Cumberland Landing.

CAMP OF CHRISTIAN COMMISSION AT WHITE HOUSE LANDING.

RUINS OF BRIDGE ACROSS PAMUNKEY RIVER, NEAR WHITE HOUSE LANDING.

GEN. FITZ JOHN PORTER AND STAFF.

ST. PETERS CHURCH, NEAR WHITE HOUSE, WHERE GEN. WASHINGTON WAS MARRIED.

CAMP AT CUMBERLAND LANDING.

under Fitz John Porter, was sent to Hanover Court House. Starting on May 27, by way of Mechanics-ville, General William H. Emory lead Porter's advance with two regiments of regular cavalry and Bonson's light battery, the main column consisting of Butterfield's, McQuade's, Warren's and Martindale's brigades, with three field batteries, under Captain Griffin, closely following. As usual, no sooner had Porter fairly started, than a heavy fall of rain drench-ed the roads, making pro-

BRIDGE ACROSS CHICKAHOMINY RIVER, BUILT BY 15TH NEW YORK ENGINEERS.

gress slow and difficult. It used to be a proverb in the old Army of the Potomac, that it had not only invaded the State of Virginia several times, but had actually waded through it. An old Confederate officer once remarked to the writer that he " did think Virginia was the muddiest State in the whole Union, at least Lee's Army had found it to be so."

The Confederate pickets were uncovered at McKinsey's Cross Roads, six miles from Hanover Court House, but they retired, and Emory did not halt until he was near the Court House. Then Butterfield advanced in good style, the Seventeenth New York capturing a field piece during the charge. Martindale meanwhile had pushed on as far as Peake's Station, on the Virginia Central Railroad, and after driving the Confederate force from his front, in the direction of Ashland, he turned towards the Court House. Then he met a fresh body of Confederate troops, which was sufficiently strong to break his centre and imperil his flanks. Porter, however, soon got his brigades together and a general engagement followed, ending in the capture of the Confederate camp, seven hundred prisoners and a consider-able quantity of small arms and supplies. The Federal loss was fifty-three killed, and three hundred and twenty-six wounded and missing. Having destroy-ed the track and the bridges on the Virginia Central Railroad, Porter with-drew, it being then known that McDow-ell was not coming up.

McClellan's army was now straddling the Chickahominy River, his line being broken by White Oak Swamp. General Casey held the left at Fair Oaks Station, on the York River Railroad, while the right lay beyond Savage Station under Porter. On the night of May 30, a heavy rain storm deluged the swamps

TRACK AND BRIDGE DESTROYED ON VIRGINIA CENTRAL RAILWAY.

GENERAL MC QUADE.
GENERAL. BUTTERFIELD.

GENERAL MARTINDALE.
GENERAL WM. H. EMORY.

and the net works of creeks which form the Chickahominy. The river soon overflowed, many of the bridges, were washed away including the pontoon structures thrown across by the Federal engineers, thus cutting the Army of the Potomac into several fragments. This was what Johnston had been waiting for, and he moved on McClellan's left early on May 31, General Hill's division striking Casey about noon. A spirited engagement followed, notwithstanding the fact that Casey had lost part of his camp, the Confederate advance being a complete surprise. The panic that at first seized the pickets was checked, and a brisk artillery fire on Hill's leading brigades, gave Casey time to form a tolerable good line. Regan's, Bates', and Spratt's batteries held Hill in partial check, until General Naglee came up with the Fifty-Sixth, Ninety-third and One Hundredth New York, the Fifty-Second and One Hundred and Fourth Pennsylvania and the Eleventh Maine. Generals Wessel and Palmer were on the left and centre. Keyes' corps was at Seven Pines, while Heintzelman's covered White Oak Swamp.

The Confederates now gathered strength, Longstreet's corps coming up, and they attacked Keyes, the movement putting Casey's artillery in danger, so Naglee charged in good style, but he was met by a tremendous musketry volley which shattered the line. A counter charge was then made by Rains, and as the Federal batteries had exhausted their ammunition, Casey was compelled to retire to the second line, occupied by Couch. Captain

FIELD HOSPITAL AT SAVAGE STATION, JUNE, 1862

OFFICERS OF BRIGADE HORSE ARTILLERY

GEN. STONEMAN AND STAFF

GEN. STONEMAN, GEN. NAGLEE AND STAFF OFFICERS

GEN. STONEMAN, GEN. NAGLEE AND OTHER OFFICERS AT HEADQUARTERS ARMY OF THE POTOMAC.

Spratt lost two of his guns after they had been spiked, and General Rhodes captured the pieces in the redoubt and turned them on the Federals. Couch's division lay across the Williamsburg road, his right resting on the York River Railroad, in rear of Fair Oaks Station, and he met the onslaught very firmly, while Heintzelman hurried up to his support, arriving on the ground about four o'clock in the afternoon. Being the ranking officer, he assumed command.

A brief pause ensued, after which the Confederates advanced on

ENGINEER CORPS MAKING CORDUROY ROADS.

CAMP LINCOLN.

FORT SUMNER.

FORT RICHARDSON.

ON CHICKAHOMINY RIVER.

Couch, striking his right flank, and doubling it up. General Johnston now appeared, and personally directed his men. By a series of clever flank movements, he broke Heintzelman's line in several places, driving him back, Kearney's division being almost flung into White Oak Swamp. When the battle began, McClellan was at New Bridge, at the extreme right of his army, but Sumner lay within striking distance, so he advanced to Heintzelman's relief, crossing a slender bridge he had thrown across the Chickahominy the day before. This

NEAR FAIR OAKS, JUNE, 1862.

MAJOR-GENERAL SILAS CASEY AND STAFF.

Grapevine Bridge, as it was afterwards known, enabled Sumner to reach Heintzelman, as Longstreet and G. W. Smith renewed the attack, and he opened fire with several brass Napoleon guns, which mowed down the enemy with rapid discharge of grape and canister. A desperate struggle then ensued, Brigadier-General A. Davis and Colonel Riker were killed, while Brigadier-General Pettigrew was wounded and taken prisoner, his horse being killed. Sedgwick, O. O. Howard, Burns, French, Meagher and Sickles were soon hotly engaged and the battle raged until sunset, when General Joe Johnston was wounded, the Confederate command falling to General Smith. Both armies slept on the ground and the following morning, at dawn, Smith made an advance all along his line, intending to pierce the Federal centre, and then defeat it in detail. The most deadly fighting was done by Pryor's and Mahone's brigades on the Confederate side, against the brigades of Howard and Meagher. Pryor had advanced on French's brigade and did such execution that the Federal line must have broken, had not Howard rushed forward. This began to turn the tide of battle, when "Little Skin and Bones," as Mahone's men called him, came running up and strengthened Pryor, so that Howard found himself overwhelmed. This was Thomas Francis Meagher's opportunity and he was quick in accepting it. Waving

COLONEL RIKER.
GENERAL NAGLEE.

GENERAL J. W. PATTERSON.
BRIG.-GENERAL PALMER.

BURYING THE DEAD, AND BURNING HORSES AT FAIR OAKS.

his sword over his head, and unconsciously adopting the brogue, as he often did when he was excited, the General exclaimed, " Now byes, here you've been grumbling all day, becase ye had'nt a dacint chance for a foight.   By the Lord Harry, you are loikely to get your belly full of it now.   Move forward, me darlings, and give 'em a taste of your quality for the sake of dear ould Ireland." The "boys" laughed at their General's characteristic speech, and then with a wild yell, the famous Irish brigade plunged into the deadly melee, like a lot of schoolboys at play. Meagher's arrival enabled Howard to hold his ground. It was a curious sight to see this Christian soldier riding up and down his line, encouraging the men in their deadly work. Howard was as calm and cool as he would be on parade, yet there was a glow on his cheek which betokened that fierce rage that invariably possesses the soldier in close combat. Howard had two horses shot

ON THE CHICKAHOMINY RIVER.

GENERAL JAMES LONGSTREET, C. S. A.

under him and he received a severe wound in the arm, but he refused to leave the field, consenting only that the wounded limb be bound by a handkerchief. When General Howard again rode at the head of a column of troops, he wore an empty sleeve.

Being fresh and naturally impetuous, Meagher's men dashed forward so earnestly that both Pryor and Mahone had to fall back, and the entire right wing of the Federals was so straightened and strengthened that the Confederates found it impossible to break though. On McClellan's left, Hooker's division, assisted by Patterson's and Sickles' brigades, presented a solid front, and after delivering a withering fire, finally succeeded in pushing back the Confederate columns. This ended the battle of Fair Oaks, but while the Confederates retired on that Sunday afternoon they were soon to return with more deadly effect.

There were two or three Federal reconnaissances in force towards Richmond, but they

BRIG.-GEN. J. J. PETTIGREW, C. S. A.

GENERAL G. J. RAINES, C. S. A.
LT.-GENERAL D. H. HILL, C. S. A.

MAJOR-GENERAL W. MALONE, C. S. A.
MAJOR-GENERAL R. E. RODES, C. S. A.

SICKLE'S BRIGADE COMING INTO LINE.

HOUSE USED AS HOSPITAL FOR HOOKER'S DIVISION.

HOUSE NEAR WHICH OVER 400 SOLDIERS WERE BURIED.

QUARLES HOUSE.

HOUSE USED AS HOSPITAL.

EARTHWORKS AT EXTREME FRONT.

BATTLEFIELD OF FAIR OAKS.

HEADQUARTERS ARMY OF POTOMAC, AT SAVAGE STATION, JUNE, 1862.

did not reveal the presence of any hostile force, as the Confederates had retired to their previous defensive position.   This two day's battle was a very costly one to both armies. The Confederates lost their general and four thousand two hundred and twenty-three officers and men, while the Federal loss was two Generals, one Colonel, and five thousand seven hundred and thirty-nine men killed, wounded and missing.

MARYLAND HEIGHTS, HARPERS FERRY.

BATTLE OF WINCHESTER, VA.

CHAPTER XIX.

STONEWALL JACKSONS' CAMPAIGN MANŒUVRES.

From the day he entered the field of hostile operations, in May, 1861, until the day of his death at Chancellorsville, May 2, 1863, General Thomas Jefferson Jackson was a sharp thorn in the side of the Federal Government. He possessed that rare faculty of being able to plan a brilliant campaign, and then successfully carry it out. He excelled in rapid movements, for he frequently fought one day in the Shenandoah Valley, and within forty-eight hours forced another army on the other side of the mountain range. This occurred at the Battle of Bull Run, and "Stonewall" was now to repeat the effort, and so save the City of Richmond from capture.

It will be remembered that Jackson's threatening movement against Washington prevented McDowell's corps joining the main army under McClellan, and it will be necessary to here give an outline of his wonderful campaign in order that the reader may understand its importance in the many strategic moves made in the wide area of territory over which these opposing armies were manœuvreing. While McClellan was carrying his magnificent body of troops to the Peninsula, Jackson retired up the Shenandoah Valley for the double purpose of keeping in touch with the Army of Northern Virginia, and drawing after him the Federal force, under General James Shields. On

GENERAL T. F. (STONEWALL) JACKSON.

March 22, a skirmish occurred near Winchester, between General Turner Ashby's Confederate cavalry and one of Shields' brigades, during which the Federal General was hit by a fragment of a shell, which inflicted a painful wound, but he refused to leave the field. Believing that Jackson would not attack in force, General Banks left Shields and repaired to Washington. The next morning the wounded General found Jackson's entire command on his immediate front. Conducting the subsequent engagement at Kenistown, from his bed of suffering, Shields succeeded in driving back his antagonist with heavy loss.

GENERAL R. S. EWELL, C. S. A.

Banks hastily returned, and taking command, pursued Jackson to his stronghold at Mount Jackson, forty miles beyond Winchester. There Jackson was joined by General R. S. Ewell and General Edward J. Johnston, who brought up two strong divisions of infantry and several field batteries, thus increasing Jackson's effective strength to nearly twenty-one thousand men.

The disposition of the Federal forces in the East at that moment was as follows:—McClellan was

threatening Richmond along the line of the Chickahominy, Banks occupied the Shenandoah Valley and the line of the upper Potomac, McDowell stood at Fredricksburg, and Fremont was further west among the West Virginia mountains. The whole Federal force under Fremont, McDowell and Banks, was about sixty-one thousand men, McDowell having fully two-thirds of the entire strength, including Shields' division that had been taken from Banks. In face of so formidable a line, Jackson planned

GENERAL EDWARD J. JOHNSTON, C. S. A.

a most brilliant series of manœuvres. Knowing that Fremont was pushing forward to join Banks, the Confederate General advanced to meet him, leaving Ewell to hold Banks' attention. Meeting Fremont a few miles east of Stanton, Jackson compelled him to retire with loss, and then swiftly returned over the Shenandoah mountains in time to prevent Banks entering Manassas Gap on his way to join McDowell. It was this movement which took McDowell's corps from McClellan. Falling with crushing force on Colonel Kenly and his garrison, at Front Royal, Jackson wounded the commander, took seven hundred prisoners, two cannon and the Federal supply train. Banks was at Strasburg, and when he found that Jackson's twenty-one thousand men were advancing on his eleven thousand, he made a rapid retreat to Winchester, reaching the town at midnight of May 24. At daylight the following morning, a furious battle began, but Banks was only covering his retreat to the Potomac, at Martinsburg, twenty-two miles above Harper's Ferry. The Confederates, however, took three thousand prisoners and nine thousand muskets. To show what fatigue trained soldiers can endure, and yet accomplish long distances, it may be mentioned that Banks' division marched and fought over fifty-four miles of roads, during forty-eight hours. Though tolerably orderly in their retreat, the Federals were glad enough when they found the Potomac between them and Jackson's advance. General Banks thus describes the fording of the Potomac: "The scene at the river, when the rear guard arrived, was of the most animating and exciting description. A thousand camp-fires were burning on the hill-side, a thousand carriages of every description were crowded upon the banks, and the broad river rolled between the exhausted troops and their coveted rest. There were never more grateful hearts in

MAJOR-GENERAL J. C. FREMONT.

the same number of men than when, at midnight on the 26th, we stood on the opposite shore."

Moving down to Harper's Ferry, Jackson prepared for a descent upon Washington, for nothing seemed too formidable or hazardous to his fearless mind. But he soon learned that McDowell and Fremont were moving to intercept him, so he made another retrograde movement up the Valley. Starting during the night of May 29, Jackson left Ewell at the Ferry as a temporary rear guard, the latter maintaining a heavy cannonading during the

BRIG.-GEN. JAMES SHIELDS.

MAJOR GENERAL E. V. SUMNER.

whole of the following night, in order to convey the impression to the Federals that a battle was in progress. This curious device was carried out amidst a furious storm of rain, accompanied by terrific flashes of lightning and heavy rolling thunder. With their batteries perched on Bolivar heights, just above the town, Ewell's gunners seemed to be mocking the artillery in the heavens. The swish of the heavy drops of rain as they were hurled in the faces of the men by the howling wind; the mighty peals of thunder rolling along the mountain peaks; the vivid flashes of blinding electricity suddenly illuminating the scene, and the next instant leaving it in utter darkness, were Nature's contribution to the spectacle. Amidst it all, Ewell's

BATTLE OF CROSS KEYS.—OPENING OF THE FIGHT.

cannon went on shelling Loudon and Maryland Heights, and as each gun gave tongue, and the shells burst on the mountain sides, it seemed as if Heaven and Earth were contending for the mastery. Such a scene recalls Milton's lines:

> " Clash'd on their sounding shields the din of war,
> Hurling defiance toward the vault of Heaven.
> There stood a hill not far, whose gusty top
> Belch'd fire and smoke."

The vicissitudes of war had now reversed the programme, for Jackson's movement up the Valley was as precipitate as had been Banks' hurried retreat. Indeed so rapidly did the Confederates race for a place of safety, that, though Fremont reached Strasburg about noon of June 1, they had passed through the town several hours before, and the division of

GENERAL BANKS' DIVISION RECROSSING POTOMAC TO ATTACK "STONEWALL" JACKSON.

General Shields, which had been sent by McDowell to join Fremont, did not get there until June 2. Stung by Jackson's wonderful escape, Fremont pursued with vigor. Putting his own troops in motion on the Harrisonberg turnpike, he sent Shields along the south fork of the Shenandoah River, as it passes between the Blue Ridge and Massanutten Mountain ranges. Jackson burned all the bridges as he crossed them, thus retarding pursuit, and he reached Harrisonburg in safety on the morning of June 5.

General Jackson was a sincere Christian. He did not parade his religious convictions, but they gave him a tremendous hold on the affections of his troops. Most men are profane when they are angry, but with Stonewall it was different. He could reprove without an oath passing his lips, yet the effect was quite as satisfactory. As a military commander, he deserved the high niche in history his achievements won for him. Had it not been Jackson's habit to make his own investigations, he would probably have lived to see Appomattox, though his fate was perhaps as kind to him as he could have wished, for he died at a moment when his side was victorious. The Lieutenant-General was a great horseman. He sat the saddle easily, while there was a sort of abandon visible which showed his familarity with horseflesh from boyhood. His seat was very erect, and though it had none of the stiffness of the cavalry style, it was very correct. His stirrups were shortened to give a slight bend to the knee and enable him to adjust his body to the movements of his steed without apparent exertion. As a soldier he ranked with Lee, for he was a born fighter, and never knew when he was defeated. His men adored him, and their part of the battle, was sure to be the hottest corner of the field.

Fremont passed through Harrisonburg a few hours after Jackson's rear guard, and

BATTLE ON THE ROAD FROM HARRISBURG, BETWEEN THE FEDERALS UNDER GEN. FREMONT AND THE CONFEDERATES UNDER GENERALS JACKSON AND EWELL.

two miles beyond the town, Colonel Percy Wyndham, commanding a few squadrons of cavalry, struck Ashby and his troopers. The Confederate General halted and gave battle, his movement being so swift that Colonel Wyndham and two entire Federal squadrons were made prisoners. Their infantry then came up under Colonel Kane and opened fire, which caused General Stewart's brigade to halt in order to support Ashby. The skirmish was a hot one, for General Ashby was killed and Colonel Kane was wounded and made a prisoner. Leaving General Ewell with five thousand men, consisting of Stewart's, Elzy's and Trimble's brigades at Cross Keys, Jackson pushed on towards Port Republic. As Ewell was only a few miles from Harrisonburg, where Fremont's main force lay, the latter moved out for attack. The Federal line consisted of the brigades of Generals Schenck, Cluseret, Milroy, Stahl and Bohlen, while General Blenker's division held the position of reserve. The engagement opened about eleven o'clock of June 8, and was fought on both sides with stubborn courage until four in the afternoon, when just as Milroy's brigade were

BATTLE OF CROSS KEYS, JUNE 8, 1862.

on the point of seizing the batteries on Ewell's centre, Stahl's men gave way before heavy musketry, and compelled Fremont to retire. The losses on both sides were severe, the Federals losing an unusual proportion of officers, Kane's Bucktails not having even a corporal left in their ranks.

While the battle of Cross Keys was in progress, the head of Shield's column reached Port Republic, when Colonel Carroll, with his cavalry, captured the bridge, but omitted to destroy it. General Tyler, coming up, drove back Jackson's right, but when Fremont arrived on June 9, in pursuit of Ewell, the bridge was burning and the river too deep for fording. The consequence was that Tyler had to retreat and Jackson had succeeded in preventing the threatened junction of Fremont and Shields. Leaving them in derision, the Confederate General started to join the Army of Northern Virginia to aid in breaking up McClellan's Peninsular campaign.

MAJOR-GENERAL R. C. SCHENCK.

BVT.-MAJOR-GENERAL T. L. KANE.   MAJOR-GENERAL R. H. MILROY.   BRIG.-GENERAL H. BOHLEN.
MAJOR-GENERAL J. STAHL.   BVT.-MAJOR GENERAL E. B. TYLER.

GENERAL HEINTZELMAN AND STAFF.

CHAPTER XX.

BEGINNING OF THE SEVEN DAYS' BATTLE BEFORE RICHMOND.

After the battle of Fair Oaks, McClellan resumed his favorite pursuit of throwing up formidable fortifications, while Robert E. Lee, who had succeeded Johnston in the command of the Army of Northern Virginia, prepared for a final blow which was to crush McClellan. General Lee was a remarkable man. Highly educated, and thoroughly trained in the art of war ; he was a true soldier in every sense of the word. As aide to Lieutenant-General Scott for several years before the war, he learned staff duty in the most thorough manner, and his studies made him a great tactician. This is shown by the methods of the Antietam and Gettysburg campaigns. In the former he actually marched an army, ninety thousand strong, only provided with ammunition, for he depended on the invaded territory for the support of his men. Those who saw the dexterous and sweeping forage of the Confederates remember how hay, grain, live stock, flour and other necessaries of life were rapidly gathered and carried across the upper Potomac. Though foraging was necessarily permitted, the discipline established by Lee

GENERAL ROBERT E. LEE.

was so effectual, that his soldiers committed no excesses, a statement that can only be made of American troops. The tales told of the French, Russian, and other European armies under such conditions, are in vivid contrast with the conduct of Northern and Southern musket bearers during their campaigns against each other.

While directing his army on the field, General Lee presented a neat and soldierly appearance, and he had a very graceful carriage in the saddle. When in motion he sat erect and composed, but he seldem rode at a faster gait than a canter. He had a curious habit of laying his hands on the pommel, on halting, to converse with anyone. Leaning gently forward, Lee's attitude was at once courteous and engaging. But there was always a look of sadness in his eyes, noticeable in no other General on either side. The

MAJOR-GENERAL JOE HOOKER.

writer once saw Lee while going to the Confederate rear as a prisoner, and I was struck by the courtesy he displayed towards us. He asked a few questions, but receiving unwilling answers, he politely lifted his hat and rode away. No General in the Confederate service held so warm a place in the hearts of his soldiers, and that fact proves the true nobility of the man, for, as their commander, he had to force his men to the greatest extremity, but for every surviving veteran of the Army of Northern Virginia, it is always a proud boast that he fought with Bob Lee, and every Federal veteran will fully appreciate that sentiment, for they entertain the same feeling for their own commanders.

General Jackson, on leaving Port Republic, as described in the last chapter, marched to Ashland, where he arrived June 25, having gathered up all of his detached commands until he had a collective force of fully thirty-five thousand men. It is so happened that General

BATTLE OF GAINES' MILLS, JUNE 27, 1862.

MAJOR-GENERAL J. F. REYNOLDS.

McClellan had on the same day sent General Heintzelman with his corps and the brigades of Hooker and Kearney on a reconnoissance beyond his extreme right. Heintzelman advanced as far as Oak Grove, sometimes known as King's Schoolhouse, where he uncovered Jackson's movement and retired. On learning from the few prisoners taken that they had come from the Shenandoah Valley, Porter took ground on Beaver Dam Creek, where he placed McCall's Pennsylvania Reserve, with Seymour's and Reynold's brigades, and plenty of artillery. Leaving Reynolds in command of that part of the line, Porter practically abandoned Mechanicsville, and waited for the attack he knew he could not long be delayed. It was the unexpected presence of Jackson, and his annoyance over the non-arrival of McDowell's forty thousand men, that led McClellan to finally seek refuge on the James River.

It is no reproach to McClellan to say that Lee was his superior as a strategist, for the latter was the equal of Grant and Sherman. Consequently, when he began the offensive, Lee found it comparatively easy to confuse his antagonist. General McClellan knew that the position of the Army of the Potomac was untenable, and he actually prepared for changing bases before Lee attacked. Immense quantities of commissary and ordnance supplies had been gathered at White House, and General Ingalls was astonished one day by receiving orders to carry all he could find transports for down the York and Pamunkey Rivers, and up the James River, and destroy the remainder. This was the first sign of the projected movement. Ingalls did his best, and as McClellan's reserve artillery and wagon trains were crossing the Chickahominy River, a dense volume of smoke informed the Federals that their base had been abandoned. Among the stores destroyed was a pile of hard bread, three hundred feet long, fifty feet wide and thirty feet high. Hundreds of artillery charges were opened, and the powder scattered over the pile, while barrels of oil were poured out. The match being applied to this inflammable material, the flames burned fiercely for two days and nights, while tents, wagons, tools and other supplies were destroyed in like manner.

Lighted by the pillow of fire at White House, that night the army assumed its new position. The Fifth Corps, under Fitz John Porter, stood at Gaines' Mills, being attacked early on the morning of June 27. Sykes, Regular division, which included the Fifth New York (Duryee's Zouaves), held the extreme right, and received the first blow. Captain J. H. Weed's regular battery being posted on the Cold Harbor Road opened fire on the head of A. P. Hill's column, and then Sykes wheeled into line and drove it back with heavy loss. Longstreet, who was to make a feint attack on Porter's left, was compelled

BVT.-MAJOR-GENERAL TRUMAN SEYMOUR.

GAINE'S MILLS. VA.

UNBURIED DEAD ON BATTLEFIELD GAINE'S MILLS.

ELLISTON MILLS, MECHANICSVILLE.

MECHANICSVILLE, VA.

UNBURIED DEAD ON BATTLEFIELD GAINES MILLS.

Scenes at and near Gaines' Mills.

MAJ.-GEN. W. B. FRANKLIN.

BVT.-BRIGADIER-GENERAL O. H. HART.

MAJOR-GENERAL E. D. KEYES.

to do so in earnest, and while he was arranging his line, "Stonewall" Jackson arrived and took position on Hill's left. The three corps, or divisions, then advanced in splendid style and strong force, but Porter's steady volleys of musketry decimated the Confederate ranks, and they were falling into disorder, when General Cobb came up and reinforced their line. Cobb made several charges without success, though the Nineteenth Carolina performed prodigies of valor, losing nearly all of their officers, and no less than eight color bearers. Despite the steadiness of his troops, Porter felt that he was being outnumbered, and in danger of having his right flank completely turned. He therefore asked McClellan for reinforcements, when Slocum's division was dispatched and came upon the ground late in the afternoon. The battle now grew in severity, the Confederates making a series of desperate charges, each being repulsed with terrific slaughter. Then Jackson, with Whiting and Longstreet dashed upon Porter's left, facing a terrific discharge of grape and canister, which mowed down the leading

BRIDGE ACROSS CHICKAHOMINY RIVER, ON MECHANICSVILLE ROAD.

GENERAL INGALLS

line, yet so determined was the movement that the Federals were on the point of falling back, when the brigades of Meagher and French came across the river and dashed in.

Butterfield's brigade becoming isolated, fought for nearly an hour all alone, but being overwhelmed, it was forced back, leaving the batteries of Weedon, Edwards, Hart and Allen so exposed that they had to retreat, abandoning several guns for want of horses to drag them off the field. With the sun rushing towards the horizon, Porter discovered that he was really fighting the bulk of Lee's army, so called up his reserve artillery of eighty guns to cover his retreat across the Chickahominy. At that moment, General St. George Cook made a foolish charge with his cavalry on the Confederate flank, but being repulsed his men came rushing through the Federal batteries then going into action. Supposing that they were charged by Confederate cavalry, these Federal gunners were panic-stricken and limbering up their guns, galloped after the infantry, now heading for the pontoon bridges. It was an awful scene of confusion, but just then French and Meagher came trotting up from the river, and passed to the rear in splendid shape and magnificent spirits. Their appearance restored confidence, the Federals re-formed, and checking Jackson's headlong advance, managed to get across the River during the night and join McClellan's main body. The losses at Gaine's Mills were very heavy, the Federals leaving behind them over nine thousand men killed, wounded or prisoners, besides twenty-two cannon, ten thousand small arms and many wagons, containing ammunition and food. The Confederate loss was twelve thousand killed and wounded.

McClellan now decided to push across the Peninsula to the James River. General Keyes was directed to hold the White Oak Swamp Road, while Porter, McCall, Sumner, Franklin and Heintzelman moved through the swamp, carrying with them five thousand wagons, and the reserve and siege artillery, besides an immense drove of cattle and other supplies. Slocum's division held Savage's Station until this movement was accomplished. The Confederates, supposing that McClellan was still in force in front of White House, advanced in that direction, finding the depot in ruins, and acres upon acres of embers where the Federal supplies had been committed to the flames by Stoneman and Emory, who had gone to Yorktown. The retreat of McClellan was now revealed, and the pursuit at once began.

The Federal commander was not only compelled to sacrifice his White House stores, he had also to destroy vast quantities at Savage's Station, among them a train of railroad cars loaded with ammunition. This was first

GENERAL SYKES AND STAFF.

Scene of Operations in Eastern Virginia, July, 1862.

MAJOR-GENERAL W. S. HANCOCK.

MAJOR-GENERAL H. W. SLOCUM.

set on fire, then sent, with the locomotive throttle valve open, to fall over the broken river bridge, each car exploding as it reached the surface of the sluggish stream. Scarcely had his entire army got across the Chickahominy, than McClellan found Lee close on his heels, but he was so elated by the success attending the movement that he sent an impertinent dispatch to Secretary Stanton, in which he said: "If I save this army now, I tell you plainly that I owe no thanks to you, or any other person in Washington. You have done your best to sacrifice this army."

Both armies now entered on their race to the banks of the James River, a series of desperate battles by day and night being the natural result.

BVT.-MAJOR-GENERAL O. EDWARDS. BVT.-MAJOR-GENERAL R. ALLEN. BVT.-MAJOR-GENERAL P. ST. GEORGE COOK.

GRAPE VINE BRIDGE.

COMMENCEMENT OF THE RETREAT.

CHAPTER XXI.

MCCLELLAN'S RETREAT TO THE JAMES RIVER.

The Federal retreat from the Pamunkey and the Chickahominy being uncovered, General Lee immediately began a vigorous pursuit. He ordered the division under

LT.-GENERAL R. E. LEE AND STAFF OFFICERS.

General Hill and Longstreet to cross the Chickahominy River at New Bridge, and advance along the Long Bridge and Darbytown roads, "Stonewall" Jackson being instructed to pass over by Grape Vine Bridge, and follow the South bank of the Chickahominy. General Huger was sent down the Williamsburg road, and General Magruder took the Charles City road. These manœuvres gave apparent opportunity for striking General McClellan's flank and rear. So rapidly did these pursuing columns move, that Magruder reached the neighborhood of Savage's Station on the afternoon of June 29, in time to strike Sedgwick's division as it stood deployed across the railroad. General Sumner, being in command, formed line of battle, and vigorously engaged Magruder. The latter supposing that the Federals intended advancing instead of retreating, he halted and sent for reinforcements, but discovered his error before they arrived, and at once moved forward to the attack. The brunt

GENERAL HUGER, C. S. A.

of the Confederate assault fell upon the brigades under Generals Hancock, Brooke and Burns, their artillery support being very effective. Despite the strong effort made by Magruder, the Federals held to their line, being greatly aided therein by the grape and canister used by the batteries of Captains Osborn, Pettit and Bramhall. Meagher's Irish brigade again distinguished itself here, making no less than three separate charges at critical moments. This engagement at Savage's Station ended at dark, and Sumner crossed White Oak Swamp and the creek during the night, burning the bridge behind him. The Federals lost nearly nine hundred men, the Confederates over four hundred.

General Jackson's column was delayed by having to rebuild Grape Vine Bridge, so they did not reach Savage's Station until noon of June 30, but found nearly three thousand sick and wounded Federals who had been left behind, besides considerable military property that had not been destroyed for want of time. Without pausing Jackson pressed forward on McClellan's rear, being joined by Longstreet and Hill, while Huger and Magruder took the Charles City road, with the intention of striking the flank of the Federal army. But General McClellan now showed the excellent fighting qualities he really possessed, when driven into a corner. As soon as all the corps had crossed White Oak Swamp, and the supply trains were well forward, the General decided to halt and give battle. Selecting an advantageous line near Willis Church, he placed General Hancock on the extreme right, and Fitz John Porter on the left, Sumner's and Heintzelman's corps occupying the centre. Scarcely had this disposition been made, when Jackson's division appeared, finding the bridge destroyed, while the road was covered by Captain Romeyn B. Ayres with his own and two of the reserve batteries. Jackson himself came up about noon, and at once opened fire on Hancock, while his troops attempted to repair the bridge, but they were

driven back, even after several Confederate batteries had gone into action. Finding it impossible to replace the bridge, Jackson made the desperate resolve to wade the river, though it was nearly breast deep, but he did not succeed, for Hancock poured in a deadly musketry fire and Ayres' guns used grape and canister at awfully close range. It is impossible for men, however brave, to advance through deep water, while exposed to a storm of iron and leaden missiles, so the Confederates fell back.

Meanwhile Hill and Longstreet had reached Nelson's Farm, two miles to the right of Jackson, finding Sumner and Hooker on the Federal right, McCall in the centre and Phil

LTS. JONES, BOWEN AND CUSTER.

BATTLE OF WHITE OAK SWAMP, JUNE 30, 1862.

Kearney on the left. General Lee was on the ground, accompanied by President Jefferson Davis, who had come to witness the operations. McCall and his Pennsylvania reserves were first attacked, but he drove back the Confederates, killing and wounding nearly three hundred men, and taking almost as many prisoners. Reinforced by fresh troops Longstreet again advanced, and so pushed the Federals that they retired until Hooker's division appeared. The fighting now grew desperate, though the Federal line remained unbroken, until General Wilcox's Alabama brigade dashed across a wide field, on McCall's left wing. Randall's battery opened a galling fire, but Wilcox had gained such headway that he succeeded in taking both Cooper's and Randall's batteries. Meagher's Irish Brigade had now achieved such a reputation for sudden charges, it was ordered up to recapture the guns. "The Irish Divils," as Meagher called his command, made a most gallant effort, but the guns were not secured until a final movement was made by the entire Federal line. At sunset the Confederates retired to the shelter of the woods, leaving the

BATTLE AT WILLIS CHURCH.

Federals in full possession of their original position. This battle of Willis Church cost McClellan nearly eighteen hundred men, the Confederates loss being about the same. The Federal General, Meade, and Colonel Simmins were among the wounded, the latter mortally, and General McCall was made a prisoner.

But there was no rest for the Army of the Potomac. Scarcely had night set in when the several columns were in motion. Worn out by fatigue and ill-provided with food, owing to the necessity of keeping their supply trains in the advance, McClellan's men had marched every night, and fought every day. On the morning of July 1, McClellan had massed his army at Malvern Hill. The position was well chosen, being admirably adapted for defensive purposes, for it was like a half moon, both ends extending towards the James River, which was clearly in sight. Remarkable tactical skill was shown by McClellan in the disposition of his troops. Sykes' and Morell's divisions occupied the extreme left;

MAJOR-GENERAL PHIL. KEARNEY.

next came Couch's, then those of Kearney, Hooker, Sedgwick, Richardson, Smith, Slocum and Casey. The flanks were also protected by the gunboats that had come up the James River to clear the way for the supply transports. Along the semi-entrenched line, seventy pieces of cannon, among them eight large siege guns, commanded the approaches to the several positions. A war correspondent thus describes the attitude of the Federal Army : " There were crouching cannon waiting for the enemy, and ready to defend all the approaches. Sheltered by fences, ditches, ravines, were swarms of infantry. There were horsemen picturesquely careering over the noontide and sun-scarred field. Tier after tier of batteries were grimly visible upon the slope, which rose in the form of an amphitheatre. With a fan-shaped sheet of fire, they would sweep the incline—a sort of natural glacis —up which the assailants must advance. A crown of cannon was on the brow of the hill. The first line of batteries could only be reached by traversing an open space of from three to four hundred yards, exposed to grape and canister from the artillery, and musketry from the infantry. If that were carried, another and still another more difficult remained in the rear."

General Lee decided to storm McClellan's centre, despite the expostulations of his subordinate Generals. Massing the bulk of his command on McClellan's right, Lee scattered his artillery in such a way as to give a concentrated cross fire, by which means he expected to silence the tremendous array of batteries on McClellan's front. These formidable preparations occupied considerable time, so it was not until half-past three o'clock that the Battle of Malvern Hill was begun by a furious storm of shell and shot from Lee's guns, which fell mainly on Keyes' and Heintzelman's division. Then Hill

MAJOR-GENERAL J. SEDGWICK.   BVT.-MAJOR-GENERAL J. R. BROOKE.   BRIG.-GENERAL W. W. BURNS.

MAJOR-GENERAL JOE HOOKER.

moved forward, striking Couch's brigade, but by some mistake, only Moorman's battery had been directed to accompany him. Moorman was soon driven away by heavier metal, the other batteries, that came up at Hill's urgent request, meeting the same fate. The Confederate infantry encountered such a concentrated musketry volley that human nature could not stand up before it, and the line fell back in confusion. Heintzelman improved his opportunity and assumed an advanced and more advantageous position.

The crash of musketry caused by Hill's assault was taken by Magruder as a signal for his own movement, and he at once began a desperate and furious attack on Fitz John Porter, who was holding McClellan's left wing. So sudden was the movement that two brigades of McLaw's division actually charged up to the muzzles of Porter's guns, being met by an awful shower of grape and canister at a distance of less than one hundred yards. The effect was a terrible one, for the jagged iron missiles tore wide gaps in the charging line, literally covering the ground with dead, dying and wounded men. Of course the assault by Magruder was repulsed, as were others equally desperate, at different points in the opposing lines. Then the fighting became general, the triple serried lines of Federal guns poured out thousands of shells and the infantry made Malvern Hill appear to be on fire, for there was no cessation in their steady volleys of musketry, shattering the advancing columns as if they were struck by lightning. Finally there was a pause, and as the sun went down, the Confederates fell back. The Federals supposed the battle to be at an end. In that they were mistaken

General Lee was convinced that the campaign could only end successfully for the Confederates by driving McClellan into the river and so annihilate his army. He therefore decided that Malvern Hill must be taken, no matter what sacrifice it might occasion, and an advance of his entire line took place at six o'clock. The fighting that ensued was of the most extraordinary character, for the antagonists were frequently so close that they exchanged musket volleys at the distance of ten or twenty yards, the execution being most deadly. The artillery fire was also very severe, that of the Federals being increased by ten-inch

MAJ.-GEN. I. B. RICHARDSON.

MAJOR-GENERAL G. W. MORRELL.

shells from the gunboats in the river, their huge missiles falling upon the masses of Confederates and harrassing their supply trains. Lee's men performed the task set them to the best of their ability, but failed to shake the Federal Army from its defensive position. Disheartened, but not dismayed, Lee finally abandoned the attempt, and at nine o'clock withdrew his line. General McClellan, in his report to the Secretary of War, thus describes the battle of Malvern Hill: "Brigade after brigade formed under cover of the woods, started at a run to cross the open space and charge our batteries, but the heavy fire of our guns, with the cool and steady volleys of our infantry, in every case sent them reeling back to shelter, and covered the ground with their dead and wounded. In several instances our infantry withheld their fire until the attacking columns—which rushed through the storm of canister and shell from our artillery—had reached within a few yards of our lines. They then poured in a single volley, and dashed forward with the bayonet, capturing prisoners and colors, and driving the routed columns in confusion from the field."

GENERAL MC LAWS, C. S. A.

JEFFERSON DAVIS.

GENERAL WILCOX, C. S. A.

The fatigues endured by McClellan's soldiers during this six days' and six nights' movement, was of the most severe character. Compelled by the steady pressure of Lee's columns to fight almost every hour of daylight, and frequently until far into the night, and then march amid the darkness to some new position, men actually walked in their sleep, and dozed in the presence of active hostile batteries. Despite every effort to push forward the supply trains it was necessary that nearly one thousand wagons should remain with the marching corps, in order that supplies of ammunition and food might be within reach. These wagons were, however, continually in the way, and the Federal artillery found their progress very difficult at times, owing to the roads being in possession of the trains. There was no time for building bridges, everything passing over the creeks and rivers on pontoons, which added to the impediments of the army. The infantry suffered the most hardship, because they had to be content with footpaths on the edge of the roads. Plodding wearily forward with their muskets, ammunition, hard-tack, and blankets, the soldiers stumbled along in the darkness, over sand in the roads, through mud in the swamps, and up to their waists in water wherever a stream crossed the route. Footsore, hungry and haggard for want of sleep, these young men, who two years before had never heard a shell or a bullet in the air, followed their Generals without a murmur, without

HEADQUARTERS OF SIGNAL CORPS CAMP

MAJOR MYERS, LT STRYTHER AND LT MORTON

GROUP OF OFFICERS U.S. MILITARY ACADEMY

AT HARRISON'S LANDING.

complaint, though most of them knew that grievous mistakes had been made by the men holding authority over them.

The men who fought at Gaines' Mills and Cold Harbor marched all that night, and fell in line of battle at dawn. So it was during the entire movement. "Halt!" would be the word, then "Load" ran down the line, and as the clatter of the steel ramrods ceased, a bugle would sound, and away would go the line, through dense woods, across open fields, through brook or swamp, until a sudden blaze of light flashed out in front, and the angry

hum of bullets saluted the ear. Then it was fire and reload, and fire again, as fast as cartridge could be bitten, and rammed, and sent home. This sort of thing would go on for an hour or two, fresh boxes of ammunition being brought up to replenish the men's belt pouches. By and by, the artillery fire would grow too hot, the lines shake, and then there came a charge by the Confederates. As the Southern yell broke on the air, the Federal line would stiffen and its volleys grow heavier and more vengeful. Shells were bursting everywhere overhead, or crashing among the trees, a storm of bullets buzzed in the air like an army of angry hornets, but the rage of the battle was in every heart and so the fight grew more intense and destructive.

TRANSPORT AND MONITOR ON JAMES RIVER.

Five or six hours of this sort of work would exhaust the strength of the men on both sides. A lull would finally come, a few changes be made in the line, wounded men be sent to a surgeon, and then the battle would break out again, and continue until long after night had set in. As the several corps marched in their turn, the muttering of distant cannon told that the rear guard was doing its duty, and that the pursuit was untiring. Hundreds of wagons broke down, and were either burned or flung into the nearest river. Disabled cannon were dismounted and pitched into swampy holes, where many of them are, no doubt, still lying. Destruction and havoc was visible everywhere, and as the remnant of the one hundred and sixty thousand men who landed during March and April at Fortress Monroe,

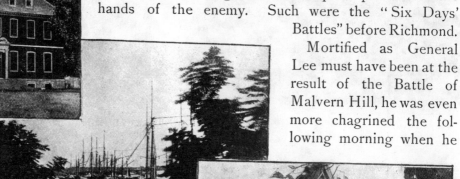

WESTOVER HOUSE.

amid so much pomp and display, moved from battlefield to battlefield, the men wondered what it all meant. The dead were left unburied as they fell, the wounded had to be abandoned for lack of vehicles to carry them, and no man knew how soon it might be his own fate to lie a corpse on the grass, or a helpless prisoner in the hands of the enemy. Such were the "Six Days' Battles" before Richmond.

Mortified as General Lee must have been at the result of the Battle of Malvern Hill, he was even more chagrined the following morning when he discovered that General McClellan had retreated during the night, leaving him in empty possession of the field. The

WESTOVER LANDING.

GENERAL W. W. AVERELL AND STAFF,
AT WESTOVER LANDING, JAMES RIVER.

Federal movement, though successful, was performed amid much hardship, for scarcely had Lee withdrawn his battalions, than a terrific rain storm began, so that the men were soon drenched to the skin, and they actually waded through mud. How the troops managed to march at all, after six such days of constant skirmish and battle few could realize. It should be said here that the abandonment of the Hills of Malvern—how rich is the soil of Virginia with English historic names—was not made by McClellan without earnest protests from his corps and division commanders. Porter, Heintzelman, Hooker, Meade, Kearney, Sumner and Couch, all of them graduates of West Point, were astounded when McClellan unfolded his plan. They reminded the commanding General that the battle just fought on the afternoon and night of July 1, had so torn and shattered the Confederate army that it was impossible for it to again assume the offensive, but McClellan could not be shaken. Phil Kearney, who had left an arm in Mexico, and was to meet a soldier's death before the end of that summer, swung his empty sleeve, and exclaimed, " As an old soldier, I, Philip Kearney, enter my solemn protest against this order for a retreat. We ought, instead of retreating, to follow the enemy, and take Richmond ; and in full view of all the responsibilities of such a declaration, I say to you all, such an order can only be prompted by cowardice or treason."

Kearney was not placed under arrest for his intemperate speech, and the retreat was made, McClellan's army reaching Harrison's Landing about daylight of July 2, having marched at the rate of a mile per hour. To say that the men were disheartened by the extraordinary campaign they had passed through, is only half the truth, for, being accustomed to criticise their commanders, these men saw that notwithstanding every battle they had fought during the past week had really resulted in a victory by their being left in possession of the position, the "strategy" of their General had converted it into a positive defeat. It was in this mood that the army read with amazement the bulletin issued by McClellan on the Fourth of July. Adopting a truly Napoleonic style, the General thus addressed his troops: "Your achievements of the last ten days have illustrated the valor and endurance of the American soldier. Attacked by superior forces, and without hope of reinforcement, you have succeed-

GEN. SEDGWICK, COL. SACKETT AND LT.-COL. COLBURN, AT HARRISON'S LANDING, AUGUST, 1862.

ed in changing your base of operations by a flank movement, always regarded as the most hazardous of military expedients. You have saved your material, all your train, and all your guns, except a few lost in battle, taking in return guns and colors from the enemy.

GROUP OF OFFICERS BELONGING TO THE IRISH BRIGADE, HARRISON'S LANDING, JULY, 1862.

Upon your march you have been assailed day after day with desperate fury by men of the same race and nation, skillfully massed and led. Under every disadvantage of numbers, and necessarily of position also, you have, in every conflict, beaten back your foes with enormous slaughter. Your conduct ranks you among the celebrated armies of history. No one will now question that each of you may always with pride say, 'I belong to the Army of the Potomac.' You have reached a new base, complete in organization and unimpaired in spirit. The enemy may, at any time, attack you. We are prepared to meet them. I have personally established your lines. Let them come, and we will convert their repulse into a final defeat."

In utter contrast to McClellan's address to his army, Jefferson Davis issued another to Lee's troops in which he said ; "I congratulate you on the series of brilliant victories which, under the favor of Divine Providence, you have lately won, and, as the President of the Confederate States, do heartily tender to you the thanks of the country, whose just cause you have so skillfully and heroically served. Ten days ago an invading army, vastly superior to you in numbers and the material of war, closely beleaguered your capital and vauntingly proclaimed its speedy conquest ; you marched to attack the enemy in its intrenchments ; with well-directed movements and death-defying valor, you charged upon him in his strong positions, drove him from field to field over a distance of more than thirty-five miles, and despite his reinforcements, compelled him to seek safety under the cover of his

McCLELLAN AND HIS GENERALS.

gunboats, where he now lies cowering before the army so lately derided and threatened with entire subjugation."

The losses during the Six Days' Battles as they will be known in History, were very great, for the Federals lost fifteen thousand, two hundred and forty-nine men killed, wounded and missing, while the Confederates sustained a loss of nineteen thousand three hundred and seventy, an aggregate of thirty-four thousand six hundred and nineteen. Of these not more than seven thousand were subsequently able to re-enter the field.

McClellan's Peninsula campaign was strategetically a failure, but it had one good effect, for the Southern troops learned that the "Yankees," could fight, while the Federals began to realize that the war would last for a year or two longer. From that time the two armies in the East entertained a high respect for each other.

Burning of the White House, Va., and Departure of Flotilla for the James River.

GENERAL VIEWS OF CULPEPPER, VA., AUGUST, 1862.

SCENE ON ACQUIA CREEK.

CHAPTER XXII.

BEGINNING OF POPE'S VIRGINIA VALLEY CAMPAIGN.

During his operations on the Virginia Peninsula, McClellan received nearly one hundred and sixty thousand men. When President Lincoln reviewed the army at Harrison's Landing, on July 7, he saw only eighty-six thousand. The remainder had been removed by disease or casualties on the field. Fully fifty thousand fell victims to malaria and fever. The President and his cabinet now decided that an older and wiser soldier should be placed at the head of all the Federal armies, and as General Henry Wager Halleck had shown ability in the West, he was summoned to Washington, and appointed Commander-in-Chief. Halleck visited McClellan, who demanded fifty thousand additional troops in order that he might again move on Richmond, but as Halleck did not approve of the plan, he refused to furnish the reinforcements, and finally ordered McClellan to transfer his army to Acquia Creek, on the Potomac. Halleck had become convinced that the Virginia Valley was the true base of operations against Richmond, and so had Secretary Stanton. It was therefore decided to consolidate the army under

MAJOR-GENERAL JOHN POPE.

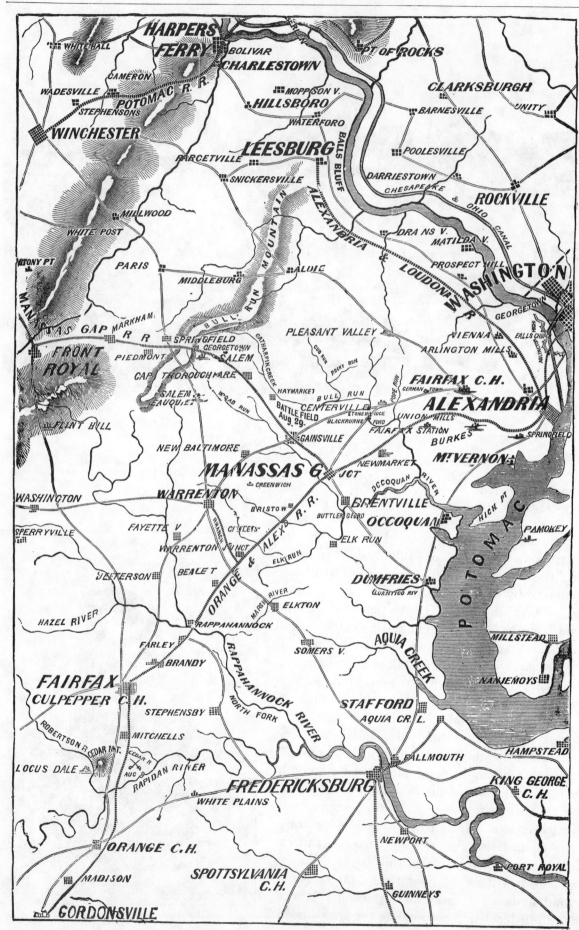

MAP OF POPE'S MILITARY OPERATIONS IN VIRGINIA, AUGUST AND SEPTEMBER, 1862.

BATTLE OF SLAUGHTER MOUNTAIN, AUGUST 9, 1862.

McClellan with the Army of Virginia, then under command of General John Pope, who had risen into prominence by his services in the West at New Madrid, Island Number Ten, and the siege of Corinth.

General Pope fell into the error that the Confederate Generals in the East were on a par with General John R. Floyd. He also entertained a poor opinion of the Eastern Federal Generals, because Halleck, Sigel, and himself had been summoned from the West. There was some excuse for this overweening vanity, as the armies under Fremont, Banks and McDowell had been reduced to the rank of corps, and Pope was given the chief command. Fremont resented this arrangement, and was relieved at his own request, General Sigel succeeding him. The total force was about forty-five thousand men, of all arms, being subsequently increased by the arrival of Burnside with ten thousand more. But instead of being concentrated, the troops were scattered along an extended line from

STREET VIEWS, CULPEPPER, VA., AUGUST, 1862.

Fredericksburg, on the Rappahannock River, to Centreville, near Manassas, and also in the Shenandoah Valley. Pope was instructed to cover Washington, guard the Shenandoah entrance to Maryland, and make a diversion in favor of McClellan, rather a heavy task for one man. It should be noted here that Pope coincided with McClellan that the Peninsula was the true base of operations against Richmond, and offered to take his entire force over-land if McClellan would act simultaneously. But the latter treated Pope very coldly, and both Generals came to grief. Pope assumed command July 28, when he issued a bombastic bulletin to his troops, which only made them smile. Among other things he said:

"I have come to you from the West, where we have always seen the backs of our enemies—from an army whose business it has been to seek the adversary, and beat him when found ; whose policy has been attack, and not defense.   In but one instance has the enemy been able to place our Western armies in a defensive attitude.   I presume I have been called here to pursue the same system, and to lead you against the enemy.   It is my purpose to do so, and that speedily.   I am sure you long for an opportunity to win the distinction you are capable of achieving ; that opportunity I shall endeavor to give you. In the meantime I desire you to dismiss certain phrases, I am sorry to find, much in vogue amongst you.   I hear constantly of taking strong positions, and holding them—of lines of retreat and basis of supplies.   Let us discard such ideas.   The strongest position a soldier should desire to occupy is one from which he can most easily advance against the enemy. Let us study the probable line of retreat of our opponents, and leave our own to take care of itself.   Let us look before us and not behind.   Success and glory are in the advance—

BATTLE OF CEDAR MOUNTAIN.

disaster and shame lurk in the rear.   Let us act on this understanding, and it is safe to predict that your banners shall be inscribed with many a glorious deed, and that your names will be dear to your countrymen forever."

General Pope was a fine horseman, and looked exceedingly well in the saddle.   He was also a good soldier, except his fondness for general orders, which promised more than could be performed.   As a subordinate commander he always did well, but as an independent general he failed.   His last order was to the effect that from that date "headquarters would be in the saddle."   Judging him by subsequent events, his soldiers used to say that Pope's hindquarters were in the saddle and his headquarters nowhere.   But soldiers are always sarcastic.

While the Federal Generals were quarrelling among themselves, thereby destroying the morale of their troops, the Confederates entered upon a more vigorous scheme of operations. Hitherto they had acted in the defensive, but as conscription had greatly enlarged their armies, it was decided that Bragg should advance on Louisville and Cincinnati, while Lee was to invade Maryland, and push for Washington, Baltimore and Philadelphia. The idea was that by capturing these three cities, the Independence of the Confederacy would be assured. Lee had now ready one hundred and fifty thousand men

BATTLEFIELD OF CEDAR MOUNTAIN.

at his command, and he decided to take two-thirds of this number on his campaign of invasion. Then Pope issued orders, directing his troops to subsist upon the country in which they were operating, and that the cavalry were to have no supply or baggage trains. He also announced that the inhabitants along the lines of railroads and telegraphs would be held responsible for any damage done, with many other intemperate and absurd provisions.

BATTLEFIELD OF CEDAR MOUNTAIN, FROM PHOTOGRAPHS TAKEN AT THE TIME.

The Confederate General issued retaliatory orders, and there seemed some danger that subsequent operations would not be conducted on the recognized lines of civilized warfare.

While McClellan was slowly and reluctantly transferring his troops to Acquia Creek, and John Pope was issuing his ridiculous bulletins, which secured for him the soldiers' nickname of "Saddle-Bag John," the Federal Government summoned six hundred thousand more men into the field. Owing to the slowness of recruiting, a system of bounties was unwisely resorted to, as it added to the expenses of the war without materially quickening the patriotic ardor of the young men in the several States, for in the

RAPPAHANNOCK BRIDGE.

end, compulsory drafts had to be resorted to, in order that the armies might be properly strengthened.

When Pope arrived at Culpepper, Va., on August 8, he learned that a strong Confederate force was advancing across the Rapidan River, and he at once prepared for battle with the twenty-eight thousand men he had on the ground. He ordered Banks to take possession of Slaughter Mountain, not knowing that the sagacious Jackson, who knew almost every foot of the territory, had anticipated him. Ewell's division was concealed in a dense mass of woodland, while Hill's lay in the rear. Fighting began early in the morning

TROOPS BUILDING BRIDGE ACROSS NORTH FORK RAPPAHANNOCK RIVER, NEAR FAUQUIER SULPHUR SPRINGS.

of August 9, but Banks was outnumbered, and had to fall back from Cedar Run, which was as far as he got, losing eighteen hundred men, Brigadier-General Prince being made a prisoner, while Brigadiers Augur, Carroll and Geary were wounded. The following day was the Sabbath, and as the Confederates had fallen back, the Federals recovered their

lost ground and buried their dead. Then the Confederates entirely disappeared, leaving their dead and wounded behind.

An autograph letter of General Lee's, revealing his intention to fight Pope before McClellan could join him, fell into the hands of the Government. Pope was accordingly ordered to fall back beyond the Rappahannock River, his command in the field being reinforced by Reno's division, of Burnside's corps, General Stevens, with ten regiments from Port

FAUQUIER SULPHUR SPRINGS HOTEL.

FEDERAL BATTERY FORDING A TRIBUTARY OF THE RAPPAHANNOCK RIVER, ON DAY OF
BATTLE OF CEDAR MOUNTAIN.

Royal, and General King's brigade, belonging to McDowell's corps. Though Pope's army was now forty thousand strong, he obeyed and retreated, beginning the retrograde movement during the night of August 18. Sending foward his immense train of ammunition and commissary wagons, with all the other cumbersome camp equipage, the General forbade the lighting of camp fires, and sent instructions to the brigade commanders that the movement of the troops must be secret and silent. So accurately were these orders obeyed, that the entire army had passed through Culpeper, and the advance was crossing the Rappahannock River by noon of the 19th, all of the trains being well on their way to Warrenton Junction.

Though it was really a retreat, the scene was a brilliant one. Heavy masses of infantry marched steadily over the plain, a cloud of active cavalry covering the rear, while the ponderous batteries rumbled over the dry earth as they toiled in one massive column through the dust, raised by the feet of the foot soldiers. Far in advance, the snowy covers of the supply wagons extended for miles, the patches of white canvas glistening in the hot sunshine. The artillery crossed the river over the railroad bridge at Rappahannock Station, but the infantry waded through the water at Beverly Ford. General Sigel was in the advance, Generals McDowell and Banks were in the centre, and Reno brought up the rear. By noon of August 20, all of the columns were north of the Rappahannock, though the

VIEWS IN WARRENTON, VA.

Confederates were in heavy force on the other side, General Bayard, who commanded the Federal rear guard, having frequent skirmishes with Lee's advance.

During the next two days there was considerable fighting, principally artillery exchanges, the Confederates seeking possession of the fords and bridges, but Pope held them until General James Ewell Brown Stuart made a wide detour with his cavalry, and came out in Pope's rear at Catlett's Station, on the Orange and Alexandria Railroad, only

RAPAHANNOCK STATION.

FUGITIVE NEGROES FORDING RAPAHANNOCK RIVER, ESCAPING FROM ADVANCE OF CONFEDERATE ARMY.

thirty-five miles from Washington. Here Stuart found most of the Federal trains, of which he destroyed all that could not be carried off, the feat being a peculiarly daring and successful one.

General Stuart (best known as "Jeb," from the initials of his name) was the Pleasonton or Sheridan of the Confederate Army. As a raider he had few equals, and his cavalry command proved to be a terror in Pennsylvania and Maryland during the Antietam and Gettysburg campaigns. A good fighter, an experienced tactician, and a daring raider, Stuart naturally won a high rank among the Generals of the South.

By the destruction of Pope's trains, the Confederates had inflicted a mortal blow, for Stuart's raid had a demoralizing effect on both the Federal General and his troops. They had been moving along so nicely and regularly, it was really humiliating to find that their line of communications had been successfully cut. Pope also discovered that Lee was moving in force on his right, and telegraphed urgently to Washington for reinforcements. These were promised, but there were unavoidable delays and Pope was in a perilous position. His strategy had proved defective, and he was soon to learn a lesson he probably never forgot.

BRIG.-GENERAL G. D. BAYARD.

DESTRUCTION OF RAILROAD AT MANASSAS.

CHAPTER XXIII.

THE BATTLES OF GAINESVILLE, SECOND BULL RUN, AND CHANTILLY.

General Robert E. Lee was now fully prepared for his descent into Maryland and Pennsylvania, and as the first step in his matured plan of operations was to double up Pope and so clear his path, the Confederate commander proceeded to do it. "Stonewall" Jackson started on a flank movement around the Bull Run range of Mountains, and passing around Thoroughfare Gap, reached within striking distance of Bristoe Station at sunset of August 26, having made a wonderful march of some fifty miles, over difficult roads, in the short space of thirty-six hours. At the same time Longstreet was advancing by way of Gainesville, so that not only did Lee threaten Pope's right flank, but he stood in a position to cut off his direct communications with Washington. In other words Pope's wings stood in the air, neither having a secure resting place.

HEAD-QUARTERS OF GEN. JOHNSTON, C. S. A., AT MANASSAS.

But Pope proved equal to the emergency, and he soon got his forces well in hand. Hooker had advanced towards Manassas Junction, where he encountered Early, and had a hot engagement. Reynolds, Sigel and McDowell were trying to intercept Longstreet, while Reno and Kearney were in the direction of Greenwich. Fitz John Porter, who had come up from McClellan, at Acquia Creek, received orders to stay at Warrenton Junction until Banks could relieve him. On the evening of August 27, Colonel George D. Ruggles, who was General Pope's chief-of-staff, sent a dispatch to Fitz John Porter, saying: "The Major-General commanding directs that you start at one o'clock to-night, and come forward with your whole corps, or such part of it as is with you, so as to be here by daylight to-morrow morning. Hooker has had a very severe action with the enemy, with a loss of about three hundred killed and wounded. The enemy has been driven back, but is retiring along the railroad. We must drive him from Manassas, and clear the country between that place and Gainesville, where McDowell is. If Morell has not joined you, send word to him to push forward immediately; also send word to Banks to hurry forward with all speed to take your place at Warrenton Junction. It is necessary on all accounts, that you should be here by daylight."

HEADQUARTERS OF GENERAL McDOWELL NEAR MANASSAS JULY 1862.

YELLOW HOSPITAL, MANASSAS, JULY 1862.

OUR PHOTOGRAPHER NEAR MANASSAS, JULY 1862.

But the overweening self-confidence of Pope is shown by his subsequent dispatches. To General Kearney he wrote: "At the very earliest blush of dawn push forward with your command with all speed to this place. I want you here at day-dawn, if possible, and we shall bag the whole crowd. Be prompt and expeditious, and never mind wagon trains or roads till this affair is over." General McDowell received the following: "At day-light to-morrow morning, march rapidly on Manassas Junction with your whole force, resting your right on the Manassas Gap Railroad, throwing your left well to the east. Jackson, Ewell, and A. P. Hill are between Gainesville and Manassas Junction. We had a severe

CONFEDERATE FORTIFICATION AT MANASSAS.

MAJOR-GENERAL McDOWELL AND STAFF.

fight with them to-day, driving them back several miles along the railroad. If you will march promptly and rapidly at the earliest dawn of day upon Manassas Junction, we shall bag the whole crowd." With the last words uppermost in his mind, Pope wrote to General Reno: "March at earliest dawn of day, with your whole command, on Manassas Junction. Jackson, Ewell and A. P. Hill are between Gainesville and that place, and if you are prompt and expeditious, we shall bag the whole crowd." But the Confederates were not to be so easily bagged, as the sequel showed.

To the military student it must be evident that the positions of both Lee and Pope were now critical. Pope was cut off from his supplies, while Lee's columns were extended over a long line and compelled to act independently. Jackson, finding himself threatened, decided to evacuate Manassas, and join the Confederate main body at Centreville, but Kearney overtook him on August 28, and drove the Confederates out of Centreville. Turning towards Thoroughfare Gap, over the Warrenton road, Jackson struck McDowell on the evening of August 28, when a desperate engagement ensued. Doubleday's and Gibson's brigades bore the burden of the fight, the desperate character of which is shown

CONFEDERATE FORTIFICATION AT CENTREVILLE, AFTER EVACUATION, MARCH, 1862.

CONFEDERATE BARRACKS AT CENTREVILLE AFTER EVACUATION, MARCH, 1862.

by the fact that two Confederate Generals, Ewell and Taliaferro, were desperately wounded, the former losing a leg.

The main body of Pope's army was now between Jackson and Thoroughfare Gap. His three divisions, under Reynolds, Sigel and McDowell, had a collective strength of twenty-five thousand men, sufficient to prevent Jackson joining Longstreet. Pope intended that Reno, Kearney, Hooker, Heintzelman and Porter should strike Jackson with their united divisions before Longstreet could come up. But the latter had been making forced marches, and reached the Gap before the Federals were in force, consequently the Confederates united and presented a bold front, Pope's advanced divisions being compelled to retire. On the morning of August 29, Hooker and Kearney struck Jackson near Groveton, as they were pushing forward from Centreville, and a sharp engagement followed, Jackson falling back to form a new line on the Gainesville and Leesburg roads.

ENGAGEMENT AT GAINESVILLE.

Nearly all the Federal divisions were engaged, one after the other, but nothing decisive occurred until late in the afternoon, when Heintzelman and Reno moved in. The onslaught was a furious one, the Federals carrying everything before them, though their losses were very heavy, Grover's brigade, in Hooker's division, suffering the most. But McDowell, who had been ordered towards Sudley Springs, did not come into line until near sunset, and Porter did not appear for an hour after, consequently the Confederates recovered part of their lost ground by driving back Kearney on the Warrenton Turnpike. This battle of Gainesville has always been claimed as a victory by both Confederates and Federals, but being indecisive, it must be considered as a drawn battle, though a very costly one, for the loss on each side was nearly seven thousand men. As the opposing forces were not over sixty thousand, one fourth were either killed, wounded or made prisoners —an appalling result.

Pope's position had now become desperate. He had only forty thousand men left, while the Confederates were able to put forward over sixty thousand. The loss of his

The Confederates Crossing the Potomac.

The Horrors of War.

GENERAL PHIL. KEARNEY.

supply trains further crippled Pope, for his men were without food, and their ammunition was running short. Still he decided to risk another battle, hoping to sufficiently cripple Lee, to render him unable to advance on Washington, no one having realized that the Confederate General really aimed at a campaign of invasion. General Lee had now reached the scene, and assumed command with more troops.

The battle of Manassas, or the Second Bull Run, as it is usually called, occurred on August 30, and it proved to be a disastrous one for the Federal General and his Government. During the entire previous night Lee's forces had been pouring through Thoroughfare Gap, but so cleverly was the movement masked that Pope believed that Lee was in reality retreating. McDowell was then ordered to take his division and Porter's along the Warrenton Turnpike. Porter, being in advance, suddenly came upon a very heavy force under Jackson, who, adopting his customary tactics, had massed his men in a heavy wood, and so was able to strike Porter's left and double it up. While Porter's line was staggering under this assault, the

THOROUGHFARE GAP.

FEDERAL BAGGAGE TRAIN OF POPE'S ARMY MAKING ITS WAY THROUGH THE MOUNTAINS TO MANASSAS JUNCTION.

CONFEDERATE FORCE ADVANCING ON RAPPAHANNOCK STATION, AND COMMENCEMENT OF THE BATTLE OF GAINESVILLE.

Confederates opened on the Federal flank, which in its turn was shattered.   McDowell then sent Reynolds from Porter's left to support Milroy and Schenck, the transfer leaving a gap in the line, which Colonel Warren, of the Fifth New York regiment, very promptly filled.   The fighting now became general and assumed a formidable character.   All of the Federal brigades displayed great bravery, returning every Confederate charge by another, but General Towers' brigade was the most conspicuous.   For a time it seemed as if Pope would win the day, for Jackson's line was slowly giving way.

Longstreet now assumed a commanding position on Jackson's right, and as he had a large number of heavy guns he opened with a terrific discharge of shell and grape which tore the Federal ranks into tatters. To add to the horrors of the scene, Porter's men were saluted by missiles, that caused an unearthly

GENERAL J. B. HOOD, C. S. A.

GEN. W. B. TALIAFERRO, C. S. A.

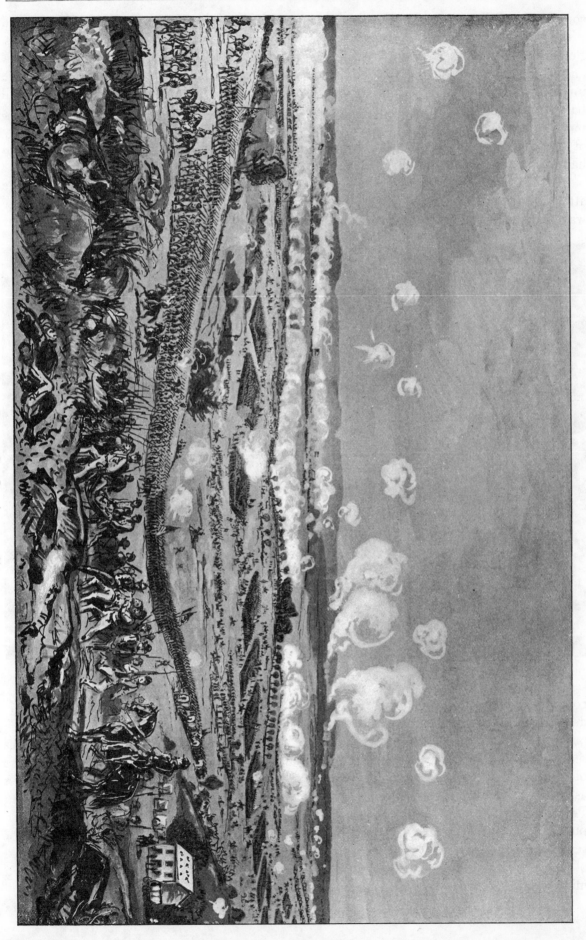

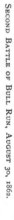

Second Battle of Bull Run, August 30, 1862.

sound as they flew through the air, for one of Longstreet's batteries had been supplied with pieces of railroad iron. Cowering under this hideous shower, for a few moments, Porter's division renewed the fighting. Then Reno passed from the centre to the left, and stemmed the tide that was then beginning to turn, but the effort proved to be unavailing, for Lee now began moving forward on his whole line, and the Federals fell back in tolerably good order, keeping possession of the Warrenton Turnpike. Darkness put an end to the fighting, and that night Pope crossed Bull Run, and retreating by way of Stone Bridge, finally took position on the heights around Centreville, where McDowell had formed in 1861 for the first battle of Bull Run.

In his report on the battle Lee says: "The enemy, being reinforced, renewed the attack on the afternoon of the 30th, when a general advance of both wings of the army was ordered, and after a fierce combat, which raged until after nine o'clock, he was

BVT.-MAJOR-GENERAL O. B. WILCOX AND STAFF.

completely defeated, and driven beyond Bull Run. The darkness of the night, his destruction of the Stone Bridge after crossing, and the uncertainty of the fords, stopped the pursuit." Pope's description was as follows: "The enemy's heavy reinforcements having reached him on Friday afternoon and night, he began to mass on his right for the purpose of crushing our left, and occupying the road to Centreville in the rear. His heaviest assault was made about five o'clock in the forenoon, when, after overwhelming Fitz John Porter, and driving his forces back in the centre and left, mass after mass of his forces was pushed against our left. A terrible contest, with great slaughter, was carried on for several hours, our men behaving with firmness and gallantry, under the immediate command of General McDowell. When night closed, our left had been forced back about half a mile, but still remained firm and unshaken, while our right held its ground."

Pope's retreat created consternation in Washington, because it led to a complete evacuation of the Virginia Valley. General Banks destroyed a large quantity of military material at Bristow Station and joined Pope, while Burnside retired from Fredericksburg and Falmouth, burning bridges and the railroad. Acquia Creek was also abandoned, every Federal corps and division hastening to Washington, then believed to be in instant danger of attack. The arrival of Banks, Franklin and Sumner brought Pope twenty-four thousand fresh troops, so he was able to make a bold front with fifty-three thousand men.

August 31 was Sunday, and Lee began a new movement. Jackson's and Ewell's divisions crossed Bull Run at Sudley Springs, and started for Little River Turnpike, with the intention of cutting round to Fairfax Court House and so gain Pope's rear. The aim of this movement was discovered by Pope in time for him to make a change of front. Hooker and Reno were thrown forward over the turnpike, towards Chantilly, the remainder of the divisions holding to the Warrenton Turnpike. On the morning of September

RUINS OF BRIDGE AT BLACKBURN'S FORD

MRS. SPINNER'S HOUSE NEAR CENTREVILLE

BRIDGE ACROSS BULL RUN. BUILT BY ENGINEERS OF McDOWELL'S CORPS.

BATTLEFIELD OF MANASSAS.

2, Reno struck Jackson near Germantown, and, Hooker coming up rapidly, an engagement began, which raged furiously despite the heavy rain that was falling. Finally Jackson, who was determined to carry his point, concentrated on Reno, falling with tremendous power on General Stevens' brigade. Undismayed by the attack, General Stevens led his command on a charge, but was shot dead at the head of his men, who fell back in confusion. Kearney, Hooker and McDowell rushed to Reno's assistance, and repulsed Jackson with heavy loss. Just as the day was closing Kearney inadvertently passed through his picket line, and approached that of the Confederates. A volley was fired and the General fell dead from his saddle. Kearney and Lee had been personal friends before the war, therefore it was a gracious act when the latter sent the body of his antagonist to Pope's headquarters under flag of truce.

Thus ended the three week's campaign, which began with so much flourish, for General Halleck ordered the Army of Virginia to retire within the defenses of Washington.

THE INTELLIGENT CONTRABAND.—"JOHN HENRY," A WELL-REMEMBERED SERVANT AT HEADQUARTERS, ARMY OF THE POTOMAC.

Pope's losses footed up thirty thousand men, thirty guns, twenty thousand small arms, and immense quantities of commissary supplies and war material. Lee's losses are estimated at fourteen thousand men, but he took more than that number of Federals as prisoners. The most painful incident of the entire campaign was the unjust condemnation of General Fitz John Porter. A scapegoat being wanted, Porter was selected, because he did not arrive on his appointed ground at the Battle of Gainesville as soon as Pope thought he should. There was another reason for disgracing Porter. Both Halleck and Pope disliked McClellan, and as Porter was believed to be his favorite, the unfortunate General was subsequently tried for alleged disobedience of orders and dilatory conduct. Being found guilty, despite his gallant service at Turner's Gap and Antietam, Porter was dismissed the service. It was not until General Grant became President that General Porter received the tardy justice of restoration to his rank in the army, and the barren honor of retirement as a Colonel without pay. This treatment of Porter will forever be a blot on the escutcheon of Halleck. Had "Fitz," as his men in the old Regular Division loved to call him, escaped this cruel, crushing and entirely unmerited punishment, he would undoubtedly have carved a higher reputation for himself than the opportunity given him permitted.

BELLE PLAIN LANDING.

DEFENCE OF WASHINGTON.—FORT TOTTEN; VIEW OF INTERIOR.

CHAPTER XXIV.

OPENING OF THE ANTIETAM CAMPAIGN.

The situation of affairs was now a serious one for the Northern States.   Though the

Hatteras Inlet, Port Royal and Roanoke Island expeditions had placed most of the Secession seacoast in the hands of the Federal Government, the National Capital, with all its archives, stood in danger.   While the capture of New Orleans had opened the Lower Mississippi, and the armies of the West had control of its upper section, no one could disguise the fact that Lee could march direct for Washington with every chance of success.   It was all very well to have the Crescent City, but what if the Confederates captured Washington, Baltimore and Philadelphia?   That was the thought of every thoughtful man.   No wonder that a momentary panic seized the public mind.

FORT CORCORAN.—LOADING BIG GUN.

U. S. COLORED INFANTRY TAKEN AT FORT LINCOLN.

GOVERNOR CURTIN OF PENNSYLVANIA.

General Lee had orders from Jefferson Davis to carry the torch of war into Maryland and Pennsylvania, for it was believed that the people of the former State would welcome the Confederate Army and reinforce the ranks by willing enlistment. Though General Lee was well aware that a direct attack upon the National Capital was entirely feasible, he preferred to first cross the Potomac, and entering Maryland, get in rear of Washington. Moving from Leesburg his main body crossed the river and advanced to the City of Frederick, his line of camps occupying the banks of the beautiful and winding Monocacy River. By September 8 all of his divisions were up and Lee issued an address to the inhabitants. Under the mistaken idea that the announcement of his presence would bring thousands to his standard, the Confederate General said : " The people of the Confederate States have long watched with the deepest sympathy, the wrongs and outrages that have been inflicted upon the citizens of a Commonwealth allied to the States of the South by the strongest social, political and commercial ties, and reduced to the condition of a conquered province. Under the pretense of supporting the Constitution

but in violation of its most valuable provisions, your citizens have been arrested and imprisoned, upon no charge, and contrary to all the forms of law. The Government of your chief city has been usurped by armed strangers ; your legislature has been dissolved by the unlawful arrest of its members ; freedom of the press and of speech has been suppressed ; words have been declared offenses by an arbitrary degree of the Federal executive ; and citizens ordered to be tried by military commissions for what they may dare to speak. Believing that the people of Maryland possess a spirit too lofty to submit to such a Government, the people of the South have long wished to aid you in throwing off this foreign yoke, to enable you again to enjoy the inalienable rights of freemen, and restore the independence and sovereignty of your State. In obedience to this wish, our army has come among you, and is prepared to assist you with the power of its arms in

DEFENCES OF WASHINGTON.

regaining the rights of which you have been so unjustly despoiled. This, citizens of Maryland, is our mission, so far as you are concerned. No restraint upon your free-will is intended, no intimidation will be allowed, within the limits of this army at least. Marylanders shall once more enjoy their ancient freedom of thought and speech. We know no enemies among you, and will protect all of you in every opinion. It is for you to decide your destiny, freely and without restraint. This army will respect your choice, whatever it may be ; and while the Southern people will rejoice to welcome you to your natural position among them, they will only welcome you when you come of your own free will."

To Lees amazement the Marylanders made no response, either in men or supplies. On the contrary, many of the conscripted soldiers in his ranks deserted. But in

GREAT FALLS, POTOMAC RIVER.

Pennsylvania there was the wildest excitement. Every man capable of bearing arms prepared to do so. Business and manufacturing were suspended, church bells were rang as a summons for the people to meet and perfect some method of defense. On September 11,

Governor Curtin called for fifty thousand men, and he telegraphed to the Mayor of Philadelphia in the following strain : "We have reliable information this evening that the Rebel generals have moved their entire army from Frederick to Cumberland Valley, and their destination is now Harrisburg and Philadelphia. We need every available man immediately. Stir up your population to-night. Form them into companies, and send us twenty thousand to-morrow. No time can be lost in massing a force on the Susquehanna to defend the State and your city. Arouse every man possible, and send him here."

Spurred by this example, the Governor of Maryland issued a similar

VIEW ON CABIN JOHN RIVER.

CHAIN BRIDGE, POTOMAC.

proclamation, and as nearly one hundred thousand men were mustering, the bright hopes of the Confederates that they would be able to dictate a treaty of peace in old Independence Hall, began to fade away.

General Halleck was compelled, by the exigencies of circumstances, to summon General McClellan to the command of the consolidated Federal armies in the East. Much as he hated his predecessor in the chief command, the danger was too great, the necessity too pressing. On September 2, as Pope's shattered columns fell behind the Alexandria fortifications, General McClellan was placed in command of all the troops in and around Washington. The announcement was hailed by the army with enthusiasm, for no General on the Federal side obtained or exercised so strong a personal influence over his troops as did "Little Mac." Had this really excellent soldier learned less about

BLOCK HOUSE NEAR AQUEDUCT BRIDGE, POTOMAC RIVER.

NEAR GEORGETOWN FERRY.

NEAR AQUEDUCT BRIDGE.

GEORGETOWN D.C.

FOOT BRIDGE NEAR CHAIN BRIDGE POTOMAC.

AQUEDUCT BRIDGE POTOMAC.

VIEW ON THE POTOMAC.

military engineering and had he a harder heart in his body, McClellan's name would undoubtedly have stood highest among American Generals on the page of history.

General Pope departed for the West, and General Lee started for Maryland. The latter had only begun to cross the Potomac when McClellan put his troops in motion. By September 7, he had nearly ninety thousand on the march, and on the 12th they were in possession of all the Potomac fords below Berlin. The movements of the Army of Northern Virginia were so cleverly masked by Lee, and the people of Maryland were in such a state of excitement and confusion, owing to the rapidity with which the Confederates stripped the country, McClellan found it difficult at first to ascertain where Lee had really

CENTRAL SIGNAL STATION, WASHINGTON, D. C.

gone to. By one of those lucky accidents which sometimes change the fate of Empires, one of the Federal scouts entered the farmhouse that had been used that morning by one of the Confederate division commanders. On the centre table of the farmer's parlor lay a few newspapers, and the scout idly turned them over. Suddenly his eyes rested on an official order, issued by General Lee to his Corps and Division Generals. At a glance the scout saw that it revealed the entire Confederate scheme of operations, and he rode so desperately to McClellan's headquarters at Damascus, Maryland, that his faithful steed dropped at the General's feet, and had to be mercifully shot.

Lee's order disclosed the fact that he had abandoned all idea of invading Pennsylvania, but that he would cling to Maryland as long as possible. The country through which the opposing armies were manœuvering is one of the loveliest on the continent of North America. The valleys that lie on either side of the South Mountain Range are extremely fertile, and, as the broad stretches of cultivated land are broken here and there by masses

of woodland, the scenery is enchantingly picturesque. So are the valleys formed by the Catoctin Range, and it was with delight that Confederate and Federal marched over the wide, smooth roads. The early frosts had already touched the maples and beeches, thus painting the beautiful and everchanging landscape with colors too vivid for the palette of an artist. Across the upper Potomac, at Martinsburg, passed southward a steady of heavily laden wagons, and immense herds of cattle, all of which were to serve as supplies for Lee's men. Through the Shenandoah Valley, beyond Cedar Mountain, went these Maryland spoils, for having failed to welcome Lee, the people of that State were made to feel the full rigors of war.

LOUDON HEIGHTS, HARPER'S FERRY.

When Lee made his advance across the Potomac, there was a large Federal garrison in possession of Harper's Ferry. McClellan, being familiar with that section of the country, advised the evacuation of the Ferry, but Halleck declined to order it. General Wool had sent General D. S. Miles there during August with orders to fortify Maryland Heights, but for some unexplained reason Miles neglected to do so, except to put Colonel Thomas H. Ford in command of the Heights, but gave him no tools. Jackson's advance had compelled the Federal garrison at Martinsburg to fall back to Harper's Ferry, thus increasing Miles' strength to thirteen thousand men. On September 6, Jackson appeared in front of Bolivar Heights in full force, Walker had seized Loudon Heights and McLaws was attacking Maryland Heights. The latter compelled Ford to spike his guns and retreat to the Ferry. By September 14, the place was completely invested and a furious cannonade was opened by the Confederates from their commanding positions. Knowing Miles' peril, McClellan wrote: "Hold on to the last extremity, and, if possible, reoccupy Maryland Heights with your whole force. The Catoctin Valley is in our possession, and you can safely cross the river at Berlin."

But Miles was unequal to the task, for he sent away two thousand cavalry and hoisted a white flag in token of surrender. The signal had been flying for half an hour before it was perceived amid the cannon smoke, and General Miles was killed by the fragment of a shell, thus paying the forfeit of his life for his incapacity. General White, the next in command, with eleven thousand six hundred officers and men, were made prisoners. The spoils of the Confederates consisted of seventy-three cannon, thirteen thousand muskets, two hundred wagons and immense quantities of military stores and supplies. All of the prisoners were paroled and allowed to take their personal prop-

GENERAL D. S. MILES, KILLED AT HARPER'S FERRY.

erty. Among these troops were the Twenty-second, New York militia. The author of this Federal disgrace being dead, Halleck punished Colonel Ford by dismissing him from the service, though it now appears, that like Fitz John Porter, he did his duty. But Halleck was a schoolmaster and believed in using the birch.

The condition of the two armies was about alike, for the Confederate troops were already beginning to feel the strain of insufficient supplies that they so heroically labored under during the remainder of the war. With them everything had to be sacrificed for arms and ammunition; food and clothing being the last consideration. No troops in the world went so lightly laden as were these soldiers of Northern Virginia. They carried no knapsacks, no overcoats, and not every man had a blanket. Many a charge was made on battlefields in hopes of capturing a Federal camp, or to pick up the knapsacks and blankets

GENERAL VIEW, HARPER'S FERRY.

scattered over a field. In this respect the reorganized Army of the Potomac was not a whit better off than their opponents The destruction of Pope's trains, and the hot haste with which the several columns passed through Washington, gave no time for the issuance of shoes, socks or other necessaries. Men who had tramped through the Chicka hominy swamps, or raced down the Virginia Valley, could get along with ragged blouses and vizorless caps, but broken shoes made it difficult to march. Mc-Clellan's men, however, forgot that their feet were bleeding, or that their trousers were hardly

decent, when they heard the magic voice of " Little Mac."   Only those who served under
this remarkable and much ill-used General can appreciate the Napoleonic influence exercised
by him over the men he led to battle.   The writer has seen a corps limping along a dusty
and stony road, the men hungry, weary and disconsolate, when word came flying along the
line from the rear, " Give ground to the right."   Then a mighty cheer would rise and
sweep forward as a cavalcade of horsemen rode rapidly to the front.   The leading brigades
knew then that the General was coming, and joined in the cheers as he passed.

McClellan had that rare faculty of being able to apparently address himself to every
man within sound of his voice, and he was constantly finding occasion for saying
something pleasant and encouraging.   " The old Fifth Corps is doing splendidly," said he

MARYLAND HEIGHTS, HARPERS FERRY.

the day before the battle of South Mountain; " Boys, I gave you the longest route
because I knew you could cover it best."   Then as he galloped on, every pain was
forgotten, every limping foot touched the ground with firmer tread; the praise of their
General was so delicious to these footsore soldiers.   " And how are the Zouaves this
afternoon ?" asked " Little Mac," as he met the Fifth New York, one of his favorite
regiments.   " First rate, General," responded one of the men, " only we are living on
supposition."   " Supposition ?   Why, what do you mean by that ?" queried the General.
" Well, you see, General," said the Zouave, " we were to have received our rations this
morning, but we didn't get them, and now we are living on the supposition that we did."
McClellan laughed heartily, then turning to an aid gave an order in a low tone.   An hour
after ten wagons came thundering up the road and the brigade was duly victualled.   On
another occasion the General overtook a solitary cannon creeping over the road with only
two horses, and both of them lame.   Telling the Corporal in command to be of good

GENERAL McCLELLAN LEAVING FREDERICKSBURG FOR TURNERS AND CRAMPTON PASSES.

cheer, he wrote an order for fresh horses, and before nightfall the artillery-men were trotting cheerfully over the road, to overtake their battery. In these deft touches on the hearts of his soldiers, McClellan was indeed unequalled.

The disposition made by Lee of his several columns, as revealed in the captured order, showed that the Confederate leader intended to defend the South Mountain passes, and so prevent McClellan getting into Pleasant Valley. But the Federal commander possessed the key to his opponent's movements, and acted accordingly. The main body of the Army of the Potomac lay in and around the City of Frederick, when intelligence of the fall of Harper's Ferry came to McClellan. He at once recalled the column that was on its way to succor Miles, and concentrating his forces started for Turner's and Crampton's Passes. There was now no danger that Pennsylvania would be invaded, for Lee had abandoned the idea. It therefore remained to drive him out of the Passes and across the upper Potomac.

"GOPHER HOLE."—BOMB-PROOF.

MAJOR-GENERAL A. PLEASONTON.

CHAPTER XXV.

THE TWO BATTLES IN THE SOUTH MOUNTAIN GAPS.

Early on the morning of Sunday, September 14, the two armies met half a mile from Middletown, the contest being for the possession of a bridge spanning the Catoctin River. General D. H. Hill was in command of Turner's Gap, but owing to the heavy pressure made by Reno, he retired up the mountain, posting his men in strong force on all of the three roads that run through the wild and picturesque mountain gorge. General Pleasanton and his division of cavalry were in the Federal advance and came within striking distance of Hill's line on the afternoon of September 13, but they had to wait for the infantry which arrived the following day. McClellan's disposition of his troops was as follows: General Burnside commanded the right wing, consisting of McDowell's First corps, led by Reno. The left wing consisting of the Sixth Corps and Couch's division, and was commanded by General Franklin. The centre, under General Sumner, comprised the Second Corps and the Twelfth Corps, commanded by Mansfield—General Banks having been left in command at Washington. Porter's corps came up on the 14th having made a two days' forced march from the National Capitol.

While Franklin passed round the Catoctin range and headed for Crampton's Gap, which is about six miles from Harper's Ferry, the remaining corps proceeded straight to Turner's Gap, by way of Boonsboro. Reno sent Cox's Division along the Southern road. As they reached the foot of the Pass, Simmon's and McMullen's batteries opened a brisk fire, under cover of which Sturgis, Wilcox and Rodman led their brigades up the mountain-side, encountering Garland's brigade of Hill's Corps. So determined was the Federal musketry that the Confederates were unable to stand before it, but they did not finally retire until General Garland was killed. As it was evident to Hill that he was facing McClellan's main force, he sent word to Longstreet, who had hurried up from Hagerstown, and assumed command, so that by noon the Confederates had thirty thousand men on both crests, and in the Gap.

When Hooker moved on the Confederate position, followed by Meade, he advanced along the Hagerstown road. The other commands went to the left of the Federal line.

GEN. SAM. GARLAND, C. S. A., KILLED AT SOUTH MOUNTAIN.

This disposition occup ed several hours, and it was not until four o'clock in the afternoon that the general engagement began. Viewed from the valley below, the battle was a picturesque and interesting one. Climbing up the steep sides of the mountain in a brigade line, the several Federal divisions were nearly half way up before Longstreet and Hill saluted them. The bright rays of the sun illumined the scene, and we could see the dark lines of Hooker's, Meade's and Reno's men steadily clambering up, only a few stray musket shots betraying the deadly character of the imposing movement. Suddenly a bright and almost blinding flash sprang from the crest of the towering range, and our ears were deafened by the fierce crash that followed it, as twenty thousand muskets opened fire on the advancing lines. The Confederate volley was returned, and the fighting that ensued was almost hand to hand. There was a slight breeze passing along the side of the mountain and it carried the musketry smoke with it in a heavy pencil-like cloud. As the two opposing lines opened fire, McClellan's batteries, that had been distributed along the line, at every advantageous position, began a furious discharge of shell which did considerable execution. The Confederate artillery replied, but their gunners could not sufficiently depress their pieces, consequently their fire was ineffective.

For over an hour the musketry continued, a cloud of smoke rolling down into the valley, tinged here and there with broad bands of gold and rosy tints, as the descending sun began reddening the western horizon. Crash after crash came to our ears, followed by brief pauses of silence, then there would be a sullen muttering, as the lines changed positions, when again the air would be shaken by sudden roar of musket and cannon. Bit by bit, the Federals pressed forward, but they did not gain the crest until the sun had set and darkness began to creep over the mountain tops. As the shadows of the September evening descended on the scene, a vivid flash of light illumined the entire range, a faint

GENERAL HOWELL COBB, C. S. A.

cheer came to the ears of the reserve, telling them that the Battle of South Mountain was over. The desperate character of the Federal advance is shown by the fact that General Jesse L. Reno was killed, General Hatch, Lieutenant-Colonel Hayes, and Colonel W. P. Wainwright being among the wounded. The Federal loss was nineteen hundred and sixty-eight, of which three hundred and twelve were killed. The Confederate loss was about sixteen hundred killed and wounded, there being also nearly fifteen hundred men taken prisoners.

While the battle was progressing at Turner's Gap, Franklin had entered Crampton's Gap, six miles away. He found himself opposed to General Howell Cobb, who was President Buchanan's Secretary of the Treasury. When Franklin reached Barkittsville, he found the Confederates strongly posted behind loose stone wall defences, but he succeeded, after three or four hours of hard fighting, in gaining the crest and the possession of the Pass. Cobb's retreat was so precipitate that he left behind him three thousand muskets and two cannons, over three hundred of his men surrendering with their three regimental standards. Had General Miles held out at the Ferry he could have been relieved by Franklin. The Federal loss at Crampton's Gap was one hundred and fifteen killed, four hundred and twenty wounded and missing.

The following morning, McClellan moved up his reserves at Turner's Gap, but the advance that bivouacked on the crest discovered at daylight that Hill and Longstreet had retreated into the valley beyond. Orders were at once given for a vigorous pursuit, Franklin being directed to avoid Harper's Ferry and march straight up Pleasant Valley. By this manœuvre, Jackson was compelled to evacuate Harper's Ferry and ford the Potomac near Charlestown, where John Brown had been hanged, and after a wide detour join Lee's army, then massing along the line of Antietam Creek.

Desperate as had been the fighting in the mountain passes, it was insignificant compared with the battle that was to be fought between the opposing armies now rapidly assembling on ground that was to be forever historic.

A BOMB-PROOF.

ANTIETAM BRIDGE, LOOKING UP STREAM.

CHAPTER XXVI.

THE DESPERATE BATTLE ON ANTIETAM CREEK.

There is no question that the diversion of so large a portion of his army for the purpose of capturing the garrison and stores at Harper's Ferry, was really the cause of Lee's failure to carry out his purpose of invading Maryland. After the lapse of so many years, when all the facts are known, it is easy to see that in making so rich a capture Lee was dropping the meat for its shadow. But when it is remembered that he knew that his overthrow of Pope, at Manassas and Chantilly, had thrown the Federals into dire confusion, it will be readily conceded that he could not anticipate so vigorous a movement on their part in opposing his passage through the South Mountain Range. Neither did he know that McClellan had possession of the secret key to his proposed movements. But in war, as in everything else, there are many unknown chances, any one of which may overturn the best laid and most careful plans. Finding out his error when it was too late, General Lee, with characteristic courage, prepared for a decisive engagement. With this end in view, and while the Army of the Potomac was advancing

MAJ.-GEN. J. K. F. MANSFIELD, KILLED AT BATTLE OF ANTIETAM.

through Crampton's and Turner's Gaps, during September 15, Lee withdrew his columns to the vicinity of Sharpsburg, and waited for Jackson's arrival.

The advance of the Federal Army was a brilliant spectacle.   As the troops descended the more gentle slopes of the mountain on the Antietam side, the morning sunlight was reflected by the muskets of the infantry, their regimental colors fluttering gracefully in the cool autumnal breeze.   On the left came Franklin's troops, their route laying in shadow. Looking down from the crest, where Reno had so gallantly died, and the Confederates as bravely fought, the sight of these long columns of troops was thrilling and inspiring.   For miles in advance the glitter of steel could be discerned, while nearer at hand a long line of artillery covered the ground, the Pass itself being still occupied by the rear guard, and an

MAJOR-GENERAL W. H. FRENCH.

MAJOR-GENERAL G. L. HARTSUFF.

BVT.-MAJOR-GENERAL G. H. GORDON.

endless train of supply wagons, which after toiling up the steep roads, where rows of new made graves attested the severity of the previous day's battle, went down at a headlong, reckless pace.   By nightfall the entire command had reached Pleasant Valley

Lee's position was well chosen.   He found a rolling crest along the western margin of Antietam Creek, with masses of out-cropping rock as it approached the Potomac.   He thus had the creek on his front, the Potomac in his rear.   But he was now acting on the defensive.   Jackson, with his customary rapidity, joined Lee in time for the approaching battle, for McClellan did not advance until the 16th, though he had laid out his plans. This was a grievous error, as it gave Lee time to gather up all his troops and establish a formidable line.   General Walker, with two brigades, held the extreme right at Shaveley's Farm, Longstreet came next, D. H. Hill being on his left with Hood holding the left flank.   Jackson was behind Hood, in reserve, protected by "Jeb" Stuart's cavalry.

ANTIETAM BRIDGE

SHARPSBURG, MD., SEPT., 1862.

When the Federals drew near the creek, Hooker took ground on the right, with Sumner and Porter in the centre, Burnside being on the extreme left. Mansfield stood behind Hooker in reserve, but Franklin had not yet come up. Crossing Antietam Creek were three small stone bridges. Hooker, Mansfield and Sumner commanded one, Porter another, and Burnside a third. The latter was to prove historic. General McClellan's plan was to attack Lee's left, which lay on and beyond the Hagerstown Road. He hoped, by turning the Confederate's flank, to double it up, and then by moving on his centre and right, drive Lee into the Potomac River. Late in the afternoon General Hooker with Meade's, Doubleday's and Rickett's division, crossed over the bridge in front of him, meeting very little opposition. Mansfield was ordered to cross during the night, and did so, while Sumner was to follow at daybreak.

When Sumner began moving, he was two miles behind Mansfield, and the latter was a mile from Hooker's bivouac line. With his customary impetuosity Hooker fired at dawn, the Pennsylvania Reserves, under Meade, being the first to go into action. During the night Jackson had discovered the scope of the Federal movement, and at once posted himself on Lee's left, taking position along some ledges of lime-

GENERAL J. E. B. STUART, C. S. A.

ANTIETAM BRIDGE.

VIEWS ON ANTIETAM CREEK.

stone that cropped all around what is known as the Dunker Church. Hooker's advance was supported by numerous batteries on the other side of the creek, the combined artillery and musketry fire cutting up Jackson's brigades, so that they were compelled to fall back to their reserves beyond the church. Scarcely had this taken place when Jackson re-formed his line, and fell with furious rage upon Hooker. The combat that ensued was of the most awful description, for the men loaded and discharged their muskets at less than one hundred yards range, the carnage being terrific. There stood the two lines, neither giving way, but each withering under the deadly storm of bullets. Finally Hooker asked Doubleday for assistance, when Hartsuff's

SIGNAL STATION ON ELK MOUNTAIN.

BURNSIDE BRIDGE.

BATTLE OF ANTIETAM.

brigade was sent him. In half an hour Hartsuff fell, severely wounded, and his brigade was cut to pieces, for he tried to cross a wide cornfield in order to reach Hooker. Then the First Texas and the Fourth Alabama made a heroic charge upon Doubleday's guns, but were driven back after a desperate hand-to-hand fight.

On hearing Hooker's guns, Mansfield had pushed rapidly up the Hagerstown road, reaching the scene of conflict soon after seven o'clock, and the divisions of Williams and Green began deploying. Then D. H. Hill's division emerged from the woods beside the Dunker Church, and drove Mansfield back, the old General being killed while trying to stem the tide of battle. General Williams now assumed command, and joining Hooker, a combined effort was made to take the key to Jackson's position, a woody elevation to the right of the church. Crawford's and Gordon's brigades dashed forward and secured it, the men being animated by the presence of

VIEW OF PART OF FIELD ON THE DAY OF BATTLE.

GENERAL HOOKER'S HEADQUARTERS DURING THE BATTLE.

Hooker, who by the reckless exposure of his body, here earned the title of "Fighting Joe." The General was sometimes on foot, and he personally directed every movement. Just as Gordon and Crawford were rushing forward a bullet struck Hooker in the foot, the missile passing clean through, and he was carried off the field.

General Sumner had now arrived and assumed command of that part of the line. Seeing the perilous position of Crawford and Gordon, who were holding their ground against heavy odds, Sumner ordered in French, Sedgwick and Richardson about nine o'clock. McLaws and Walker now joined Jackson, so that the main battle surged around the Dunker Church. The Confederates held to their limestone ledges, and mowed down the Federals as they advanced. General Sedgwick received three wounds and had to retire. Crawford met the same fate. Hooker's corps had been shattered, and its ammunition was exhausted; Mansfield's corps had also suffered terribly, while Sumner saw his own men falling in every direction. He knew that Jackson must have suffered heavily, for the ground had as many dead Confederates stretched upon it as there were Federals, so he sent McClellan word that he could hold his position, but needed reinforcements for a forward movement.

BODIES OF DEAD CONFEDERATE SOLDIERS NEAR SHERRICK'S HOUSE.

BATTLE OF ANTIETAM.

BURYING THE DEAD.

General Franklin arrived about noon, and was at once sent to Sumner's support. Smith's and Slocum's divisions were in the advance. Their artillery opened and the columns swept on, Irwin's brigade forcing the Confederates beyond the road. In this final charge, the Vermont and Maine regiments fought with remarkable courage. But the battle had cost many lives. From the time Hooker first began the fight around the Dunker Church, until Smith's division closed the struggle, there had been no less than four charges and countercharges. Each army had taken and re-taken the ground until it was literally carpeted with dead and dying men. Writing of the battle, General "Stonewall" Jackson says: "The carnage on both sides was terrific. At an early hour, General Starke, commanding the Stonewall division, was killed; Colonel Douglas, commanding Lawton's brigade, was also killed. General Lawton, commanding division, and

GRAVES OF FEDERAL SOLDIERS AT BURNSIDE BRIDGE.

BODIES OF DEAD CONFEDERATE SOLDIERS ALONGSIDE FENCE ON HAGERSTOWN ROAD.

GENERAL LAWTON, C. S. A.

Colonel Walker, commanding brigade, were severely wounded. More than half the brigades of Lawton and Hays were either killed or wounded, and more than a third of Trimble's. All the regimental commanders in those brigades, except two, were either killed or wounded. Thinned in their ranks, and their ammunition exhausted, I had to withdraw them, and Hood's division of Longstreet's command, took their place."

On Sumner's left, French's and Richardson's division began fighting D. H. Hill, who was holding Jackson's right. The Federal brigades of Meagher, Weber, Caldwell, Morris, Brooks and Kimball, did the fighting, while General Anderson had reinforced Hill with two brigades. Pushing back the Confederates to the Piper house on the Sharpsburg road, General Richardson was wounded by a cannon ball, so Hancock, going to the head of the division, pressed forward. Then General Meagher was wounded, darkness fell and the right wing of McClellan's army rested.

During the movement on Jackson, the corps under Porter, which occupied the centre of the Federal line, had been active. The Regular division, under Sykes crossed the middle stone bridge and silenced the Confederate sharpshooters, who were picking off Pleasanton's gunners, his horse batteries having greatly annoyed that part of Lee's line. Then Warren went to the left, and supported Burnside's right. The hero of Roanoke Island had four divisions under him, those of Cox, Rodman, Sturgis and Wilcox. He received orders at eight o'clock, just about the time old General Mansfield was killed at the church, to force the bridge in front of him, seize the height beyond, and push the Confederates back upon Sharpsburg. For some reason that has never been clearly explained, Burnside did not make any decided move until after one o'clock in the afternoon, despite the urgent commands of McClellan, who finally sent his aide, Colonel Sackett, to see that Burnside obeyed. By this time A. P. Hill, who, following Jackson from Harper's Ferry, had arrived, and assumed Lee's right, which had been weakened to meet the onslaught on the Confederate left. Had Burnside moved two hours earlier, he would have found Longstreet with only two thousand men; now he had to face fresh troops. The Federal charge on the stone bridge was a gallant effort, and three times did the men take the bridge and twice were they driven back. Finally the height, was taken and several pieces of Confederate artillery were captured, when suddenly the division of A. P. Hill rushed in and turned Burnside's left flank. Stubbornly trying to hold their new position, Burnside's men were finally forced back until they reached the bridge,

MILLER'S HOUSE, ANTIETAM.

VIEW IN THE FIELD WHERE SUMNER CHARGED, AND IN THE DITCH ON THE RIGHT, SHOWING MANY DEAD CONFEDERATES.

BVT.-MAJOR-GENERAL N. KIMBALL.

MAJOR-GEN. W. T. H. BROOKS.

BVT.-MAJOR-GENERAL J. C. CADWELL.

GENERAL RODMAN, KILLED AT BATTLE OF ANTIETAM.

where, being protected by their batteries, tney stood fast. During this part of the engagement, the Federal General, Rodman, and the Confederate General, L. O'B. Branch were killed.

Thus ended the Battle of Antietam. It cost Lee over fourteen thousand men, three thousand being killed. McClellan had two thousand and ten killed, nine thousand four hundred and sixteen wounded, with one thousand and forty-three missing, a total of twelve thousand, four hundred and sixty-nine. Lee had lost by battle and desertion of conscripted men, fully thirty-five thousand since crossing the Potomac River. His campaign of invasion had ended disastrously, for, on striking the balance, his losses had far exceeded those inflicted on the Federals.

The blow to the Confederate cause was a severe one, but the people of the Southern States were not subdued. On the contrary, the more they were defeated, the more desperately did they fight for supremacy and an independent form of Government.

CONFEDERATE WOUNDED AT SMITH'S BARN; DR. HURD, 14TH INDIANA, IN ATTENDANCE.

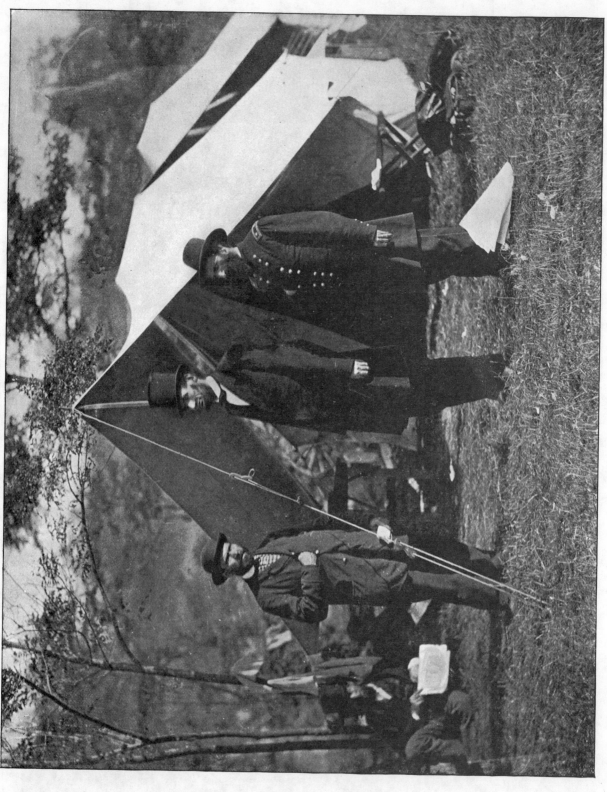

Photo. by M. B. Brady and Alexander Gardner.

McClellan and His Generals

CHAPTER XXVII.

LEE'S RETREAT AND MCCLELLAN'S RETIREMENT.

There has been a great deal of criticism of McClellan's conduct before, during and after the battle of Antietam. He has been blamed for not forcing a general engagement on September 18, because it was subsequently ascertained that Lee was in no condition to meet a determined attack. The fact was recalled that just before sunset of the 17th, McClellan received fourteen thousand fresh men, under Generals Humphrey and Couch, which might have been advantageously used in heading the pursuit. It was also remembered that McClellan had eighty-seven thousand men, while Lee would not muster at one time. more than forty-five thousand. In the light of later information, concerning the shattered condition of the Army of Northern Virginia, the government and the people of the North forgot the delight caused by McClellan's official announcement " That no less than thirteen guns, thirty-nine colors, upwards of fifteen thousand stand of small arms, and more than six thousand prisoners are the trophies which attest the success of our arms in the battles of South Mountain, Crampton's Gap and Antietam; not a single gun or color was lost by our army during these battles."

The Comte de Paris, who served on General McClellan's personal staff, thus writes concerning Antietam: " The issue of the contest, however, would probably have been different if A. P. Hill, instead of arriving at three o'clock in the afternoon, had been able to take part in the struggle early in the morning, and add his efforts to those which kept the Federal right so long in check.   There were however, many other causes which prevented McClellan from achieving a more complete victory, and taking advantage of the opportunity to strike an irreparable blow at Lee.   The first is to be found in the moral condition of his troops.   The army which had been entrusted to him was partly composed of the vanquished soldiers of Manassas, and the remainder consisted of soldiers who had been only one or two weeks in the service, who had never marched, never been under fire, and knew neither their commander, nor their comrades.   They fought with great bravery; but they could not be expected to perform what Lee easily obtained from his men.   Their

MAJOR ALLEN PINKERTON AT SECRET SERVICE
QUARTERS, OCTOBER, 1862.

ranks had not that cohesion which enables a commander to follow up a first success without interruption. The Union generals may be censured for having divided their efforts on the right in successive attacks, and thereby impaired their effectiveness. The corps of Hooker, Mansfield and Sumner—in all from forty to forty-four thousand men—instead of being brought into action one after the other for the space of four hours, might have been united so as together to strike the Confederate left, which

they would, no doubt, have crushed.   Burnside, by his long inaction also upset Mc-Clellan's plans, enabled Lee to mass all his forces on his left, and thus deprived the Federals of the principal advantages which a more energetic action on his part would certainly have secured."

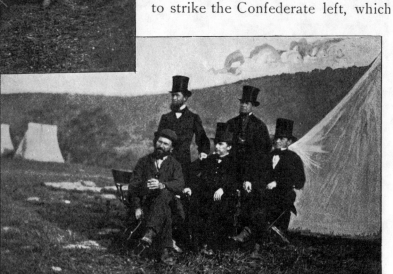

GROUP AT SECRET SERVICE HEADQUARTERS, ARMY OF POTOMAC, OCTOBER, 1862.

General McClellan consulted with his corps commanders as to the advisability of renewing the attack on the 18th, or to defer it.   Franklin and others urged an immediate forward movement, while Sumner, who had displayed great personal courage during that day, strenuously opposed the suggestion.   The whole of the 18th was therefore devoted to burying the dead and caring for the wounded, seven thousand Confederates being among the latter.   The army was reorganized, revictualled and duly supplied with ammunition. At dawn of September 19, General Pleasanton's cavalry columns advanced over the several roads, and in an hour news came to McClellan that the Confederate Army had dissappeared.   Lee had imitated McClellan's move at Malvern Hill, and, taking advantage of the Federal halt, had escaped across the Potomac by the Shepherdstown Ford, carrying with him not only his entire army, but vast quantities of supplies that had been gathered up in Maryland by his active raiders. Lee had twenty hours' start, and he went over the river and passed into the Shenandoah Valley, bag and baggage, leaving General Pendleton with forty pieces of artillery on the river bank to check pursuit. Porter's corps followed, captured four of the guns, but fell afoul of A. P. Hill's division, which forced the Federals to recross the river.

During September 21, Lee marched along the line of the Potomac as far as Martinsburg, destroying the track and bridges of the Baltimore and Ohio Railroad. The next day one of his divisions recrossed the Potomac, but was driven back by Couch. During the following two or three days Maryland Heights and Harper's Ferry were reoccupied by the Federals and the bridges reconstructed. On October 1, President Lincoln visited McClellan* and urged a forward movement, remarking that the General

PONTOON BRIDGES AND RUINS OF STONE BRIDGES ACROSS POTOMAC RIVER, AT BERLIN, OCTOBER, 1862.

had then one hundred and fifty thousand men under his immediate command. Lee was at that time near Winchester, in a very sad condition. McClellan promised to move, but not doing so General Halleck telegraphed under date of October 6, the following brief order: "The President directs that you cross the Potomac, and give battle to the enemy, or drive him South. Your army must move now, while the roads are good."

Four days after receiving this order, McClellan learned that the Confederate cavalry general, "Jeb" Stuart had made a complete circuit of the Federal Army lines. He penetrated into Pennsylvania as far as Chambersburg, where he found an immense quantity of supplies, railroad trains, machine shops and other property, all of which he destroyed by fire. "Jeb" then crossed the Potomac below McClellan, and escaped by way of Leesburg, into the Loudon Valley, through Aldie Gap. Amid the indignation at Stuart's daring and really wonderfully successful raid, Halleck telegraphed on October 21,

*See illustration Page 23.

SCENES AND INCIDENTS AT HEADQUARTERS ARMY OF THE POTOMAC.

as follows : "The President does not expect impossibilities, but he is very anxious that all this good weather should not be wasted in inactivity." Finally, goaded into action, General McClellan crossed the Potomac by the lower fords on November 2, Lee's advance having reached Culpepper.

On November 7, General Buckingham arrived at McClellan's headquarters and handed him an order from the War Department, relieved him of his command, and transferring it to General Burnside. The next day "Little Mac" issued his parting address to the army he had twice reorganized. "In parting from you, I cannot express the love and gratitude I bear you," said he, "As an army you have grown up in my care. In you I have never found doubt or coldness. The battles you have fought under my command will probably live in our nation's history. The glory you have achieved over mutual perils and fatigues ;

PONTOON BRIDGES AND RUINS OF STONE BRIDGE ACROSS POTOMAC RIVER AT BERLIN, OCTOBER, 1862.

POST OFFICE, HEADQUARTERS, ARMY OF THE POTOMAC.

the graves of our comrades fallen in battle and by disease; the broken forms of those whom wounds and sickness have disabled—the strongest associations which can exist among men unite us by an indissoluble tie."

Never before or ever after was such a scene witnessed in any army as the one enacted by the Federal soldiers of the Potomac, when General McClellan personally took leave of his officers and men, before finally retiring from the field of active duty. Those who had read the life of Napoleon Bonaparte were reminded of the leave-taking at Fountainebleu. At the head of his brilliant staff, and seated on a magnificent steed, the General rode rapidly along the lines. Lifting his cap to the regimental colors as they fell in salute to him, his eye kindled and his smile had the same old magnetism. Whole regi-

SHARPSBURG, MD., SEPT., 1862.

BATTERY No. 8.

ments dropped their muskets from the position of salute, to cheer their General, none of the Colonels seeking to control the enthusiasm of their men, or compel the decorum of discipline. Many were moved to tears, and General McClellan was himself shaken by emotion on seeing it displayed by his soldiers. On Tuesday, November 10, the General rode to Warrenton, where a train awaited him. An artillery salute was given him at the Junction, and as he stood on the rear platform, he said to the soldiers gathered around him: "Boys, I want you to stand by General Burnside as you have stood by me. Good bye."

CHAPTER XXVIII.

OPERATIONS IN THE SOUTHWEST.

The campaigns of invasion made by McClellan and Lee against Richmond and Washington, in 1862, had the effect of dwarfing the coincident movements in the Southwest. The peril in which the cities of Philadelphia, Baltimore, and Washington were placed by the Confederate advance across the upper Potomac concentrated the attention of the Federal Government and the people of the North, but the operations beyond the Tennessee and Missouri rivers had an equally important bearing in the general scope of hostile demonstrations. The assignment of Halleck to the chief command of the Federal armies again gave Grant command of the Army of the Tennessee. Buell was near Chattanooga, facing Bragg, who was threatening Louisville. Rosecranz had command of Pope's troops, now called the Army of the Mississippi, and occupied Alabama and Northern Mississippi. Grant's line extended from Memphis to Bridgeport, Tennessee, along the Memphis and Charleston Railroad. On his immediate front stood Van Dorn and Price, with a heavy force. These Confederate generals aimed at recovering Corinth, which they rightly considered the military key to Tennessee.

On September 1, 1862, Price advanced to Jacinto with twelve thousand men. Rosecranz had removed from Tuscumbia to Iuka, thence toward Corinth. Price captured Tuscumbia and Iuka, finding a large quantity of stores, which the Federal commander, Colonel R. C. Murphy, neglected to destroy. General Grant saw that Price hoped to occupy his attention while Van Dorn struck his flank and turned it. But Grant decided to make a rapid dash upon Price at Iuka, beat him, and get back to Corinth in time to meet Van Dorn.

Grant and Rosecranz began moving on September 18, and on the following day encountered the Confederate outposts. The ground was very difficult, being cut up by ravines and tangled thickets. Hamilton's division began the attack, and desperate fighting ensued. The Eleventh Ohio Battery's guns were lost and retaken three times. Colonel Eddy fell mortally wounded, and his regiment was thrown into disorder, the entire battery being captured, with nearly all of its officers and men killed or wounded. Then Stanley's division went in, led by the Eleventh Missouri, and the Confederates were driven into the ravine. The next morning Price had disappeared. The Federal loss at Iuka was seven hundred and thirty killed and wounded, and the Confederates lost nine hundred men, General Little being among their dead.

BVT.-MAJOR-GENERAL JEFFERSON C. DAVIS.

When General Beauregard retreated from Shiloh to Corinth in April he constructed extensive fortifications. During the summer of 1862 General Halleck had so scattered his troops in a series of disconnected operations, Grant found that the Beauregard intrenchments were entirely beyond the capacity of his army. An inner line was therefore erected, and it was finished during the month of September.

On October 3 the advance of Van Dorn's army arrived under General Mansfield Lovell. Pushing up the Chewalla road, Lovell attacked with such impetuosity that part of Rosecranz's line was driven back. A desperate struggle followed, during which the Federals lost heavily, General Hackelman being among their killed, and General Oglesby severely wounded. When night put an end to the battle Van Dorn had arrived with his entire army of forty thousand men, and as the Federals had fallen back from the Beaure-

BVT MAJ GEN, A. BAIRD.

BVT MAJ GEN, A. WILLICH.

BVT MAJ GEN, D. S. STANLEY.

BVT MAJ GEN, R. W. JOHNSON.

gard intrenchments to those designed by Grant, the Confederate commander believed that he had Rosecranz in his grasp.

Having thrown up several batteries within one thousand yards of the Federal lines, the Confederates opened fire the following morning, receiving a quick response. The territory around Corinth consists of low hills interspersed with swamps, only a few open fields here and there giving opportunity for the deployment of troops. The Federal line was protected on the right by Battery Williams, and on the left by Battery Robinette, a new fort called Fort Richardson having been completed in the centre during the previous night, Battery Powell being to its right. As soon as Van Dorn's guns opened fire their shells fell in the streets of the town, causing much confusion among the residents. Then Captain Williams opened with twenty-inch Parrott guns, silencing the Confederate batteries.

Under cover of the cannonading, Lovell had moved round to Rosecranz's left, while

Price massed his strong divisions on the centre. At nine o'clock Price advanced along the Bolivar road and charged upon Battery Powell, when General Jefferson C. Davis opened fire. The road over which Price's men were pressing forward in solid columns was swept by a cross fire of artillery, causing great havoc, but the Confederates pushed on. Then the Federal guns used grape and canister with deadly effect, yet the charging columns moved up and Davis' men became temporarily panic-stricken. Price then seized Battery Powell, and actually penetrated to the heart of the town, capturing Rosecranz's headquarters. As the Confederates were carrying everything before them Rosecranz appeared, and by his example restored order. A section of Jumel's battery now galloped forward and delivered three or four rounds of grape and canister at the distance of a dozen yards. One hundred men fell before this terrible discharge, and the Confederate line was shaken. Be-

CONFEDERATE DEAD IN FRONT OF FORT ROBINETTE, CORINTH.

fore they could recover, the Fifth Minnesota and Tenth Ohio opened a deadly musketry fire. This incident was closed by a magnificent charge by the Fifty-sixth Illinois, which recaptured Battery Powell. Hamilton's battery now went into action, and the streets of Corinth were cleared of Confederates, except those who were dead or wounded. So complete was the repulse that Price could not restrain his men until they had reached the woods.

Rosecranz's success upset Van Dorn's plans, for, having undertaken to conduct the attack on the Federal left, he was not aware of Price's defeat until it was too late. Van Dorn formed Lovell's corps into four columns and placed his artillery at convenient points to cover their advance against Forts Williams and Robinette. As the infantry appeared the Federal guns opened with a murderous discharge of shell, followed by grape. The bravery of the Confederates was unequalled. Facing a deadly storm of shell, grape, and bullet, which mowed them down by section and company, these Southern soldiers ran up almost to the muzzles of the cannon. The front line got within one hundred and twenty feet of Fort Robinette, when the Ohio Brigade delivered a tremendous volley. The advancing lines withered under this shower of lead and fell back to the woods. Reforming, the Confederates made a second effort, their momentum being sufficient to carry the front rank up to the parapet.

This charge was a most gallant effort, and stands as a rare example of human courage. Colonel Rogers, of the Second Texas, led the column, and scaled the breastwork, falling inside. The Twenty-seventh Ohio and Eleventh Missouri went to the rescue of the Federal gunners, and again drove back the Confederate line.

General Grant had ordered General McPherson to join Rosecranz, and he reached Corinth as the Federals were repulsing Van Dorn at Fort Robinette. His presence led to a

GENERAL BRAXTON BRAGG, C. S. A.

Confederate retreat. Ord and Hurlburt were also coming up, and encountered Van Dorn as he was crossing the Hatchie River, ten miles from Corinth, but, being too weak, were compelled to withdraw, General Ord being wounded during a brief engagement. Rosecranz began a pursuit, but Grant ordered him back. The Federal loss at this battle of Corinth was three hundred and fifteen men killed, eighteen hundred and twelve wounded, and two hundred and thirty-two missing. The Confederate loss in killed was one thousand four hundred and twenty-four officers and men. Their wounded exceeded five thousand, and they lost two thousand two hundred and sixty-eight as prisoners.

General Buell had been ordered to take the Army of the Ohio and move on Chattanooga, the possession of which would shut the Confederates out from Kentucky. Buell began his march on June 11, and as General Morgan had seized Cumberland Gap, the route was open. But Buell moved so slowly that General Bragg reached Chattanooga first, on July 28, the Federal advance being twenty-five miles away, on Battle Creek. Bragg had fifty thousand men, in three corps, under Polk, Hardee, and Kirby Smith, the latter being at Knoxville. Bragg's northward movement compelled Buell to fall back to Nashville, finally moving to Louisville, but did not arrive there until September 25. It had taken Bragg six weeks to cover the distance between Chattanooga and Frankfort. Buell's arrival at Louisville gave him fresh reinforcements, and he had fully one hundred thousand men. Then an order came from Washington transferring the command to General George H. Thomas, but at his earnest solicitation Buell was retained. General Thomas was really one of the best of the Federal commanders. Once he assumed a position, he held to it with dogged pertinacity, for he never seemed to know when he was beaten. He always carried out a plan intrusted to him with rare faithfulness, yet with a sound judgment which enabled

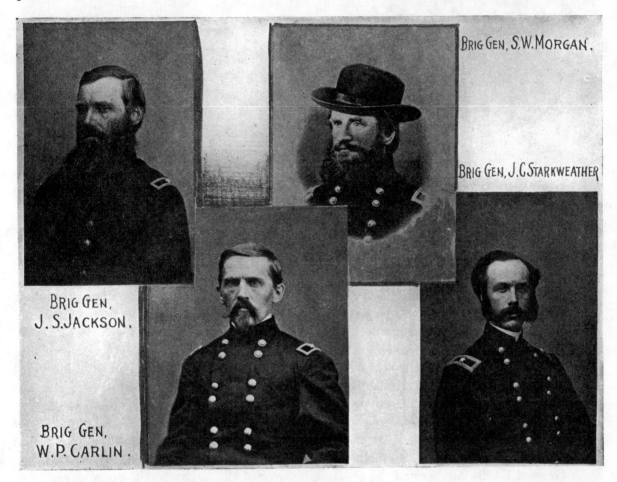

BRIG GEN. S. W. MORGAN.

BRIG GEN. J. C. STARKWEATHER

BRIG GEN. J. S. JACKSON.

BRIG GEN. W. P. CARLIN.

him to take advantage of any favorable change in the situation. His soldiers obeyed him because they trusted implicitly to his sagacity and coolness.

Bragg was meanwhile stripping Kentucky of supplies. It was said at the time that his wagon trains were forty miles long, but this was one of the current exaggerations.

Buell then assumed the offensive, and began his pursuit on October 1. Dividing his immense army into three grand corps, he moved on Bardstown. General Crittendon had the right wing, accompanied by Thomas as second in command to Buell, and went to Shepherdsville. The left wing, under McCook, approached Frankfort, while the centre, under Gilbert, moved over the Mount Washington road. Bragg having crossed the Kentucky River, the two armies manœuvred for nearly a week, when the Confederate general concentrated his forces at Perryville. Bragg's army consisted of five corps, Hardee having two, the others being under Buckner, Cheatham, and Anderson, all three

BRIG.-GEN. P. A. HACKELMAN, KILLED AT BATTLE OF CORINTH.

being commanded by Polk, the ex-bishop. Kirby Smith was far in the rear with the accumulated supplies.

Fighting began during the afternoon of October 7, and was resumed at dawn the following morning. The brunt of the battle fell on General McCook's corps, who stood some three miles from Perryville. He had only Rousseau's and Jackson's divisions. Posting a battery with adequate infantry supports, McCook left Generals Jackson and Terrill to hold the line and proceeded to his right, which firmly rested on Gilbert's left.

Thirty minutes after, General Cheatham's division fell upon Terrill, who held the extreme left, and a most desperate engagement followed. General Terrill fell mortally wounded, dying before sunset, and General Jackson was instantly killed by a fragment of a shell. The loss of their generals completely demoralized the Federals, and they fled in shameful confusion. Then the Confederates, having driven back McCook's left, struck Rousseau's division with tremendous force. Bush's and Stone's batteries, gallantly supported by Starkweather's brigade, held Cheatham in check for nearly three hours, but had finally to withdraw.

General Bragg led the Confederate assault in person, believing that he had his antagonist on the hip. But the Confederate commander was now to meet a Federal officer who was subsequently to rise to high command. Brigadier-General Philip H. Sheridan occupied Gilbert's left with his brigade, and when Rousseau's men broke he discovered that he had suddenly become the extreme left of Buell's line. Knowing that he held the key to the Federal position, Sheridan decided to retain it as long as he had a shell left. Turning his batteries on the advancing Confederates, Sheridan checked them, and throwing forward his line, opened a terrific musketry fire. By this he held his position intact until Carlin's brigade arrived and strengthened him. Finding himself reinforced, Sheridan ordered a charge. Sheridan's counter-attack was a surprise, and the Confederates were compelled to fall back. Sheridan saw his advantage, and he drove the Confederates clear through Perryville, capturing eighteen or twenty wagons of ammunition and supplies, some artillery caissons, and several hundred men.

General Buell only learned the severe character of the engagement when it was over, but he sent one of Crittendon's divisions to McCook's support. Then night ended the battle. Buell made preparations for renewing the engagement at daylight, only to find that Bragg had disappeared.

Hastening through Cumberland Gap with his entire army, the Confederate commander did not pause until he reached Chattanooga. This retreat surprised the North and the South, Bragg's excuse being that he wished to save the supplies he had gathered in Kentucky.

Bragg's retreat gave Buell a chance to redeem himself, but his pursuit was tame, so Bragg went off with his Kentucky supplies. General Thomas was ordered by Buell to take route for Nashville, while he returned to Louisville. Then came another change in commanders. Rosecranz succeeded Buell, the name of the command being changed to that of the Army of the Cumberland.

CHAPTER XXIX.

THE BATTLE OF MURFREESBORO', OR STONE RIVER.

General Rosecranz had now achieved the height of his ambition, an independent command, and the hero of Iuka and Corinth began at once to prepare for a vigorous campaign. He put his army in good fighting trim in the short space of a week, and rebuilt the Louisville and Nashville Railroad, establishing his headquarters at Nashville. General Bragg was well informed regarding Rosecranz's operations, but supposed the Federals were going into winter quarters. Bragg therefore put his men into huts at Murfreesboro', and sent Wheeler's cavalry into Western Tennessee, where Grant was operating against Vicksburg, another cavalry column crossing into Kentucky on an extensive raid.

Permitting his troops to enjoy Christmas Day in camp, Rosecranz put them in motion on the following morning. Despite a cold rain, the Army of the Cumberland moved with such celerity that the Confederates could not destroy the bridges, and the Federals advanced to the line of Stone River where it enters the Cumberland just above Nashville.

Rosecranz had, on December 30, forty-three thousand men on the ground. He placed McCook on his right, with Davis, Johnson, and Sheridan as division commanders. General Thomas held the centre with Rousseau's and Negley's divisions, while Crittendon occupied the left with Palmer's, Van Cleve's, and Wood's divisions. The left flank of the Federal army rested on the river, the right extending beyond the Franklin road.

General Bragg's army was sixty-two thousand strong. He put the four divisions of Cleburne, Cheatham, McCown, and Withers on the west side of Stone River, with Breckinridge's division on the eastern side to protect Murfreesboro'.

Both Bragg and Rosecranz meditated attack. The Confederate commander intended to swing round on his right as a pivot and face the Federal right and centre, take possession of the railroad, and so cut Rosecranz's line of communications. Rosecranz contemplated throwing his left and centre on Breckinridge's isolated division, drive it through the town, and get in Bragg's rear. The two movements were identical. Before sunrise on December 31, 1862, Rosecranz's army was in motion.

McCleve's division crossed Stone River without opposition, and Wood was following with his division, when deafening artillery and musketry broke out on the Federal right. So tremendous was the volume of sound that both Wood and McCleve halted, the earth fairly trembling beneath the awful detonations. It was Bragg's assault, for he had massed his men under cover of the Winter fog and fallen with resistless momentum upon Johnson's division of McCook's command. So unexpected was the movement that Johnson lost two of his batteries before either of them could go into action. The next instant the entire division was flying to the rear, Brigadier-General Willick being taken prisoner. General Kirk was wounded, and one-third of the division were made prisoners.

This movement uncovered the division commanded

MAJOR-GENERAL W. S. ROSECRANZ.

by Davis, and his men also gave way, leaving behind several pieces of artillery. Bragg now believed that victory was in his hands, so strengthened his line and fell upon Sheridan's division. Rosecranz soon discovered that his gambit had been interfered with, so Rousseau's division was detached from Thomas and sent to Sheridan's support, while the advance of the left wing across Stone River was temporarily checked.

Sheridan had anticipated the uncovering of his flank, and placed his three batteries in positions to command the advance of the Confederate columns. Withers' division rushed down on Sheridan's flank in columns, but was met by a heavy discharge of shell and canister. Withers' men paused, then gathering strength, charged in a massive body, but the Federals poured in a deadly volley of musketry at forty yards' range, and the Confederates reeled, then broke and rushed to their breastworks. Having turned the tide of battle, Sheridan

GEN CLEBOURNE. C.S.A.

GEN. WITHERS. C.S.A.

GEN MᶜGOUN. C.S.A.

rapidly changed front to face McCown's and Cleburne's divisions. This change of front brought Sheridan's line almost at right angles to his previous one. Cleburne and McCown now fell upon the heroic Federal division, but they were met by a steady fire. For over an hour the Confederates charged and recharged, but they failed to shake the Federals. The fighting on both sides was of the most determined character, and the field was literally carpeted with dead and dying men. Sheridan learned, on sending for more ammunition, that the ordnance train belonging to McCook had been captured. He then wheeled round so as to cover Negley's right flank and continued the battle.

Hardee and Polk next advanced with their full force, when Sheridan expended the rest of his ammunition and fell back in good order. His three brigade commanders, Shaeffer, Roberts, and Sill, had been killed, and he left nearly seventeen hundred of his men lying where they had fallen. "This is all that is left of us," said he, sadly, on reaching Rosecranz. It now came Thomas' turn to meet the onslaught, and gallantly did he do it. Both Rousseau's and McCleve's divisions held their positions in some cedar brakes, pouring in fierce musketry volleys on the advancing columns. But the Confederates were in overwhelming numbers, and were enabled to overlap Thomas' flank and get into his rear, where they delivered such a tempest of lead and iron that Thomas decided to assume position in the Nashville turnpike road. He succeeded, but lost terribly. On reaching the road he held it with the tenacity of a bulldog. Again and again did Bragg's division generals try to dislodge Thomas, without effect.

The Federal army was now in a perilous position. Rosecranz's entire right wing had been annihilated, and Thomas' tenure of the flank was exceedingly weak. Rosecranz, however, displayed rare military genius. When the Federal right had been so suddenly attacked

BATTLE OF MURFREESBORO', OR STONE RIVER.

by a force twice its strength, he ordered McCook and Thomas to hold as much of their ground as possible, promising a counter-movement to relieve the pressure. Sheridan, Rousseau, and Negley obeyed, and having checked the Confederates, waited for the next move of their commander.

With full confidence that McCook and Thomas would do their duty, Rosecranz gathered up his batteries and placed them in solid array on a knoll commanding the Murfreesboro' wood and the fields beyond it. He then began changing front, but while doing so Palmer's division of Crittendn's corps became the right wing, the five divisions under McCook and Thomas having fallen back to reform and receive a fresh supply of ammunition. The right and centre brigades belonging to Palmer were now attacked and scattered.

MAJOR-GENERAL J. M. SCHOFIELD.

But Colonel W. B. Hazen's brigade stood firm, though fully half of the men fell dead or wounded during those awful sixty minutes.

Ignorant of Rosecranz's plan, General Bragg decided that he had won the battle, and ordered an advance along his entire line. Cheatham, McCook, Cleburne, and Withers moved forward in magnificent shape. Then the Federal batteries opened with a terrific storm of shells, followed by grape and canister, the infantry delivering a steady musketry fire. The effect was an awful one, for the Confederate line melted away. Three times Bragg's men reformed and faced the deadly torrent, but finally fell back, shattered and discomfited.

Bragg now brought Breckinridge's seven thousand fresh men into the field, but their assault upon Rosecranz's left was so well met that Breckinridge had to retire. That was the end of the engagement. The battle of Murfreesboro' was claimed as a victory by both the Federal and Confederate generals, but history gives the victory to the former, because Bragg finally retreated.

There was more fighting on New Year's Day, and on the following morning, but it did not change the result. On January 2 Breckinridge made a headlong assault on Van Cleve, on the Federal right, but he was driven back with a loss of one-third of his men. On Sunday, January 4, Rosecranz discovered that Bragg had disappeared, leaving two or three thousand wounded men in hospital. Rosecranz entered Murfreesboro', but further pursuit was impossible, owing to the exhausted condition of his troops. The Federal loss was sixteen thousand men; that of the Confederates, over fifteen thousand. Rosecranz lost part of his supply train and twelve or fifteen pieces of artillery. He had, however, shown his ability to hold the line of the Cumberland Mountains.

Subsequent to the defeat of General Van Dorn by General Curtis at Pea Ridge, there ensued a long series of over one hundred minor engagements and skirmishes throughout the Mississippi Valley. The Federal troops, under General J. M. Schofield, operated in small bodies, the fighting being of a sanguinary character, for the opposing forces were natives of Missouri. Very little quarter was given. The destruction of public and private property was very great, and as Indian warriors were employed by both Federal and Confederate commanders, they infused an element of barbarity into this guerilla kind of warfare that was appalling. The loss in killed and wounded was very heavy, no accurate estimate being attainable. Among the Federal officers directing these remarkable operations were Colonels McNeil, Merrill, Ben Loan, Warren, Guitar, and Hughes. The Confederate leaders were Generals Cobb, Porter, Poindexter, and others.

Then Schofield concentrated his forces and entered on a more vigorous campaign, being confronted by forty-five thousand men under General Thomas C. Hindman. The latter had complete control of Arkansas, and waited in the passes of the Ozark Mountains for Schofield's advance. General Blunt joined Schofield, and the Federals succeeded in driving in the Confederate outlying divisions until they reached the old Pea Ridge battle ground, finally crossing the White River Mountains. General Herron also came up, and increased Schofield's strength to some twenty thousand men. A battle occurred at Boston Mountain which compelled Hindman to withdraw. But he crossed the Arkansas River on December 1, and gave battle at Prairie Grove. General Herron was overwhelmed for a time, but Blunt, who proved himself a vigorous fighter, came to the rescue, and striking the Confederate flank, turned the tide of victory. General Stein, one of Hindman's brigadiers, led a charge to retrieve the day, but was killed at the head of his men.

Owing to the then sparsely settled condition of Arkansas and Texas, there were numerous guerilla bands moving about, their ostensible object being to aid the Confederate cause, while in many instances unscrupulous men used the device for concealing robbery. On August 19 a band of Sioux fell upon the village of New Ulm, on the Minnesota River, when they massacred every human being who fell into their hands, among the victims being one hundred and sixteen women and children. There being no survivors to tell the tale, no record has been left concerning the horrible scenes that were enacted. But evidence of their dreadful character was abundant, for the winding street of the picturesque

BVT. MAJ GEN. J. N. PALMER.

BVT MAJ GEN. VAN CLEVE.

BVT MAJ GEN T. J. WOOD

MAJ GEN. F. T. HERRON.

BVT MAJ GEN A. P. BLUNT

village was strewn with corpses, gray-haired women, pretty maidens, and innocent children being heaped together, just as they had fallen under the cruel tomahawks of the savage warriors. It recalled the Colonial days, when England employed Indian braves as auxiliaries to her troops.

Colonel Sibley, the inventor of the circular tent that was used by the Federal forces during the first year of the war, was ordered to avenge this atrocity. Starting from Fort Ridgely on September 19 with the Third, Sixth, and Seventh Minnesota regiments, he met the Sioux near Yellow Medicine Creek on September 23. The Sioux, led by Little Crow, charged on both of Sibley's flanks, but his musketry and artillery discharges were too much for the Indians, and they were defeated with great slaughter. This lesson was sufficient to keep all the Indian tribes quiet, and they very sensibly decided to let the white men fight out their own quarrel without interference by the red man.

CHAPTER XXX.

THE INITIAL MOVEMENTS AGAINST VICKSBURG.

Though the Federals had captured New Orleans and Island Number Ten, the Mississippi River remained closed to navigation by formidable earthworks in front of the city of Vicksburg. This point on the mighty stream was important to the Confederacy, because it was the first high ground below Memphis. Indeed, Vicksburg is still known as

MAJ GEN. C. S. HAMILTON.   MAJ GEN. FRANK P. BLAIR.

MAJ GEN. A. J. SMITH.

"The City of Terraces." There were other fortified points between Vicksburg and Port Hudson, but their fate rested on the safety of the former.

Farragut had ascended the Mississippi with part of his fleet and four thousand infantry under General Thomas Williams to attack Vicksburg. A desultory bombardment, covering ten weeks, ensued, the troops meanwhile endeavoring to cut a canal behind the city in order to change the channel of the river. But the project failed, and Farragut decided to go down the river again, so the Mississippi blockade remained unbroken.

Three weeks after the battle of Corinth, Grant was placed in command of the Department of the Tennessee, when he began the series of operations that were to raise him to the rank of Lieutenant-General. He had long contemplated moving against Vicksburg, but it was only in November that he felt strong enough to do so. General John C. Pemberton, a native of Pennsylvania who had joined the Confederate service, succeeded Van

Dorn, and assembled a strong force on the banks of the Yallabusha and Tallahatchie rivers, just above where they unite and form the Yazoo. Grant was at LaGrange, a few miles west of Grand Junction.

Just as Grant had made all his arrangements he received orders from Washington to divide his command into four army corps, with General McClernand to command one of them and to be assigned to that part of the army which was to operate down the Mississippi. As this interfered with his plans, he decided to take the field in person, in order that only one head, his own, should direct the subsequent operations. It was this

COMMODORE, AFTERWARD REAR-ADMIRAL, D. D. PORTER.

tenacious grasp of the chief command that made Grant so successful a general. The Federal line at that time held the Mobile and Ohio Railroad from Corinth north to Columbus in Kentucky, the Mississippi Central from Bolivar north to its junction with the former road, the Memphis and Charleston Railroad from Corinth east to Bear Creek, and the Mississippi River from Cairo to Memphis. Grant realized that the line was too long for defensive purposes, so decided to assume the offensive.

The fighting strength of Grant's forces was about forty-five thousand men. General Sherman commanded the right wing, General McPherson the left, and General C. S. Hamilton the centre. Pemberton was fortified at the Tallahatchie, but occupied Holly Springs and Grand Junction on the Mississippi Central Railroad. On November 8 the Federals

MAJOR-GENERAL W. T. SHERMAN.

occupied Grand Junction and LaGrange, and the next day Grant's cavalry entered Holly Springs, the Confederates falling back to the Tallahatchie, where they threw up breastworks.

General McPherson had driven back General Lamar, holding open the road for Grant. On December 5 Sherman arrived at College Hill, and on the 8th he and Grant met at Oxford, when the final details were arranged. Having been so successful in using the naval branch of the Federal service on the Tennessee and Cumberland rivers, Grant asked for the co-operation of Commodore Porter, who had succeeded Commodore Foote on the Ohio and Upper Mississippi. This was freely given, every available gunboat being placed at his command. A large fleet of transports was also sent from St. Louis by General Allen.

General Sherman was placed in command of the river expedition, consisting of four divisions, which was to proceed down the Mississippi under the protection of Porter's gunboats, and the orders were to open up the mouth of the Yazoo River and attempt to capture Vicksburg in the rear. In the meantime, Grant was to push on to Jackson and offer Pemberton battle. McClernand was to proceed to Vicksburg and co-operate with Sherman. These movements necessarily exposed the Federal line of communication and supply, but Grant had left Colonel R. C. Murphy at Holly Springs, his chief depot and hospital, with an adequate garrison.

On December 20 General Van Dorn swept down on Holly Springs, when, to the astonishment of the Federal garrison, Colonel Murphy offered no resistance, and accepted a parole for himself and his men, except the Second Illinois Regiment, which fought its way through the Confederate lines. Van Dorn thus came into possession of military property and supplies valued at nearly two millions of dollars, and destroyed everything he could not carry away. While Van Dorn was approaching Holly Springs in one direction a Federal force of four thousand men was marching to reinforce Murphy, and it arrived only four hours after the cowardly capitulation. Grant very properly dismissed Colonel Murphy from the service.

Simultaneous with Van Dorn's capture of Holly Springs, General Forrest's Confederate cavalry tore a path through to Jackson, Tennessee. Passing swiftly along, Forrest captured Trenton, Dyer's, Humboldt, Rutherford, Kenton, and other railroad stations. Applying the torch as he went along, the Confederate raider completely destroyed Grant's line of communication and all of his supplies. General Grant was thus compelled to recross the Tallahatchie River, finally reaching Grand Junction and LaGrange, and regaining communication with Memphis and Corinth.

General Sherman started from Memphis on December 20, having embarked twenty thousand men on river steamers. His promptness was occasioned by the desire to escape being superseded by General McClernand. The latter happened to be a warm personal friend of President Lincoln, and being ambitious to obtain an important independent command, he descended to intrigue, and came very near attaining his object.

On December 21 Commodore Porter joined Sherman with three gunboats: the Black Hawk, his flagship; the Conestoga, commanded by Captain Selfridge, and the Marmora, under Captain Getty. On the same day the Federal troops at Helena marched on board their waiting transports, and reported to Sherman, at Friar's Point, thus increasing the General's force to thirty thousand men. The remainder of Commodore Porter's fleet being already at the mouth of the Yazoo River, the joint expedition moved majestically down the river. So large a body of troops required the services of no less than sixty river steamers, for Sherman had forty regiments and eleven batteries, made up entirely of Western soldiers.

As is usual at that season of the year, the Mississippi River was running full, from bank to bank, and these transports were lashed together in groups of from four to six, each loaded to its full capacity with men, horses, cannon, and stores. Keeping up a steady, regulated speed, this enormous fleet of river craft floated on the broad and muddy stream, its appearance being an imposing one. The gunboats led with their pieces ready for instant action,

GEN. T. H. HOLMES. C.S.A.

GEN. LAMAR. C.S.A.

GEN. S.T. CHURCHILL. C.S.A.

GEN. N. B. FOREST. C.S.A.

and the transports swept down the great river in close and regular order. On the forward lower deck of each steamer were massed the artillery field pieces and caissons, while the remainder of the deck was occupied by horses or the stores of hay, oats, hard bread, coffee, sugar, barrels of beef and pork, live cattle, ordnance supplies, tents, wagons, and all other necessaries for an army. The upper decks were allotted to the troops, and as the steamers passed around the broad bends of the river the Federal soldiers sang army songs. Few signs of human habitation were visible, for the desolating hand of War had been already laid on that part of the disputed territory. On board the fleet there was life and gayety, for both officers and men felt the influence of the pomp and circumstance with which the movement was being made.

General Sherman was a great, an ideal soldier, the idol of those who followed the feathery fringe of the skirmish smoke and faced the open-mouthed cannon, winning victories along the advancing lines as they marched with him. He was of a highly nervous organization, and was often fitful and wayward, but only in light and trivial matters. When it came to anything of consequence to his fellow-men, or to the country, he was as firm and unshaken as a rock.

Seen at the head of a column of troops, or giving orders for their disposition on the field, Sherman presented a remarkable figure. Riding along the road, he was constantly gazing about him, noting the lay of the land passed over, as if mentally planning how a battle could be fought there. When preparing for an engagement Sherman was in an excited mood, though his orders were clear and concise, despite the nervous manner of their delivery. For the moment, the General was stern and sharp in his demeanor. Corps and divisions were sent here and there with rapidity, showing that the entire plan of opera-tions had been quickly formulated in his active brain. Though generally courteous to his subordinate generals, Sherman could at times show considerable temper if things did not go

DRILLING IN THE FORTS.

exactly as he wanted, or when some mistake had been made. Then he would straighten his lean figure and utter a good deal of the language they often used in Flanders. This generally had its effect, and Sherman gradually grew quiet and composed.

General Sherman, on active campaign, used to wear one of the rustiest uniform coats that was ever seen. It was the old one he had ordered made when first commissioned a Brigadier in 1861. When he started from Atlanta on his march to the sea the old coat had assumed two or three distinct tinges of color, for the rain and sunshine of half dozen campaigns had done the garment up brown, blue, and green. The silken threads in the buttonholes were quite white, while the shoulder straps of his rank as a Major-General had assumed the hue of rusty copper, instead of brilliant gold. But the coat was dear to the heart of the old warrior, and he seemed to be more at home in it than in the more correct one needed for parade. A few weeks before the General's death I asked him about the old coat. "Got it yet," he replied. "That coat saw its share of service, didn't it?"

CHAPTER XXXI.

BATTLE OF CHICKASAW BAYOU AND CAPTURE OF FORT HINDMAN.

Sherman's expedition reached Milliken's Bend on Christmas Day, 1862, Burbridge's brigade being sent to destroy the railroad between Vicksburg and Shreveport, Louisiana, a task that was soon accomplished. Leaving A. J. Smith with his division to wait for Burbridge, the remaining three divisions proceeded to the mouth of the Yazoo River, the troops disembarking at Johnson's plantation. Steele's division took position just above the mouth of Chickasaw Bayou, M. L. Smith's being below, with Morgan's in the centre. The Federals were really on an island, separated from the Walnut Hills, on which the city of Vicksburg stands, by a broad, shallow bayou, called Old River, it having once been the channel of the Yazoo.

Reconnaissances on December 27 and 28 satisfied Sherman that the bayous interfered with his contemplated movement, so he changed front. It was during these reconnaissances that Morgan L. Smith was severely wounded, the command of his division falling to Brigadier-General D. Stuart. On the morning of December 29 everything was ready for attack, A. J. Smith's division having arrived. The Confederate force lying between Vicksburg and Haine's Bluff was about fifteen thousand strong, under command of Generals Martin Luther Smith and Stephen D. Lee.

Sherman's plan was to attack all along his line, while the army broke across the bayou at two selected points where there was tolerably good footing. Morgan's division was to lead this movement, and when Sherman pointed out the place where he could cross, Morgan gallantly replied: "General, in ten minutes after you give the signal I'll be on those hills." But he failed to keep the promise. Steele's division was to follow and support Morgan's. The passage across the bayou was very narrow, and immediately in front of it the Confederates had erected a battery, only three hundred yards away. A strong force of infantry was posted on the spurs of the hill. In order to draw attention away from this point, Sherman ordered an attack on both of his flanks.

About noon of December 29 the Federals opened a heavy artillery fire along their whole line, it being briskly replied to by the Confederate batteries. Then, as De Courcey's brigade, of Morgan's division, crossed the bayou, Lee's infantry began a withering fusillade, which prevented De Courcey from going forward. Frank Blair's brigade, of Steele's division, then crossed the bayou, when it encountered a severe artillery cross-fire. Being unsupported, Blair was compelled to fall back, leaving behind nearly five hundred men killed, wounded, and prisoners. Among the wounded was Colonel Thomas Fletcher, of Missouri, who afterwards became Governor of his State. The Sixth Missouri got across, but could do

ARRIVAL OF NEGRO FAMILY IN THE LINES.

nothing except scoop out caves in the bank, under a Confederate battery, using their hands and bayonets, the Thirteenth Regulars acting as sharpshooters and keeping the cannoniers quiet. There has been no explanation why J. W. Morgan did not obey orders and cross the bayou. His failure to do so prevented Sherman continuing the assault, because his objective point had been discovered by the Confederates.

Commodore Porter and General Sherman had become personal friends, and they co-operated in perfect harmony. Finding that the Confederates were reinforcing their line, Sherman decided to consult Porter and try some other point of attack. Sitting down

Battlefield of Chicasaw Bluffs.

Poison Springs on Battlefield.

Chicasaw Bayou, Mississipi.

on the flagship, the soldier and the sailor agreed on a plan. During the next day, December 30, a sufficient number of steamers were selected and their captains ordered to get up steam. These river men and their pilots, learning that another move was contemplated, became demoralized, so it was necessary to place guards over them, in order to be sure that they would be at their posts. That night Steele's division, which had been quietly massed on the river bank during the afternoon, was marched on board the transports. The steamers were to proceed up the Yazoo River to Haine's Bluff and disembark at daylight. Sherman had meanwhile strengthened his position on Chickasaw Bayou, in order to renew the assault on that part of the line simultaneously with the one intrusted to

A CAMP SCENE.

Steele. During that day the fleet had been busy at Haine's and Snyder's bluffs, when Captain Gwin was mortally wounded by a round shot.

At midnight a dense fog settled down on the river, and it was impossible for Steele to move, and after daylight a steady rain began falling. Sherman had sufficient experience regarding these Western rivers to know that a few hours' rain would inundate the bayous and render his position untenable. He noticed that the high-water mark on the huge cottonwood trees stood fifteen feet from the ground, and as the rivers frequently rise from five to six feet in a single night, he lost no time in ordering all the stores re-embarked, and the troops were directed to be ready to join their respective boats during the night of January 1, 1863. While Sherman's army was thus preparing to withdraw there were heavy reinforcements pouring into Vicksburg, having been sent by Pemberton, who was then at Grenada. At sunrise of January 2 Sherman's entire force was afloat, his loss during the movement having been seventeen hundred and thirty men killed, wounded, and missing. Then McClernand arrived at the mouth of the Yazoo, and on meeting Sherman handed him an order from the War Department which gave McClernand command of the expeditionary force on the Mississippi. This reduced Sherman to the position of a corps commander. The army name was also changed to the Army of the Mississippi.

The first thing McClernand did was to order the expedition to return to Milliken's Bend, and thus the simultaneous movement against Vicksburg by Generals Grant and Sherman came to an inglorious end. Six months after, these two Federal commanders tasted the fruits of victory.

General McClernand seems to have entertained the idea that he was destined to be the most successful general in the Federal service, and as he had the ear of the President, and was not at all backward in criticising everybody but himself, he made considerable mischief. He talked grandiloquently about what he was going to do, but it was evident to his corps commanders that he had no settled plan how to "cut his way to the sea," as he expressed it.

While General Sherman was on his way to attack Vicksburg in December the steamer Blue Wing, that had been sent down the river with a full freight of coal and ammunition on barges, had been captured by the Confederate garrison at the post of Arkansas. A boy who had been on board escaped by swimming ashore. He made his way to Milliken's Bend and gave General Sherman the details. Seeing the importance of capturing the garrison, Sherman went to McClernand and asked permission to take one division and go up the Arkansas River in order to seize the post. McClernand at first objected, but finally consented to see Commodore Porter, who was at the mouth of the Yazoo, in his flagship the Black Hawk.

When they arrived at midnight Sherman was surprised to see Porter treat the new commander very brusquely. He therefore took the future admiral into the forward cabin and demanded what he meant by it. Porter replied that he did not like McClernand, for he had met him in Washington, and said something profane and uncomplimentary. Sherman begged Porter, for the sake of harmony, to put his prejudice into his pocket and assist in getting up the Arkansas River expedition. The Commodore stroked his long black beard, laughed, and good-naturedly gave in. The difficulty about coal being got over, Porter volunteered to accompany the expedition, instead of sending a subordinate officer. This delighted Sherman, who supposed that he was to command the land forces, but to his mortification McClernand decided to take the entire army and so have all the glory.

Accordingly, the four divisions proceeded, under convoy of three ironclads, up the Mississippi River to the mouth of White River, reaching that point January 8. On the following day the expedition ascended White River to what is called "The Cut Off," passing through which it entered the Arkansas. Disembarking below Fort Hindman,

By permission of the artist.   *From the painting by Gilbert Gaul.*

BRINGING UP THE GUNS.

Stuart's division advanced on the morning of January 10, encountering a strong Confederate force lying behind a line of intrenchments extending from the river bank to a swamp. Sherman took Steele's division, and passing over a road through the swamp, was moving around to the rear of Fort Hindman when McClernand galloped after him and said that the Confederates had fallen back and re-entered the fort. Sherman was then ordered to retrace his steps and join Stuart.

Four miles below the fort the Federals passed through the abandoned works and got so near to the fort that they could hear the sound of axes. On the morning of January 11 they discovered that the Confederates had thrown up a new line of breastworks which connected Fort Hindman with an impassable swamp. Sherman's corps stood on the right of a road that divided the peninsula, Morgan's being on the left. McClernand remained on board the steamer Tigress, and sent a man to climb a tall tree and observe the movements.

About half-past ten o'clock Porter's ironclads moved up and opened fire on the fort This was the signal for Sherman and Morgan, and they advanced in fine style. Morgan and the gunboats paid strict attention to the fort, while Sherman's men faced the new breastwork. The Federal line moved steadily forward, delivering sharp musket volleys and a fierce artillery fire.

Then a white flag was hoisted, and Sherman entered the fort, finding the interior almost a complete wreck. Fort Hindman was a square bastioned work, with a ditch fifteen feet wide and a parapet eighteen feet high. It mounted two eight-inch, one nine-inch, and nine six inch guns. General I. J. Churchill was in command, and he had a garrison of five thousand men. When Churchill notified General T. H. Holmes, who commanded the Confederate forces at Little Rock, that the Federals were advancing in force, the latter replied, " Hold on until help arrives, or until you are all dead." But Churchill found the odds too great, for he was facing twenty-six thousand men, therefore surrendered. In fact, the surrender was brought about in a very curious manner. While the Confederate general was considering what was best to be done, as nearly all of his artillerymen were dead or wounded, a staff officer went to Brigadier-General Garland, whose brigade was facing Sherman, and said Churchill's orders were to hoist a white flag. When Sherman entered the fort there was an angry altercation going on between Garland and Churchill, the latter insisting that he had given no order to surrender.

Ever watchful for an opportunity to wound the feelings of his subordinates, McClernand now hit on the fertile expedient of keeping Sherman outside the fort, while the honor of occupying it was given to one of Morgan's division commanders, though he knew very well that Sherman and his corps had been the first to enter. By this act McClernand ignored one of the courtesies of military etiquette. The Federal loss at Fort Hindman was nine hundred and seventy-seven killed and wounded, among the latter being General Hovey. The Confederate loss was five thousand one hundred and forty. The dead being buried and the prisoners despatched to St. Louis, the fort was completely dismantled and the parapet destroyed by explosion. A small expedition under General Gorman and Lieutenant J. G. Walker ascended still further up the White River, sweeping away the redoubts at Duval's Bluff, St. Charles, and Des Arc. On January 13 the Army of the Mississippi dropped down the Arkansas River as far as Napoleon.

GENERALS BURNSIDE, HANCOCK, AND STAFF OFFICERS.

MAJOR-GENERAL A. E. BURNSIDE AND STAFF, WARRENTON, VA., NOVEMBER, 1862.

CHAPTER XXXII.

GENERAL BURNSIDE'S ADVANCE UPON FREDERICKSBURG.

General Ambrose E. Burnside assumed command of the Army of the Potomac distrustful of his own ability, for he said : " With diffidence for myself, but with a proud confidence in the unswerving loyalty and determination of the gallant army now intrusted to my care, I accept its control." Such an utterance was not calculated to inspire confidence, for men usually judge others by their own estimate, until proved incorrect.

It is only justice to Burnside to say that like all of the Federal commanders in the East, he was hampered by Halleck, who was always interfering.

Instead of adopting the organization of the army as left him by McClellan, it consisting of six separate and easily handled army corps, Burnside's first step was to form three grand divisions of two corps each, commanded by Generals Sumner, Franklin, and Hooker. General Sigel was given an unattached body of troops as a reserve. On November 14 the army was set in motion.

Then occurred one of those lamentable mistakes which often marked the campaigns of the Army of the Potomac. Burnside decided to move one column toward Rappahannock Station and so lead Lee to expect an advance near Gordonsville, while in reality he intended to enter Fredericksburg and march for Hanover Court House. Acquia Creek was to be the new base of supplies, and as the Fredericksburg bridges had been burned, Burnside asked for a pontoon train with which to cross the river. Halleck agreed, but when told that the departure of Burnside's columns from Warrenton should be delayed five days in order to give time for transporting the ponderous pontoon trains the commander-in-chief not only refused to delay the army, but actually kept Burnside in ignorance of the fact that he was to be hindered by the non-arrival of the huge boats. By this act Halleck caused the useless sacrifice of thousands of brave men. The verdict of history is that for this act he deserved dismissal from the service, a medicine he was fond of administering to others. This may seem harsh criticism, but it has been made time and time again by distinguished generals in the presence of the author. As it was, Burnside had to shoulder all the responsibility and blame.

On a bright November morning the three grand divisions began their new campaign. The roads were good, the air cool and comfortable. Every man had good clothing, the armament was in first-class condition, so the Federal soldiers marched forward with a feel-

MARYE'S HOUSE, ON MARYE'S HEIGHTS
IN REAR OF FREDERICKSBURG;
RIFLE PITS IN FRONT.

ing of hope and expectancy. There was, however, an element which received very little attention from the authorities at Washington, and that was the abundant and unchecked sources of information which the Confederates always enjoyed in the East. It was natural for the Confederates to take advantage of their opportunities, but it does seem remarkably strange that the Federal Government did not ferret out the spies in official quarters. Under these circumstances it is not surprising that Burnside had scarcely got in motion when Longstreet appeared on the railroad between Acquia Creek and Fredericksburg and destroyed it.

On November 17 the head of Sumner's division reached Falmouth, opposite Fredericksburg, Franklin and Hooker coming up on the 19th. At that time the Rappahannock might have been forded, but the attempt was not made, Burnside preferring to wait for his

Clerks at Commissary depot.

Quartermasters Office.

Wharves.

Wharves

AQUIA CREEK LANDING

Group at Hospital

Officers at Landing

Employees at Quartermasters wagon camp.

SCENES AT ACQUIA CREEK LANDING, ARMY OF THE POTOMAC, NOVEMBER, 1862, TO JUNE, 1863.

EMBARKATION OF NINTH CORPS AT ACQUIA CREEK LANDING.

promised pontoons. Then a heavy rain swelled the river and rendered fording an impossibility. This delay cost Burnside the possession of Marye's Heights, which stand behind the city and command it, for on November 22 the Confederates appeared in strong force and began fortifying that position.

"Where are my pontoons?" telegraphed Burnside.

"They will start to-morrow," was the cool reply. The consequence was that these boats did not begin to reach Falmouth until November 25, and it was the 10th of December before the engineers were ready to build their bridges. This fatal delay enabled Lee to gather his whole army on Marye's Heights, his eighty thousand men being thoroughly intrenched. The Confederate position was like a half-moon, each point reaching the river. Here the Army of Northern Virginia waited at its ease. The morning of December 10 broke raw and cold, with a dense fog covering the river and plain. The work of building five bridges across the Rappahannock was begun under a galling musketry fire from the opposite bank of the river. Almost every blow of a hammer or axe cost a human life. Burnside grew impatient, and gave orders for his artillery, already massed on Stafford Heights, to open fire on the city. Again was the Demon of Destruction stalking abroad.

"Batter the place down, if necessary," said General Burnside. "Silence those sharpshooters and finish the bridges."

His order was promptly obeyed. In less than twenty minutes no less than one hundred cannon, many of them of the largest calibre, opened fire on Fredericksburg. Battered by solid shot, and set on fire by exploding shells, the city soon grew untenable, for five thousand rounds were expended, and Fredericksburg became a mass of ruins. But the Confederate sharpshooters were not driven away, and the bridges were yet to be completed. The artillery having failed, volunteers were called for to cross the river in boats as a forlorn hope. The Nineteenth and Twentieth Massachusetts and Seventh Michigan stepped forward to a man, and a line of pontoon boats was soon crossing the river. The Confederate riflemen were speedily driven from their shelters, and the bridge-building went on with celerity.

Sumner got across the river by sunset of December 11, using the upper bridges. He was followed by Hooker, who took about one-third of his troops, leaving the remainder to cross in the morning. Franklin had the two lower bridges, and was in full force on the other side soon after dusk. None of these grand divisions met any resistance, General Lee preferring to await attack in his intrenched position. In silence, Burnside's army took up its position outside of the city, facing Marye's Heights, the rear columns marching over the bridges during the night. At dawn of December 12, 1862, both armies stood stripped for the combat that was to prove one of the bloodiest battles of the Civil War.

Wharves.

Distant View.

Quartermaster's Office.

Distant View.

Lacey's House.

Distant View.

Lacey's House.

Phillips House.

Commissary Depot.

SCENES AT ACQUIA CREEK LANDING, ARMY OF THE POTOMAC, NOVEMBER, 1862, TO JUNE, 1863.

Copyright, 1887, by L. Prang & Co.

BATTLE OF FREDERICKSBURG.

CHAPTER XXXIII.

THE SANGUINARY BATTLE OF FREDERICKSBURG.

The position assumed by Lee's army was on a table land, with two ridges rising one above the other. These Marye's Heights, as is their generic name, stand nearly one mile from the city of Fredericksburg, the plain in front being almost level. South of these heights are a series of irregular hills, following the line of the Massapomax River, until it falls into the Rappahannock. Prospect Hill stands at the southern extremity, Lee's Hill at the northern end, and Bernard's Cabin near the centre. Every hill had its share of cannon, so that the Army of the Potomac stood before three hundred guns of all calibres, without protection or proper position for its own batteries. Yet General Burnside prepared to dash his magnificent command against this formidable obstacle.

As has been said, Lee had eighty thousand men, Burnside's force being one hundred and ten thousand. To give the reader some idea of these imposing numbers, it may be said that if Lee's army had been placed in a straight line in the city of New York it would have extended from the Battery to the Obelisk in Central Park, while Burnside's line would have run from the Battery to High Bridge. These two enormous bodies of men were, however, massed within a space of less than three square miles. By the morning of December 12 Lee had made the following disposition of his troops: A. P. Hill's division occupied the extreme right from Hamilton's Crossing to Bernard's Cabin; Hood's division stood on the crest of the heights between Deep Run and Hazel Run; Pickett's division crouched under the hills between the Telegraph Road and Hazel Run, forming Lee's centre. On

Panoramic Views.

View from Tyler's Battery.

Lower End of Town.

House on Maryes Heights Showing effect of Shells.

Houses Showing Effects of Shells Dec. 13, 1862

FREDERICKSBURG

the left of Pickett the division of McLaws had possession of the hills, while Anderson's division rested on the Rappahannock River. Marye's Hill, commanding the Plank Road, was held by Ransom's division, and it bristled with cannon.

Burnside had, at first, no intention of facing the awful array of Confederate artillery. That had been his original plan, until he decided to send two of Hooker's divisions to Franklin, giving the latter half of the army for the task of turning Lee's right flank, when the rest of the Federal line was to move forward. Franklin expected to start at daylight on the morning of December 13, but to his surprise Burnside sent orders that he was to keep his troops in readiness for a rapid movement down the Richmond road after first seizing Hamilton Crossing and the Massapomax Heights.

That General Burnside was unequal to the command of so large a body of troops is shown by his contradictory orders. Having tied up Franklin, he surprised Sumner by

VIEWS IN FREDERICKSBURG.

ordering him to move forward and attack Lee's centre, thus suddenly and unexpectedly changing the preconcerted plans and hopelessly confusing his generals.

A more gloomy battle morning could not be imagined. The air was raw and chilly, the dense fog that wrapped the hills, fields, and woods in its moist and clammy embrace adding to the discomfort of the troops. Men move with spirit into deadly combat when rosy dawn gives token of a bright and sunny day, but here at Fredericksburg colonels lost sight of their regiments in the heavy mist, while brigade commanders learned with difficulty which was the right or the left of their line. To the Confederates it was also cheerless, but they had already taken up their positions, and knew the ground, while the Federal army was groping through the rolling vapor like a blind man.

Franklin began the battle by sending Meade's division forward to attack the Massapomax Heights. General Reynolds, of the Fifth Corps, placed Doubleday's divi-

Scenes Photographed at Headquarters
Army of Potomac Nov 1862 June 1863

sion on Meade's left, while Gibbon occupied a similar position on Meade's right. The troops stumbled along in the wet fog over ground full of narrow gullies and clumps of trees, but the fog began lifting, and at ten o'clock Meade's men, who had advanced beyond the Richmond road, caught sight of the Confederate line. The opposing bodies of infantry were scarcely three hundred yards apart, and at that range the Confederates poured in a deadly series of musketry volleys. At the same time "Jeb" Stuart's mounted artillery opened fire on the Richmond road. Staggering before this sudden onslaught, Meade's division gathered itself together and returned the volleys. This stand-up fight continued for nearly half an hour, when Doubleday came up and deployed, silencing Stuart's guns, so that Meade was able to move forward as far as the railroad, where A. P. Hill's division was concealed. As the Federal division approached Prospect Hill it was met by a cross-fire of artillery from Walker's guns and Jackson's centre. There was another pause while

WOUNDED FROM THE WILDERNESS, AT FREDERICKSBURG.

BURYING THE DEAD AT FREDERICKSBURG.

SOLDIERS DRAWING WATER FOR THE HOSPITALS.

WOUNDED FROM THE WILDERNESS, AT FREDERICKSBURG.

SOLDIERS DRAWING WATER FOR THE HOSPITALS.

FREDERICKSBURG, VA.

the Federal batteries endeavored to silence the Confederate artillery. The duel that ensued was a terrible one, the infantry on both sides receiving shells at point-blank range.

Meanwhile, General Birney, from Stoneman's corps, had hurried up with his division, and, as the fire from Prospect Hill visibly slackened, Meade went forward. So sudden was the rush of these Pennsylvania regiments that the Confederates under General Brock-enborough were driven back, the Federals crossing the railroad to a new road that had been cut by Lee for his interior line of communication. As they passed into this road Gregg's South Carolina brigade was encountered. The Confederate general, supposing Meade's advance to be a part of Lee's army, held his fire, and the next instant his brigade received a volley from three thousand muskets scarcely one hundred feet away. General Gregg fell mortally wounded, and his command was nearly annihilated. But Meade was not being supported, as Doubleday had advanced along the Richmond turnpike, while Gibbon stopped at the railroad. Then Ewell's division rushed into the breach, the Confederate line was reformed, and struck Meade's flank with such fury that he had to fall back under cover of his artillery, Birney coming forward and turning the tide. The Confederates were again forced back, but their line was unbroken, and the gap had been closed; thus, all that Meade had gained was lost. The two divisions under Gibbon and Meade suffered heavily, the latter general being wounded.

The remainder of Burnside's army stood to arms in their several positions, listening to Reynolds' attack on the left of the Federal line. Sumner, with Couch's Second Corps, occupied the town, while Wilcox's Ninth Corps held the ground between Fredericksburg and Franklin's line. Hooker stood on the right, near the river. The booming of Franklin's and Jackson's cannon finally died away, the fog disappeared, and at the noon hour a flood of bright sunshine brightened what was soon to be a frightful battlefield.

BATTLEFIELD OF FREDERICKSBURG—VIEW OF MARYE'S HEIGHTS.

Finally Burnside gave the signal, and General French's division, consisting of Kimball's, Anderson's, and Palmer's brigades, emerged from the town and entered the open plain in front of Marye's Heights. Scarcely had the heads of the columns shown themselves, when all the Confederate batteries on the opposite hill opened on Fredericksburg, setting fire to many of the houses, shattering others, and compelling the Federal engineers to blow up several in order to prevent the flames spreading. Then, when French began forming his line, the muzzles of Lee's guns were depressed, the Confederate shells falling thickly among the assembling lines. Behind French's division was Hancock's, with Howard's in reserve. The heavy Federal guns on the other side of the river now opened on the Confederate batteries on Marye's Hill, in hopes of silencing them, but the range was too great, so the gunners reluctantly abandoned their effort. Meanwhile, the men under French began the awful task assigned them. From the spot where they formed in line of

AMBULANCE TRAIN OF ENGINEER BRIGADE.

battle to the foot of Marye's Hill was less than a mile. The ground was almost level, yet the Federal infantry was expected to march across this narrow plain in the face of one hundred cannon and thirty thousand muskets.

The sun was shining clear and bright, not a cloud floated in the steel-blue sky, and there was a shimmer on the frostened grass which gave it a golden hue. In a few short minutes this yellow tinge was changed to dark crimson, for thousands of brave men dyed it with their blood. As Burnside's reserve guns on Stafford Heights ceased their useless clamor, French's and Hancock's divisions, each nearly six thousand strong, began advancing. Scarcely had the brigade and regimental flags begun fluttering in the cool breeze than the guns on Marye's Hill increased their fire. Shell and round shot were hurled upon the advancing columns, cutting ghastly gaps in the ranks, but the Federal line moved steadily onward. So heavy was this Confederate artillery fusillade that the Federal batteries could not advance. When half the distance had been covered the two divisions rushed forward, French's men getting within fifty yards of the stone wall behind which crouched the Confederate infantry. Then a blinding flash of light sprang forth, followed by the crash of a tremendous volley of musketry. The front line melted away and Hancock's men passed over it to meet the iron and leaden tempest. In fifteen minutes his division shared the fate of French's, and out of the twelve thousand men who started on the awful charge scarcely four thousand returned. Nearly four hundred field and line officers fell among the dead and wounded.

With that stubbornness that marked every battle between these Northern and Southern soldiers, General Howard next moved into the breach and charged on Hancock's right, while Generals Sturgis and Getty dashed across Hazel Run on the extreme right. But they were met by the same steady, merciless volleys of grape, canister, and bullet, and the lines were driven back, leaving the ground thickly covered with more dead and dying men.

Every subordinate general on the field now supposed that Burnside would pause, and dispositions were made to give the troops some slight shelter. But Burnside seemed to be seized by a spasm of insanity, for he paced up and down the terrace of the Phillips House on the northern bank of the Rappahannock, muttering, "That crest must be carried to-day." Ignoring the awful carnage among his troops, he sent Franklin orders to attack with all his force, while Hooker was directed to repeat the effort just made by French, Howard, and Hancock.

Hooker, quickly moving forward with Humphrey's and Sykes' divisions, advanced on Marye's Hill. But when told by French and Hancock what he was about to face he sent an aide to Burnside asking that the order be countermanded. The commanding general reiterated his orders. Then Hooker crossed the river and made the appeal in person. But the only reply was, "That height must be carried this evening."

General Hooker returned to his command at four o'clock, hearing a sharp outburst on the right of Lee's line as he galloped across the pontoon bridge. The Confederates had endeavored to regain possession of the railroad and the Richmond turnpike, but were repulsed by Meade and Birney, the Fifty-seventh North Carolina leaving nearly every officer and man behind. Posting a couple of batteries on his right and left, Hooker ordered the guns to open a rapid fire. Then Humphrey's men dropped their haversacks and knapsacks, and throwing off their overcoats, they made the assault with empty muskets, for there was no time to load. With fixed bayonets, the men rushed forward, actually getting within fifteen or twenty yards of the fatal stone wall. Another flash saluted them, the ranks were shattered, and the division fell back crushed and broken. In fifteen minutes seventeen hundred and sixty men were killed or wounded. Darkness now fell upon the bloody field and mercifully put an end to the slaughter.

On Sunday, December 14, Burnside proposed to renew the assault, but the consensus of opinion among his generals was against it, so he withdrew, and Lee re-entered the town. Burnside lost thirteen hundred and eighty-seven men killed, nine thousand one hundred

MAJ GEN. G. W. GETTY.

MAJ GEN. J. GIBBON.

MAJ. GEN. D. B. BIRNEY.

wounded, and three thousand two hundred and thirty-four missing. Lee's loss was over six thousand.

Burnside immediately formulated another plan of operations. He proposed a feint attack at Kelley's Ford, above the junction of the Rapidan and Rappahannock rivers, while moving his main force below Fredericksburg. But Mr. Lincoln forbade the movement, so Burnside tendered his resignation, which the President refused to accept. Then permission was given him to cross the Rappahannock at United States and Banks' fords. The several grand divisions were to march at dawn of January 20, 1863, but a storm of snow, rain, and sleet deluged the roads and made them impassable. The Federal army started for the river in due time, and floundered through mud and rain for three days, being finally compelled to return to Winter quarters. The heavy rains had so softened the earth that cavalry, artillery, and infantry had to wade for miles through deep mud, while the ammunition and supply trains could not proceed or join their several columns. "The Mud March" was the soldiers' nickname for this remarkable and insane movement, these three words telling their own story.

DR. LETTERMAN, MEDICAL DIRECTOR, AND OTHER OFFICERS, ARMY OF
THE POTOMAC.

The rich soil of that fertile region is held in place by the outcropping masses of rock, which stretch out from the massive Blue Run range of mountains like the surface roots of a gigantic tree. Wherever the engineers of the roads had cut through these rocky ridges to reduce the grade the hollows were filled to the depth of eight or ten feet with loose earth, which, though solid enough for hoof and wheels in dry weather, became quagmire pits in the presence of long-continued rains. The consequence was that the artillery and supply wagons were soon up to the hubs in the clinging mud.

During this movement the author's brigade had halted on the slope of a hill for rest, and we watched the movement of a long train of wagons that came plunging along the road. The leading wagon went gallantly down the steep incline, the driver evidently hoping to gain sufficient headway by his rapid descent to ascend the upward grade with comparative ease. But, unhappily, his brake broke, and the team of six mules found the heavy wagon sliding on to their heels. The brutes, in positive terror, made a sudden plunge to the right, and in less than a minute all of the unfortunate animals sank into the mire and disappeared from sight. The driver only escaped by climbing to the top of his canvas roof, from which he was rescued with difficulty. Three months after, I passed over the same road, and saw the imbedded wagon, though the six mules lay buried beneath the then hardened earth.

The people of the North were irritated, Halleck was criticised, and Burnside condemned. The latter made charges of insubordination against Generals Brooks, Cochrane, Hooker, and Newton, and wanted them dismissed the service. He wrote out the order, adding that Generals Ferriss, Franklin, Smith, and Sturgis were deprived of their commands. President Lincoln refused to sign the order, and Burnside resigned. General Hooker was given the command, General Sumner being relieved at his own request, and General Franklin was transferred to another sphere.

FREDERICKSBURG, VA., MARCH, 1863.

MAJOR-GENERAL JOE HOOKER AND STAFF.

CHAPTER XXXIV.

HOOKER'S FLANK MOVEMENT AGAINST LEE.

While Hooker was reorganizing and recruiting the Army of the Potomac, Lee sent Longstreet to the Blackwater River, where he was joined by Hill, their aggregate force being forty thousand men. The Confederates at once besieged Suffolk, Virginia, then in possession of a Federal force under General John J. Peck. This siege continued for twenty-four days, being raised on May 3. Its importance lay in the fact that Lee was deprived of the services of Longstreet's corps during the Chancellorsville campaign. Hooker assumed his command on January 26, 1863, and divided the army into. seven corps, the First, Second, Third, Fifth, Sixth, Eleventh, and Twelfth, commanded by Generals John Fulton Reynolds, D. N. Couch, Daniel E. Sickles, George G. Meade, John Sedgwick, O. O. Howard, and Henry W. Slocum. The cavalry was consolidated as a corps under General George Stoneman. Each corps was given a distinctive badge, which was worn by the men on their caps and was emblazoned on their banners. New regiments were poured into the army, the hospitals were emptied, and scattered commands drawn in, until Hooker had one hundred and thirty-six thousand men at his disposal.

President Lincoln visited Falmouth early in April, and reviewed the Federal army. It was a magnificent spectacle, the strange devices of crosses, stars, crescents, and trefoils on the headquarter banners giving the scene a touch of that barbaric splendor historians ascribe to the steel-clad Crusaders on the sands of Palestine. The glitter of bayonet and sabre, the fluttering folds of regimental and brigade colors, the roll of drums, and the crash of music filled the eye and the ear as President Lincoln rode along the massed lines. The plain selected was in full view of the Confederate army, as it stood on the opposite bank of the Rappahannock, the men in butternut watching with curious interest the holiday evolutions of the men in blue.

General Lee's line at that time extended from Banks' Ford to Port Royal, a distance of twenty-five miles, his cavalry holding the line of the upper Rappahannock. He had strengthened his position in Marye's Heights in such a way that he was apparently entirely safe from attack in front of Fredericksburg. His lines of retreat were by the railroad or the Gordonsville turnpike. General Hooker decided on a flank movement to compel Lee to fight him on new ground. The Fifth, Eleventh, and Twelfth corps, with General Meade in chief command, were sent on a long détour into Lee's rear. On April 22 General Stoneman started with twelve thousand sabres to destroy all the railroads and bridges along Lee's lines of communication with Richmond. He performed this duty in the most effectual manner, drawing after him the Confederate cavalry, thus making it possible for the three corps under Meade to cross the Rappahannock at Kelley's Ford without detection. So rapid was the march of this flying column that it crossed the Rapidan during the night of April 28.

Meade's movement was a wonderful one, for he had marched his men nearly forty

miles inside of thirty-six hours, and stood in the rear of Lee's right flank. The scene at Germanna and Ely's fords during that night was an exhilarating one, for the troops were in excellent spirits, every man recognizing the success of the movement. So confident were Geneals Meade, Howard, and Slocum that they permitted their men to build immense fires by which to dry themselves and get warm after their passage through the cold water. For miles these fires burned, lighting up the banks of the Rapidan, their reflection being the first indication General Lee had of the presence of so large a body of troops in his rear. General Hooker was so enthusiastic over the success of the movement that he said to his staff: "The rebel army is now the legitimate property of the Army of the Potomac. They may as well pack up their haversacks and make for Richmond, and I shall be after them." His boast was a vain one, however, for bitter defeat awaited the Army of the Potomac and its vainglorious commander.

The plan of operations, as sketched by General Hooker, was an ingenious one. By placing three corps on the south side of the Rapidan River, he expected to throw Lee into confusion, then attack him on both front and rear. While Meade, Howard, and Slocum were marching to the Rapidan River, Couch, with two divisions of the Second Corps, threatened United States Ford, and Sedgwick made a feint nine or ten miles below Fredericksburg with the First, Third, and Sixth Corps. Having crossed the Rapidan, Meade marched through woods and fields for United States Ford. The Confederate guards were driven in, the ford uncovered, and Couch joined Meade. During Thursday, April 30, the right wing of Hooker's army was massed near the Chancellorsville House, while Sedgwick had crossed the river, with part of his command, below Fredericksburg. Sickles was ordered up to Chancellorsville, and Reynolds followed, while Sedgwick and the Sixth Corps remained to engage Lee on his old line. Lee's situation was apparently a precarious one, for he was compelled to change front to face seventy thousand men, with the Rappahannock, held by forty thousand men, in his rear, his communications with Richmond being in the hands of Stoneman's cavalry. Yet Lee coolly faced the emergency, and by superior strategy dealt his opponent a stunning blow.

On May 1 Hooker was ready for battle, but he wanted to get out of the dense woods and gain a wide stretch of open country near Robertson's Tavern. The Fifth Corps formed the left, Griffin's and Humphrey's divisions marching up the old river road, while Sykes' division of regulars advanced along the turnpike, closely followed by Hancock's division of the Second Corps. Slocum took an old plank road. All of these troops reached the neighborhood of Banks' Ford without firing a shot. When about a mile east of the Chancellorsville House Sykes encountered a tolerably strong Confederate force, but he drove it back and took the position assigned him.

During this brief engagement an incident occurred which aptly illustrates the life of a soldier. Little Tommy Cullen was a drummer, and had caught a pony during the march from Kelley's Ford to the Rapidan. By permission of his colonel, the boy retained the animal to carry drums and knapsacks. When a Confederate battery opened on Sykes' division the Federal line advanced, Tommy and his pony being left in the rear with the rest of the drummers, on the banks of a small creek, where the surgeons had stationed their field hospital. As the fight grew hot the boy mounted and crept up to the battle line on his little steed. The artillery fire becoming severe, the Federal line had to fall back a few hundred yards, and when Tommy's colonel saw him he ordered the boy to go back. But just at that moment the boy missed the face of his brother in the company they both belonged to. Asking what had happened to Jim, he was told that the young man had been wounded and was lying on the ground between the opposing lines. Away dashed Tommy, his sturdy pony carrying him over the grass in fine style. In a few moments he reached the line of dead and wounded men, soon finding Jim. Quickly dismounting, the little drummer assisted his brother to mount the pony, when back they came in safety, the boy running beside the animal to guide him. The six or seven thousand men who witnessed the gallant act cheered the brave little drummer most lustily, and it was voted that Tommy should keep his pony to lighten the fatigues of subsequent marches.

Hooker's right had meanwhile taken up a strong position on a high ridge which overlooked the fields in the rear of the heights around Fredericksburg. Here the Federal commander seemed to have Lee in his grasp, but, to the astonishment of his corps commanders, Hooker suddenly decided to fall back on Chancellorsville, throw up intrenchments, and assume the defensive.

CHANCELLORSVILLE.

CHAPTER XXXV.

FIRST DAY'S BATTLE OF CHANCELLORSVILLE.

When General Lee learned, on April 29, that a strong Federal force had arrived on the line of the Rapidan, Jackson's Corps was at Hamilton's Crossing, near Massapomax Creek, McLaws' division stood at Fredericksburg, while Anderson lined up to face Meade. That night McLaws was ordered to join Anderson, leaving Barksdale's brigade to guard Fredericksburg. At daylight of May 1 Jackson started in the same direction with three divisions, to take command in that part of the field, Lee remaining to watch Sedgwick. General Early was placed on Lee's right, near Hamilton's Crossing. It will thus be seen that both armies had been split in two.

General McLaws joined Anderson at dawn of May 1, and Jackson arrived about eight o'clock, when he began advancing to the right. This was while Hooker was falling back on Chancellorsville. Jackson soon discovered that Hooker's right did not extend to the Rappahannock River, so he decided to attack the Federal right while Anderson and McLaws kept the left and centre busy. To do this necessitated a march of fifteen miles, and cutting Lee's army into three sections. To conceal this counter flanking movement Stuart's cavalry made several feints, while McLaws and Anderson showed considerable activity. Jackson started with twenty-two thou-

MAJOR-GENERAL T. R. ANDERSON, C. S. A.

sand men early in the morning of Saturday, May 2. The columns marched with great speed and secrecy, but did not entirely escape the attention of the Federals, for Jackson's ambulances and ammunition wagons were seen passing over a hill in front of General Sickles' line, and General Birney detected a body of Confederates crossing Lewis' Creek. At first it was believed that the Confederates were retreating, so Sickles was ordered forward with two divisions to learn what was really going on in that direction.

Birney's and Whipple's divisions, with Barlow's brigade, of Howard's corps, and Randolph's battery, advanced briskly and engaged, capturing three or four hundred officers and men. As it was evident that Jackson was in strong force, Sickles made a vigorous assault, but Colonel Thompson Brown uncovered an entire battalion of artillery and opened a terrific fire, which seriously checked Sickles. By this time Jackson's main body had gained such

VIEWS AT CHANCELLORSVILLE.

momentum that he could not be stopped. Pressing forward through the dense forest, this indomitable man passed on and reached his chosen ground an hour before sunset.

Having reached the Furnace Road, Jackson's troops proceeded through the woods in silence until they came to the old plank road over which Slocum's Twelfth Corps had marched the day before. Here the Confederate general ascended a commanding height and coolly surveyed the Federal position, then ordering General Fitz Lee's cavalry brigade and General Paxton's infantry brigade to go forward over the plank road. Jackson led his main body through some dense undergrowth until he arrived at the turnpike. Here the strictest orders were given for secrecy.

Moving along the turnpike until he was near Chancellorsville and on Howard's flank, Jackson formed his command in three lines. Rodes', Dole's, Colquitt's, and Iverson's brigades made the first line; Colston's, Nicholls', and Jones' brigades the second, and A. P. Hill's division, the third line. One section of a mounted battery from Stuart's cavalry trotted quietly down the battered old turnpike in order to open the proposed surprise party in good style. Having massed his twenty thousand men, Jackson instructed General Rodes to make a rapid, headlong assault, while Colquitt and A. P. Hill were to move in on close support.

The right of the Federal line was occupied by the Eleventh Corps under General Howard, his division commanders being Generals Devens, Schurz, and Steinwehr. As the setting sun began reddening the horizon the Federals were cooking supper, and complete silence reigned all along the line. Suddenly bugles began their shrill clamor in the forest outside the breastworks, and before the Federals could fall in under arms Rodes'

GEN. WILCOX, C.S.A. GEN. COLQUITT, C.S.A. GEN. SEMMES, C.S.A. GEN. COLSTON, C.S.A.

GEN. DOLE, C.S.A. GEN. FITZ HUGH LEE, C.S.A. GEN. NICHOLS, C.S.A.

division leaped over the parapet and opened a merciless musketry fire. Both Colquitt and Hill followed. The Eleventh Corps broke and ran like a flock of sheep. The Fifth Corps had held the right of the line during the night of May 1, while Howard's men built their breastworks. At dawn Meade proceeded to Hooker's extreme left. When the crash of Jackson's musketry broke out on the cool evening air Meade's bugles soon sent his brigades racing down a narrow wood road toward the scene of conflict. Louder and louder grew the terrible musketry, followed by sharp and constant cannonading.

The point of Jackson's attack was at Dowdall's Tavern, and as Howard's flank was completely turned, the three Confederate lines of battle smote the Federal ranks such terrific blows that the men threw away knapsacks, overcoats, muskets, and, in many instances, their haversacks. Then these demoralized troops rushed pell-mell across the fields, with ammunition and commissary supply wagons, artillery pieces, caissons, mules, horses, and cattle all mixed up among them. This miserable mob was closely followed by the Confederates, who opened a deadly fire from musket and cannon which did horrible execution. It was an awful and disgraceful scene for the Federals. Hooker's first effort to preserve his line was to send General Berry's division to the right, and it checked Jackson's further advance, Captain Best's batteries doing good service in the sudden emergency. Then, despite the growing darkness, a fierce battle was begun. General Sickles had hurried up from the Furnace, accompanied by Pleasanton and his cavalry. Coming up as Howard's corps rushed past, General Birney threw forward the Eighth Pennsylvania, only to see it almost annihilated, and its colonel fall, riddled by bullets. Pleasanton's artillery then galloped on the field, and twenty or thirty field pieces were soon at work. This artillery fire was responded to by the Confederate batteries as their infantry

HANCOCKS AND SEAVYS POSITION, FROM TOP OF CHANCELLORS HOUSE.

GENERAL VIEW OF BATTLEFIELD.

VIEW OF BATTLEFIELD.

VIEWS AT CHANCELLORSVILLE.

formed for the charge. But the effort was fruitless, for Pleasanton met the assault with grape and canister. Then night fell, and the rank and file of both armies supposed that the fighting for that day was over, but for the first time during the war a battle was fought in these dense Virginia woods until near dawn, the movements of the various bodies of troops being made by the light of a tender May moon and the fitful flashes of cannon and musket volleys.

As the Fifth Corps emerged from the woods the Eleventh Corps stood huddled together in a sort of pocket in the woods, where the axe of the settler had eaten a little deeper into the virgin forest. The leading regiments of Meade's corps used the bayonet as they tore a path through the struggling and cowering mass. There was no time to waste, no thought of mercy. Maddened by the sight of so much confusion, the Fifth Corps rushed through and deployed in line of battle, delivering a steady and effective musketry fire. In the gathering darkness we could see Rodes' division advancing in triumph across the fields. Word then ran along the Fifth Corps line to fire low, and as the musket volley was delivered the Confederate column melted away. Just then Weed's battery came thundering up, and as the pieces wheeled into position by sections on a knoll to the right of Sykes' division they opened a very rapid discharge of grape, which drove Rodes back in some confusion.

The Fifth Corps now formed its line more deliberately, and we could see that the Eleventh Corps was being driven into our road, in order to get it out of the way. Then, as the moon rose above the tops of the trees, several Confederate batteries opened on our front, their shells crashing through the woods, but doing but little other damage. Three

ROOM IN WHICH STONEWALL JACKSON DIED.

HOUSE IN WHICH STONEWALL JACKSON DIED.

WHERE STONEWALL JACKSON DIED, RICHMOND, VA.

Federal batteries galloped forward and replied, the effect being a weird and striking one, for as the flashes of the cannon revealed the gunners at work the rolling smoke hid the moon and deepened the darkness.

While this was going on Lee had grown active on his right, in order to engage Hooker's attention, but the effort was too feeble to be of any importance. General Berry's division, with Best's artillery, now attacked Jackson on the plank road, and so vigorous was the Federal movement that several of Howard's lost field guns were recaptured, and the Confederates were repulsed, being compelled to fall back nearly half a mile. Then the struggle ceased, only a few stray cannon on either side keeping up a muttering series of shell discharges.

When this sanguinary night work began General Jackson was sitting on his horse in the middle of the turnpike road, anxiously waiting for A. P. Hill's division to come up.

Just before General Hobart Ward's brigade made its charge Jackson rode forward with most of his staff to personally reconnoitre, first giving strict orders that his troops were not to fire unless cavalry approached. This was a fatal order. Riding through his picket lines, the General advanced to the Van Wert House, and then turned back over a side road. As he neared the Confederate picket line the General's mounted party was mistaken for Federal cavalry, and, true to the orders received, three hundred muskets were discharged. Two of Jackson's aides fell dead from their saddles, and several others were wounded. Quickly turning, the General plunged through a dense undergrowth, only to receive another and more deadly volley, at a distance of thirty paces. Three bullets struck

MAJ GEN, A. W. WHIPPLE.

BVT MAJ GEN,
A. P. HOWE

MAJ GEN, F. C. BARLOW

Jackson, one passing through his right hand, the others shattering his left arm and severing the artery. Having passed through the lines, Jackson's men recognized their general, and he was lifted from his horse and laid under a tree. Then the Federals charged, actually passing Jackson in the darkness, but the Confederates wanted their general, so they returned the charge furiously, and succeeded in regaining the ground long enough to pick him up. As the men were placing the wounded general on a litter a charge of grape and canister came tearing down the turnpike and killed one of the bearers. His fall threw the litter to the ground and increased Jackson's injury. He was carried to a hospital, where the arm was amputated, but he died on Sunday, May 10.

CHAPTER XXXVI.

THE SECOND DAY'S BATTLE OF CHANCELLORSVILLE.

The position of the Army of the Potomac had now become a very critical one, for it was compelled to act strictly on the defensive, despite its superiority in numbers. Sedgwick was still below Fredericksburg, with nearly twenty-four thousand men, so Hooker sent him orders, late on Saturday night, to occupy the town, seize Marye's Heights, and advance up the Chancellorsville plank road, which would bring the Sixth Corps in rear of Jackson's command. In the meantime the Federal army took up a new A-shaped line, it being so shortened that the wings rested securely on the Rappahannock River. Reynolds' First Corps occupied the extreme right, Sickles' Third Corps and Slocum's Twelfth Corps being in the centre, and Howard's Eleventh Corps, now reorganized into something like shape, being on the left. Meade's Fifth Corps lay behind Sickles' in reserve, while further in the rear stood two divisions of Couch's Second Corps, ready to move to either face of the A. Thus, sixty thousand muskets were facing forty thousand. The assault by Jackson, though successful, had cost the Confederates dearly, for Lee's most trusted lieutenant was dying and Hill had been wounded by the fragment of a shell. "Jeb" Stuart had temporarily succeeded Jackson, he being the ranking officer, but when he left his cavalry corps to take charge of the infantry Stuart hesitated regarding his movements, and sent an aide to Jackson asking instructions and advice. But the dying general could only say "He must use his own judgment," for he knew that for him there were to be no more battles.

The morning of Sunday, May 3, found these one hundred thousand men facing each other in grim lines, but Hooker had made another fatal mistake in ordering Sickles to abandon his commanding position at Hazel Grove, because it was really the key to the Federal line. Scarcely had the Third Corps retired when Stuart seized the ground, recognizing its importance. Then began a battle that was terrible in its aspect and awful in its carnage, for the Confederates opened fire from over thirty cannon on the fields around the Chancellor House. After an hour's cannonading the Confederate infantry advanced in three strong lines. As their batteries paused for a moment the Federal troops could hear the fierce yells of Lee's men as they came forward. Every field piece in the Confederate centre again opened, and amid a fierce shower of shells Sickles' men stood waiting for the charge.

MAJOR-GENERAL H. G. BERRY.

It was six o'clock, and a deafening crash of musketry drowned even the sound of the opposing cannon as twenty thousand muskets were discharged in a simultaneous volley. Sickles' corps, consisting of Birney's, Whipple's, and Williams' divisions, bore the brunt of this onslaught, standing firm and doubling the volume of sound as they returned the volley. Captain Best had massed forty pieces of cannon in front of the Chancellor House, and was sweeping the road over which the Confederate column was advancing. Despite the storm of lead and iron poured upon them, these Southern soldiers pressed onward. On—on they went, until Generals Birney and Berry massed their divisions on the right and left of Sickles' line and charged. The shock was tremendous, and the roar of weapons terrific, for here were forty thousand men in close combat, with nearly ninety cannon at work. Brave General Berry was killed at the head of his command. The Confederates stood fast, and for nearly an hour the awful musketry continued without cessation. Then the Federals reformed, and again charged, under cover of a furious artillery fire from Sickles' and Slocum's batteries, which decimated Stuart's ranks and drove him from his position. With that tenacity so often displayed on these American battlefields the Confederates reformed in their turn, and charging with impetuous fury, precipitated a fiercer struggle.

Another hour passed, the fields and woods were filled with dead and wounded men, yet still the hot fighting continued. Backward and forward ebbed and flowed the tide of battle ; now the Federals seemed victorious, then the Confederates gained ground, when finally Stuart sent in every available man, and after a desperate struggle succeeded in capturing Sickles' position.

While Stuart was thus active Lee had ordered McLaws and Anderson to unite on Stuart's right, at the same time opening on Slocum's line with several batteries posted at Hazel Grove, which shook that part of Hooker's line. Anderson then rushed up the plank road and struck Slocum, while McLaws attacked Hancock's division, which stood between Howard's and Slocum's corps. McLaws failed to shake Hancock, being in reality repulsed, but Anderson succeeded, after a desperate contest, in getting past the apex of the Federal A line, and so formed a junction with Stuart. Then Lee ordered a general advance along his entire line, and the battle raged with even greater fury. Slocum and Sickles were now compelled to give way, and they formed line around the Chancellor House. The engagement had been continued for over five hours, and the cannonading and musketry did not pause for an instant on either side from six o'clock in the morning until two in the afternoon. The shrieks of shells as they flew through the air by hundreds, the steady rolling musketry as whole divisions and corps opened fire, the crashing sound of falling trees as they were shattered by solid shot, the sudden reverberations of exploding ammunition or artillery caissons, the screams of disabled horses, the groans of wounded and dying men, the shrill bugle notes, the hoarse commands of colonels—all these horrid and confusing sounds deafened the ears of those Federal soldiers who were not called on to join in the dreadful *mêlée*.

During the movement made by Generals Anderson and McLaws a solid shot struck one of the pillars of the Chancellor House. General Hooker happened to be leaning against it, and he was knocked down and stunned. This was a misfortune, for the Federal army had, practically, no commander for nearly an hour, and thus it was that neither Couch nor Meade had been ordered up to support Sickles and Slocum. As soon as Hooker revived he asked if Sedgwick had come up, and being answered in the negative, ordered a new and shorter defensive line to be assumed. His left now extended beyond the Ely's Ford road to Hunting Run, while his right rested on Scott's Dam, along Mineral Spring Road. Then there was a pause and silence in those Chancellorsville woods as the Federals and Confederates rested.

Meanwhile, what had become of Sedgwick and his twenty-four thousand men ? Having received orders at midnight of Saturday to seize Marye's Heights and advance over the plank road, Sedgwick got in motion, and entered Fredericksburg at daylight, where Gibbon's division of Couch's corps joined him. General Gouverneur K. Warren, who was Hooker's chief engineer, had been sent to see the movement executed. It should be remembered that Jackson had left Early's four brigades and Barksdale's brigade from McLaw's division to guard Marye's Heights. As General Newton's division advanced under cover of a fog it reached the stone wall that had proved so fatal at the previous battle in December. The Confederate brigades under Barksdale and Hays then opened a strong musketry volley, which compelled Newton to retire. Sedgwick next attempted to turn Early's flanks, sending Gibbon along the river bank to attack the Confederate left, while Howe advanced on Hazel Run, which formed Early's right. Gibbon proceeded as far as the canal, finding it too full of water to cross, and as he was exposed to a heavy cannonading from Taylor's Hill the Federal general was compelled to withdraw. A similar fate was encountered by Howe; consequently, both movements failed. Four hours had now been consumed, and Sedgwick decided to make a direct attack. Selecting Newton's division, it was sent forward, while Howe was to renew his effort on Hazel Run. Newton's columns consisted of the Thirty-ninth, Forty-third, and Sixty-seventh New York regiments,

BATTLE OF CHANCELLORSVILLE.

the Seventh Massachusetts, the Sixty-first and Eighty-second Pennsylvania. The right-hand column was commanded by Colonel Spear; the left one, by Colonel Johns. They advanced over the plank road, while Colonel Burnham took four regiments to the extreme left, against the base of Marye's Heights. When within three hundred paces of the Confederate line Early's batteries began firing canister, and as the Federals pressed on they were met by a murderous volley of musketry. Staggering for a moment, the Federals rushed forward, and by a desperate effort seized the crest, Colonels Spear and Johns and Majors Faxon, Bassett, and Haycock being killed. General Howe was equally successful, for he captured Lee's Hill, and as the Confederate position was no longer tenable, they fell back. Sedgwick now prepared to advance and join Hooker, who had by that time been driven to the position last described.

General Lee was preparing to again attack Hooker, hoping to drive him to the river, when a staff officer galloped up and announced Early's defeat. It was an awful emergency, but the Confederate commander met it promptly. On the instant Wofford's, Kershaw's, Mahone's, and Semmes' brigades were sent, under General McLaws, to Early's assistance, with orders to intercept Sedgwick and prevent his further advance. The latter was now pressing forward toward Chancellorsville, and met McLaws at Salem Church, about five miles from Fredericksburg, the Confederates being posted in a line perpendicular to the plank road, with their artillery so arranged as to cover the flanks and enfilade the road.

It was about four o'clock in the afternoon when Sedgwick ordered Brooke's division to deploy across the road and advance, Newton being placed in support, while the Federal batteries opened fire up the road, shelling the woods on either side. This apparently had an effect, for McLaws' skirmishers fell back precipitately, and his artillery slackened its fire. Believing that he was still fighting Early's men, Sedgwick ordered a charge by Bartlett's brigade. Away went the line with a cheer, meeting no obstacle until it arrived within ninety paces of the church, when the Confederates delivered a blinding volley slap in the faces of Bartlett's men. For a moment the Federals were checked, but, obeying the shrill notes of their general's bugle, the brigade gathered itself together, and with another cheer dashed on and surrounded a little schoolhouse, capturing all the Confederates ensconced there, the main force falling with such force upon a Confederate regiment which was endeavoring to hold the road that Wilcox's brigade wavered, and a moment after the Federals had taken the position.

Wilcox now threw forward the Ninth Alabama, which had been standing in reserve, and as they rushed on Bartlett, delivering volleys at the distance of a few yards, they succeeded in breaking the Federal line. Having turned the tide by this supreme effort, the Alabama men were promptly supported by the remainder of McLaws' line, and a general engagement followed, both sides fighting with desperation and bitter rage. Despite their valor and pertinacious grasp of the crest, the Federals were slowly but steadily driven back to the toll gate, where the battle had begun. Indeed, so furiously did McLaws' infantry burst through the woods—their favorite method of fighting—that Sedgwick might have been driven clear to the river. The Sixth Corps batteries, however, found advantageous ground just then, and sent such showers of shells with short-cut fuses that the Confederates were compelled to halt. A few sullen volleys of musketry were then exchanged by the opposing lines as the shades of evening mercifully drew a curtain over the bloody field, and the men of both armies flung themselves on the earth, exhausted by the dreadful fatigues of the day.

When the sun rose on Monday morning, May 4, Sedgwick found himself not only cut off from joining Hooker, but facing the main body of Lee's army, for the Confederate commander had detached Anderson's entire division and sent it to assist McLaws and Early. This left only Jackson's three divisions on Hooker's front, of which fact the Federal general was, of course, ignorant, for he remained cooped up in his intrenchments before a force not half his own strength. At sunrise, General Lee, who had arrived in person at Salem Church, made up a new line, which threw Sedgwick in sudden peril. The latter soon became aware that heavy bodies of Confederates were rapidly passing from their left to their right, and he asked General Hooker for assistance. Chafing under his own failure, Hooker curtly informed Sedgwick that he must get out of his scrape the best way he could, for no help would be sent him.

Early speedily got to work and recaptured Marye's Heights without much difficulty or loss, so that Sedgwick was compelled to shorten his line and cover Banks' Ford, in anticipation of recrossing the Rappahannock River. Anderson's division did not arrive at

Salem Church until noon, the subsequent manœuvres preparatory to an attack occupying the remainder of the afternoon. At six o'clock, however, Lee was ready. Considerable skirmishing had been going on, and as the Confederate musketry grew heavier Sedgwick saw that he was to be attacked on both his front and rear. Notifying Hooker that he could no longer hold his precarious position, the commanding general gave an ungracious permission for the Sixth Corps to recross the river.

Lee now advanced in splendid style, and his men made a spirited charge, which was stubbornly resisted by the Federals, both commands suffering considerable loss. Though it fought hard, the Sixth Corps was slowly pressed toward the river, barely succeeding in retaining possession of Banks' Ford. Night falling, the fighting again ceased, and before dawn of Tuesday Sedgwick had placed the Rappahannock River between him

PRESIDENT LINCOLN IN CAMP.

and Lee. During the three days he had been trying to reach Hooker General Sedgwick had lost over one-fifth of his strength.

The strange spectacle was thus presented of an army of seventy thousand men dividing another one hundred thousand strong and whipping each section in detail. General Lee had taken desperate chances. He had cut his own army into three parts, turning Hooker's flank with the one under Jackson; then, uniting his left and centre, he drove the Federal army half-way to the river. Next he transferred his centre to his right and smashed Sedgwick, rendering him unable to join Hooker's main force. It was a brilliant exhibition of strategy, supported by the devotion and courage of his troops.

Tuesday morning, May 5, found Hooker still inactive, and although his corps commanders were anxious for another advance with the entire army consolidated, the General decided to retreat. Unknown to the men, the engineers and axemen were set to work cutting roads through the woods toward the river, and they repaired and strengthened the bridges on the turnpike and plank roads for the passage of artillery. Meanwhile, the troops were kept busy erecting breastworks from Hunting Run to Scott's Dam, a distance of over three miles.

Having seen that Sedgwick had crossed the river, Lee repeated his old movement and sent McLaws' and Anderson's divisions back to Chancellorsville, intending to attack Hooker with every man he could muster. But as McLaws and Anderson were compelled to march slowly, the Confederate army did not assemble at Chancellorsville until nearly noon. Then a heavy rain began falling, and continued until after nightfall. The creeks soon overflowed, and the flats became shallow lakes, so military movements were impossible.

The rain storm placed Hooker's army in greater peril than ever, for the Rappahannock began rising so rapidly that the Federal pontoon bridges were in danger of destruction. The question now was, could the several corps get across before communication was cut off? A council was called, and there was a wide difference of opinion among the generals. A few of the more stubborn insisted that the army should remain and fight; others were sick of the indecision displayed by their commander, and wanted to retire while there was time. This counsel best suited Hooker, in his anxious and perturbed condition, so the order was given, and the splendid army must confess itself beaten.

CHURCH BUILT BY THE ENGINEERS.

CHAPTER XXXVII.

RETREAT OF HOOKER'S ARMY ACROSS THE RAPPAHANNOCK.

In the midst of a pouring rain which soon reduced the soft Virginia roads to that sticky mud so familiar to Northern and Southern troops the ammunition and commissary wagons began moving toward the river. As strict orders had been given to make the movement as quietly as possible, the Federal teamsters displayed unusual patience with their teams as the poor brutes struggled through the mud, now hub-deep. It took the whole afternoon for the reserve trains to get across the river, for the pontoon bridges were very shaky and unsafe. None of the fighting corps knew that a retrograde movement had been decided upon, even the brigade and regimental commanders being kept in ignorance until almost the last moment. Sullen and disconsolate, the soldiers of the Army of the Potomac stood all day shivering around their spluttering fires and listening to the rain-drops pattering overhead among the tender leaves of the trees. A heavy mist made the air raw and cold ; a deep silence prevailed, in utter contrast to the turmoil of the previous days. It was then remembered that during Sunday these woods had caught fire, when hundreds of wounded Confederates and Federals were burned to death.

Late in the afternoon a change occurred in the disposition of the different corps, but the men took very little interest in it. This change left the centre of Hooker's line uncovered, so the Fifth Corps was ordered forward to fill it. By this time the rain had slackened and the fires burned a little brighter, making the men more comfortable and cheerful. Then darkness crept slowly over field and forest, and the soldiers waited for orders. The road in which the Fifth Corps was resting had remained empty all day long. Hour after hour passed, yet there were no signs of a hostile movement such as had been made by the Confederates during the previous nights, and it was nearly midnight before anything happened to break the monotony of the long vigil. Then there was a curious muffled sound in the distance which surprised the men who remained awake, for it was unlike anything they had ever heard since donning the uniform. Closer and closer came this strange sound, until finally the tread of horses could be distinguished. As the sleeping men roused up and listened with their comrades the advance of the reserve batteries of artillery came in sight. When the first cannon and caisson passed the men noticed that the heavy wheels were wrapped in blankets. The muffled sound was now explained, and a murmur ran along the line of the corps—"A retreat! We are going back to Falmouth!"

Such, indeed, was the fact, and for over an hour did these ponderous batteries occupy the road. Then came ordnance supply trains, the wagon wheels also swathed in strips of blankets. Before these canvas-covered vehicles had all passed in the uncertain light of the now deserted fires a column of infantry went hurrying past. It was the Third Corps, and the men told us that the right of the army line had been abandoned. A feeling of sadness now seized every heart, for it was then known that all our

MAJOR-GENERAL O. O. HOWARD.

fatigue had been endured for no purpose, that the thousands of lives lost had been wasted, that our wounded comrades were groaning without hope of that recompense which comes with the knowledge that victory has been won.   As the Third Corps turned down a narrow side road leading to United States Ford the Second Corps appeared from another direction and marched straight through the dense forest, following, as we subsequently discovered, a "blazed" path carefully selected for them by the engineers.   Then came more artillery and ordnance wagons pressing forward in eager haste, with the First Corps tramping beside them, to follow the Second in its woody road.   The movement had evidently been carefully planned, for there was no apparent confusion, only a constant, feverish hurry.

While the men of the Fifth Corps were wondering when their turn would come to move to the rear, orders were passed along the line to replenish the fires and make them burn brighter.   As the soldiers gloomily tore down the interior supports of the breastworks and piled the logs on the glowing embers the sky on our right became illuminated by a great glow, showing us that similar work was going on there.   So large did the Fifth Corps line of fires become that the road was clearly defined, and we could see every face as it hurried past.   By three o'clock in the morning only a few weary stragglers and a disabled wagon were to be seen.   Then the order came to "fall in," and in a few minutes the Fifth Corps was in motion, on the route taken by the First and Second corps, which was easily discerned, for the tread of so many thousands of armed men had brushed aside the accumulation of dead leaves, leaving a black path along the line of blazed trees.   Soon after entering the forest we came to the rude tables built for the surgeons.   Around these structures lay ghastly heaps of human legs and arms.

Just as the day began breaking a drizzling rain fell, and by the time the corps passed into some open fields dotted with young pines the drops grew heavier.   Forming line of battle to protect the ford, we could discern the other corps moving rapidly and irregularly toward the pontoon bridges.   But no sign of any Confederate force was to be seen, though it was now broad daylight, and the entire army got safely across the swollen and muddy Rappahannock River, the Fifth Corps remaining on the Fredericksburg side.   Finally General Meade came riding along the rear of the line, and as he passed, brigade after brigade broke off and headed for the ford, until at length the whole command got across.   The retreat had been accomplished, and every regiment received orders to march to its respective camp.

By nine o'clock the rain ceased, but the roads to Falmouth were almost knee-deep in mud, so the troops took to the woods, leaving the roads filled with staggering wagons and toiling cannon.   Then demoralization seized the entire army.   Regiments missed their brigade headquarter staffs, colonels lost their regiments, captains their companies.   The reins of discipline were broken, every man and officer became a straggler.   Had Lee pushed forward over the river that day he could have captured thirty thousand men with ease, but the Army of the Potomac had left its stern imprint upon the Army of Northern Virginia, and the Confederates were content to see their opponents go away in peace.   The appearance of the Federal army during that memorable day was in woful contrast to the one it made when President Lincoln had reviewed it in holiday attire only a fortnight before.   Some of the men did not reach camp until the third day, and colonels were pleased if they had enough muskets to furnish details for the pickets.   But scarcely had the commands fairly assembled than the entire army recovered, and with wonderful elasticity resumed its perfect organization and mobile power.

The Chancellorsville campaign had been a costly one to both armies.   General Hooker's loss was seventeen thousand one hundred and ninety-seven men killed, wounded, and missing, of which nearly six thousand had been captured by the enemy, together with fourteen cannons and over nineteen thousand muskets.   General Lee lost nearly fifteen thousand men, of whom thirty-five hundred were prisoners in the hands of the Federals.

Scenes Photographed at Headquarters, Army of the Potomac from November 1862 to June 1863.

CAPTAIN GEORGE A. CUSTER AND GENERAL PLEASANTON.

CHAPTER XXXVIII.

GENERAL LEE'S SECOND INVASION OF MARYLAND AND PENNSYLVANIA.

Hooker's and Lee's armies remained quiet during the remainder of May, 1863, for neither command was in a condition to assume an offensive attitude. The Army of the Potomac lost all of its two years' service men, and its strength did not reach one hundred thousand. The Army of Northern Virginia was, however, reinforced by Longstreet's corps and a rigid conscription throughout the South, so that Lee mustered nearly ninety thousand men. Jackson being dead, the Confederate army was reorganized into three corps, under Ewell, Hill, and Longstreet. In the beginning of June Hooker became convinced that Lee intended an active movement, but could not discover his purpose. With the double purpose of watching his antagonist and removing his troops from their Winter camps, Hooker threw his seven corps along the banks of the Rappahannock from Franklin's Crossing, below Fredericksburg, as far up as Kelley's Ford.

The Confederate Government had been endeavoring for months to induce England to recognize it as a separate nation, but learned that it must first conquer Northern territory. Led by this *ignis fatuus*, General Lee was instructed to again invade Maryland and Pennsylvania. In order to mask his proposed movement and gain headway, Lee started two of Longstreet's divisions on June 3, under Hood and McLaws, toward Culpepper Court House. Ewell's corps marched after them during the next two days, while A. P. Hill remained at Fredericksburg to hold Hooker's attention. On June 6 Sedgwick crossed the river and made a reconnaissance, but was met by Hill with such stubbornness that the Federals were completely deceived.

On June 9 General Pleasanton started with Buford's and Gregg's divisions of cavalry, and crossing at Kelley's and Beverley fords, rode forward toward Culpepper, only to find the Confederate cavalry marching toward Brandy Station to cover the advance of Longstreet's and Ewell's corps. General Buford was on Pleasanton's right, and began fighting General Jones' brigade, which retired until Wade Hampton's and W. H. F. Lee's brigades came to its support. Then a good-sized battle ensued, as Gregg, coming up from Kelley's Ford, struck Stuart's rear. The Confederate general turned like a tiger and flung his whole force upon Gregg, but Buford was not so easily shaken off. The result was a genuine cavalry combat, in which fully twenty thousand sabres and carbines were used. The Federals seized the heights of Brandy, and, as the Confederates fell back, Pleasanton retired across the Rappahannock.

Captain George A. Custer was a member of General Pleasanton's staff. He was even then noted for his daring and fearless bravery. At a critical moment during this battle Custer was called upon to perform a brilliant and dangerous feat. The Confederate cavalry had succeeded in breaking a part of the Federal line on Pleasanton's right, and Stuart threw forward a couple of his batteries to enfilade the Federal centre, in hopes of throwing it

MAJ GEN, D. M. M. GREGG.   MAJ GEN, J. BUFFORD.

into confusion. The shell and shot were beginning to tell, when General Pleasanton turned in his saddle and called Custer.

The young captain was by the General's side in a second, with his hand at the visor of his braided cap.

"Mr. Custer," said the General, quietly, "will you please ride over to our right and get some of our batteries in position to reply to these infernal Rebel guns?"

Captain Custer bowed as he put spurs to his steed, which speedily dashed over the field in response to the harsh summons. A heavy bank of white smoke had begun to hide the Confederate artillery, but through its density bright flashes were visible as each gun was served. On—on, Custer galloped. Shell and round shot, bullets and grape, shrieked and whistled through the air, but the young officer seemed to bear a charmed life, for he remained untouched. The thunder of the cannon and the crash of musket and carbine volleys deafened the ear, and it seemed impossible that the aide could escape.

"I wonder if he will be able to get there," muttered Pleasanton, as he gnawed his mustache and watched Custer through his field glass.

Whole ranks of horse and infantry went down as the howling shells burst over their heads, yet Custer passed on unharmed, until he was finally lost to view in the distance.

"Oh, if he only reaches the batteries," exclaimed General Pleasanton, as he turned to see what the enemy was doing on his left.

Five minutes passed, then ten, yet no sign of the Federal batteries to take their part in the contemplated duel. Custer must have fallen, and the anxious general looked again for another aide to send.

"I'm afraid Custer has been hit," said he to young Dahlgren, who had ridden up. "I wish you would——"

"The batteries are coming up, sir," answered Dahlgren, pointing to the Federal guns as they emerged from the bank of smoke and began rapidly wheeling into position, each piece being loaded and fired as the caissons dropped to the rear.

"So they are," replied General Pleasanton. "It's all right."

"The guns have gone into action, sir," said Captain Custer, with another salute, as he rode up to the clump of trees.

"So I see, sir," responded the General. "Thank you, Mr. Custer."

There was nothing more said, for a battlefield is full of danger, and Captain Custer had merely done his duty.

General Hooker's scouts soon confirmed Pleasanton's information regarding the Confedeate movements, and he at once set his corps in motion along the line of the Rappahannock Railroad, the troops again passing over ground that many remembered seeing during Pope's campaign. Lee's actual movement had begun on June 10, Hooker's on the 13th. Three days after, the Federal army was massed at Fairfax Court House and Manassas, the Fifth Corps being at Aldie Gap, supporting Pleasanton, who commanded the cavalry corps. Early was now crossing the Potomac, and the remainder of the Army of Northern Virginia was between Winchester, in the Shenandoah Valley, and the Gunpowder River, but nobody could tell what Lee was aiming at, his movements being somewhat different from those adopted in the Antietam campaign.

While Imboden's division was sent toward Romney, Rodes' division advanced on Winchester, where General Milroy stood with seven thousand men and a few pieces of artillery. Milroy fought Rodes with vigor, but Longstreet coming up, the Federal general tried to reach Harper's Ferry, but was surrounded and compelled to surrender with four thousand men, the remainder making their escape. The Confederates also captured three hundred wagons and over one thousand horses and mules. Harper's Ferry and Maryland Heights were soon occupied, and Lee's army crossed the Potomac into Maryland.

The same feeling of panic seized the people of the Northern States as had been exhibited on Lee's first invasion. President Lincoln called on the State of Pennsylvania for fifty thousand militia; Ohio, thirty thousand; New York, twenty thousand; Maryland and West Virginia, ten thousand each. This call was promptly responded to, while in Baltimore, Harrisburg, and Pittsburg the wildest excitement prevailed.

By June 26 the entire Confederate army was across the Potomac, and Hooker advanced to Frederick. Then there came another of those disputes between Halleck and his subordinates. General Hooker had succeeded in obtaining Halleck's consent that the troops under Heintzelman and Schenck should be added to his army, but when he suggested that Slocum and his corps be sent into the Cumberland Valley for a demonstration on Lee's rear Halleck protested. It was a sad dilemma. The Army of the Potomac lay massed in and around the city of Frederick, while Lee was rushing toward the Susquehanna. As Halleck would not budge, Hooker resigned his command, requesting instant release from further responsibility. There being no time to lose, the President accepted Hooker's resignation, and appointed General George G. Meade, of the Fifth Corps, to the chief command. Thus in an hour the army changed leaders, though in the midst of an important and momentous campaign.

SCENES AT HEADQUARTERS, ARMY OF THE POTOMAC, JUNE, 1863.

MAJOR-GENERAL G. G. MEADE AND STAFF.

CHAPTER XXXIX.

THE FEDERAL AND CONFEDERATE ARMIES MANŒUVRING FOR BATTLE.

It was with curious emotions that the Army of the Potomac broke ranks after listening to the bulletins of the retiring general and his successor. Sitting around their fires, the men freely discussed the situation, finally reaching the conclusion that everything would come out all right. General Sykes, who had so long headed the Regular Division, succeeded Meade in command of the Fifth Corps, and Romeyn B. Ayres filled Sykes' old position. Hancock was given the Second Corps, Couch being assigned to the Department of the Susquehanna. It was soon noticed that the soldiers were cleaning their weapons and overhauling their ammunition, a silent and pregnant sign that they were ready for another battle.

General Meade was of a very modest nature. When the command of the Army of the Potomac was thrust upon him he accepted the trust with reluctance, for Meade had made for himself an honorable record as a corps commander, and he did not seek higher or greater responsibility. But once he took command of the famous army his mind began to expand, and he seemed to visibly grow in physical and mental stature.

"I shall never forget," said he to the writer at Cape May, in 1870, while we were enjoying the hospitality of the New York Seventh Regiment and discussing the declaration of war between France and Germany, announced that day—"I shall never forget the day I received President Lincoln's order to relieve Hooker. As you will remember, we had advanced as far as Frederick City, and our movements seemed to be all right, but the removal of Hooker was a great surprise to me. When I met him, Joe said he was glad to

RUINS OF RAILWAY BRIDGE, DESTROYED BY THE CONFEDERATES.

MT. ST. MARY'S COLLEGE, EMMETSBURG, PA.

RAILWAY STATION AT HANOVER JUNCTION, PA.

HANOVER JUNCTION, PA.

FARMERS HOTEL, EMMETSBURG, PA.

ST. JOSEPH'S ACADEMY, EMMETSBURG, PA.

EMMETSBURG, PA.

SCENES AT HANOVER JUNCTION, PA., AND EMMETTSBURG, MD.

know that I was to be his successor, but he added, 'George, you will find it an awful responsibility.' Joe Hooker never spoke a truer word than that. I know, as no other man knows, what a weight I carried through that Gettysburg campaign. I thank God we won, but I can assure you no man was more grateful than myself when Lieutenant-General Grant decided to remain with me during the 1864 campaign, and so take from my shoulders the influence of Washington. Whatever fame I may have gained during that awful Summer movement from the Rapidan to the James was easier won than that I received for the battle of Gettysburg and the movements that followed it. Only those who have borne the burden of high military command can understand its crushing weight. It is not the sacrifice of human life that appalls a general. It is the fear that he may not succeed after making the sacrifice, and the knowledge that failure means the loss of thousands upon thousands of additional lives."

Meade was one of the most perfect riders in the service. He sat erect at all times, and it was an inspiring sight to see him gallop past a halted corps. In answer to the tumultuous cheers that invariably greeted him on such occasions, he would lift his braided cap, and, holding it high above his head, pass through the ranks of his men like a meteor.

VIEW OF GETTYSBURG

Meade took good care that his chargers were capable of speed and endurance, and he was very careful of them. He was born at Barcelona, Spain, his parents happening to reside there at the time. At the age of twenty he graduated from West Point, in 1835, and resigned from the army in 1836. He re-entered the service in 1842, and won distinction during the Mexican War, especially at Monterey and Palo Alto. During the Civil War he had already distinguished himself on the Peninsula and at Antietam under McClellan, at Fredericksburg under Burnside, and at Chancellorsville under Hooker.

During the forenoon of June 29 Meade gave the order for his several corps to march out of Frederick City. The First and Eleventh corps were to move to Emmettsburg, the Second to Frizzleburg, the Third and Twelfth to Taneytown, the Fifth to Union, and the Sixth to Windsor. As it was desired that the men should see their new commanding general, and there being no time or opportunity for a review, the corps marched from their bivouac camps into the quaint old-fashioned town and passed before General Meade and his staff. There was no cheering, no fuss, but as the General lifted his cap now and then to a corps, division, or brigade commander those who carried muskets took the act as a salute to the entire command. From that hour Meade had won the love and admiration of his troops.

By two o'clock in the afternoon the whole army was in active motion. The sound of bugle and drum filled the air as regiment after regiment passed into the road selected for it and fell into its brigade position.   The scene was an inspiring one, for never before in its history had the Army of the Potomac set out for a battle-ground in one grand movement.   Each command had its separate route, but as the several corps got clear of Frederick City the men of the Fifth Corps, being on a high ridge, could see the whole army as it advanced.   Just below, to the left, marched Sedgwick's Sixth Corps, beyond it, on a diverging road, was Hancock's trefoil banners, while further on rode Sickles with the Third Corps.   On the right of the Fifth streamed the long column of the Eleventh Corps under Howard, and in the fields beside him tramped the Twelfth, with Slocum at its head. Away off in the far distance beyond the Third Corps could be distinguished the glitter of the muskets of the old First Corps, under Reynolds, while between it and its neighbor rose a swiftly moving cloud of dust which betrayed the rapid movement of

GEN. MEADE'S HEADQUARTERS

GEN. MEADE'S HEADQUARTERS DISTANT VIEW SHOWING HORSES KILLED BY ARTILLERY FIRE.

GEN. LEE'S HEADQUARTERS ON NIGHT OF FIRST DAY NEAR CHAMBERSBURG PIKE.

THREE CONFEDERATE PRISONERS.

GETTYSBURG, PA.

Pleasanton's cavalry, as the four great divisions of veteran horsemen rode forward to cover the advance of the army and uncover Lee's movements.

With the rays of the setting sun glistening on thousands of muskets and sabres, and brightening the faded colors in the various brigade and regimental ensigns, with the sound of many voices filling the warm afternoon air, the martial picture was one never to be forgotten by those who saw it.   The most striking feature of this imposing march was the reserve artillery, which rumbled along a wide turnpike road in close order.   There were over two hundred and sixty guns, with their attendant caisson carriages and forges.   This line of cannon was fully six miles long.   On other roads were passing three or four long lines of canvas-covered wagons, carrying ammunition, food, and other necessary supplies. With such a broad expanse of canvas, these wagons had the appearance of a field of tents in motion. Thus did the army start under its new commander to try issue once more with the brave and resolute antagonist it had so often faced on Virginia and Maryland battlefields. Stripped for battle, every man in the full vigor of manhood, strong and healthy, the Army of the Potomac was on that day a magnificent body of soldiers, one hundred thousand strong. During that afternoon and part of the night the several corps reached their different destinations, and after a few hours' rest and sleep, the columns were in motion before daylight of June 30.

Both Meade and Lee were ignorant of each other's purpose or position. Lee supposed that the advance of the Federal army was at South Mountain, while Meade believed that the Confederate columns were pushing northward to the Susquehanna River. Instead of this, Lee was concentrating his forces on the east side of the South Mountain range. The advance on Harrisburg was given up, Longstreet and Hill being ordered to march from Chambersburg through the mountain passes toward Gettysburg. Ewell was also countermarching from York and Carlisle to the same point of rendezvous.

Meade was meanwhile extending a counter-movement against the threatened Susquehanna invasion, but learning from a scout, at a late hour on the night of June 30, the true meaning of Lee's operations, he changed the direction of his own marching columns. General Reynolds was ordered to hold Gettysburg with his own corps, and those of Howard and Sickles, as a mask for the rest of the army to take position along the line of Pipe Creek. Sedgwick's Sixth Corps was sent to Manchester, Slocum's Twelfth and Sykes' Fifth Corps moved to Two Taverns and Hanover, Hancock's Second Corps going to Taneytown, where Meade established his headquarters. Accustomed as was the army to rapid and long marches, these apparently confused movements taxed its strength and endurance to the utmost, for all of the corps had covered from twenty-five to thirty-five miles each day since leaving the Rappahannock River.

Early on the morning of July 1 the First and Eleventh Corps reached Marsh Creek, four miles from Gettysburg; the Fifth was thirty-odd miles from Hanover, crossing a spur of the Catoctin mountain range; the Sixth was really marching away from Gettysburg, for when Sedgwick received his summons he had to cover thirty-eight miles in order to reach the battlefield. Slocum's Twelfth and Sickles' Third Corps were within striking distance of Reynolds, while Hancock was ten miles from Taneytown and twenty-three from Gettysburg. Lee's troops had passed through the South Mountain gaps the night before, and were pushing forward to strike the Army of the Potomac before it could concentrate. Both the army commanders were now fencing for an opening.

GENERALS OF THE ARMY OF THE POTOMAC.

CHAPTER XL.

GETTYSBURG—THE FIGHT ON SEMINARY RIDGE.

None of the corps commanders had instructions to bring on an engagement. Consequently, when Reynolds did meet the enemy he aimed more at holding his own command together than making a decided fight. But on that eventful Wednesday morning, July 1, events were so shaping themselves that Gettysburg became forever an historical name. General Buford's division of cavalry had been occupying the town for two days, and as his videttes reported the approach of a strong Confederate column Buford advanced his brigades to the vicinity of Willoughby Run, his line crossing the Chambersburg road. Seminary Ridge was on his west and rear, nearly two miles away. Scarcely had the cavalry division assumed its position when General Heth's division, of Hill's corps, came up the Chambersburg road, the rest of Hill's and Longstreet's commands being in the rear.

General Buford saw at a glance that battle was inevitable. Sending an aide galloping to General Reynolds with a message that he was about to engage, and would endeavor to keep the Confederates in check, Buford made a skilful deployment

MAJOR-GENERAL GEO. G. MEADE.

and opened fire. Heth did not make a vigorous response, for he was waiting for Hill to come up, so Buford had not lost much ground when General Reynolds arrived on the scene with General Wadsworth's division. As Wadsworth's men went forward the cavalry was being pressed, so the division rapidly deployed, and Reynolds sent word to Howard to come up as speedily as possible. Hall's battery took position alongside the Cashtown road and began work. Cutler's brigade formed line of battle on the right of the road, while Meredith's brigade went into a bit of woods that skirted Willoughby Run, on the left. As soon as the line was formed General Reynolds gave the order to charge, going forward himself. The brigades obeyed with a cheer, when suddenly Reynolds fell from his saddle, mortally wounded. A bullet had cut the jugular vein in his neck, and the General died before he could be removed from the field.

MAJOR-GENERAL G. G. MEADE'S STAFF AT GETTYSBURG, PA.

The command now fell to Doubleday, who continued the movement. Meredith's brigade struck Archer's brigade on the flank as it was crossing Willoughby Run, the appearance of the Federal infantry being such a surprise to the Confederates that General Archer and over four hundred of his men were taken prisoners. Cutler's brigade met a determined resistance, and the struggle was a hot one. As Hall's battery was delivering a galling fire, the order was given by General Heth to seize it, but as the Confederates advanced on the Federal guns the Sixth Wisconsin and the Fourteenth New York charged, being joined by the Ninety-fifth New York. As the two lines came together two Mississippi regiments were surrounded and captured with their battle flags.

Desperate as had been the fighting, it was merely the prelude to a more sanguinary combat, for both Federals and Confederates were receiving reinforcements. Rowley's and Robinson's divisions of the First Corps were the first to come up. Robinson took position on Seminary Ridge, while Rowley went to the assistance of Cutler and Meredith. General Hill had by this time arrived, bringing with him Pender's division. Both sides were busy forming line as General Howard galloped on the ground, when, being the ranking officer, he took command of the Federal forces. He was followed by Barlow's and Schurz's divisions, the latter temporarily under command of General Schimmelpfennig, Schurz having gone to the head of the corps. Both divisions were sent to the right of the First Corps, thus prolonging the Federal line on the approaches to Gettysburg, while Von Steinwehr's division went to Cemetery Ridge as reserve. These dispositions were in accordance with the plan laid down by Reynolds just before he was killed.

Howard did not reach the field until one o'clock, and it was two before his line was perfected. At three, Ewell's corps (formerly Jackson's) came up the York Road, turned into the woods, and fell upon Howard's right. Early's division struck General Francis C.

Major Gen. John Newton. Brig. Gen. J. S. Wadsworth. Brig. Gen. S. Meredith. Brig. Gen. L. Cutter. Brig. Gen. J. C. Robinson.

Major Gen. J. F. Reynolds.

Brig. Gen. G. R. Paul. Brig. Gen. H. Baxter. Major Gen. A. Doubleday. Brig. Gen. E. A. Rowley. Col. Roy Stone. Brig. Gen. G. J. Stannard.

COMMANDING GENERALS, FIRST ARMY CORPS, AT GETTYSBURG, PA.

Barlow, while Rodes' division formed a junction with Hill's corps. Rodes succeeded in getting possession of Oak Hill, which enabled him to deliver a destructive artillery fire. The Confederates then advanced all along their line, and as they were two to one, both of Howard's wings had to give way after a stubborn resistance. General Barlow was severely wounded and made a prisoner. For a time he believed he was dying, and calmly gave his last instructions to a tender-hearted Confederate officer. Ewell now doubled up the Federal line, and drove it through Gettysburg, capturing nearly five thousand prisoners. Doubleday, Robinson, and Wadsworth kept the First Corps together, but when Howard's corps was driven back Doubleday abandoned Seminary Ridge and joined Howard, the movement being neatly and successfully performed.

The Confederates being in possession of the town of Gettysburg, Howard decided to mass his two shattered corps on Cemetery Ridge, where General Steinwehr had made admirable disposition of his artillery and infantry. Here the five divisions rested.

General Meade was at Taneytown when aides galloped up to announce the opening of a decisive battle and the death of Reynolds. General Hancock's corps was resting near by, so Meade ordered it put into motion, telling Hancock to leave his command with General Gibbon and hurry forward in an ambulance to decide what should be done. It was nearly four o'clock when Hancock reached Cemetery Ridge, finding that Howard was making good disposition of his troops. To Hancock's surprise, the Confederates contented themselves with the possession of the Gettysburg town. About sunset General Slocum arrived with the Twelfth Corps, and assumed command, as senior officer on the field, Hancock returning to Meade with his report. As soon as the commanding general understood the gravity of the situation he put all of his army corps in motion. The First, Eleventh, and Twelfth were already on the ground; the Third arrived after sunset, the Second about

COMMANDING GENERALS, SECOND ARMY CORPS, AT GETTYSBURG, PA.

midnight. The Fifth Corps was at Hanover, Pa., eighteen miles away; the Sixth at Manchester, thirty-eight miles distant. Meade ordered the commissary and ordnance trains to Westminster, and reached the battlefield about one o'clock on the morning of July 2.

The Fifth Corps had descended the Catoctin Hills during the afternoon of July 1, having marched thirty-eight miles since daybreak. The sun was rushing to the horizon in a sea of golden and ruby-tinted clouds, the air was hot and oppressive, and the men seemed exhausted by fatigue, for this was their third consecutive day's march, during which the corps covered one hundred miles of dusty roads. Then the little town of Hanover came in sight, its pretty church steeples embowered in foliage, the valley being a perfect picture of rural peace and plenty. Wide meadows on the right had just been mowed, the fresh-dried grass standing in haycocks ready for the wagon, while in front stretched a broad field of standing wheat almost ripe enough for the reaper. Smiling orchards, huge barns, groups of cattle, and a few scampering horses in a pasture near a brook completed the pastoral scene. Like an avalanche, the corps descended into the valley. The infantry marched into the wheat field, trampling down the ripening grain, while the artillery seized the meadows and the hay. Tents were put up, and the men were quietly eating their suppers, when the news ran from fire to fire that the First and Eleventh corps had struck the enemy, and that General Reynolds had been killed. Twenty minutes after, the bugles began winding the call "Strike tents and march away." The bugle notes had scarcely ceased before the entire corps of sixteen thousand men was in line for a night march of eighteen miles. The route ran through a succession of small villages. The houses were all illuminated, while among the cherry trees, beside the road, stable lanterns had been hung. The inhabitants exhausted their stores of bread, honey, coffee, milk, and

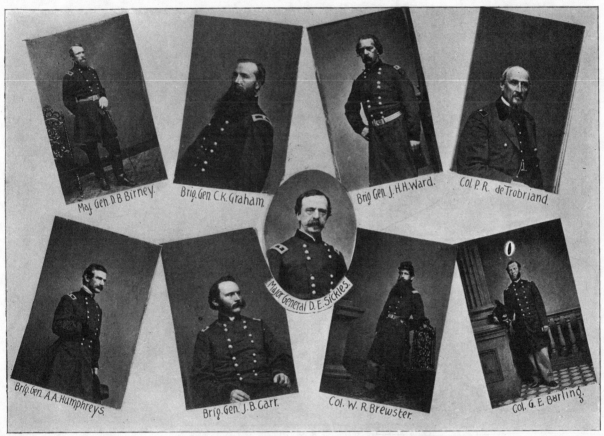

Maj. Gen. D. B. Birney.   Brig. Gen. C. K. Graham.   Brig. Gen. J. H. H. Ward.   Col. P. R. de Trobriand.

Brig. Gen. A. A. Humphreys.   Major General D. E. Sickles.   Brig. Gen. J. B. Carr.   Col. W. R. Brewster.   Col. G. E. Burling.

COMMANDING GENERALS, THIRD ARMY CORPS, AT GETTYSBURG, PA.

cheese by giving it freely to the men in the marching column. All night these people stood at their garden gates watching the solid masses of infantry tramp steadily forward.

It was two o'clock in the morning when the Fifth Corps was halted in an open field. Then word was passed for bivouac, so the men stuck their bayoneted muskets into the soft earth and threw themselves on the ploughed ground, almost instantly falling into slumber. There were a few houses near by, and those of us who remained awake learned from a countryman that we were on the outskirts of a town called Gettysburg. At five o'clock the brigade bugles began again, and the men rose wearily from their warm blankets. Building small fires out of fence-rails to boil their coffee, these veterans munched hardtack and waited for orders. Everybody knew that marching was over for a time, for even at that early hour brisk, crackling musketry was going on somewhere in front, showing that the pickets had found something to do. As the corps moved out into the road a few pieces of artillery gave tongue, the reverberations of the cannon having a muffled sound as we marched through the mists that were rising from the damp earth. Coming to a culvert, the line diverged into the fields, leaving the dusty road for the reserve artillery. Over on the left of the road long lines of canvas-covered wagons could be seen in the gloom. A few hundred yards further on we came to a beautiful evergreen hedge, six feet high and carefully trimmed. Just then a battery came crashing through the hedge, each section cutting its own path. As the column of infantry opened to give passage for cannon and caisson I noticed how completely the hedge had been destroyed, for there were three broad gaps showing where the heavy pieces had cut down the neatly trimmed plants.

But it was no time for sentiment, so on we went until the sun rose bright and warm. We had now re-entered the road, and followed it for nearly a mile, when the leading brigade turned into a piece of woodland. Here the corps was again halted, and the men,

COMMANDING GENERALS, FIFTH ARMY CORPS, AT GETTYSBURG, PA.

finding that no movement was intended, stretched themselves on the ground and fell asleep. We remained quiet for two or three hours, when the bugles again sounded, and the troops listened to the bulletin issued by General Meade. It reminded the veterans of the McClellan days, and they smiled grimly as they listened. But, to the astonishment of all, the bulletin simply said that it must be a soldiers' battle, not the general's. This was something new, and coming, as it did, from the man who had so long commanded the Fifth Corps, it meant a good deal to the men of the Maltese cross. Scarcely had the bulletin been read than the corps was again in motion.

Moving leisurely through the woods, we came to a broad open meadow, and while crossing it the musketry and cannonading on the battle line grew more fierce and vengeful, showing that the enemy was growing active. But the men gave very little heed to the uproar, knowing that their turn would come soon enough. On the other side of the meadow were more woods. It was now eleven o'clock, and eyelids were still heavy for lack of sleep, so in less than ten minutes nearly every man was dreaming.

BATTLE OF GETTYSBURG—COMMANDERS OF ELEVENTH, TWELFTH, AND CAVALRY CORPS.

COMMANDING GENERALS, SIXTH ARMY CORPS, AT GETTYSBURG, PA.

CHAPTER XLI.

GETTYSBURG—THE STRUGGLE FOR LITTLE ROUND TOP.

When General Hancock left the field at sunset of July 1 to report to General Meade the Federal line consisted of the First Corps, under General Newton; the Eleventh, under General Howard, and the Twelfth, under General Slocum. Hancock's Second Corps, arriving about sunset, was ordered by Slocum to take position on the left of the established line, and when Sickles marched up with the Third Corps he was directed to extend the line further to the left, along Cemetery Ridge. General Meade personally examined the ground at dawn of July 2. He found no occasion for changes, as the corps generals had taken advantage of every obstruction in placing their men. The country around the picturesque town of Gettysburg is of a rolling character, consisting of a series of ridges. Gettysburg nestles at the base of these, and it is the centre of radiating roads. All of these were full of Confederate and Federal troops or wagon trains, so that a section of country fully twenty miles square was under the pressure of vast bodies of armed men and cumbrous impedimenta of war.

The configuration of the ground on which these two imposing armies were to meet in the mighty shock of

GENERAL ROBERT E. LEE, C. S. A.

battle is admirably suited for that purpose. Cemetery Ridge lies south of Gettysburg, and is some four miles long. Its general outline is that of a fish-hook. The shank consists of Big and Little Round Top, the first four hundred feet high, the latter nearly two hundred and eighty. The stem is Culp's Hill, the point is called Wolf's Hill. At the base of the Round Top flows Plum Run Creek, and between Culp's and Wolf's hills meanders Rock Creek. The entire ridge is broken up by numerous rocky ledges and outcropping strata, mingled with huge boulders. On the west of Cemetery Ridge extends a narrow valley, through which passes the Emmettsburg road. On the other side of this valley, fated to be deeply dyed with human blood, rises Seminary Ridge, from which General Buford and his cavalry division had been driven the day before. In

BATTLE OF GETTYSBURG—COMMANDERS FIRST ARMY CORPS, C. S. A.

the centre rises Oak Ridge. The outline of Cemetery Ridge is that of a crescent, over five miles long.

While General Meade was examining the Federal line with General Warren, his chief engineer, and General Hunt, his chief of artillery, Generals Lee, Hill, and Longstreet were consulting on Oak Ridge, which gave them a clear view of the opposing army. Having planted their batteries along the Ridge, the Confederate line was formed, Longstreet's corps being on the right, opposite the Round Top, Hill's in the centre, confronting Howard and Hancock, while Ewell held Lee's left and stood against Slocum on Culp's Hill. It is a curious fact that this disposition of Lee's eighty thousand men left an opening in his line almost a mile in width.

It was evident to the Confederate generals that the Federals intended to stand on the defensive, Meade's principal reason being that he did not have his whole force on the ground, as Sedgwick was miles and miles away and French remained at Frederick watching the Potomac Fords. In fact, even when the Sixth Corps did arrive the effective Federal strength was only eighty-four thousand, as the cavalry was of little use on the field.

The sun now rose above the tops of the woods and poured its fierce heat on the scene. A soft breeze fluttered the tree-leaves and made the standing wheat in the fields wave like ripples on a sheet of water. It did not seem to be a battlefield until the careful eye de_ tected, here and there, long lines of butternut or blue, as the Confederate or Federal bri- gades assumed some new position. Next there came to the ear a few dropping shots of musketry as the pickets fell within range, and now and then a cannon would give an angry bark and a shell go flying through the morning sunshine. So carefully did General Lee

BATTLE OF GETTYSBURG—COMMANDERS SECOND ARMY CORPS, C. S. A.

prepare for the attack he contemplated that it was four o'clock in the afternoon before he made any decided movement. There had been a feint by Ewell during the forenoon, but it came to nothing, as Slocum was alert.

When General Sickles had been ordered to extend the Federal left his instructions were to keep close connection with Hancock's line. Instead of doing so, he advanced to the Emmettsburg road, thus throwing his line into the air, a proceeding that came near proving fatal.

Sickles' advanced line was accordingly selected for the Confederate point of attack. While Meade and Sickles were discussing the position Longstreet's artillery opened in most furious fashion. Seeing at a glance that the battle had opened, General Meade hurried off to send Sickles some assistance. Humphrey's division formed Sickles' right, along the Emmettsburg road; Birney's division had been thrown forward into a peach orchard, where Graham's brigade was posted, the brigades under De Trobriand and Ward moving in an oblique line toward the Little Round Top. Under the protection of a terrific artillery fire, which wrapped the Third Corps in a mantle of flame, Longstreet swept forward with twenty-five thousand infantry, Hood's division being on his right. Suddenly the Confederate line swayed to the right, evidently bent on seizing the Round Top. Thus

BATTLE OF GETTYSBURG—COMMANDERS THIRD AND CAVALRY CORPS, C. S. A.

it was that Ward's brigade received the first shock, but soon the whole corps was desperately engaged. For an hour did the struggle continue, until both of Sickles' flanks were partially enveloped. The Third Corps fought determinedly to hold its ground, but was slowly forced back, until there seemed great danger that the left of Meade's army line would be turned and overthrown.

When the fierce crash of cannonading broke out on Sickles' front the men of the

Fifth Corps were sleeping or resting. Then the hot air was shaken by rapid exchanges of cannon shots, accompanied by vengeful bursts of musketry. "What has happened?" was on every lip. A few minutes after, a staff officer rode up to General Sykes, who was conversing with Generals Ayres and Weed in a little dell, and the writer noticed that his face was covered with blood. He had uttered only a few words when Ayres and Weed galloped off, and the corps headquarters bugler began an alarm, the refrain being quickly taken up by the division and brigade bugles. In less time than it takes to write it the entire nine brigades were on the double-quick and going in the direction of the uproar that had now become almost deafening.

Turning into a narrow road, the Fifth Corps raced along, there being no need for the colonels to urge their men forward, for all realized that a critical moment had come and the sooner we got to the scene of threatened danger the better. As the column passed over a rise in the road I could see a dense cloud of white smoke, which was illumined by fitful flashes as the batteries barked angrily and the infantry poured in a leaden hail. Twenty minutes of this headlong pace brought us a mile nearer the fight, and in ten minutes more we were right in its midst. Descending a sharp pitch in the road, we saw a confused mass of men struggling for the mastery. The blue and the gray seemed inextricably mixed, and how we were to distinguish between friend and foe was a puzzle. But the three divisions here separated, the First, under General Griffin, going to the right in columns; the Second, under Ayres, keeping to the road, while Crawford and his Pennsylvania Reserves were halted for an emergency.

Pell-mell went the First and Second divisions, cutting their way through the Third Corps and forming in line to confront Longstreet, who had doubled up Sickles' left flank and flung it back on his centre. Just before making the charge, a litter was carried past our moving column, and the bearers whispered that they carried their general, who was to lose his leg. We charged a battery and captured it. As the guns were being dragged away I saw that Griffin's brigades had struck Longstreet's main force, but just at that moment our brigade line broke away on the left, and we soon found ourselves clambering a rocky hill which we subsequently learned was the Little Round Top. It proved to be an awful hard climb, for the hill was mainly rubble-stone, which made footing uncertain. At every step men fell dead or wounded before the volleys that were poured into our faces from the apex of the hill. Up—up we struggled, and on reaching the summit the leading line gave a hoarse cheer, for Longstreet had lost the Little Round Top, never to regain its possession. The two brigades under Vincent and Weed, which won the position, had, however, suffered heavily, among their killed being the two brigadier-generals and Colonel O'Rourke of the One Hundred and Fortieth New York. Captain Hazlitt, who had succeeded General Weed in command of his famous battery, hastened to the side of his old commander, who was mortally wounded by a Confederate sharpshooter after the position had been taken. The General was lying on a stretcher among some boulders, and Hazlitt bent over him to receive his dying instructions and private letters.

"Weed," said Hazlitt, "I hope you will be able to carry home these messages yourself." "Why do you say that?" replied the General, faintly. "Don't you see I am as dead as Julius Cæsar?"

As he uttered these words a bullet from the same death-dealing rifle crashed through Hazlitt's skull, and the artillery captain fell forward on his knees, a corpse, across the form of the dying general. Weed, turning his eyes downward to look at his friend, said, sadly: "Poor Hazlitt! he has gone before me," and then expired.

It was General Hood's favorite Texan brigade that had seized the Little Round Top, but Plum Run Creek had delayed their movement, so that these Texan veterans had not time enough to establish a line before they were assailed by the Fifth Corps. Being

LITTLE ROUND TOP AND BIG ROUND TOP.

LITTLE ROUND TOP.

FEDERAL ENTRENCHMENTS ON LITTLE ROUND TOP.

"VALLEY OF THE SHADOW OF DEATH" OR THE SLAUGHTER PEN, BETWEEN THE TWO ROUND TOPS.

BIG ROUND TOP, SHOWING FEDERAL ENTRENCHMENTS ON LITTLE ROUND TOP IN FOREGROUND.

BATTLEFIELD OF GETTYSBURG, PA.

driven back, General Vincent's brigade, consisting of the Twentieth Maine, Colonel Chamberlain ; Forty-fourth New York, Colonel Rice, and the Sixteenth Michigan, Lieutenant-Colonel Welch, formed line along the crest of Big Round Top, on the left of Little Round Top, while Weed's brigade, now under command of Colonel Garrard, consisting of the One Hundred and Fortieth New York and the One Hundred and Forty-sixth New York, held the Little Round Top, supported by some regulars. Back came the Texans with other brigades from Hood's division, uttering fierce yells. In three lines rushed the Confederates, but they were met by a withering musketry volley, accompanied by rapid rounds of grape from the depressed guns of Hazlitt's battery, which had climbed up the Round Top. Again were they driven back, only to return and be beaten once more. For nearly an hour did the struggle continue, with awful slaughter on both sides, until finally the Texans fell back beyond a ledge of rocks on the other side of the hollow, afterwards given the name of "The Devil's Glen."

It was General Gouverneur K. Warren, the Chief Engineer of the Army of the Potomac, who really saved the Round Top, for he took the responsibility of sending Vincent and Weed to fight for its possession. General Warren was of an extremely nervous temperament. His bravery was undisputed, but in the midst of a battle he seemed querulous and excited. He invariably and intuitively grasped the situation at a glance, but grew so excited that his simplest order was uttered in a passionate manner. Nothing angered him so much as a mistaken interpretation of his commands, and if a brigadier failed to carry out the movement he had planned his passion knew no bounds.

Warren was an ungainly horseman. His engineering studies and tendencies rendered him careless of his equitation. If he had a position to reconnoitre he would leap out of the saddle in order to clamber on top of a rock scarcely any higher than his horse's back. There on foot, with solid ground under him, Warren could plan at leisure and with ease. Neither was he particular regarding the sort of horseflesh at his command. His rank gave him a right to the best, and the quartermaster always saw that he was well mounted. He paid no attention to the matter. The animals might be changed daily and the fact entirely escape Warren's attention, so long as the old saddle remained.

But neither Longstreet nor Hood gave up hopes of finally securing the Round Top, for, withdrawing from in front of General Griffin, the Confederates formed in solid mass in the woods, and advanced at sunset. Scarcely had the first line shown itself when Griffin's batteries opened a flanking fire of grape which shattered it. Then a second and a third line came pouring out of the woods and rushed across the glen. Again did the Federals open with vengeful volleys of lead and iron, compelling the Confederates to sullenly retire. Desperate as was the struggle for the possession of the Round Top, the fighting along the line of the Third Corps was still angry and vengeful. When Sickles was wounded, Birney assumed command, there being no time to summon Humphrey, the ranking division commander. Birney found McLaws' division and several regiments from Anderson's division opposed to him, Longstreet's evident intention being to crush the apex of Sickles' ∧-shaped line.

Sweitzer's and Tilton's brigades of the Fifth Corps now rallied to Birney's support, but the Confederates had succeeded in advancing a couple of light batteries, which enfiladed the Peach Orchard. Birney's men fell back, and took a new position on a wooded knoll lying between a wheat field and the Round Top. Here the fighting was resumed with the same headlong dash and fury that had characterized all the movements during the day in that part of the field. Both Birney and Hancock saw the pressing necessity for closing the gap between them, and the latter sent Caldwell's division to extend the line and support Birney. Away went the men of the Second Corps, Cross's and Kelley's brigades being in advance. As these fresh troops rushed into the flame and smoke of battle Long-

VIEW AT TROSTLE'S BARN.

VIEW AT TROSTLE'S BARN

FEDERAL ENTRENCHMENTS LITTLE ROUND TOP.

FEDERAL ENTRENCHMENTS LITTLE ROUND TOP.

LITTLE ROUND TOP.

FEDERAL ENTRENCHMENTS LITTLE ROUND TOP.

LITTLE ROUND TOP.

FEDERAL ENTRENCHMENTS LITTLE ROUND TOP.

BATTLEFIELD OF GETTYSBURG, PA.

street's men gathered in heavy force and met them with a frightful volley of musketry and grape. General Cross was killed at the head of his brigade, and the Federal loss was a very heavy one. Seeing the line faltering, Zook's and Brooke's brigades sprang forward with a loud cheer, and the battle raged with even greater fury. Foot by foot the Confederates were forced back, but the musketry on both sides was so steady that the fighting soldiers found it difficult to avoid their dead and wounded comrades who were falling thickly among them. The angry buzz of bullets, the cruel swish of grape and canister, stunned the ears of these contending troops, while above these murderous sounds rose the piercing shrieks of shells thrown from Longstreet's reserve batteries on his right and from the Round Top on Meade's left.

Here General Zook fell mortally wounded, but Brooke carried forward both brigades and drove the Confederates from their position. McLaws and Anderson were not to be entirely shaken off, however, for they quickly reformed and charged through the Peach Orchard with every available man. So impetuous was the onslaught that Caldwell's entire division was compelled to retire, which brought the Confederates on Sweitzer's brigade, when it in turn was torn and hurled back. At this supreme moment General Ayres came up with the brigades of Regulars, who stemmed the tide for a time, but McLaws had gathered his men into a compact mass, and it was impossible to stop their progress. So back went Ayres and Caldwell and Birney to form a new line along a ledge of rocks on the right of the Round Top. This brought McLaws' and Hood's men together right in front of Round Top, and another effort was begun to seize that elevated position.

At this moment General Warren was on the Round Top, standing on a boulder, regardless of the sharpshooters' bullets that were whistling about his ears. As General Crawford's Pennsylvania Reserves, the Third Division of the Fifth Corps, had not yet fired a shot, Warren decided to call upon them, for, as he afterwards said, Pennsylvania troops could be relied upon to fight on the soil of their own State. Sending for Crawford, the Chief Engineer pointed into the Devil's Glen, where Longstreet's divisions were visibly forming for a charge. Then Warren exclaimed, in a harsh, sibilant voice:

"Crawford, there's your chance; I want those brigades driven back—do you think you can do it?" The former surgeon of Fort Sumter stroked his long, luxuriant whiskers and calmly replied, "We can try."

Then there came a long line of men, each wearing a bit of fur in his cap. With a cheer, these famous "Bucktails" spread themselves along the face of the Round Top and went scrambling down the slippery declivity. At the same moment there was a sudden movement in the road as the remainder of the division rushed into the glen. Seizing a flag, Crawford led the Reserves on a headlong, resistless charge. The struggle that ensued was a desperate one, the troops on the Round Top seeing the General still mounted and waving the flag over his head. For fully twenty minutes these Pennsylvanians, Texans, and Carolinians fought with the fury of demons. Finally the Confederate line gave way, and it fell back to the shelter of the woods, broken and confused. Then the Federal line from the Round Top to Hancock's left was filled up and straightened, and the battle on that part of the field ended, for darkness soon fell on the scene, and the exhausted troops on both sides rested.

CEMETERY GATE, LUNETTES THROWN UP TO PROTECT GUN OF BATTERY B, U.S. ARTILLERY.

BRYAN'S HOUSE, IN 2ND CORPS LINE NEAR PICKETT'S CHARGE.

CEMETERY HILL, SHOWING POINT OF ATTACK OF LOUISIANA TIGERS.

SHOWING POSITION OCCUPIED BY 9TH MASS. BATTERY AND THEIR DEAD HORSES.

TROSTLE'S HOUSE.

GROUND OVER WHICH LOUISIANA TIGERS ADVANCED TO ATTACK FROM STEVENS KNOLL.

CULPS HILL, IN THE FOREGROUND BALTIMORE PIKE AND LUNETTES PROTECTING GUNS OF REYNOLDS BATTERY.

GETTYSBURG, PA.

GETTYSBURG, PA.

CHAPTER XLII.

GETTYSBURG—THE CONFEDERATE ASSAULT ON CULP'S HILL.

The Sixth Corps arrived on the field of Gettysburg while the brigades of the Fifth Corps were rushing to the left of Meade's line. Sedgwick's men had been on foot since eight o'clock the previous night, having marched sixty-eight miles in thirty-one hours. The Fifth Corps covered sixty-six miles in thirty-two hours. Every musket-bearer carried, besides his nine-pound weapon, a bayonet, one hundred rounds of ball cartridge, six days' rations, an overcoat, blanket, a piece of tent, and a hatchet or a frying pan. The marches made by these troops illustrate the tremendous strain frequently placed upon soldiers.

While Hood and McLaws were fighting the Third and Fifth corps the division under Anderson was moving toward a depression in Cemetery Ridge. When Sickles advanced his line to the Peach Orchard Humphrey's division was facing to the right, so that when Longstreet's three divisions moved forward Humphrey was exposed to a severe cross-fire, but he held his ground until orders came to fall back to the Ridge. Then Anderson hurled the brigades of Perry, Wilcox, and Wright upon that part of the Federal line. These three brigades were perfectly fresh, and drove Humphrey's men up to Round Top Ridge, which brought the Confederates within close range of the Second Corps. Hancock's men rose from behind a stone wall and poured in so destructive a volley of musketry that Anderson's division reeled under it and finally withdrew, leaving the ground thickly covered with dead and wounded men.

General Slocum's Twelfth Corps at that time stood on Meade's extreme right, on Culp's Hill, with Howard's Eleventh Corps and Wadsworth's division of the First Corps. In front of them was General Ewell, who had received orders to make a simultaneous assault with Longstreet. But Ewell did not attack until late in the afternoon. Consequently Meade transferred Slocum's corps to the left, leaving only Greene's brigade. Lying between Culp's Hill and the right of Cemetery Ridge is a small ravine. On the right of this gully stood Stevens' Maine battery, while on the left Howard's corps was sheltered by a stone wall, Ricketts' and Wiedrich's batteries being posted on the summit of the Ridge. As the men on the Federal right were listening to the turmoil attending the struggle for the Round Top several of Ewell's batteries on Benner's Hill, a little to the north of

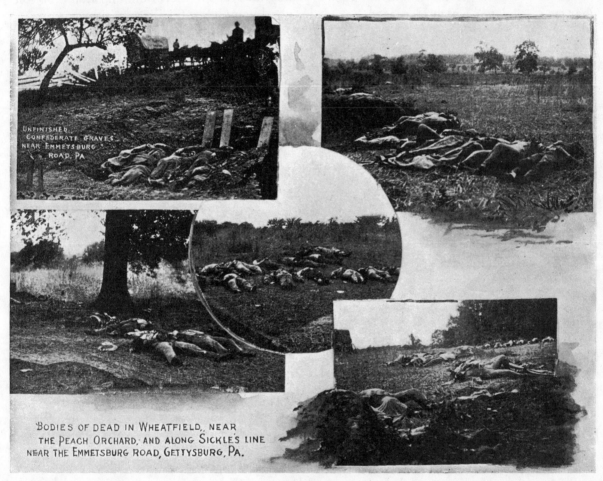

UNFINISHED CONFEDERATE GRAVES NEAR EMMETSBURG ROAD, PA

BODIES OF DEAD IN WHEATFIELD, NEAR THE PEACH ORCHARD, AND ALONG SICKLE'S LINE NEAR THE EMMETSBURG ROAD, GETTYSBURG, PA.

BATTLEFIELD OF GETTYSBURG, PA.

Culp's Hill, opened a furious cannonading. The hour was six o'clock, and the attack was unexpected. The Twelfth and Eleventh corps batteries responded briskly, and succeeded in silencing the opposing guns. At sunset General Ewell massed his two divisions of infantry under Early and Johnson, and sent them to assault the Federal positions, Early going against Howard and Johnson moving on Culp's Hill.

General Early had Hoke's and Hays' brigades, including the Louisiana Tigers. These troops marched up in splendid shape, until within six or seven hundred yards of Howard's line. Then all of the Federal batteries on both sides of the gully opened with grape and canister, the charges tearing wide gaps in the Confederate ranks. But Early's men pushed on until they were within musket range of Howard's stone wall. Then a flash of hot flame sprang up, and a dense white cloud of smoke wrapped the wall as the

Eleventh Corps poured five thousand bullets into the advancing column. Early's left and centre was shattered by this deadly discharge of leaden hail, and fell back, but his right managed to press forward and leap over the wall. A desperate hand-to-hand contest followed, the Federal artillery being helpless, for the gray and the blue were mingled together. So impetuous was this part of the Confederate charge that Wiedrich's battery was captured, many of his men being bayoneted over their guns. Onward swept the line until Ricketts' battery was reached, when another sanguinary conflict ensued, but the artillerists saved their guns by heroic personal effort. Hancock now sent over Carroll's brigade, which found the Eleventh Corps in a state of confusion. Rushing into the mêlée, Carroll's men delivered a well-directed volley, which decimated the Confederate line and forced it to retire. Ricketts' battery then resumed its fire, the men ramming home double charges of canister, which increased Early's loss and completed his discomfiture.

BATTLE OF GETTYSBURG.

As Early moved forward Johnson essayed to take Culp's Hill. Johnson's first line of battle consisted of Jackson's old "Stonewall Brigade." Wadsworth's division and Greene's brigade had fortified the hill during the day, being tolerably well protected. Johnson's division lost no time in crossing Rocky Creek, in water about knee-deep, and gained the dense woods along its banks. The Federal skirmishers retreated to the main body, while the Confederates formed a more orderly line. As yet there had been no musketry, beyond the scattering shots of the discomfited Federal skirmishers, and Johnson's men emerged from the woods in one grand line. Then Greene and Wadsworth opened fire, their volleys being rapid and well delivered, compelling the Confederates to pause. Seeing that Greene's right flank was wholly unprotected, the Confederate general made it his point of attack. Throwing his main force to his left, Johnson gained a foothold on the hill. This brought the brunt of the fight on Greene's brigade, which was being slowly pressed back, when Wadsworth rushed in and drove Johnson's division off the hill and into the woods beyond the creek.   Then there was another of those pauses which are so ominous during an engagement.   The shadows of that hot July evening blotted out the rifts of sulphurous smoke still lingering in the hollows, the tired artillerists dropped their sponges and ram mers, the skirmish lines grew mute, and the second day's struggle was at an end.

The Confederates had failed in their efforts to shake the Federals from the Round Top, Culp's Hill, and Cemetery Ridge, but Meade had lost nearly ten thousand men, killed, wounded, and missing ; Lee, over eleven thousand.   In the wheat field, among the ripening peaches in the orchard, in the Devil's Glen, under the trees in the clumps and belts of woodland, in the shallow waters of Plum Run and Rock creeks, along the steep face of the Round Top, behind and in front of stone walls, beside dismantled cannon,

BODIES OF FEDERAL DEAD ON BATTLEFIELD.

BODIES OF FEDERAL DEAD ON BATTLEFIELD.

DEAD CONFEDERATE SHARPSHOOTER. AMONG ROCKS IN DEVIL'S DEN.

DEAD CONFEDERATE SHARPSHOOTER IN FRONT OF LITTLE ROUND TOP.

BATTLEFIELD OF GETTYSBURG, PA.

everywhere along the front of the Federal positions, lay many thousand corpses.   They were in rows and heaps, a single body here, two or three there.   Lying in every conceivable attitude, the faces of some were peaceful and calm, for death had come swiftly ; the features of others betrayed intense agony.   Some lay on their faces, others on their backs ; others, again, were still kneeling.

It was a dreadful harvest, on ground that had hitherto only resounded to the swish of the scythe or the musical rattle of the reaping machine.   These soldiers in the blue and the gray were lying peacefully together, mere clods of clay, many to sleep forever in "unknown" graves.   All night, mysterious lights could be seen moving hither and thither over the entire field, as hospital parties searched for wounded men.   The soldiers, behind the stone walls they had hurriedly built during the day, watched these relief parties as they passed to and fro, carrying groaning burdens, but, being hardened to the vicissitudes

BATTLE OF GETTYSBURG.

of war, these veterans of so many hard-fought battles boiled their cups of coffee, indifferent alike to the present, the past, or the future.

"Here's Jim Manning, he's got it bad," said one of the men in a hospital party, as they laid a wounded man on the ground occupied by their company. "Here are the boys, Jim." And then the soldiers forgot their coffee-pots and their suppers as they gathered around their wounded comrade.

"Where are you hit, Jim?" asked a sergeant, bending over the stricken man.

"Don't know exactly—somewhere in my side. I got it when we charged down through the hollow. Bob Smith lies down there. He's dead, for the bullet went through his brain, and Frank Judson's dead, too. Tom Griffith got hit in the leg, and crawled back. Where's the captain?"

"Dead; we buried him under the tree, yonder, this afternoon. Here's some hot coffee, Jim; try and drink it."

"Ah! that tastes good. Well, good-bye, boys. We drove them back, didn't we?" and then the fatigue party disappeared in search of a field hospital behind the battle line. Such scenes occurred all along the Federal positions, the work of gathering up the wounded lasting until after midnight, but no attempt was made to bury the dead—that must be left for daylight, if no fighting ensued.

BATTLE OF GETTYSBURG.

PICKETT'S CHARGE.

CHAPTER XLIII.

GETTYSBURG—THE HEROIC CHARGE OF PICKETT'S DIVISION.

The Twelfth Corps returned to the right of the Federal line when the second day's fighting was over. But Johnson's division had crept up in the darkness close to the Federal position and occupied the works on Greene's right. Wholly unconscious that the Confederates had possession of a part of Culp's Hill, General Geary placed some batteries on the higher ground and advanced his division to occupy the abandoned line. A sudden volley of musketry revealed the presence of Johnson's division, so Geary took position on Greene's right, Ruger bringing up Williams' division to face Johnson's flank.

About three o'clock on the morning of July 3 there were signs of activity all along the Confederate right, and General Geary decided not to wait for an attack. The men were awakened and ordered into line, and at four o'clock General Geary discharged his revolver as a signal. On the instant, five thousand Federal muskets opened fire, the fierce volley being succeeded by the deafening roar of twenty pieces of artillery. Then the sun rose, and the battle grew more determined. Ewell's division made several efforts to take Culp's Hill, but was beaten back with heavy loss.

The heat was terrible that morning, and as the men's canteens soon became empty, they suffered greatly from thirst. The gunpowder smoke clung to the ground, but still the fighting went on. Suddenly the woods and the glen and the hill rang with a fierce yell, as Ewell's veterans rushed forward in a solid mass. On they went, down the glen, across the creek, and up the slope of Culp's Hill, until they were scarcely two hundred yards from the Federal breastworks. Then up rose Geary's, and Ruger's, and Greene's men, and poured down a deadly volley, the batteries above their heads throwing thirty double charges of canister right into the charging columns. The effect was magical, for several

Confederate battalions melted away before the terrible discharge, the line shook for a moment, and then Ewell's corps fell back. The position seized by Johnson was then re-occupied by Geary, and Meade's right flank was once more secure.

This struggle had occupied over five hours, the roar and racket rousing the entire Federal army, and as these men on the left and centre stood to arms, along Cemetery Ridge and on the Round Top, every musket was loaded, the throat of every cannon crammed with canister or shell. As no signs of an attack were visible on Meade's centre or left, the men coolly cooked their coffee and satisfied their hunger, careless of the fact that to many of them it was the last meal they would have occasion for.

The forenoon was passing, yet no further movement was visible along Lee's lines. The Federals strengthened their rude stone breastworks and calmly waited for orders. About ten o'clock it was noticed that a few guns had taken position in the open field on the centre of Seminary Ridge, but very little attention was paid to the incident until it was discovered that other Confederate batteries were wheeling into line. Very soon field

JOHN BURNS THE "HERO OF GETTYSBURG" SITTING IN FRONT OF HIS DOOR WITH RIFLE AND CRUTCHES.

SHATTERED ARTILLERY CAISSON NEAR PEACH ORCHARD.

SANITARY COMMISSION HEADQUARTERS.

GETTYSBURG, PA.

officers who carried glasses reported that fully sixty pieces were in view. The massing of these cannons portended some important movement, and Meade's entire army watched this assembling of Confederate artillery with curious interest. Battery after battery came forward and leisurely assumed its place in the bristling line, but not a shot was fired until after the hour of noon.

The Confederate batteries being now in line, numbering nearly two hundred guns, there was an ominous pause, the Federal artillery being busy meanwhile in bringing up every piece that room could be found for along Culp's Hill, Cemetery Ridge, and the Little Round Top. Battery after battery rattled forward, until we had fully one hundred and thirty cannon in bristling array. As Meade's army watched the enemy's preparation a single shot was fired from the right of Lee's line. The shell flew through the hot July sunshine with a piercing shriek and burst over the centre of Hancock's position. Then another and yet another followed, until thirty or forty guns had gone into action, and as the remainder joined in the work Meade's batteries also opened a rapid fire. The roar of this double bombardment now became deafening, for the pieces on either side of the wide field were served with surprising celerity and precision.

For an hour this artillery duel continued, yet there was no abatement in the terrible shower of shot and shell that each of the confronted armies was receiving.

It was now one o'clock, and there were soft shadows passing over the ground between the two armies, as the clouds of white smoke floated in the warm breeze which fanned but did not comfort the opposing troops. Then another hour passed, but the cannonading lost none of its vigor or destructive force. Cannon after cannon was dismounted on either side, or the batteries were withdrawn to grow cool and get more ammunition, their places being taken by fresh batteries, while long lines of wounded men streamed to the Federal and Confederate rear. In front of Cemetery Ridge patches of dead men could be seen, while in our own ranks, on Little Round Top, the losses in dead and wounded were very heavy.

The third hour showed no decrease in the awful discharge of iron hail, and it was not until nearly four o'clock in the afternoon that the fire from the Confederate batteries visibly

BATTLE OF GETTYSBURG.

slackened. Twenty minutes after, it had died away until only three or four cannon were in action, the Federal artillerists dropping their ramrods as the Confederate shells ceased to fall among them.

Then all was silent, even the skirmish lines remaining mute, for no musket had been fired in presence of the heavier metal that had been so long employed. This silence was really more appalling to our ears than the crash and boom of cannon, for we had grown accustomed to the awful din during those perilous three and a half hours. It will never be known how many shells were expended by both armies, but the number has been estimated at over twenty thousand. The light wind had died away, and the smoke lay along the ground like a hot mist, concealing nearly every object on the historic field. Both armies knew that the fierce artillery practice was only the prelude to a more deadly struggle.

As the heavy banks of cannon smoke began rising and melting in the hot sunshine we could see that many of the Confederate pieces were dismounted, while all along the line there lay a thick row of dead men. Half an hour passed, but still no musket shots were fired. There were none of those sounds in the air one hears in field and forest on a summer's day, for the awful detonations of those twenty thousand shells had destroyed all bird and insect life, or hushed it into silence. The reader can have but a faint conception of the contrast between the tremendous thunder of those three hundred and thirty cannon and the absolute absence of sound that followed the artillery combat. The suspense was finally broken by the appearance of a white horse, which passed along the edge of the woods on Lee's left. Then the horseman came galloping back again, and a line of troops emerged from under the trees and formed in beautiful order. As the horseman disappeared behind the woods in which we knew Hood's and McLaws' divisions still lurked this battle line advanced two or three hundred paces. Then a second line left the shelter of the woods, and behind it a third line. Even at that distance, this cool preparation for a charge presented a magnificent spectacle.

General Pickett's division had reached Gettysburg the previous evening, and it had not fired a shot. Lee and Longstreet, Hill and Ewell, had been in consultation during the forenoon of July 3. They had discovered that there was a "fault" in the formation of Cemetery Ridge, and so a charge was decided on that point. Pickett's division consisted of Garnett's, Armistead's, and Kemper's brigades. On his right was Wilcox's brigade, from Hill's Corps, and on his left one of Hill's divisions, under Pettigrew. The Confederate line having been arranged, a few bugle notes floated across the broad field of torn and tattered wheat, and on came that magnificent body of men. The distance to be covered was a little over a mile, but what an awful mile to march, exposed to the enfilading fire of ninety pieces of cannon! It seemed madness to attempt such a task, yet these Virginia veterans moved across the fields as if on review. But when the three lines of battle had fairly got in motion the air was again rent by a furious discharge of artillery, as Meade's guns opened. Contrary to our expectations, the Confederate batteries made only a feeble reply, for Lee's ammunition was running short.

Keeping perfect alignment, the charging body of men moved over the ground until half the distance had been covered. At almost every step men were falling, as the Federal shells exploded over their heads, but the gaps were quickly filled and the lines kept marching on. On reaching the centre of the wide dip between Seminary Ridge and Cemetery Ridge more bugle calls were heard, and the Confederates quickened their pace. This was taken by the Federal batteries as a signal to use grapeshot and canister. Every puff of smoke in front of the Confederates was followed by a wide gap as the charges struck down a dozen or twenty men. Into a dip in the ground went the leading line, closely followed by the others. Then as they again appeared these Virginia troops marched steadily through the yellow wheat-stalks until they crossed the road.

While the Federal artillery was playing havoc with Pickett's command the three corps under Hancock, Newton, and Slocum were preparing to receive the charge. Doubleday's division was on the left of the Federal centre, and Stannard's Vermont brigade was on his right, so far advanced as to be on an angle with Hancock's line, consisting of Hays' and Gibbons' divisions. It was expected that Doubleday's division would be the first attacked, but the enfilading fire from the batteries assembled on the Round Top compelled the Confederates to swerve, so they struck Stannard first. The Green Mountain boys stood fast in the grove and allowed the Confederates to go past their position before opening fire. Then a flame of fire sprang from among the trees, followed by another and another. So terrible was the effect of these volleys that nearly one thousand men surrendered.

Unconscious of this disaster, the main body of Pickett's line swept straight onward, toward Gibbons and Hays. Both the Federal generals rode composedly along their division lines, saying, "Don't be in a hurry, men; wait until they get near enough." Then the Federal batteries, occupying the rugged crest of Cemetery Ridge, flung double-shotted

BODIES OF DEAD IN WOODS, LITTLE ROUND TOP.

BODIES OF DEAD COLLECTED FOR BURIAL, McPHERSON'S WOOD'S.

DEAD CONFEDERATE SHARPSHOOTERS HOOD'S DIVISION:

BATTLEFIELD OF GETTYSBURG, PA.

volleys of canister at the foe. Scarcely had the cannon smoke rolled over the heads of Hays' and Gibbons' men than they rose from their stone walls and poured in a withering fire. Now for the first time the Confederates used their weapons, and a deadly battle began at a range of two hundred yards.

General Stannard's unexpected flanking musketry fire had the effect of pushing Heth's division of Hill's corps, temporarily commanded by General Pettigrew, on the right of Hays' line. It was composed of North Carolina troops, few of whom had been in battle before, and they had been told they were marching to meet raw militia. But when Hays' men rose and lifted their ragged battle flags Pettigrew's men discovered that they were facing the Potomac veterans. Woodruff's battery, happening to occupy an advanced position, reopened with grape and canister, which had such an awful effect that the North Carolinians broke, and nearly two thousand threw down their muskets and became prisoners.

BATTLE OF GETTYSBURG.

But the Virginians were not so easily shaken, for, despite the storm of bullets and grape they were passing through, Pickett's own division pressed forward. General Gibbons had placed Owen's brigade, now commanded by General Webb, behind his batteries. The brigade consisted of the Sixty-ninth (Irish) Pennsylvania, the Seventy-second, Colonel Baxter, and the Seventy-first, under Colonel R. Penn Smith. As Pickett's men rushed for the batteries Owen's brigade opened with steadiness, but so impetuous was the Confederate charge that the first of the Federal lines gave way and fell back on the se ond. Pickett's men leaped over the breastworks, and a fierce hand-to-hand struggle ensued, many of the Federal artillerists being bayoneted beside their guns. It was in this bloody angle that Lieutenant Cushing was mortally wounded while superintending his battery. Feeling his life rapidly ebbing away, the young officer ordered the nearest piece to be reloaded, then, leaning over the trail, he pulled the lanyard and fell back dead.

But it was a last despairing effort on the part of Pickett's division, for Pettigrew's line had been broken and was falling back, and Wilcox had failed to give the support expected of him.   Seeing that his line had been pierced, Hancock now flung Hall's and Harrow's brigades into the breach, Colonel Mallon's Forty-second New York and Colonel Devereux's Nineteenth Massachusetts, of Gates' brigade, also going forward, followed by two of Stannard's Vermont regiments.   By the time these reinforcements reached the scene of conflict their formation was greatly broken, owing to the difficult nature of the ground and the haste with which they moved.   It therefore happened that the Federals and Confederates were fighting by company and squad, instead of by regiment or brigade.   This made the battle all the more deadly.   For half an hour this combat continued, the Federals rapidly outnumbering and surrounding the Confederates, whose general vainly looked for reinforcements.   But no more Confederate lines came marching across the wheat field, and as the odds were growing heavier every minute, these brave men wisely gave up

BATTLE OF GETTYSBURG.

the unequal struggle.   Falling back, another effort was made by Pickett and Wilcox, but it proved too feeble, and resulted in more loss.   Out of the eighteen thousand men who started on the charge nearly five thousand became prisoners, and as not more than eight thousand returned, there were five thousand killed or wounded.

This was one of the many heroic charges that occurred during the Civil War.   The divisions of French, Howard, and Hancock made one on Marye's Heights under Burnside, the Fifth Corps made another at the battle of the Wilderness, and Barlow's division distinguished itself in the same way at Spottsylvania.   Hooker's ascent at Lookout Mountain was a desperate effort, while Thomas's corps covered itself with glory at Chickamauga.   The charge of Burnside's men at Antietam Bridge may be mentioned in the same category.

Such movements are sometimes a necessity, but are always hazardous, because the chances of success are exceedingly slender.   It is now known that Pickett's charge was entirely General Lee's idea.   When General Pickett had formed his line he sought General Longstreet to receive final orders.   He found Longstreet sitting on the top rail of a fence whittling a stick.   General Pickett saluted and said, "General, my column is ready to charge.   Shall I charge?"   Receiving no answer, and waiting a reasonable time, Pickett returned to his command and again rode through the ranks. A second time he reported to the General, with the same result. A third time he reported. General Longstreet was still sitting on the fence. As he received no answer, Pickett remarked, "General, if I am to make the charge it must be made now, or it will be too late. Shall I make the charge?" Without saying a word, Longstreet simply bowed his head. Pickett immediately rode off and led his troops forward.

The battle of Gettysburg was now practically at an end. On the Federal side, General Reynolds had been killed, while Generals Hancock, Sickles, Barlow, and Gibbon were among the wounded. On the Confederate side, Generals Garnett and Armitage were killed, General Kemper was severely wounded and became a prisoner, as were fourteen colonels and majors.

There had also been some fighting between Pleasanton's and Stuart's cavalry toward

BATTLE OF GETTYSBURG.

Bardstown. In the fields near Plum Run Creek General Gregg made a brilliant sabre charge upon Hood's brigade of infantry, which was supported by Stuart's advanced cavalry. In this charge Colonel Farnsworth was killed. This brought the hostilities to a final close.

General Hancock obtained great fame at Gettysburg, and deservedly so. He was an ideal soldier, brave in action yet cool and collected under the most trying circumstances. When emergency arose he showed that fire and headlong courage which so strongly appeal to the musket-bearer, for when the General straightened his splendidly developed figure, and waved his sword to the men behind him, they were ready to follow Hancock wherever he led. It was this personal magnetism, coupled with the dauntless bravery of the man, that gave Hancock that influence over his soldiers for which he was famous. Hancock was an exceedingly genial man, and he was a popular officer to the day of his death, while his memory is warmly cherished by many a grizzled veteran. But I have seen the time when there was no smile on Winfield's face, for if his command was not holding its own his eye grew dark and there was an ominous frown which told of the passion that for the moment agitated him. But scarcely had the tide of battle changed than Hancock's expressive features lighted up and became serene. He looked exceedingly well in the saddle. Those who only saw him after his hair became gray can have no idea of the change in his personal appearance. During the war Hancock had a swarthy complexion, the result of being so much in the open air. His dark hair and huge goatee gave his face a look of sternness, though it was frequently lighted up by a pleasant and engaging smile. His figure was rather slender then, which made him seem taller than he really was.

General Lee's defeat at Gettysburg was the turning point in the war. From that day the Confederate cause waned. The fall of Vicksburg and Port Hudson, to be described hereafter, had the same importance. There was scarcely any firing during the Fourth of July, the national holiday being occupied by both armies in burying the dead. The Confederate loss was five thousand men killed, twenty-three thousand wounded, and eight thousand taken prisoners. The Federals lost two thousand eight hundred and thirty-four killed, thirteen thousand seven hundred and thirty-three wounded, and six thousand six hundred and fifty-three missing or prisoners. There were, therefore, nearly eight thousand killed during the three days, and fully five thousand more died of their wounds during the succeeding ten days. Few battles of modern times have shown so great a percentage of loss. Out of the one hundred and sixty thousand men engaged on both sides, forty-four thousand were killed or wounded.

General Lee executed a masterly retreat over the South Mountain Range, and, crossing the upper Potomac at Falling Waters, escaped into the Shenandoah Valley. Meade's pursuit was feeble and purposeless, though he pushed Lee beyond the Rapidan River. The campaigns in Virginia during the remainder of 1863 were of no importance, the tide of battle drifting to the West.

BRIG. GEN. A. P. HOVEY.

BRIG. GEN. S. ROSS.

BRIG. GEN. J. S. CROCKER.

BRIG. GEN. JOHN E. SMITH.

CHAPTER XLIV.

GRANT'S EXTRAORDINARY MOVEMENT AROUND VICKSBURG.

When General Grant began his operations against Vicksburg in January, 1863, he had four army corps at his disposal, McClernand's Thirteenth, Sherman's Fifteenth, Hurlbut's Sixteenth, and McPherson's Seventeenth. Ordering Sherman's and McClernand's corps

LT.-GENERAL U. S. GRANT.

LEVEE AT VICKSBURG.

to Young's Point, and McPherson's to Lake Providence, Grant proceeded to Memphis and made the necessary arrangements for holding his rear communications. Hurlbut's corps held the Memphis and Charleston Railroad, but the Mississippi Central was abandoned, as were also all the posts on the river, except Columbus, every available soldier and gun being sent to Young's Point. Grant arrived there on January 30, and, assuming active command, ordered McPherson to cut the levee at Lake Providence, hoping to make a new water route to the Mississippi through the Red River at Port Hudson, which is four hundred miles below Vicksburg. Lake Providence is part of the old bed of the Mississippi, is six miles long, and its waters pass through Bayou Macon, Bayou Baxter, and the Tensas, Washita, and Red rivers. This project proved a failure. The old canal, begun by General Williams in 1862, was also deepened and widened, but on March 8 a dam broke and filled up the channel, so it, too, was abandoned. Fort Pemberton stood at the junction of the Tallahatchie and Yallabusha rivers, where they form the Yazoo. It was so low that Grant ordered the levee to be cut opposite Helena, but the water did not swamp the fort. General Ross, with his brigade and two gunboats under command of Lieutenant-Commander Watson Smith, had previously passed through the cut levee, but they could not reduce the fort.

Grant accordingly tried Steele's Bayou, which enters the Yazoo near its mouth, thirty miles above Young's Point. Steele's Bayou connects with a chain of navigable waters known as Black Bayou, Deer Creek, Rolling Fork River, and Big Sunflower River. On March 14 Porter explored this waterway as far as Deer Creek, and found the route apparently feasible. The next day, he and Grant started with five gunboats and four mortar boats. The passage was difficult, owing to the overhanging timber. On February 16 Sherman proceeded on river transports to Eagle Bend, where Stuart's division marched to Steele's Bayou and re-embarked on the smaller steamers. Porter's gunboats got too far ahead, and were attacked, the result of the expedition being finally a failure, and thus ended the fourth attempt to get in rear of Vicksburg. Grant next determined to get below Vicksburg as soon as the subsidence of the spring freshets would give him solid ground to march upon. True to his reticent nature, he did not reveal this plan until the time came for its execution. Commodore Porter entered into it with zeal and alacrity, he and Grant deciding that the gunboats and a sufficient number of river transports should run past the Vicksburg batteries. The steamers' boilers were protected by bales of cotton and hay tightly packed on the decks and along the guards.

At ten o'clock on the night of April 16 Porter started, his flagship, the Benton, leading. The gunboat fleet consisted of the Rice, Lafayette, Louisville, Mound City, Pittsburg, and Carondelet. The river steamers Forest Queen, Silver Wave, and Henry Clay followed, each towing barges full of coal for use by the fleet below. The gunboat Tuscumbia brought up the rear. The Confederates expected the movement, and it was not long before nearly all of their batteries opened fire, the gunners being aided in sighting their pieces by blazing huts or bonfires, which illuminated the surface of the river. For over two hours the Federal fleet was under bombardment, but all the vessels made the passage safely, except the Henry Clay, which caught fire from the explosion of a shell among her cargo of cotton, and she was burned to the water's edge, soon after floating down to Carthage.

In order that the difficulties encountered by the Federals may be understood, it should be stated that Vicksburg stands on a high bluff, which begins on the left bank of the Yazoo River, thence runs in a southerly direction to the Mississippi, continuing down the latter river to Warrenton, six miles below Vicksburg. The Yazoo empties into the Mississippi nine miles above Vicksburg, and the entire bank had been strongly fortified from Haine's bluff, on the Yazoo, to Warrenton, a distance of seventeen miles. The rest of the country is flat and cut up by a labyrinth of bayous, creeks, and swamps. During the winter season these water courses invariably overflowed, so that the movement of large bodies of troops was then impossible.

General McClernand had been sent on March 29 with his four divisions to New Carthage, by way of Richmond, Louisiana, with orders to capture Grand Gulf. The roads were scarcely above water, and McClernand's movement was very slow, for at Bayou Vidal he had to collect boats or construct them in order to ferry his troops across, so that only one division reached New Carthage by April 6, with the remainder of the corps perilously strung along the entire route. But by making a détour and building several bridges the remaining three divisions reached their destination by April 20. McClernand having made a route for the army, General Grant began moving his troops, McPherson's corps being on hand. The march was to be rapid, consequently tents were dispensed with, except a sufficient number for the protection of rations and account books, the generals, officers, and men being compelled to bivouac. As the wagon trains could not carry sufficient rations, six transport steamers and twelve barges were loaded and sent down past the batteries. One steamer and five barges were sunk by the Confederate guns. All these river craft were officered and manned by the troops, a fact which shows the adaptability of Americans. No matter what emergency arose, the soldiers were ever ready to meet it; they built bridges, repaired steamboats, laid railroad tracks, patched boilers, rebuilt locomotives, remounted cannon, made harness, mended muskets, baked bread, reshod horses—in fact, the Federal generals always found men in the ranks who were able from experience to undertake any work that was needed. This rule did not apply in the same ratio to the Confederates, they being more accustomed to agricultural pursuits.

McClernand being on the march, Grant ordered the Seventeenth Army Corps, under McPherson, to follow as fast as the road was opened, and the Fifteenth Corps, under Sherman, was to proceed when McPherson had cleared the way. In order to avoid several swamps and bayous, the route was made from Smith's plantation to the Perkins place, which lengthened the line of march to nearly forty miles. When Sherman had got in motion Grant's entire force was stretched along these forty miles, infantry and artillery toiling along through water and mud. During this laborious movement the cavalry, under Colonel Benjamin H. Grierson, performed brilliant service. Grierson had some seventeen hundred horsemen. He started from La Grange, Tennessee, on April 17, and succeeded in getting in the rear of the Confederate forces. Frequently riding for miles through water up to their horses' bellies, Grierson's men passed over every road, cutting down telegraph poles, burning bridges, destroying railroad tracks, depots, cars, factories, and stores of every description. In fifteen days they marched six hundred miles, and reached Baton Rouge on May 2. Colonel Grierson was deservedly promoted to the rank of Brigadier-General, and he subsequently became a famous cavalry officer.

It was Grant's intention to cross the Mississippi at Hard Times, twenty-two miles below Perkins' plantation, in order to make a landing at Grand Gulf, a strongly fortified position on the east side of the river, just below the mouth of Big Black River. This was the extreme left of the Confederate works protecting Vicksburg on the south. By March 29 McClernand's corps had arrived opposite Grand Gulf; McPherson was in sight, with Sherman close behind. McClernand's corps embarked on transports and barges, Porter's gunboats moving up to cover the movement. The fleet was soon engaged, and cannonading continued for nearly six hours, until finally the shore batteries were silenced. But the forts on the crown of the hill could not be touched by the gunboats, and as the hills were honeycombed with rifle pits and filled with marksmen, Grant reluctantly abandoned the direct attack and decided to move down to Rodney.

Commodore Porter then repeated his feat of running past the batteries. The passage was safely made, though the gunboats suffered considerable damage. There is a long tongue of land extending from the Louisiana side of the river toward Grand Gulf, and the only practical road for the troops was the top of the levee. A landing was finally made at Bruinsburg, a few miles above Rodney, where a good road was found leading to Port Gibson, twelve miles in the interior.

Grant, seeing the necessity of keeping General Pemberton cooped up in Vicksburg, ordered Sherman to make a diversion by going up the Yazoo River to attack Haine's Bluff. So well timed were the orders that Sherman began bombarding on the day McClernand and Porter attacked Grand Gulf. On May 1 Sherman received instructions to leave Haine's Bluff and resume his march for Hard Times. The position of the Federal army was then as follows: Grant's supply depot was at Perkins' plantation, McClernand and the gunboats were at Bruinsburg, McPherson's advance division had arrived at Hard Times, while the remainder of his corps and two of Sherman's divisions were following.

On April 30 Grant had with him McClernand's Thirteenth Corps and two brigades from the Seventeenth Corps. During the ensuing week he was joined by four more divisions, which gave him thirty-three thousand men, with the Mississippi River rolling between him and his base of supplies, but he was on dry ground, and on the same side of the river with his opponent. The Confederate force under Pemberton was about sixty thousand strong, all inside formidable fortifications. General Grant named his command "The Army in the Field," for he had not only cut loose from his base of supplies, but also from all communication with Washington, a display of nerve very characteristic of the man.

McClernand's corps was put in motion on the morning of May 1, and it struck the Confederate forces eight miles from Bruinsburg. Very little opposition was made, General Bowen falling back toward Port Gibson. The section of country through which the Federals were now marching "stands on edge," to use General Grant's expressive phrase, for all the roads were on ridges, and nearly all the land was covered by a dense growth of timber and brush, every ravine being choked with cane brakes and wild vines. The roads to Port Gibson ran over twin ridges, so McClernand had to divide his forces, the divisions under Carr, Hovey, and A. J. Smith going by the right-hand road, while Osterhaus' division proceeded by the left. When Grant arrived at the front he found that Osterhaus had been repulsed, so McPherson was ordered to send John E. Smith's brigade to his assistance, the men plunging through the ravine and striking the Confederate flank, Logan's division pressing forward on the centre. This movement compelled the Confederates to fall back, though McClernand, as usual, began calling for reinforcements, much to Grant's disgust, for he knew that they were not needed.

At daylight of May 2 Grant prepared to push forward. Bowen, having burned the bridges on both roads, had retreated past Port Gibson, which was soon occupied by the

Federals. In order to get across the South Fork of the Bayou Pierre, Grant's men had to build a raft-bridge of logs and material taken from buildings and fences. The entire army crossed the swift current that day and advanced as far as Hankinson's Ferry. Then Grand Gulf was evacuated by the Confederates, and the Federal base of supplies established there. General Grant's little son, Fred, then not quite thirteen, was with the army, and foraged for himself. Charles A. Dana, Assistant Secretary of War, was also present.

On May 7 all of the divisions, except Blair's, had arrived at Grand Gulf and Hankinson's Ferry. Blair was at Milliken's Bend, guarding supplies until fresh troops, ordered from Memphis, could relieve him. A nondescript train was formed of wagons, carriages,

GEN. J. S. GREEN, C.S.A.

GEN. VILLEPIGUE, C.S.A.

GEN. M GREGG, C.S.A.

GEN. JOHN BROWN, C.S.A.

GEN. COCKRELL, C.S.A.

GEN. W. W. LORING, C.S.A.

GEN. L. P. WALKER, C.S.A.

and carts drawn by horses, mules, and oxen, in plough harness, straw collars, rope lines, and other fixtures. The men had been given two days' rations on crossing the river, and they were told the food must last five days, unless supplies could be gathered on the advance. The only thing allowed on the ramshackle train was ammunition, and as there was plenty of it, the vehicles were loaded to their full capacity.

So far, everything had gone well. Grant had succeeded in turning the Confederate flank, and all of his army was together. He had intended to co-operate with General Banks, then advancing from Baton Rouge on Port Hudson, by sending him McClernand's corps, but as Banks sent word that he could not reach Port Hudson until May 10, and had only fifteen thousand men, Grant decided to cut loose from everybody, march into the interior, destroy the Confederate rear lines, and then invest Vicksburg.

CHAPTER XLV.

GRANT'S ADVANCE ON VICKSBURG, AND THE BATTLE OF CHAMPION HILLS.

By May 7 all of Grant's army was across the river, including Blair's division of Sherman's corps and Lanman's division of Hurlbut's corps, making his effective strength about forty-six thousand men. McPherson and McClernand had gone to Rocky Springs, ten miles beyond Hankinson's Ferry, the latter continuing his march to Big Sandy. On May 12 McClernand and Sherman had reached Fourteen Mile Creek, while McPherson was at Raymond. The Federals had thus penetrated thirty miles into the interior, and

BATTLE OF CHAMPION HILLS.

were living off the country. Grant was now entirely cut off, and on May 11 he telegraphed to General Halleck that weeks might elapse before he would again be heard of. A bold proceeding, truly.

General McPherson encountered a Confederate force near Raymond on the morning of May 12. The enemy was six thousand strong, under Generals Walker and Gregg, who took position on Farnden's Creek, and placed batteries to command the two roads over which McPherson's corps was advancing. Logan's division received the first volley, when DeGolyer's battery was ordered up and opened fire, the Confederate artillery making a vigorous response. Suddenly, part of Gregg's brigade made a dash on the Federal guns, but DeGolyer's guns delivered a withering fire of grape at short range, which shattered the Confederate ranks and compelled them to withdraw beyond the creek. McPherson then sent in Dennis' brigade. They were stubbornly met, and suffered severely, the

MAJOR-GENERAL J. B. M'PHERSON.

Confederates maintaining their line. Then the Eighth Illinois, under Colonel Sturgis, rushed forward so impetuously that the Confederates broke and retreated.

Sherman's and McClernand's corps were now moving toward the Vicksburg and Jackson Railroad, over parallel roads. The Thirteenth Army Corps was approaching Edward's Station, the Fifteenth was near Bolton. When Grant learned of McPherson's brilliant little victory he knew that the defeated force would fall back on Jackson, where General Joseph Johnston was expected with several divisions. He therefore ordered McClernand and Sherman to march on Raymond while McPherson pressed forward to Clinton, which town he entered during the afternoon of May 13, and destroyed several miles of railroad track, thus cutting off communication with Vicksburg. Then McPherson and Sherman started for Jackson, where Johnston had arrived in advance of his troops, leaving only Gregg's and Walker's defeated brigades to oppose the Federal movement.

Johnston did not realize that Grant was moving all of his corps at once, and imagined that the battle of Raymond had been fought by a heavy reconnoitring force. He therefore ordered Pemberton to throw himself on the Federal rear by advancing to Clinton. But Pemberton objected to any movement that would uncover Vicksburg, and he procrastinated and lost the opportunity. Meanwhile, Grant's columns marched steadily on, the advance entering Jackson on May 14, Johnston having retreated toward Canton. One of those terrific rain-storms so common in the West at that season of the year now hampered the movements of both armies, but Grant having learned that Johnston had peremptorily ordered Pemberton to cross the Big Black River, he determined to push on through the mud and force a battle. His troops were then in such a position that concentration in the neighborhood of Edward's Station was quite feasible, and it was so swiftly performed that on the morning of the 16th McClernand's corps found Pemberton taking hurried position on Champion Hills, five miles from Baker's Creek. So accurate had been Grant's entire movement that no courier from Johnston reached Pemberton, who, supposing he was going to meet only part of the Federal force, made his advance leisurely. As the Thirteenth Corps came in sight Pemberton received a message from Johnston telling him that he must move northward or they could not unite their forces. Pemberton accordingly prepared for a retreat, and had already sent his wagons to the Big Black, when he found himself compelled to stand and accept battle. Pemberton's right was commanded by General W. W. Loring, his left by General Carter L. Stevenson, and his centre by General John Bowen, each hurriedly throwing up breastworks.

Though Grant had General Hovey's division on the road, with two of McPherson's divisions on the right, and Blair's and Smith's on his left, he decided to wait for the remainder of McClernand's corps before opening fire. But despite the fact that several staff officers were sent to McClernand, urging him to make haste, that general did not reach the ground until the battle was all over. The Confederates, discovering Grant's hesitation, began forcing the fighting, and by eleven o'clock the entire line was engaged. Hovey's division made a charge on two Confederate batteries, stationed on a ridge to the right of the road, and captured one, but Pemberton massed his men on his centre and pressed Hovey very heavily, so he was compelled to abandon his captured guns and fall back half a mile. In this emergency Grant sent first one and then another brigade from Crocker's division of McPherson's corps, thus enabling Hovey to hold his position.

General Grant was sitting on a stump beside the road over which McClernand was expected. He was half a mile in rear of Hovey's line, and he listened to the cannonading and musketry while vainly looking for some sign of the Thirteenth Army Corps. Suddenly General John A. Logan came galloping up a side road, and flinging himself from his saddle, strode over to General Grant.

"General," said Logan, "the road over which my division is advancing turns sharply to the left and will carry us round Pemberton's flank, and slap up in rear of his centre. If Hovey will make one more effort and keep the Confederate line busy I will be able to open on their rear in half an hour."

"You are quite sure the road turns sharply to the left?" said Grant.

"Quite. One of our officers who was captured early in the day managed to escape, and came in over the road. It was he who suggested the movement."

"His name?"

"Captain Norton, Thirteenth Indiana."

"Tell him that I will see he is promoted to the rank of Major. Go and push your division forward as rapidly as possible. I will join Hovey and make the diversion. If you succeed, Logan, we will win this battle without McClernand."

"In twenty minutes you will hear my guns going," said Logan, and he disappeared.

Grant also galloped to the front, for he had become infected by Logan's enthusiasm. Briefly explaining the situation to General Hovey, he rode among the troops and told them what he expected them to do. The men cheered lustily, and when the order came they moved forward so steadily that the Confederate centre found it difficult to maintain its position. Suddenly the roar of cannon broke out on Pemberton's rear, and a few of Logan's shells came flying over the heads of Hovey's men. Then panic seized Bowen's division, for Stevenson's line had broken and came rushing along the centre. The whole line now retreated in confusion, Hovey and Logan pushing forward and gathering up prisoners. General Loring, who held the left of Pemberton's position, found himself entirely cut off, and was compelled to leave all of his field pieces on the ground.

With the cheers of the victorious divisions ringing in his ears, General McClernand came up with Carr's and Osterhaus' divisions. · Without deigning to ask an explanation for his tardiness, Grant ordered the Thirteenth Corps to take up the pursuit. Spurred into retrieving his error by the knowledge that an important engagement had been won without him, General McClernand entered on the pursuit with ardor. He had reached the field at four o'clock in the afternoon, and his two fresh divisions pushed forward until after nightfall, when they bivouacked near Edward's Station, and resumed their movement on the following (Sunday) morning, until the Confederates were encountered in some strong earthworks protecting the railroad bridge on the Big Black River.

The Federal force actually engaged in this battle of Champion Hills was fifteen thousand men; the Confederate, nineteen thousand. Grant's loss was twenty-four hundred and ten; Pemberton's, over six thousand. Loring's division was so completely cut off from the main body that it never reached Vicksburg. Pemberton got safely across the Big Black River, but he had lost thirty pieces of field artillery.

BATTLEFIELD OF BIG BLACK RIVER.

CHAPTER XLVI.

THE BATTLE OF BIG BLACK RIVER, AND THE ASSAULTS ON VICKSBURG.

A notable characteristic of General Grant was his vigorous method of pursuit. No sooner did he win a battle than he wanted to have another. So it was not surprising that, having driven Pemberton across the Big Black River, this son of a tanner prepared for fresh attack. The Federal army had now secured an assured position between the Confederate forces under Generals Joe Johnston and Pemberton, and their junction was thenceforward an impossibility. Sunday morning, May 17, saw Grant's troops well advanced toward the Big Black. Sherman had been ordered to leave Jackson and march to Bolton, thence to Bridgeport, where he was to cross the Big Black, eleven miles to the right of Grant's main position. General Blair was sent with his division to join Sherman, who thus had the entire Fifteenth Army Corps under his command. To expedite the movement, Grant sent with Blair the only pontoon train in his possession.

Early on Sunday morning General Carr's division assaulted three brigades under Generals Cockerill, Villepigue, and Green. They were holding a strong line of earthworks on the eastern bank of the river. General Lawler led his brigade to the right until he gained an open field. Then charging before a heavy fire of musketry, his men crossed a ditch, and delivering a terrific volley, clambered over the breastworks with empty muskets. The Confederates, on falling back, found that their comrades had set fire to both of the bridges, which compelled them to surrender. Two thousand prisoners, eighteen pieces of artillery, six thousand stand of small arms, and a considerable quantity of commissary stores was Lawler's reward for his men's gallantry.

The remainder of Carr's division and that of Osterhaus, then pushed forward, and compelled Pemberton's whole line to give way, General Osterhaus being wounded during the hot engagement. While the battle was going on one of General Banks' aides arrived with a letter from Halleck ordering Grant to return to Grand Gulf and co-operate with Banks. Grant read the letter, when, hearing Lawler's men cheering, he rode away, and never saw the astonished messenger again.

The destruction of the bridges enabled Pemberton to gain his main defences around Vicksburg. The Federals built bridges, using bales of cotton instead of boats, or felling trees on both banks, so that they tumbled into the stream and interlaced. All three bridges were completed by daylight of May 18, and the troops began crossing the Big Black. Sherman had reached Bridgeport the previous afternoon, and he crossed that night and the following morning. He was joined by Grant as soon as the latter saw McClernand's corps

BIG BLACK RIVER STATION, MISS.

safely over. Sherman advanced rapidly on Walnut Hills, from which he had been repulsed in December. The garrison was evacuating, and in an hour the Fifteenth Corps was in possession of the position, and a base of supplies was obtained on the Yazoo. McPherson came up by the Jackson Road, while McClernand moved to Mount Albans, and established his line on the Baldwin's Ferry Road. The position of Grant's army was then complete. Sherman stood on the right, covering the high ground overlooking the Yazoo; McPherson occupied the centre, on both sides of the Jackson Road; McClernand was on the left, his line extending toward Warrenton. During the forenoon of May 19 considerable skirmishing occurred, and at two o'clock Grant ordered an assault all along the line, which gained for his troops some advanced positions and better cover from the Confederate batteries. The next two days were occupied in constructing interior roads along the lines from the Yazoo River and Chickasaw Bayou. Rations of coffee, sugar, and bread came up, and the Federals were no longer hungry.

At ten o'clock on the morning of May 22 a furious cannonading began from all the

MAJOR-GENERAL P. J. OSTERHAUS.

BRIG.-GENERAL BENJ. H. GRIERSON.

Federal batteries, followed by a general infantry assault. The Federals behaved most gallantly, in many instances succeeding in reaching the Confederate parapets, and planting their flags, but Pemberton's men made a fierce defence, and when night came the Federals withdrew to their old position. That was the last assault attempted, for Vicksburg was now to be regularly invested.

This second assault led to McClernand's removal from his command. While Sherman and McPherson were telling their commander that they had failed, Grant received a note from the Thirteenth Corps commander informing him that he had captured a Confederate fort, and that the Union flag waved over Vicksburg. McClernand rather imperiously suggested that if Sherman and McPherson pressed forward the victory would be complete. The latter obeyed, only to lose many valuable men, for, instead of taking a fort, McClernand had only captured two lunettes, the Federals who entered them being made prisoners. Then this singular officer wrote a congratulatory order to his men. Instead of having it read to his troops, McClernand sent it to St. Louis for publication. In the document he claimed that he had actually succeeded in making a lodgment in Vicksburg, but had lost it, owing to the fact that McPherson and Sherman did not fulfil their parts. This was not only untrue, but insubordinate, so Grant removed him, giving the command of the Thirteenth Corps to General E. O. C. Ord. The deposed corps commander proceeded to Springfield, Illinois, and there was peace in Grant's military family.

This campaign will always be considered a remarkable military exploit. In twenty days Grant had crossed the Mississippi River with his entire force, had placed it in rear of Vicksburg, fought and won five distinct battles, captured the State capital, and destroyed the Confederate arsenals and military manufactories. His troops had marched one hundred and eighty miles with only five days' rations from the Quartermaster, and had captured over six thousand prisoners, twenty-seven heavy cannon, and sixty-one field pieces. The Mississippi River was now open from Vicksburg to Port Hudson, a distance of four hundred miles. All this had been accomplished by forty thousand men against sixty thousand. The Federal loss was less than four thousand ; the Confederate, fully twelve thousand. General Grant then formally began his siege of Vicksburg, receiving large reinforcements.

U.S. SIGNAL CORPS HEADQUARTERS.

BARRACKS 124TH ILLINOIS INFANTRY.

U.S. QUARTERMASTER'S CAMP, SHOWING CONFEDERATE FORTIFICATIONS IN REAR OF CITY.

U.S. PROVOST MARSHALL'S GUARD HOUSE.

HOUSE OCCUPIED AS U.S. HEADQUARTERS.

VICKSBURG.

MARKET HOUSE.

FEDERAL ENTRENCHMENTS AND "THE COONSKIN'S" TOWER.

BOMBPROOF QUARTERS OF LOGAN'S DIVISION.

STREET VIEW.

ALONG THE RIVER BANK.

VICKSBURG.

SIEGE OF VICKSBURG.

Copyright, 1888, by L. Prang & Co.

CHAPTER XLVII.

THE SIEGE AND FALL OF VICKSBURG.

The works held by Pemberton were seven miles long. Grant's lines of circumvallation extended over fifteen miles. General Halleck ordered reinforcements ·without waiting for a request, and Grant sent for every available man in his own department, brigades and divisions pouring in from West Tennessee, Kentucky, Missouri, and West Virginia. Three of these divisions were from the Sixteenth Corps, under Generals Kimball, Lanman, and Smith, another was under General Herron, and two were brought from the Ninth Corps by General Parke. The entire besieging force was seventy thousand strong, in eighteen divisions and fifty-four brigades. Grant was, however, insufficiently supplied with siege material, for he had only six thirty-two-pound guns, but he borrowed a battery of naval guns from Porter and filled the gaps with field artillery, finally placing in position two hundred and twenty cannon. Rude Coehorn mortars were made out of hard wood logs bound with iron hoops. Small shells were thrown from them with considerable success and accuracy. Commodore Porter brought down all his mortar boats, and began work so earnestly that six thousand mortar shells were flung every twenty-four hours, while the land batteries threw four thousand. This terrible fusillade continued for weeks.

General Joseph Johnston now began moving to Pemberton's relief, and on June 1 Grant prepared to receive him. General Parke's corps, with a division from the Thirteenth, Fifteenth, and Seventeenth, was placed under General Sherman, who faced to the rear, his line extending from the Big Black to Haine's Bluff. On learning the preparations

View of Vicksburg from the River.

Vicksburg.

to receive him, Johnston refrained from any further attempt. In the meantime, Famine stalked through Vicksburg. From full rations the Confederate troops were reduced to four ounces of flour, four ounces of bacon, one and one-half ounces of rice, two ounces of peas, and three ounces of sugar—scarcely enough for one good meal. On the thirty-sixth day of the siege mule and dog meat, with bean flour and corn coffee, formed the daily fare. It was, therefore, but a question of time when Pemberton must surrender.

While the bombardment was going on General McPherson had been mining. On June 25 he exploded his first mine under Fort Hill. The result was terrific, for a vast column of earth, broken timbers, gabions, fascines, and other débris rose in the air to a

GEN. FRANK GARDNER, C.S.A.

GEN. T. GREEN, C.S.A.

GEN. E.D. TRACY, C.S.A.

GEN. H.H. SIBLEY. C.S.A.

height of over one hundred feet. An enormous breach was made in the fort, into which rushed a forlorn hope of one hundred men from the Twenty-third Indiana and Forty-fifth Illinois regiments. They were met by a large force of Confederates, but the Stars and Stripes were planted on Fort Hill. When this assault was made every Federal battery opened fire, the example being followed by the gunboats and mortar boats. Nearly four hundred army and navy cannon went into action for over an hour, filling the air with a cloud of exploding shells. The earth trembled under the repeated concussions and entire forests were set on fire. The assault on Fort Hill was repulsed, however, yet there was another mine exploded on June 28, and a third on July 1, with the same result.

General Johnston finally sent a note to General Pemberton telling him that on July 7 a diversion would be made in order that he might escape. The messenger was captured and the note fell into Grant's hands. The Federal commander accordingly decided to

PEMBERTON'S HEADQUARTERS. GENERAL PEMBERTON TOOK REFUGE FROM FEDERAL FIRE IN A CAVE UNDER THIS HOUSE.

make a general assault on July 6, but on the morning of July 3 a white flag was displayed on the front of General A. J. Smith's division, in Ord's corps. It was borne by General Bowen, the division commander, and Colonel Montgomery, of Pemberton's staff. They carried a letter from Pemberton proposing an armistice, preparatory to capitulation. Grant refused, but agreed to meet the Confederate commander to discuss terms. The meeting took place that afternoon under an oak tree, but came to no result. Returning to his headquarters, Grant summoned his corps and division commanders. Their unanimous voice was for unconditional surrender, but Grant decided to parole Pemberton's army, allowing the officers to retain their side arms.

At ten o'clock on the morning of July 4 General Logan's division marched into Vicksburg and hoisted the American ensign over the Court House. Then the Federals and Confederates began fraternizing, the latter gladly accepting rations from their antagonists. During the day General Grant rode into the city, being followed by more troops. That afternoon he sent a despatch to General Halleck announcing the surrender. The fall of Vicksburg and the defeat of Lee at Gettysburg occurring on the same day lifted the hearts of the Northern people to a sense of thanksgiving, for the war was believed to be over.

The Federal loss during the siege was about nine thousand killed and wounded. The Confederates lost ten thousand killed and wounded, while thirty-seven thousand surrendered, including fifteen generals. Among their killed were Generals Tracy, Green, and Tilghman (the defender of Fort Henry). With the prisoners taken at the various battles before the siege—Port Gibson, Raymond, Jackson, Champion Hills, and the Big Black—the total Confederate loss was fifty-six thousand men. Grant also secured over sixty thousand muskets, all the heavy and light artillery in Pemberton's hands, besides a vast amount of other property, such as locomotives, cars, steamboats, and cotton.

GENERAL J. C. PEMBERTON, C. S. A.

LEVEE AT ALEXANDRIA.

CHAPTER XLVIII.

OPERATIONS ON THE LOWER MISSISSIPPI.

When General Sherman and his division commanders left General Grant's headquarters at midnight of July 3, 1863, they had to ride nearly seven miles before reaching their respective lines. Half an hour's quick trot brought these Federal generals to the interior road of communication, and they halted for a moment. There was only a faint moonlight, as clouds floated through the air, but the light was sufficient for these officers to distinguish each other's faces.

"Do you intend to enter Vicksburg to-morrow?" asked General Parke. "I should like to ride over and see how the place looks."

"Why, Parke, we have better business on hand than that," replied Sherman. "Instead of gloating over those poor devils who have kept us at bay for six months and now give in from starvation, I am going to chase Joe Johnston."

"When do we start?"

"At daylight. General Grant gave me my orders while we were discu sing Pemberton's letters. You will have just time enough, gentlemen, to reach your commands and give the necessary orders."

MAJOR-GENERAL E. O. C. ORD.

In this brief, unceremonious way were Sherman's columns set in motion.　General Ord's Thirteenth Corps was given the advance, and the orders were to move rapidly.　Ord crossed the Big Black River at the railroad bridge.　Sherman's Fifteenth Corps went by Messinger's Ferry, and Parke's Ninth by Birdsong's Ferry, all of the commands to converge on Bolton.　During July 5 and 6 Sherman caught up with Ord, but Parke was delayed at the ferry, so the advance corps had to wait for him.　Johnston received timely notice of Pemberton's surrender, and made a rapid retreat on Jackson.　As the water supply was mainly drawn from pools, the Confederate commander adopted the unusual device of driving cattle, hogs, and sheep into the pools and then shooting the animals.　This caused much suffering among the Federals.

Sherman's troops arrived at the city of Jackon on the 10th, finding the Confederates intrenchments greatly strengthened.　Quickly investing the place, Sherman placed Ord's

BUILDING THE DAM ON RED RIVER TO RELEASE THE NAVY FLEET.

FORT CURTIS, HELENA, ARK.

BUILDING THE DAM ON RED RIVER TO RELEASE THE NAVY FLEET

corps on the right, his line reaching to Pearl River below the town ; Parke's corps occupied the left, and Sherman's the centre, from the Clinton to the Raymond road.　On July 11 all the Federal batteries shelled the town, the infantry lines moving up for a charge. General Lanman carried his division too close, and was severely handled, falling back in great disorder.　General Ord was indignant, as the movement had been made contrary to his orders, so he requested Sherman to relieve Lanman.　This was done, and it ended the division general's military career.

The siege of Jackson was pressed day or night, the Federal artillery being very active, until July 17, when citizens notified General Sherman that Johnston had evacuated the town.　A pursuit was immediately ordered, General Steele's division going as far as Brandon, a distance of fourteen miles.　But Joe Johnston had secured so good a start that he could not be overtaken in such terribly hot weather.　On reporting the facts to General Grant, orders were received by Sherman to return, Parke's corps being sent to Haine's Bluff, Ord's to Vicksburg, and Sherman returned to his old encampment on the Big Black, receiving a new division under Brigadier-General W. Sooy Smith.

ADMIRAL FARRAGUT AND CAPTAIN DRAYTON ON DECK OF U. S. S. HARTFORD, BELOW VICKSBURG, ON MISSISSIPPI RIVER.

ADMIRAL FARRAGUT AND CAPTAIN DRAYTON ON DECK OF U. S. S. HARTFORD, BELOW VICKSBURG, ON MISSISSIPPI RIVER.

During the summers of 1862 and 1863 great activity prevailed on the Lower Mississippi. General Williams, who had accompanied Farragut up the Yazoo, was killed at Baton Rouge, while leading a charge. The Federal gunboats had several battles with Confederate rams, with varying result.

General Banks succeeded Butler in command of the Federal Department of the Gulf, arriving in New Orleans on December 14, 1862, with ten thousand men. Butler had twenty thousand men, some of them colored troops, so that Banks had a force of thirty thousand men, designated as the Nineteenth Army Corps. Banks' orders were to co-operate with Grant in opening the Mississippi, capture Port Hudson, take possession of the Red River region, and expel the Confederate forces from Louisiana and Texas. He entered on this extensive field of operations under somewhat discouraging circumstances, for Gen-

EXCHANGED PRISONERS BELONGING TO THE 19TH IOWA INFANTRY AT NEW ORLEANS, LA.

eral Sherman had just made his futile movement against Vicksburg on the Yazoo River, and Grant had lost his base of supplies.

General Banks, however, sent ten thousand men to Baton Rouge, under General Cuvier, and the Federals took possession of Galveston and Sabine Pass. Then a series of reverses seriously threatened the Federal occupation of both Louisiana and Texas. General Magruder, the defender of Yorktown, commanded the Confederate Department of the Gulf, and he began active operations before Banks could put his forces in motion.

Colonel Merrill had been sent with part of his Forty-second Massachusetts Regiment to serve as the garrison at Galveston. Merrill found Commodore Renshaw in possession of the city, with several gunboats. Renshaw seems to have had a very hazy idea concerning his responsibility, for after the Massachusetts men went into camp he left them unprotected. On January 1, 1863, General Magruder made an attack. The City of Galveston stands on a low, sandy island, connected with the main land by a wooden bridge, two miles long. Renshaw being evidently negligent, Magruder resolved to make a sudden move. There was a bright moon that night, and the Confederate general dashed over the bridge on a train of cars loaded with artillery and infantry, succeeding in seizing

BRIG.-GEN. THOMAS WILLIAMS.

MAJOR.-GEN. GODFREY WEITZEL.

a position for shelling Renshaw's gunboats. The Massachusetts men made a desperate resistance, finally repulsing their assailants. Magruder had fortified four steamboats by packing their guards with cotton bales, and armed them with the heaviest guns in his pos-

BRIG GEN. W. DWIGHT.

MAJ GEN. E. C. AUGUR.

BRIG GEN. GROVER.

LT. COM. R. L. LAW.

session. While his land forces were engaged, these steamboats passed down the bay and attacked the Federal fleet. General Sibley's brigade was in charge of the guns. The Bayou City and Neptune opened the battle by delivering a well-directed fire on the Harriet Lane. Despite the volleys of musketry poured upon her decks, the Harriet Lane ran full tilt on the Bayou City, tearing off her wheel guard. Then the Neptune rammed the Harriet Lane, finally sinking her, and the sixty-eight-pounder on board the Bayou City burst. The Confederate soldiers boarded the Harriet Lane, and a dreadful hand-to-hand conflict ensued, both Commander Wainwright and Lieutenant-Commander Lee being killed, after refusing to surrender.

Commodore Renshaw's flagship, the Westfield, ran aground on a bar, as did the Owasco, and the entire Federal fleet was at the mercy of the Confederates. Commodore Renshaw refused to surrender, deciding to blow up the flagship and escape with his crew on the transports. The train to the magazine burned too rapidly, and the explosion killed two boat-loads of men, among them being Commodore Renshaw, Lieutenant Zimmerman,

HOUSE OF JEFFERSON DAVIS AT DAVIS RUN, MISS.

and Engineer Green. In the confusion Lieutenant-Commander Law took charge of the fleet and escaped to sea with the Owasco, Clifton, Corypheus, and Sachem. The Forty-second Massachusetts was compelled to surrender, and the port of Galveston was again freed from the blockade. The Confederates passed down the Sabine River on January 21 with four cotton-padded steamboats and captured the Federal gunboats.

General Banks next sent an expedition to Brashear City, where Bayou Teche enters the Atchafalaya, eighty miles west of New Orleans. The combined forces were commanded by General Weitzel and Commodore McKean Buchanan, and reached Brashear City on January 11. There were several engagements, and the expedition accomplished its purpose by destroying the Confederate fleet. On March 13 Banks and Farragut advanced on Port Hudson with several gunboats and twelve thousand men. While the troops were landing Farragut tried to run past the Confederate batteries, but failed. During April there was another expedition, the Confederates being driven back to Vermillion Bayou, and the Atchafalaya River was opened to the Red River, and two thousand prisoners were taken, with twenty pieces of artillery and immense stores. General "Tom" Sherman, the hero of Port Royal, was equally successful on Lake Ponchartrain.

MAJOR-GENERAL N. P. BANKS.

CHAPTER XLIX.

SIEGE AND FALL OF PORT HUDSON.

The activity of Banks' movements finally compelled General Frank·Gardner to concentrate the Confederate forces at Port Hudson. His main batteries were admirably constructed, and stood on a high bluff, forty feet above high-water mark. Here fortifications of the most formidable character were erected, the salient angles affording opportunity for delivering an effective cross-fire from heavy guns. Other batteries extended up the river to Thompson's Creek, three miles away, with curtains and artillery lunettes connecting the forts. This wing was further protected by a swamp impassable for troops. Below the batteries there were other intrenchments and forts following a semicircular line round to Thompson's Creek, forming the rear defensive line.

General Banks decided on a general assault, the naval vessels having been cannonading for several days. Farragut had two gunboats above Port Hudson, while Commander C. H. B. Caldwell lay below with four more. The divisions under Weitzel, Grover, and Paine occupied the Federal right. Augur's the centre, and "Tom" Sherman stood on the extreme left.

At six o'clock on the morning of May 27 Banks' guns opened, the gunboats joining. Gardner replied, and a severe exchange of shells and shot continued for several hours. Weitzel and Grover advanced at ten o'clock under cover of a furious artillery fire, but neither Augur nor Sherman got their columns in motion until the noon hour. Weitzel's assault was met by so accurate a discharge of shell that he had to retire. When the entire line charged their progress was hindered by the broken character of the ground and the abatis scattered over every practicable route. After these separate attempts the Federals, under Weitzel and Grover, succeeded in crossing Big Sandy Creek, and drove the Confederates through a heavy piece of woods, finally reaching within striking distance of the rear fortifications. Augur and Sherman were equally successful, so that the Confederates had been driven to their intrenchments by sunset. Then General Gardner opened a flanking fire on Sherman's advanced line, which compelled his withdrawal, Augur also retiring when his left was uncovered. The position being untenable, Banks fell back during the night.

It was now evident that a siege must be entered upon. Orders were sent to New Orleans for heavy guns, and the troops began digging approaches and building forts. Banks soon found that twelve thousand men were not sufficient for a complete and thorough investment of Port Hudson, and asked Grant to send him reinforcements. As stated in a previous chapter, the latter found it inexpedient to do so. On June 11 Banks made an effort to gain a more advanced line, in anticipation of a final assault. The movement began at early dawn, but the attack failed. As he had reason for believing that Gardner contemplated a sortie for the purpose of cutting his way out, General Banks decided to make another effort to carry the place by storm. On June 14 everything was ready, a summons having been sent the previous day to the Confederate general demanding his surrender, but Gardner, naturally, refused, as long as he had shot and shell for defence. Two regiments were pushed into a ravine, every man carrying a six-pound grenade in one hand and his musket in the other, while the men in the companion regiment had bags of cotton, with which they were to fill the ditch, in order that the supporting columns might sweep over the breastworks.

Weitzel's division, with Morgan's and Kimball's brigades, were to begin the assault as soon as it was light enough. Paine's division was placed on Weitzel's left, ready to charge should Paine succeed in gaining the breastworks, while Augur and Dwight were to make a diversion on the right. Passing through a parallel and under cover until they had reached a point less than three hundred paces from the Confederate intrenchments, the forlorn hope sprang forward. Narrow as was the distance, it proved difficult to cross, being covered with vines, brush, and canes, and full of hollows. Knowing where the main attack would be made, General Gardner massed fully one-half of his force at that point, so when the Federals appeared they encountered a fearful series of musketry volleys, accompanied by showers of grape and canister. The men carrying grenades and bags of cotton did reach the ditch, but many of the grenades were thrown back at them and caused frightful loss. Weitzel's and Paine's divisions could make no progress in the face of so destructive a fire, consequently the entire column retreated to its parallel. The efforts of Augur and Dwight also failed, and by noon Banks had suffered a repulse along his entire line. General Paine was wounded and Colonel Abel Smith killed. The only success gained was the possession of a hill which commanded the main fort, and here Dwight rapidly intrenched himself.

That was the last of the assaults, Banks and his division generals agreeing that further sacrifice of human life would be cruel, so the siege went on until July. The Federals slowly dug their way nearer and nearer to Gardner's guns, the opposing pickets being engaged day and night within a range of forty yards. Mining was indulged in with varying success, and the Confederates were compelled to eat mule meat, and what rats they could catch. Finally the largest mine of all was completed, and the Federals were placing barrels in the chamber, when news reached General Banks and his troops that Pemberton had surrendered. The cheering along the Federal lines attracted the attention of the Confederate pickets, and when they inquired the cause, during a temporary cessation of hostilities, received the reply, "Vicksburg has fallen." That night General Gardner consulted

General Beale and Colonels Lyle, Miles, Shelby, and Steadman. They agreed that if Vicksburg had indeed fallen, surrender was the only thing left for them. The following morning Gardner sent a note to Banks asking if the news was correct. Being assured of that fact, he asked for an armistice preparatory to capitulation.

The terms accorded by the Federals were of an honorable character. On July 9 General Andrews, of General Banks' staff, entered Port Hudson with two regiments from each division. General Gardner advanced, and, with visible emotion, tendered his sword. It was declined, because his bravery entitled him to retain it. The order was then given the Confederate troops to "ground arms," and six thousand two hundred and thirty-three brave men became prisoners of war. Banks' trophies consisted of fifty-one cannon, two steamboats, seven thousand muskets, and a considerable quantity of ammunition. The capture of this Confederate stronghold, following so closely after that of Vicksburg, gave the Federals possession of the entire Mississippi River. President Lincoln, in one of his epigrammatic letters, remarked that "the mighty river now ran unvexed to the sea."

BATTLE OF PORT HUDSON.

MAJOR-GENERAL Q. A. GILLMORE AND STAFF.

CHAPTER L.

OPERATIONS IN CHARLESTON HARBOR, AND THE FALL OF FORT WAGNER.

When General David Hunter succeeded General Thomas W. Sherman at Hilton Head he began preparing for an attack on Charleston. On May 20, 1862, the gunboats Ottawa, Unadilla, and Pembina ascended the Stone River to the mouth of Wappoo Creek, six or seven miles from the city of Charleston. A land reconnoissance toward Pocotaligo resulted in the partial destruction of the Charleston and Savannah Railroad. The Confederates, under Colonel Lamar, had constructed a formidable battery at Secessionville, which General Benham attacked on June 11, but his guns proving ineffective, he retired. On the morning of June 16 Wright's and Stevens' brigades advanced over a narrow strip of land, when Lamar opened with grape and canister from a masked battery, and the Federals retired. This ended the operations under Hunter, and no further attempt was made until the following October. General O. M. Mitchell superseded Hunter in September, but he died of yellow fever on October 30. He had planned to approach Charleston by way of Pocotaligo, and General Brannan undertook to execute the movement. Starting out with five thousand men, Brannan ascended Broad River to the Coosawhatchie, thence to Pocotaligo, encountering considerable opposition, the Federals being compelled to re-embark for Hilton Head.

General Hunter resumed command of the depart-

REAR-ADMIRAL J. A. DAHLGREN.

ment after Mitchell's death, but though he had fully thirty thousand men, nothing more was attempted until January, 1863. Admiral Dupont sent Commander Worden up the Great Ogeechee River to attack Fort McAllister, a strong casement earthwork mounting nine heavy guns. Worden arrived opposite the fort on January 27 with the monitor Montauk, some gunboats, and a mortar schooner. The river being obstructed, the monitor could not get within range, so retired. The experiment was renewed on February 1, with better results, for, though the Montauk was struck by sixty large shells and shot, she was not injured, while the fort was considerably battered. The Confederate privateer steamer Nashville was meanwhile prevented from going down to the sea, and when Worden made another attack on February 27 he discovered her aground just above the

QUARTER DECK OF PAWNEE.

OFFICERS ON DECK OF PHILADELPHIA.

QUARTER DECK OF PAWNEE.

DECK AND TURRET OF KAATSKILL.

VIEWS IN CHARLESTON HARBOR.

fort. Opening fire with twelve and fifteen inch shells, the Nashville was soon in flames; one of her guns exploded, and the magazine blew up, completely destroying the privateer.

Admiral Dupont, having received more monitors, decided to see what they could do *en masse.* Accordingly, on March 3, he sent four monitors and some mortar schooners, in charge of Commander Drayton, against Fort McAllister. But the shallow water prevented three of the monitors from getting near enough to be of any use, the Passaic alone reaching a range of one thousand yards. Though nearly three hundred shells were thrown into the fort, it was not reduced. The blockading fleet had captured the English blockade runner Princess Royal on January 27, with a cargo of military arms and ammunition. The Confederates, seeing the captured vessel still at hand, determined to make an effort to recapture her. Taking advantage of a thick haze, Commander Necker and Lieutenant Rutledge ran down the harbor of Charleston with the rams Chicora and Palmetto State. Their appearance was a complete surprise to the Federal fleet. The

ADMIRAL DAHLGREN AND STAFF ON DECK OF PAWNEE IN CHARLESTON HARBOR.

steamer Mercedita was first encountered by the Palmetto State, which rammed her and sent a seven-inch shell into her steam-drum, killing and scalding many of the crew. The two rams then rushed on the Keystone State, which made a desperate resistance until a shell passed through her steam-chest. By this time the remainder of the fleet awoke to the gravity of the situation, and succeeded in making it so hot for the Confederate rams that they steamed back to Charleston.

General Beauregard, who was in command of the Confederates, had fortified the harbor in the most elaborate manner. Fort Sumter was the centre of a radius of forts mounting over three hundred guns, mostly of the heaviest calibre. With Fort Sumter guarding the main channel, there stood on Sullivan's Island Fort Moultrie, Fort Beauregard, Battery Bee, and a sand-bag battery on the extremity, covering Maffit's Channel. On James Island stood Fort Johnson, the Wappoo Battery, and Fort Ripley. Castle Pinckney lay in front of the city, and on Morris Island there were Battery Gregg, Fort Wagner, and a battery on Lighthouse Inlet. All of the channels were blocked with huge iron chains, and an immense hawser, buoyed with empty casks, extended from Fort Sumter to Fort Ripley, the entire harbor being thickly planted with torpedoes.

During the night of April 5 Admiral Dupont anchored his fifteen vessels off the bar, in the light of a full moon, and two days after prepared for action. Dupont decided to run past the Morris Island batteries and attack Fort Sumter at close range. The Weehawken, which led, had a sort of raft fixed to her bow for the purpose of sweeping away obstructions, but it proved more of a hinderance than a help. The Federal fleet passed toward the entrance to the inner harbor without a shot being fired by the Confederate forts,

THE "SWAMP ANGEL" GUN, MORRIS ISLAND.

but when Dupont's vessels encountered the hawser and chains every gun that could be brought to bear opened fire. Finding that the Weehawken could not advance, Captain Rodgers attempted to pass Fort Sumter, but was prevented by a row of piles. Then the New Ironsides was caught by the tideway and drifted, the Nantucket and Catskill falling foul of her, all three being pounded most mercilessly by the neighboring forts. At four o'clock eight of the ironclads had ranged up before Fort Sumter at a few hundred yards' distance and opened fire, while they were receiving the concentrated discharge of seventy-six cannon from Forts Sumter, Beauregard, Moultrie, Wagner, and Battery Bee. The monitors had only sixteen large guns among them. The combat lasted just forty minutes, when five of the ironclads were disabled, the fleet having received twenty-two hundred

FORT SUMTER.

heavy shells and solid shot. Yet only one man was killed, and twenty-nine wounded. Dupont then withdrew to Port Royal, leaving the New Ironsides to guard the entrance.

The Government deciding that Fort Sumter must be reduced, sent General Quincy A. Gillmore to relieve Hunter, and Admiral Dahlgren replaced Dupont, who had meanwhile captured the Confederate warship Atalanta, an English blockade runner that had been rudely armored. General Gillmore found that his force consisted of eighteen thousand men, but as he had to guard a coast of two hundred and fifty miles, his effective force was only eleven thousand, with sixty-six siege guns and thirty mortars. Dahlgren had the frigate New Ironsides and six mortars. The General and the Admiral, however, resolved to make a combined attack.

Gillmore began operations on Morris Island, hoping to capture Fort Wagner and Fort Gregg. He erected strong batteries on the northern extremity of Folly Island, General Vodges being in command of that part of the line. In order to disguise the erection

SERGEANT JOSEPH A. WOOSTER, KILLED WHILE PLANT-
ING THE FLAG ON PARAPET OF FORT WAGNER.

of these batteries, Gillmore sent General A. H. Terry with six thousand men up the Stone River to make a feint attack on James Island, while Colonel Higginson went up the Edisto with two regiments of negro soldiers to destroy a section of the Charleston and Savannah Railroad. Higginson failed, but Terry reached James Island during the night of July 9, and landed, General Strong going with two thousand men down Folly River in boats to Lighthouse Inlet. At daybreak on the 10th Terry's hastily constructed batteries opened fire on Fort Wagner, aided by the monitors, which threw fifteen-inch shells that soon crumbled the works. General Strong then advanced and gained possession of the Confederate batteries on the northern end of Morris Island. The Confederates retreated to Fort Wagner. The next morning Strong made an assault on Fort Wagner, but was repulsed.

General Gillmore now began siege approaches. He soon erected batteries across Morris Island, and on the 18th opened fire on Fort Wagner, Dahlgren shelling both Fort Wagner and Fort Sumter. Fort Wagner responded with only two guns, which led Gillmore to believe that the Confederates were demoralized, so he ordered an assault.

As the sun went below the horizon a terrific storm of rain and thunder began, in the midst of which the Federal column moved forward. The advance was held by Strong's

BATTERY REYNOLDS — FIVE TEN INCH SIEGE MORTARS.

BATTERY WEED — FIVE TEN INCH SIEGE MORTARS.

BATTERY HAYES — SEVEN 300 POUND PARROTTS.

BATTERIES AGAINST FORT WAGNER.

BATTERY RENO,
TWO 100 POUND AND ONE
EIGHT INCH PARROTT.

BATTERY STRONG,
ONE 300 POUND PARROTT.

BATTERY KIRBY,
TWO EIGHT INCH
MORTARS.

BATTERY STRONG,
300 POUND PARROTT
AFTER BURSTING OF
MUZZLE.

NAVAL BATTERY,
TWO 8 INCH
PARROTTS

NAVAL BATTERY,
TWO 80 POUND
WHITWORTHS.

BATTERY ROSECRANZ,
THREE 100 POUND
PARROTTS.

BATTERY STEVENS
TWO 100 POUND PARROTTS.

BATTERY ROSECRANZ,
BURSTED GUN.

BATTERY BROWN,
BURSTED GUN.

BATTERY MEADE,
TWO 100 POUND PARROTTS.

BATTERIES AGAINST FORT SUMTER.

brigade, and included a negro regiment, commanded by Colonel Robert G. Shaw. The supporting column consisted of General Putnam's brigade. These troops had to cross a strip of sand eighteen hundred yards long. They were within two hundred yards of the fort before the Confederates opened fire with grape. With desperate courage Strong's brigade pressed forward to the edge of the ditch, when a blaze of musketry flashed from the parapet. With death staring every man in the face, the Federals began climbing the exterior slope of the fort. It was here that Sergeant Joseph Alvah Wooster, of Company C, Governor's Foot Guard, and color-bearer for the Sixth Connecticut, performed the brilliant deed of valor that cost him his life. Wooster was apparently devoid of fear, for on every occasion that his regiment had gone into action he always managed to get into the thickest of the fight. When given the colors in recognition of his bravery Wooster's colonel cautioned him against unnecessarily exposing himself. But he never heeded the advice. When the Sixth Connecticut reached the fort Wooster scrambled up all alone in advance of the

THE "SWAMP ANGEL" GUN, AFTER BURSTING.

line and triumphantly placed his flag on the parapet. Before the heroic sergeant's comrades could reach his side a Confederate soldier sprang forward, and placing the muzzle of his musket against Wooster's heart, fired. The next instant the color and its brave bearer fell, and no other flag appeared. Sergeant Wooster was a man of deep religious conviction, and always carried a small Testament in his blouse side pocket. Pasted inside the cover was a daguerreotype of his little daughter, and he happened to have another copy of the picture wrapped in paper, which had been placed in his breast pocket. The fatal Confederate bullet that pierced Wooster's heart passed through this second picture, tearing a jagged hole. Both pictures are still cherished by the daughter, now a happy wife and mother, as a sad but proud memorial of her gallant father.

The slaughter of the Federal column was a fearful one, for the entire brigade was torn to pieces, and the Massachusetts negro regiment so murderously handled that not more than sixty men escaped, no quarter being shown. General Strong was mortally wounded, and Colonel Shaw was killed on the parapet, his body being riddled by musket balls. Seeing that Strong and his brigade had been destroyed, General Putnam rushed forward with

A FULL SAP.

ASHCROFT'S BATTERY IN THE 2 PARALLEL.

FORT PUTNAM PREVIOUSLY REBEL BATTERY GREGG.

BOMBPROOF FOR TELEGRAPH OPERATOR IN THE TRENCHES A SPLINTER PROOF.

HENRY'S BATTERY IN THE 2 PARALLEL.

BIRCHMEYER'S BATTERY IN THE 2 PARALLEL.

his brigade. The effort was, however, a vain one, for Putnam was killed, with nearly every commissioned officer in the brigade. Torn and bleeding, the remnants of Strong's and Putnam's commands retired, having lost over half of their strength.

This bitter lesson taught General Gillmore to rely on his siege operations. Parallel after parallel was opened, until by August 9 the Federal cannon were within three hundred and thirty yards of Fort Wagner, the guns being trained also on Fort Sumter and Battery Gregg. The General had a small battery built in a marsh west of Morris Island, mounting an eight-inch Parrott-rifled gun. The soldiers nicknamed this piece "The Swamp Angel," and having a range of five miles, it threw its enormous shells into the city of Charleston.

During all these preparations General Beauregard's forces maintained a continuous

MAJ GEN. G. C. STRONG.

MAJ GEN. GORDON GRANGER.

MAJ GEN. A. H. TERRY.

and severe artillery fire from over two hundred guns. By August 17 Gillmore had twelve heavy batteries ready on Morris Island. On that day the batteries and monitors began a simultaneous bombardment, mainly directed against Fort Sumter. For seven days this terrible fusillade continued, over ten thousand shells and solid shot being delivered, and Fort Sumter was battered into shapeless ruins. On September 5 a combined bombardment of Fort Wagner was begun, and continued without cessation for forty-two hours. An assault was arranged for the 9th, but when daylight came the forts were found to be abandoned. It was also supposed that Fort Sumter was tenantless, and some boat-loads of sailors were sent to take possession. As they landed, a terrible musketry volley was fired, placing nearly every man *hors du combat*. The blockade of Charleston harbor was, however, assured.

EXTERIOR VIEW OF LAND FACE.

EXTERIOR VIEW FROM SANDBAR.

EXTERIOR VIEW SHOWING DESTRUCTION OF OUTER WALL.

INTERIOR VIEW.

INTERIOR VIEW.

INTERIOR VIEW SHOWING SALLYPORT.

LIGHTHOUSE ON PARAPET OF FORT.

EXTERIOR VIEW SHOWING DESTRUCTION OUTER WALL.

EXTERIOR VIEW OF NORTH FACE.

VIEW ON THE PARAPET.

VIEW FROM THE PARAPET.

INTERIOR VIEW.

FORT SUMTER.

ORDNANCE DEPOT.

NAVAL BATTERY

MORTAR BATTERY.

MORTAR BATTERY.

SWAMP BATTERY

SWAMP ANGEL BATTERY.

STEAMBOAT DOCK.

NAVAL BATTERY.

ORDNANCE DEPOT.

MORTAR BATTERY

INTERIOR VIEW.

GUARD MOUNTING.

SOUTH PARAPET.

INTERIOR VIEW, WITH QUARTERS OF FEDERAL GARRISON.

INTERIOR VIEW.

INTERIOR VIEW, WITH QUARTERS OF FEDERAL GARRISON.

INTERIOR VIEW, WITH QUARTERS OF FEDERAL GARRISON.

INTERIOR VIEW, WITH QUARTERS OF FEDERAL GARRISON.

FORT WAGNER.

CHAPTER LI.

COUNTER-MOVEMENTS OF ROSECRANZ AND BRAGG.

According to all previous rules and precedents of war, the defeat of General Lee's forces at Gettysburg, coupled with the fall of Vicksburg and Port Hudson, should have ended the war. The Confederate government was distinctly refused recognition as an independent autonomy by the European powers, and it had lost a large slice of its territory, while immense Federal armies were invading the remainder. But as many historic precedents had already been ignored by both the North and the South, their struggle was continued with greater fury and determination for nearly two more years. Severe as had been the fighting, it was to be exceeded in the display of desperate valor by the men who wore the blue and the gray. The whole of Europe, with its millions of soldiers in barracks, observing an armed peace, stood amazed at the fury and extent of this mighty American internecine struggle, which was yet to cause the sacrifice of nearly four hundred thousand human lives, and the maiming of twice as many men.

When Rosecranz took possession of Murfreesboro, Tennessee, in January, 1863, General Bragg held a formidable position on Duck River, his line extending from Shelby-

MAJOR-GENERAL N. P. BANKS AND STAFF.

ville to Spring Hill, through Wartrace, McMinnville, and Columbia. Having established his base of supplies at Chattanooga and Tullahoma, the Confederate commander placed strong outposts in Liberty and Hoover's Gaps, ten miles from Murfreesboro. For six months these two armies stood confronted, but only severe skirmishing occurred between them. In February General Wheeler attempted the recapture of Fort Donelson. Wheeler summoned Colonel A. C. Harding to surrender. The Federal colonel had only six hundred men, but opened fire with his five cannon, sending a steamer down the Cumberland River to notify the Federal gunboats. The battle continued all day, Harding having thirty-two men killed and ninety-four wounded, besides losing fifty more who were taken

MILITARY RAILROAD TRESTLE BRIDGE AND PASS IN RACCOON RANGE, NEAR WHITESIDE.

HOUSE OF JOHN ROSE, NEAR RINGGOLD GA.

THE VALLEY OF RUNNING WATER CREEK, NEAR WHITESIDE.

ARMY TRANSPORTS ON TENNESSEE RIVER.

ARMY TRANSPORTS BRIDGEPORT, ON TENNESSEE RIVER.

prisoners. Lieutenant Fitch arrived with the gunboat Fair Play just after dusk, and opened a raking fire on the Confederates, other gunboats coming up and compelling Wheeler to retreat and leave one hundred and fifty dead where they had fallen. While returning Wheeler encountered two brigades of Federal cavalry, under General J. C. Davis, and was severely handled.

General John Colburn started out on March 4, with two thousand men, to attack Bragg's outpost at Spring Hill. He encountered Forrest and Van Dorn, when half his force was captured. About the same time General Sheridan marched with his division toward Shelbyville. On March 14 he struck Van Dorn and Forrest at Thompson's Station and drove them to Duck River. On April 10 Van Dorn appeared at Franklin Station with ten thousand men, finding General Gordon Granger on the Harpeth River, strongly intrenched. With him were Generals G. C. Smith, Baird, Gilbert, and Stanley. A lively

MAJOR-GENERAL N. P. BANKS.

battle ensued, the Confederates retreating after heavy loss.

Colonel A. D. Streight organized an expedition in Nashville, and going to Dover on transports, marched to Fort Henry and passed up the Tennessee River to Eastport. A large Confederate cavalry force under Forrest and Roddy pursued Streight, who was destroying immense quantities of supplies. After several skirmishes, Streight's ammunition was exhausted and he was compelled to surrender.

The Confederate army, under Bragg, was very strongly posted at Shelbyville, Wartrace, and Tullahoma, besides holding possession of Hoover's and Liberty Gaps. Rosecranz decided to make a feint on Bragg's left and centre, while his main force was to try to turn the Confederate right flank.

On June 24 the Army of the Cumberland broke camp. A tremendous rain-storm drenched man and horse, and rendered the roads almost impassable. Rosecranz had four corps under McCook, Thomas, Granger, and Crittenden. Rosecranz directed McCook to march toward Shelbyville, Thomas to Manchester, and Crittenden to McMinnville, Granger following McCook and Thomas. All of these movements were executed with precision and success. General Sheridan was at the head of McCook's column, while Johnson and Davis turned with their divisions to the left, in the direction of Liberty Gap. Wilder's mounted infantry reached Hoover's Gap in advance of Thomas, and seizing the pass, captured one of Bragg's wagon trains and several hundred cattle. Liberty Gap was also seized by Willich's brigade, after a sharp, quick fight, in which the Federals captured the Confederates' tents, baggage, and supplies. In the meantime, Granger arrived at Christiana, where he was joined by Stanley's cavalry division. Pushing rapidly toward Guy's Gap, Granger and Stanley took the pass after a severe engagement, driving the Confederates until they halted near Shelbyville. Here Stanley charged, and the Federals entered Shelbyville, Wheeler's cavalry escaping by swimming their horses across Duck River.

All of Rosecranz's columns marched hurriedly through the several passes, and on June 27 army headquarters was established at Manchester. Bragg retired to Tullahoma General Wilder's cavalry then struck the railroad at Dechard and destroyed several miles of track, but the Elk River bridge remained intact. Bragg abandoned his position at Tullahoma on June 30, falling back to Bridgeport, Alabama.

Rosecranz had in six days driven Bragg from his fortified positions and gained possession of Middle Tennessee. The campaign had been conducted amid almost continuous rain and extraordinary difficulties. Bragg showed his generalship by saving all of his artillery and military supplies, and by destroying the railroad as fast as his trains passed over it. Bragg then crossed the Tennessee River at Bridgeport, burned the bridge, and entered Chattanooga.

When Burnside started to co-operate with Rosecranz a Confederate force of twenty thousand men, under General Simon B. Buckner, occupied Knoxville, but on Burnside's approach fell back to Chattanooga. The Federals then entered Knoxville on September 3. So precipitate had been Buckner's retreat that the Federals came into possession of all the railroad rolling stock and machine shops. On September 7 General Shackelford invested Cumberland Gap. When General Frazier, the Confederate commander, received a summons to surrender he promptly refused, but on Burnside's arrival with more troops the brave officer surrendered with his two thousand men on September 9. By these movements the entire valley lying between the Cumberland and Alleghany Mountains fell into the possession of the Federal forces.

The Federal and Confederate authorities now reinforced their respective armies in and around Chattanooga. Buckner joined Bragg, Johnston's brigades arrived from Mississippi, and Polk hastened up from Alabama with a strong force, while Lee was ordered to detach Longstreet's corps. Another conscription was made, and the men paroled at Vicksburg and Port Hudson were placed in the ranks, Bragg soon having eighty thousand men at his disposal. On the Federal side, General Hurlbut was directed to cover Corinth and Tuscumbia. Grant, Pope, and Schofield were ordered to send all the men they could spare. The two immense armies then prepared for a desperate and momentous struggle.

BRIG GEN, J.M.SHACKLEFORD.

BRIG GEN, J.T.WILDER.

BRIG GEN, A.D.STRAIGHT.

CHAPTER LII.

THE TWO DAYS' BATTLE OF CHICKAMAUGA.

It was not until August 20 that General Rosecranz's Army of the Cumberland arrived in force on the banks of the Tennessee River. Bridges were thrown across, McCook moving over with two of his divisions at Caperton's Ferry, Sheridan crossing at Bridgeport, the corps concentrating at Winston's Gap. Thomas' corps went over by three routes, one division crossing at Caperton's Ferry, another at Shell Mound, and the third at Battle Creek. They met at Trenton, and then moved by Stevens' and Cooper's Gaps, through Lookout Mountain into McLemore's Cove. Crittenden's corps crossed at Battle Creek and moved direct for Chattanooga. On September 8 Thomas occupied Trenton, and held Cooper's and Stevens' Gaps, on Lookout Mountain, while McCook was at Valley Head and Crittenden had reached Wauhatchie, with his left flank resting on Thomas. These dispositions caused Bragg to evacuate Chattanooga and mass his forces at Lafayette. General Crittenden's signal men discovered the movement, and the Federals entered Chattanooga on September 9. This bloodless entrance into Chattanooga gave Rosecranz an opportunity for crushing Bragg which he did not improve.

Intoxicated by his success, Rosecranz incautiously scattered his army throughout the mountain, instead of concentrating it. Thomas marched toward Lafayette, Crittenden went to Ringgold, and McCook moved to Summer Creek. General Thomas soon discovered that Bragg was really moving forward to the attack, while Rosecranz was occupying a line fifty-seven miles long, from Chickamauga to Alpine. Bragg also committed an error in waiting for a week before engaging, the delay giving Rosecranz time to concentrate, and on September 18 he was in tolerably good shape.

The Indian word "Chickamauga" means "The River of Death," rather an ominous one for a battlefield. The creek rises where Pigeon Mountain and Missionary Ridge join, and flows to the north, past Crawfish Spring to Lee and Gordon's Mills on the Chattanooga and Lafayette road, and finally enters the Tennessee River a mile above the town. It was along the course of this creek that the engagement was to be fought. Rosecranz occupied the west bank, his right wing resting on Lee and Gordon's Mills, while his left was near Rossville, with his reserves between Chattanooga and the right flank.

Chattanooga is a Cherokee word, and signifies "Hawk's Nest," the region being part of the Appalachian Range. The outlying spurs around Chattanooga are known as Missionary Ridge, Chickamauka Hills, Lookout Mountain, Pigeon Mountain, and Raccoon Mountain. The town stands on the south bank of the Tennessee River, at the mouth of the Chattanooga Valley. This beautiful and fertile valley is formed by Missionary Ridge on the east and by Lookout Mountain on the west, while the Chattanooga River mean-

BRIG.-GEN. W. H. LYTLE.

ders through it toward the Tennessee River. Between Pigeon Mountain and Missionary Ridge lies a smaller valley, the Chickamauga.

General Bragg had now been joined by Hood's division, of Longstreet's corps, and Buckner's from East Tennessee. He decided to throw his main body around the Federal left, to uncover Chattanooga, sending Wheeler's cavalry against the Federal right to cover his flanking movement. The weather was clear and pleasant, being an ideal battle morning. Bragg succeeded, on the night of September 18, in throwing Hood's and Falk's thirty thousand men across Chickamauga Creek before Thomas discovered the fact. At ten o'clock the head of the Confederate column was discovered, when Thomas ordered Brannan to take his brigade to Reed's Bridge and cut off the Confederates, while Baird's brigade was to move on Alexander's Bridge. Scarcely had Brannan and Baird got in motion when they discovered that they were attacking an overwhelming force. A fierce battle ensued. The Confederates were driven back, however, until Liddle's division came up, and the Federals were forced to retreat with the loss of two entire batteries and five hundred men. Lieutenant Van Pelt held his guns until he was killed. Seeing the importance of the Confederate movement, Thomas sent in Reynolds' division, while McCook ordered up Johnson's division and Crittenden sent Palmer's division. The Federals were now able to outflank the Confederates, and being the strongest, drove them pellmell on their reserves, Van Pelt's battery being retaken.

At five o'clock two Confederate divisions, under Generals Gist and Liddle, charged on Reynolds' right, while another force moved on Baird, Van Cleeve, and Johnson, so that the battle line extended from Alexander's Bridge to McDaniel's House and Reed's Bridge. The Confederate onslaught was so terrible that the Federal line began breaking in an alarming way, and Thomas' entire corps stood in sudden peril. Then one of those curious incidents occurred which so often serve to turn the tide of battle. When the Confederate flanking movement was fully developed it was suddenly remembered that four of the Federal reserve batteries, comprising twenty-one pieces, had been left on the Rossville road, beyond the left of Thomas' line, entirely without infantry supports. General Hazen's brigade was ordered to bring in the guns. Hazen found the artillery already occupying a ridge which commanded the ground on which Gist and Liddle were driving back the Federal divisions. Hastily placing his infantry under these twenty-one guns, Hazen remained silent until the Confederate flank was fully exposed. No sooner had Liddle and Gist reached his line of fire than Hazen ordered the batteries to begin. The discharge of twenty-one double rounds of canister actually tore the Confederate ranks into tatters. Blinded by the smoke of the Federal guns, Gist's and Liddle's divisions stood for a few minutes, amazed, then fell back on the creek in dire confusion. Rosecranz's left was thus saved, and at sunset the fighting ended.

On the Federal right there had been another attack, when Hood advanced three brigades and captured a Federal battery. Following this up, Hood sent two divisions against Davis, of McCook's corps, driving him back and capturing the Indiana battery. Sheridan then sent one of his brigades, under Bradley, to the assistance of Davis, when the Federals charged with such impetuosity that they drove back the Confederates, recaptured the Indiana guns, and took several hundred prisoners.

During that night General Longstreet arrived at Bragg's headquarters. Having this experienced general at hand, Bragg divided his forces into two bodies, the one on his right continuing under command of General Polk, while General Longstreet assumed control of the left wing. Polk had Breckinridge's and Cleburne's divisions, of Hill's corps; Cheatham's division, of Polk's corps, and the division commanded by General W. H. T. Walker. Longstreet's forces consisted of Johnson's, Preston's, and Stewart's divisions, of Buckner's corps; Hood's division, consisting of Lane's, Benning's, and Robertson's brigades;

Hindman's division, of Polk's corps, and Humphrey's and Kershaw's brigades, from Mc-Laws' division.

The next day was Sunday, September 20, and the sunrise had that blood-red color that betokens a hot day. While the mountain-tops were bathed in golden and rosy tints, a cool mist gathered in the beautiful valley, being densest along the line of Chickamauga Creek. Every bird and four-footed denizen of the forest had been driven away by the fierce sounds of the previous day's battle, and there was nothing to disturb the silence. In days of peace the sound of village church bells might have been heard, but they were now mute on this Sabbath morn, in the presence of two trained and opposing armies.

General Bragg decided to begin the battle at dawn, and General Polk was ordered to open the attack on Rosecranz's left, the Confederate line to move forward from right to

BATTLE OF CHICKAMAUGA.

left in swift succession. Daylight came, and the sun rose, yet there was no sound of Polk's guns. Impatient and amazed at the delay, Bragg sent an aide to ascertain the cause. The staff officer found the Bishop and his staff stretched at their ease, under some wide-spreading trees, enjoying a substantial breakfast.

"General Bragg wishes to know, sir, why you have not attacked the enemy," said the aide, astonished at the scene.

"I cannot understand myself why General Hill has not begun long ago," responded Polk, equably. "I ordered him to open the action at dawn, and I am now waiting to hear his guns. Do tell General Bragg, sir, that my heart is overflowing with anxiety for Hill's attack—actually overflowing with anxiety," and then the Episcopal soldier resumed his breakfast, the mortified aide declining to join him.

It subsequently turned out that Polk stated the exact truth, but General Hill was far in the rear at Tedford's Ford, and the order to attack did not reach him until an hour after sunrise. Meanwhile, Rosecranz had not been idle. Thomas' position on the left remained unchanged, and he had received Negley's, Palmer's, and Johnson's divisions to strengthen it. McCook was well closed up on Thomas, and Crittenden stood in reserve behind the Federal centre. About nine o'clock Breckenridge's division advanced on Thomas' line. With appalling suddenness the Confederate cannonading and musketry began, and the Sabbath silence was at last broken. Breckenridge's attack was a magnificent one, his infantry line being perfectly aligned, and as steady as a rock. General Cleburne was on Breckenridge's left, in the same excellent order. Opening fire at close musket range, Breckenridge swung round on Thomas' flank, while Cleburne moved directly against the Federal breastworks. Both the Confederate divisions encountered a galling fire, but they were not checked. Facing a continuous and most destructive series of musketry volleys, accompanied by rapid discharges of grape and canister from Thomas' field guns, the South-

VIEW ON BATTLEFIELD OF CHICKAMAUGA AT LEE & GORDON'S MILLS.

erners pushed forward. Losing men at every step, whole lines being at times mowed down, they went steadily forward. Breckenridge was sweeping round the Federal flank, and Cleburne gained considerable ground, while Thomas sent aide after aide urgently asking Rosecranz for assistance.

Bragg had set his heart on turning Rosecranz's left, and learning how well Breckenridge and Cleburne were doing their work, he rushed division after division to that part of the field. But Rosecranz was as swift in reinforcing Thomas, and the battle continued with unabated fury. Soon after the attack on the Federal left, General Sheridan discovered a gap between his division and the main body, caused by the movement of reinforcements toward Thomas. Laiboldt's brigade and two brigades of Davis' division filled it. Longstreet now began pressing forward, Davis being seriously engaged. Seeing this, Sheridan contemplated sending in Lytle's and Bradley's brigades, when he received orders to send them to Thomas, who seemed to have the bulk of Bragg's army on top of him.

Scarcely had Lytle and Bradley started when a fresh Confederate line appeared before Davis, which doubled him up and sent his men flying in confusion. General McCook ordered Laiboldt to charge, which he did in good style, but the opposing body was too strong, and his brigade also broke. Lytle and Bradley were still within call, so Sheridan threw them forward, when they met a volley which fairly shattered both brigades. McCook's corps tried next to stem the torrent, but the Federals were driven from the ridge with severe loss, among the killed being General William H. Lytle.

MAJ GEN, J. M. BRANNON.

MAJ GEN, J. J. REYNOLDS,

General Thomas' men were still fighting valiantly on the extreme left; when his reinforcements arrived they were ordered in, to give his own corps a breathing spell. Then Vanderveer's and Stanley's brigades charged Breckenridge's line, driving it back with great slaughter, the Confederate General, Helmond Desher, being killed, General D. Adams severely wounded, and the Chief of Artillery, Major Graves, mortally wounded. General Breckenridge now turned on a ridge, and putting his batteries at work, stood fast with the assistance of Cheatham and Walker, who reinforced his line. The Confederates then again moved forward, but General Thomas had taken a new position on Missionary Ridge, with his left on the Lafayette road. Knowing that McCook's and Crittenden's corps were retreating to Chattanooga in the utmost confusion, Bragg ordered Polk to press Thomas, hoping to capture his entire command. Thomas, however, doggedly stuck to his position, and could not be shaken from it.

Despite the efforts of McCook and Sheridan, the latter was finally cut off, and he had to fall back to Missionary Ridge, where he was joined by Carlin's brigade, of Davis' division, both marching to Rossville by the Lafayette road. They reached the hamlet at five o'clock, finding there eight pieces of artillery, fifty-six caissons, and a long ammunition train. Organizing an impromptu battery, Sheridan marched his column toward Thomas' position, arriving in time to cover the retreat of the left wing an hour or two after sunset.

General Longstreet had meanwhile advanced with his entire force on both McCook and Crittenden, finding them in such confusion that they were easily driven back. General Rosecranz had meanwhile ridden off to Chattanooga, so McCook and Crittenden followed, the movement being disgracefully disorderly.

Having succeeded in this movement, Longstreet now turned on Thomas, taking advantage of an opening in the hills which entered a gorge directly in rear of the Federals. Through this gully his columns poured like a mighty wave, and the heroic Thomas found himself attacked on flank and rear. General Gordon Granger, who had been waiting for orders at Rossville, knew from the increased cannonading that Thomas must be sorely pressed, so decided to go forward on his own responsibility. Arriving on the ground with Steadman's division, Granger threw his men on the crest of the hill commanding the gorge Longstreet was already entering. Steadman's guns immediately opened a rapid discharge of grape on Longstreet's two divisions as they approached in a dense mass, the effect being terrible, for the missiles destroyed the leading battalions. It was the brigades of Mitchell and Whittaker that led this Confederate charge, but they were compelled to fall back through the gorge, bleeding and broken.

This ended the battle, and Thomas withdrew in the evening to Rossville, having held

VIEW OF RINGGOLD, GA.

his lines unbroken during the entire day. In fact, Rosecranz had, in sending him nearly two-thirds of his entire force, left Thomas to fight the battle at discretion while he went to Chattanooga to prepare for the retrograde movement he had only himself made possible. The stubborn courage of Thomas and his men had, however, saved the Federal army from destruction.

The battle of Chickamauga was a victory for the Confederates, but a very costly one, like that of Bull Run and Chancellorsville. Bragg's loss was nearly eighteen thousand men, Rosecranz's over sixteen thousand, and fifty-one pieces of cannon, the Confederates also picking up seventeen thousand muskets on the abandoned battlefield. General Rosecranz was subsequently relieved of his command, two of his corps commanders, McCook and Crittenden, retiring with him.

CHAPTER LIII.

THE BATTLES OF ORCHARD KNOB AND LOOKOUT MOUNTAIN.

Not only did General Bragg administer defeat to General Rosecranz at Chickamauga, he actually shut up the Federal army and its commander in Chattanooga. While Generals Thomas, Sheridan, and Granger made their orderly retreat, the corps under Generals Crittenden and McCook were panic-stricken, and Rosecranz seems to have been as demoralized as his men. The roads were lined with abandoned cannon, caissons, and wagons, while over fields and through woods streamed disordered detachments and groups of fugitives. Had Longstreet refrained from attacking Thomas and followed Rosecranz's left wing instead, the Confederates would have undoubtedly captured the greater part of it. Having got the remnant of his army together, Rosecranz proceeded to fortify Chattanooga, and was so strongly intrenched inside of twenty-four hours that Bragg could not safely attack him. The Confederate general then decided to cut off all the Federal lines of communication. He seized the south bank of the Tennessee River at Moccasin Point, and the roads between Chattanooga and Bridgeport. By destroying the railroad, he prevented access to Nashville, where Rosecranz's base of supplies had been located. The only way the Federal general could get rations was by wagons over a circuitous road along the Tennessee and Sequatchie valleys, where the trains were so exposed to attack that they were frequently captured or destroyed by Bragg's cavalry. The Army of the Cumberland was, therefore, reduced to extremity, being soon on the verge of starvation. No less than ten thousand horses and mules perished in the effort to procure food.

General Grant was then summoned to Indianapolis, Indiana, where he met Secretary Stanton, who handed him an order from President Lincoln conferring upon him the command of the new Military Department of the Mississippi, comprising the armies and departments of the Ohio, Tennessee, and Cumberland. The hero of Vicksburg was at that time on crutches, he having sustained severe injury by the fall of his horse in New Orleans, where he had gone to visit Banks and perfect plans for advancing on Mobile. While Grant and Stanton were conversing the latter received a despatch from his Assistant Secretary, Charles A. Dana, announcing that Rosecranz contemplated evacuating Chattanooga. At Grant's suggestion, Rosecranz was at once relieved of his command, and General Grant telegraphed to Thomas that he was to assume

MAJOR-GENERAL GEO. H. THOMAS.

command of the Army of the Cumberland, adding, "Hold Chattanooga at all hazards." In an hour the wires flashed back the reply of the hero of Chickamauga, "I will hold the town until we starve."

Preparations were now made for a vigorous campaign. General Sherman was given the command of the Army of the Tennessee, and troops were hurried forward from all directions. General Slocum's Twelfth Corps and General Howard's Eleventh Corps were detached from Meade's Army of the Potomac, and, being placed under the command of General Joseph Hooker, transferred to the West. The transportation of these twenty-three thousand men, with their artillery, wagons, baggage, animals, ordnance, and commissary supplies, from the Rapidan River, in Virginia, to Stevenson, Alabama, a distance of eleven hundred and ninety-two miles, was accomplished by railroad in the short space of seven days, a most marvellous feat.

General Grant reached Nashville on October 21, where he met Rosecranz and Hooker. Two days after he was at Chattanooga, only to find the troops without shoes or clothing, all the food exhausted, and positively none in sight.

Telegraphing to General Burnside to hold Knoxville, he asked Admiral Porter at Cairo to send gunboats to convey transports carrying rations from St. Louis for Sherman's army, which was moving up the Mississippi to join him. On October 24 Grant made a personal inspection of the country, accompanied by General Thomas and General W. F. Smith, his engineer-in-chief. Grant found that Bragg's intrenched line began on Missionary Ridge, extending along the crest and across Chattanooga Valley to Lookout Mountain. Here the Confederate fortifications were very strong, and their line crossed Lookout Valley to and over Raccoon Mountain. That night the plan of operations was decided upon. General Hooker, who had reached Bridgeport with his two corps, was ordered to cross the Tennessee and march up by Wauhatchie and Whitesides to Brown's Ferry. General Palmer, with one division of the Fourteenth Corps, was to move down the river by a back road to Whitesides, when he was to cross and

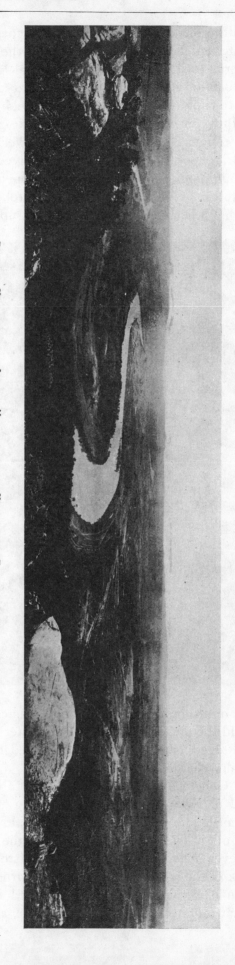

PANORAMIC VIEW FROM TOP OF LOOKOUT MOUNTAIN, SHOWING VALLEY OF THE TENNESSEE RIVER, AND CHATTANOOGA.

hold the road in rear of Hooker. General Smith, with twenty-two hundred picked men was to march during the night along the north bank of the river to Brown's Ferry, carrying material for laying a bridge. General Hazen was given eighteen hundred men, who were to float down in the darkness, in sixty pontoon boats, and on reaching Brown's Ferry, he was to capture the Confederate pickets on the south bank. These movements were successfully made on October 26, and on the following day two new bridges made the connections complete, so that the river was opened to the Federals from Lookout Valley to Bridgeport. Then the army received full rations and an abundance of clothing and ammunition. On discovering the opening of the Federal supply line, Bragg attempted to close it. During the night of October 28 Longstreet's corps attacked Geary at Wauhatchie, when Howard was ordered up by Hooker. By the time he reached Geary it

ARMY BRIDGE ACROSS THE TENNESSEE AT CHATTANOOGA.

QUARTERMASTER'S LANDING CHATTANOOGA, SHOWING WAREHOUSE.

MILITARY RAILROAD BRIDGE ACROSS CHATTANOOGA CREEK.

RUINS OF RAILROAD BRIDGE AT BRIDGEPORT AND CONSTRUCTION OF PONTOON BRIDGE.

PART OF CHATTANOOGA, SHOWING BLOCK HOUSE ARMY BRIDGE.

was quite dark, and the fighting was conducted by the flashes of the opposing muskets. Amid the uproar, the Federal teamsters deserted their mules, and the animals, becoming frightened, broke loose and stampeded toward the Confederates, who, taking it for a cavalry charge, stampeded in turn.

General Grant had a habit that frequently led him into personal danger. He was fond of riding off alone, investigating his line and that of the enemy. The day after the skirmish just described Grant rode along his line and heard a Federal picket sentinel call out "Turn out the guard for the commanding general." Grant, as usual, replied, "Never mind the guard." To his astonishment a Confederate sentinel, on the opposite bank of the creek, then shouted, "Turn out the guard for General Grant." The Confederate picket, instantly falling in, faced the Federal general and presented arms. General Grant returned the unexpected salute, and rode on. A few days after this incident the

VIEWS ON LOOKOUT MOUNTAIN.

General came to a tree that had fallen across the creek and was used amicably by the opposing pickets in obtaining clear water. Longstreet's corps at that time wore European uniforms somewhat similar in color to the Federal blue. Seeing a soldier sitting on the log, Grant rode up and began conversing with him, finally asking whose corps he belonged to. The man was very polite, touched his hat in salute, and replied, "I belong to General Longstreet's corps, sir."

On November 4 General Longstreet left Bragg's lines with twenty thousand men to move against Burnside. By this time Sherman had arrived at Bridgeport. This movement of Sherman's was a remarkable one, for it was necessary to rebuild the railroad between Nashville and Decatur, and thence to Stevenson, where the Memphis and Charleston and the Nashville and Chattanooga railroads unite. General G. M. Dodge was an experienced railroad builder. He forged the necessary tools, cut timber for ties, repaired

PULPIT ROCK WHERE JEFF. DAVIS ADDRESSED THE ARMY

VIEW FROM NEAR THE ROLLING MILL

PULPIT ROCK WHERE JEFF. DAVIS ADDRESSED THE ARMY

NORTH SLOPE

LOOKOUT MOUNTAIN.

locomotives and cars, depending entirely on the soldiers in his command for workmen. General Sherman left Vicksburg on September 27, and reached Tuscumbia exactly one month later, having two or three minor engagements on the way. The Federal plan for battle was arranged on November 18. Grant decided that Sherman should attack Bragg's right flank, and extend his left over South Chickamauga River, and so threaten the Confederate line of communication. Hooker was to enter Chattanooga Valley and advance on Missionary Ridge, while Thomas, with the old Army of the Cumberland, was to make a direct assault on Bragg's centre. As Sherman had unexpected difficulty in crossing at Brown's Ferry, the concerted attack did not occur until the 23d. General Thomas' army moved out of Chattanooga under bright sunshine, in magnificent condition. Sheridan's division was on the extreme right, with Wood's on the left, two of Palmer's divisions holding the centre, one division under Johnson being retained in the intrenchments as reserve.

Howard's corps was massed behind Granger's. When the long line of infantry moved forward the heavy guns opened fire, and it was not long before General Wood reached the base of Orchard Knob. Charging in gallant style, Wood's division carried the Knob, and a heavy battery was now sent to occupy the Knob. Meanwhile a brigade of cavalry had swept round the Confederate right, and getting into Bragg's rear, burned Tyner's Station, cut the railroad running to Cleveland, capturing one hundred wagons, and destroying considerable supplies. Sherman reached the south side of the Tennessee, while Hooker was ready for his dash through Rossville Gap on Missionary Ridge.

November 24 proved to be a drizzly day, the mist concealing the movements of the Federal forces. About three o'clock Sherman took possession of the northern extremity

BATTLE OF CHATTANOOGA.

of Missionary Ridge, and intrenched himself in a strong position. Soon after daylight Geary, of Hooker's command, began crossing the Lookout Creek, at Wauhatchie, with his division and Whittaker's brigade, while the remainder of the force threw bridges over the swollen stream. Geary surprised the Confederates, capturing their pickets, while Hooker's other divisions came up in fine style. The Federals then dashed across the valley, sweeping everything before them, until they finally reached the base of Lookout Mountain, pushing in the Confederate skirmish line, though it was well posted in rifle pits.

Hooker had now three divisions west of Lookout Creek: Osterhaus', Geary's, and Cruft's. Geary was on the right, at Wauhatchie, Cruft at the centre, and Osterhaus near Brown's Ferry. Facing these were three Confederate brigades, under General Carter L.

BLOCK HOUSE AT HIA=
WASSEE RIVER BRIDGE
K.&C.R.R.

VIEW OF TENNESSEE RIVER VALLEY FROM LOOKOUT MT.

VIEW OF TENNESSEE RIVER VALLEY FROM LOOKOUT MT.

"SUTTERS ROW" CHATTANOOGA.

BLOCK HOUSE ON TENNESSEE & ALABAMA RAILROAD.

BLOCK HOUSE ON KNOXVILLE & CHAT. RAILROAD.

VIEW OF TENNESSEE RIVER VALLEY FROM LOOKOUT MT.

Stevenson. The face of Lookout Mountain in front of Hooker was rugged, heavily timbered, and broken by deep chasms, yet it was this terrible ascent that Hooker's men now prepared to make in face of cannon and musket.

General Grant stood on the top of Orchard Knob watching Hooker's movement. From that position the General could see that his line was continuous and perfect, being in full view, extending from the Tennessee River, where Sherman had crossed, up Chickamauga River to the base of Mission Ridge, over the top of the north end of the Ridge to Chattanooga Valley, then along parallel to the Ridge a mile or more, across the valley to the mouth of Chattanooga Creek, thence up the slope of Lookout Mountain to the foot of the upper palisade. General Hooker had so well timed the movements of his divisions

that, as Geary dashed across the Creek at Wauhatchie, General Osterhaus was rapidly advancing from Brown's Ferry, with Cruft within close supporting distance. The New York and Ohio batteries now took position on Bald Hill and other eminences, and began a severe cannonading with solid shot and shell. The Confederate position that Hooker proposed to attack being perched on the mountain side, the Federal guns had to be elevated to the last twist of the screw, their fire proving very effective. Under cover of this artillery discharge, Hooker's men began climbing. Rushing up the rugged side of the mountain, leaping from one rocky ledge to another, scrambling over huge boulders, and cutting away the confused *abatis* of felled timber, the Federals drove the Confederates before them. At times the advance lines were almost at the muzzle of the enemy's cannon before the gunners gave way. As Osterhaus' division moved forward, Geary led his men along the face of the steep incline, just beneath the Confederate batteries, and then rushed up to complete the assaulting line. For over three hours did this extraordinary mountain battle continue, but, despite the desperate and stubborn resistance offered by General Stevenson's brigades, the Federals gained ground, foot by foot, until at last they reached the base of the Palisades, finding the Confederates flying down the slope toward Chattanooga Valley. Owing to the drizzly atmosphere, Hooker's movement was frequently hidden by the rifts of mist which clung to the face of the mountain, and this fact has given it the name of " The Battle Above the Clouds."

General Hooker did not deem it prudent to make a pursuit, so he established his line on the east side of Lookout Mountain. At sunset the mists disappeared, the wild landscape being bathed in bright moonlight. As a Confederate force still occupied the mountain summit, Hooker started detachments from several regiments to scale the Palisades. The Eighth Kentucky was the first to reach Pulpit Rock, finding the position abandoned, the Confederates leaving behind them twenty thousand rations, all their camp equipage, and a considerable quantity of ammunition. At sunrise of November 25 these Kentucky soldiers unfurled the Stars and Stripes on Pulpit Rock, the crisp, clear air in the valley below being filled with the cheers of their comrades.

RAILROAD DEPOT, CONFEDERATE PRISONERS WAITING FOR TRANSPORTATION

FORT SHERMAN

INDIAN MOUND IN MONUMENT GARDEN.

RAILROAD DEPOT, LOOKOUT MOUNTAIN IN DISTANCE

THE CRUTCHFIELD HOUSE

CHATTANOOGA, TENN.

CHAPTER LIV

BATTLE OF MISSIONARY RIDGE AND SIEGE OF KNOXVILLE.

The sanguinary battles of Orchard Knob and Lookout Mountain broke the Confederate investing line, while Grant's was unassailable, though much extended. The Federals now occupied a strong position from Lookout Mountain, across the Chattanooga Valley, up to the northern end of Missionary Ridge. The two gaps between Grant's centre and the right and left wings were filled by Generals Carlin and Howard. Being compelled to abandon the Chattanooga Valley, Bragg concentrated his entire army on Missionary Ridge, the Confederate line extending from Tunnel Hill to near Rossville. Hardie

VIEW OF MISSIONARY RIDGE FROM ORCHARD KNOB.

occupied the Confederate right with Cheatham's, Cleburne's, Stevenson's, and Walker's divisions. The left was commanded by Breckenridge, with Anderson's, Lewis', and Stewart's divisions.

When the Kentuckians raised the Federal flag on Pulpit Rock the sun had already risen in a cloudless sky, and as its bright rays flooded valley and mountain, they were caught and reflected by long lines of glittering steel. Missionary Ridge fairly swarmed with Confederate troops, while the summit was occupied by frowning masses of artillery. Hooker's divisions held Lookout Mountain and spread down into the valley, where Thomas' Cumberland veterans stood in solid phalanx, while on the left could be discerned Sherman's compact lines. Seldom has a battle begun under a brighter sun than that of November 25, 1863.

Grant had ordered Hooker to attack Bragg's left, while Sherman was to advance against his right, Thomas being held in reserve. At six o'clock Grant's bugler sounded

NEWSBOY IN CAMP.

"Forward," as he stood on top of Orchard Knob, the refrain being taken up until the valley was filled with martial melody. Then Hooker's men began moving down the eastern slope of Lookout Mountain, sweeping across the valley in grand lines. Sherman was quite as prompt. From Orchard Knob Grant saw that Bragg was massing his main force to meet Sherman, the opposing batteries soon beginning a fierce duel.

General Sherman found himself under fire as he moved across the valley, but his men rushed forward and seized the opposite hill, only to discover that the ground consisted of a succession of low hills, each well fortified and wooded. When Corse's brigade reached the second crest they found it commanded by a higher one, from which the Confederates delivered a plunging fire. Between these hills was a gorge, through which passed a railroad tunnel. Here a desperate struggle occurred, lasting for over an hour, neither side gaining any advantage. All that Corse could do was to cling to his position, several charges and counter-charges failing to shake either the Federal or Confederate forces from their respective crests. Generals Loomis and Smith, however, were able to get possession of the left spur of Missionary Ridge and the railroad embankment, thus relieving Corse. This part of the battle raged during the entire forenoon, and it grew more and more vengeful, until, at three o'clock, the crisis was reached. Bragg sent in column after column, and brought up every field piece he could spare, until, finally, it seemed impossible for Sherman to retain the slight advantage he had gained. Indeed, to General Grant it appeared as if Sherman was losing ground, while in reality the Federals held the ground they had seized. The line was, however, sorely pressed ; General Corse had been wounded, and help was needed. Grant expected that Thomas would support Sherman, but he was delayed, as will be hereafter explained, so the divisions under Wood and Sheridan were ordered to charge.

It was now two o'clock in the afternoon. The rapid discharge of six pieces of artillery was the signal, and as the last gun sent its shell shrieking through the sunshine both divisions moved steadily forward. The imposing line was soon saluted by a terrible storm of shot and shell, but the Federals pressed on through the timber, and, on reaching the plain, rushed forward with fixed bayonets. Not a shot was fired until after the skirmish line had been overtaken and absorbed, as the six brigades swept over the Confederate rifle pits. Then the men flung themselves on the earth for a breathing spell and to avoid the volleys of canister, grape, and musketry that were pouring down upon them. The Confederate prisoners were told to go to the rear without escort, which they did with alacrity, being exposed to the fire of their own comrades. In a few minutes the divisions were again on their feet, climbing the steep hill. The regimental color bearers entered into a rivalry as to which flag should be farthest to the front ; first one would go forward a few paces, then another would come up to it, until, finally, every standard was planted on the intermediate works.

This movement relieved Sherman of a part of the pressure upon him, and Bragg was compelled to weaken his centre. During all this time Hooker was endeavoring to carry out his part of the general plan. Pushing on to Rossville Gap, he found that the Confederates had destroyed the bridge across Chattanooga Creek, and it took over three hours to put the structure in proper shape. Then, rushing across, Hooker's men quickly occupied the Gap. General Osterhaus' division next moved along the eastern slope of the Ridge, while Geary's passed to the west, leaving Cruft's on the Ridge itself. Despite their stubborn resistance, the Confederates were steadily driven back by Cruft, until at sunset Hooker had not only pushed Breckenridge from the Ridge, but had taken several thousands of his men as prisoners.

This was Grant's opportunity, and he quickly embraced it. With Sherman holding

PANORAMIC VIEWS OF MISSIONARY RIDGE.

CONFEDERATE ARTILLERY, CAPTURED AT MISSIONARY RIDGE.

PANORAMIC VIEWS OF MISSIONARY RIDGE.

Bragg's right in check, and Hooker driving in his left, the final assault on his centre was to begin. Then General Thomas sent in Baird's and Johnson's brigades to assist Sheridan and Wood. In twenty minutes Missionary Ridge was a mass of flame, for every Confederate cannon and musket was in action; but this storm of shell and grape, canister and bullet, did not check the Federal advance. The loss was, however, enormous. A few men of the First Ohio reached the crest on Bragg's centre, under Lieutenant-Colonel Langdon, who was instantly killed; but more men came up and widened the breach, until the Confederate line finally gave way and retreated, their abandoned cannon being turned against them. This ended the battle, forty cannon, seven thousand muskets, and an immense quantity of ammunition being added to the fruits of victory.

Sherman, Hooker, and Palmer took up the pursuit early the following morning, Bragg having fallen back in the direction of Ringgold. Sherman passed Chickamauga Station, which he found in flames, while Hooker and Palmer moved over the Rossville Road.   At Ringgold General Hooker's command struck the Confederate rear, under General Cleburne, who turned and made a most desperate fight, which lasted nearly all day.   This ended the pursuit, and Grant turned his attention to Burnside, at Knoxville.   Though the several engagements on Orchard Knob, Lookout Mountain, and Missionary Ridge are usually known as the Three Days' Battle of Chattanooga, the writer has chosen to separate them, in order that the reader may gain a proper conception of the scope and importance of these combined operations.

The siege that Longstreet had entered on at Knoxville began on November 18, and it was pressed with vigor for eleven days, several engagements occurring, until, finally, the Confederates crossed the Holston River and assumed a commanding position.   Then

BATTLE OF MISSIONARY RIDGE.

news of Bragg's defeat reached Longstreet, who, knowing that Grant would send Burnside relief, decided to carry Knoxville by storm.   Fort Sanders, a work of great strength, and occupied by the Twenty-ninth Massachusetts, the Seventy-ninth New York, and companies from the Second and Twentieth Michigan, was selected as the point of attack.   The fort contained twenty-six guns.   McLaws' division, with the brigades of Anderson, Bogart, Humphreys, and Wolford, were selected for the task.   The assault was made at daylight of November 29, and the columns forced their way through a network of wire that had been wound from stump to stump of the slashed timber.   General Ferrero, who commanded the fort, used his guns with great effect, but the Confederates finally reached the parapet.   An officer sprang to the summit with the flag of the Thirteenth Mississippi, demanding surrender.   The next instant he fell dead, pierced by a dozen bullets, and his body rolled into the ditch, his nerveless fingers still clutching the flag-staff. Again and again did the Confederates charge, only to be repulsed. Then the fighting ended, a flag o truce being displayed, while Longstreet's men carried away their dead, dying, and wounded.

General Granger had been ordered by Grant to start for Knoxville with twenty thousand men, but finding, on November 28, that Granger had not moved, Grant relied on Sherman, who at once marched. He reached Knoxville on December 5, finding the siege raised and Longstreet in retreat for Virginia. General Sherman's troops had accomplished a wonderful feat. They marched four hundred miles, and fought at Chattanooga, then marched one hundred and twelve miles to compel Longstreet to raise the siege of Knoxville. General Bragg went down before the storm of indignation in the South, and was relieved from his command. On the other hand, Congress gave Grant a gold medal and a vote of thanks. Such is the mutation of human affairs—the victor is crowned with laurels; the man who suffers defeat retires covered with obloquy.

THE CREST OF MISSIONARY RIDGE.

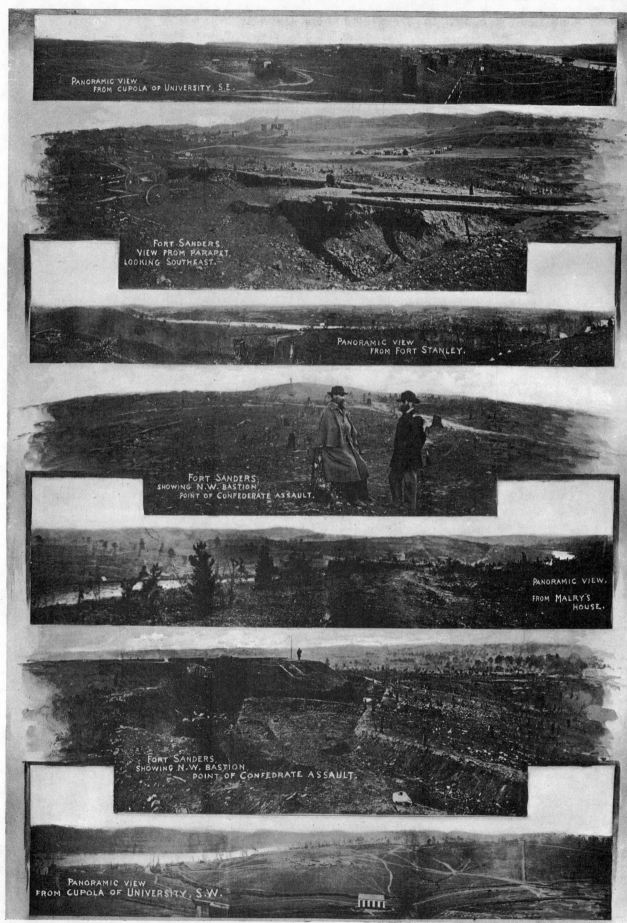

Panoramic View
from Cupola of University, S.E.

Fort Sanders
View from Parapet,
Looking Southeast.

Panoramic View
from Fort Stanley.

Fort Sanders,
showing N.W. Bastion,
Point of Confederate Assault.

Panoramic View,
from Malry's
House.

Fort Sanders,
showing N.W. Bastion
Point of Confedrate Assault.

Panoramic View
from Cupola of University, S.W.

KNOXVILLE, TENN., AND FORT SANDERS.

FORT SAUDERS, SHOWING GROUND OVER WHICH
CONFEDERATE ASSAULT ADVANCED.

FORT SAUDERS EXTERIOR VIEW.

RAILWAY BRIDGE ACROSS PLATT CREEK.

STRAWBERRY PLAINS BRIDGE

STRAWBERRY PLAINS BRIDGE.

VIEW FROM HEIGHTS

BATTLEFIELD OF STRAWBERRY PLAINS

VIEW IN VICINITY OF KNOXVILLE, TENN.

CHAPTER LV.

SHERMAN'S DESTRUCTION OF MERIDIAN AND BANKS' RED RIVER EXPEDITION.

Desultory warfare of an unimportant character marked the close of 1863, both in the East and the West. The armies under Meade and Lee went into winter quarters, with the picturesque Rapidan River rolling between them; Thomas still occupied Chattanooga; Foster replaced Burnside at Knoxville; Sherman returned to Mississippi to co-operate

GENERALS OF THE ARMY OF THE POTOMAC, CULPEPPER, VA.

with Banks. On the Confederate side, Longstreet remained in Tennessee, and Johnston replaced Bragg in command of all the Confederate forces west of the Ohio River. The Army of the Potomac made an advance on Lee's winter camp, at Mine Run, in the depth of winter, but it amounted to nothing. In February, 1864, General Kilpatrick undertook a cavalry raid, the chief incident being the death of young Colonel Uhlric Dahlgren, son of the Admiral, and a very promising officer, who had already lost a foot in the service, though only twenty-one.

This raid was Kilpatrick's first independent movement, and added to his fame. No man was as happy as he when in the saddle, though he did not present a good appearance on horseback, for he rode more like a Comanche Indian than the pupil of a school of equitation. But he could fight like a Comanche. In fact, he was always fighting, and he taught his men to do the same. When on a raid or endeavoring to intercept a Confederate supply train he moved with startling rapidity, and it was no unusual thing to find his route marked by disabled horses and dismounted men. He was a very genial man personally, though he could swear like a trooper when excited. His men called him "Kill," as suggestive of his destruction of Confederate property and his expenditure of horseflesh.

Sherman organized an expedition in February, 1864, against Meridian, Miss., a position of great importance to the Confederacy, as it controlled all the railroads in that section and the communications with Mobile and Wilmington. With seven thousand horsemen, General W. Sooy Smith started out from Memphis to destroy railroads and bridges, while Sherman began marching with four divisions from Vicksburg, one column being led by McPherson, the other by Hurlbut. General Smith failed to move on time, and

CULPEPPER, VA.

soon after crossing the Tallahatchie River was outflanked by Forrest, at Okolono, and compelled to fall back to New Albany. Sherman reached Meridian on February 14, Polk precipitately retiring to Demopolis. Ten thousand men were set at work, destroying over one hundred miles of railroad, sixty bridges, rolling stock, depots, arsenals, saw-mills, warehouses, hotels, and military cantonments. Only private dwellings were spared by the torch. The work of destruction also involved Decatur, Bolton, Jackson, Marion, Enterprize, Quitman, Hillsboro, Canton, Lake Station, and Lauderdale. This action of Sherman's raised a storm of anger throughout the South, and led to some cruel reprisals.

General N. B. Forrest had, up to this time, achieved a high reputation as a Confederate cavalry raider. After the destruction of Meridian and vicinity, Forrest tore through the country, capturing small garrisons and sustaining repulses in equal ratio. He lost a large number of men, among them General Thompson, who was struck on the breast by a

OFFICERS AT HEADQUARTERS.

OFFICERS OF SIGNAL CORPS.

GROUP OF OFFICERS.

WAGONS AND HORSES   QUARTERMASTER'S REPAIR SHOP.

QUARTERS OF Gen. PATRICK, PROVOST MARSHAL GENERAL.   HEADQUARTERS OF NEW YORK HERALD IN THE FIELD.

OFFICERS 93RD N.Y. INFANTRY.   STAFF OFFICERS 93RD N.Y. INFANTRY.

HEADQUARTERS ARMY OF THE POTOMAC, SEPTEMBER, 1863.

SCENES IN CAMP OF ARMY OF POTOMAC, AUGUST TO DECEMBER, 1863.

SCENES IN THE CAMP OF ARMY OF POTOMAC, DECEMBER, 1862.

bursting shell at Fort Anderson. Fort Pillow lay in Forrest's path, and here the General violated the honorable instincts of a soldier. Fort Pillow was occupied by three hundred and fifty white soldiers, under Major W. F. Bradford, and two hundred colored troops, under Major L. F. Booth. It stood on a high bluff, and contained six guns. Forrest attacked on April 13, the garrison resisting with great bravery, Major Booth being killed early in the day. A lull in the battle occurred at noon, and Forrest sent a flag of truce, demanding unconditional surrender. While Major Bradford was consulting with his officers two more flags were sent, but the garrison decided to fight it out. Then it was discovered that Forrest had taken advantage of the truce to place his men in positions, which enabled them to swarm into the forts.

The scene that ensued was of the most cruel and shameful character, for an indiscrim-

inate slaughter was begun. Over four hundred Federals were killed, for Forrest's men gave no quarter. Those who escaped the frightful butchery did so by plunging into the ravines on the first alarm. Even the helpless wounded in the hospital were barbarously put to death. Men were placed in convenient groups and shot to death, others were nailed to the floors of houses, and perished in the flames. Major Bradford was ordered to Jackson, Tennessee, as a prisoner, but was shot to death on the road because he was of Southern birth. This awful massacre stamped Forrest as a man unworthy to wear the uniform of a general.

General Banks began his Red River expedition in March, having received ten thousand veterans from Sherman, under General A. J. Smith, the Mississippi fleet, under Admiral Porter, co-operating. After several skirmishes Banks' force of twenty-five thousand men

U.S. ARTILLERY NEAR CULPEPPER
SEPT 1863.

DR. MURRAYS HOUSE
NEAR AUBURN, VA.

GEN. MOTT AND OFFICERS
CULPEPPER, OCT. 1863.

U.S. ARTILLERY
NEAR CULPEPPER
SEPT 1863.

PONTOON BRIDGE ACROSS POTOMAC RIVER
AT BERLIN.

GEN. PRINCE AND STAFF
CULPEPPER. SEPT. 1863.

OFFICERS OF HORSE ARTILLERY
CULPEPPER. SEPT. 1863.

OFFICERS 18TH N.Y. INFANTRY
CULPEPPER. SEPT. 1863.

HEADQUARTERS ARMY OF THE POTOMAC, SEPTEMBER, 1863.

arrived at Natchitoches on April 4, and started for Shreveport. Then orders came for Sherman's troops to return, so the expedition was abandoned. An important battle took place, however, at Sabine Cross Roads on April 7. Twelve thousand Confederate cavalry and eight thousand infantry made a concerted charge upon the leading Federal divisions, under Lee, Ransom and Landman, driving them into the woods, with the loss of several field pieces. Cameron's division, of the Thirteenth Corps, hurried forward and a new line was established. Before it was completed the Confederates made another headlong charge, fairly sweeping the Federals off their feet. Cameron's men broke, and a regular stampede followed. Colonel Vance, of the Ninety-sixth Ohio, and Colonel Webb, of the Seventy-seventh Ohio, were killed, while among the wounded were Generals Franklin and Ransom, and Colonel Robinson, of the cavalry. The Confederates captured fifteen hun-

dred prisoners, twelve pieces of artillery and nearly two hundred wagons. The Federals halted at Pleasant Grove, three miles away, when General Emory's divisions came up and advanced. The Confederates not realizing that they were now facing fresh troops, tried another charge, but Emory's men held their fire until the advancing line was within sixty yards' range, then poured in so deadly a series of volleys that Green's troops were shattered, and compelled to retire. Banks now fell back fifteen miles to Pleasant Hill, where on April 8 he met General A. J. Smith with part of the Sixteenth Corps. The Confederates were in close pursuit, and advanced on Benedict's brigade, which held Emory's left, driving it back. General Benedict was first wounded in the arm and then killed by a bullet passing through his skull. Colonel Sweitzer's Texan cavalry regiment led the Confederate charge; but meeting the reserve line of General Smith, it was cut to pieces. It was now Smith's opportunity. The Sixteenth Corps had been trained to save ammunition, and did not open fire until the Confederates were massed. Eighteen guns, double-loaded with grape and canister, and seven thousand muskets sent in a simultaneous volley at perilously short range, the Confederate's centre being swept away, nearly one thousand men being killed inside of twenty minutes. "Charge," sounded General Smith's bugle, and as the Sixteenth Corps rushed forward Emory's Nineteenth joined in the headlong movement, and the field was won, the Confederates disappearing in the woods. Taylor's and Nim's batteries being recaptured, and the Federals took five hundred prisoners, three flags, and two thousand muskets.

Considerable fighting marked the succeeding operations, and Admiral Porter fell into difficulty owing to the dangerous navigation. At one time he narrowly escaped being killed by a solid shot. On April 24 the troops were back in Alexandria, and Gen-

Bvt. Maj. Gen. J. G. Lanman.   Brig. Gen. A. W. Lee.   Bvt. Maj. Gen. T. E. G. Ransom.

eral Hunter arrived with orders from General Grant to close the campaign. Porter and his light-draft vessels were above Alexandria, and the water had fallen so low it seemed impossible to save the vessels. Lieutenant-Colonel Bailey, who was Bank's chief engineer, then offered to build dams on the river. With three thousand men and three hundred wagons he built a three hundred-foot dam, which was lengthened by sinking barges loaded with brick. In eight days the water was high enough to permit the gunboats and ironclads to pass down the river. For this feat Bailey was made a Brigadier-General, and received a gold medal from Congress.

These Red River operations included a battle between General Steele's Federal force and General Kirby Smith's command at Jenkin's Ferry, near the Sabine River, on April 27. The engagement was won by Steele after a desperate struggle, Kirby Smith having three generals killed and over two thousand men, killed, wounded, and prisoners, the Federal loss being seven hundred and thirty. Steele then abandoned the effort to join Banks and returned to Little Rock.

THE MISSISSIPPI RIVER FLEET OF IRONCLAD GUNBOATS.

THE MISSISSIPPI RIVER FLEET OF IRONCLAD GUNBOATS.

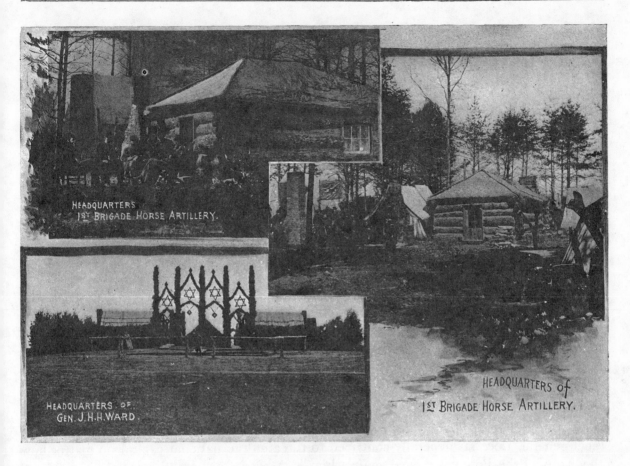

HEADQUARTERS 1ST BRIGADE HORSE ARTILLERY.

HEADQUARTERS OF GEN. J. H. H. WARD.

HEADQUARTERS of 1ST BRIGADE HORSE ARTILLERY.

CHAPTER LVI.

OPENING OF GRANT'S OVERLAND CAMPAIGN IN VIRGINIA.

The Federal Congress revived the rank of Lieutenant-General on March 1, 1864, and conferred it upon Ulysses S. Grant. This promotion placed him in command of all the United States armies in the field. General Sherman was given the command of all the Federal armies in the West. Intense activity prevailed in the Spring of 1864 on both sides of the hostile line. Sherman and Johnston concentrated their forces; Grant reinforced the Army of the Potomac, and Lee recalled Longstreet, and received reinforcements from Georgia and the Carolinas. Besides emptying the hospitals, Grant ordered to the front some of the heavy artillery regiments that had been specially raised for the defences of Washington on the Heights of Alexandria, Virginia.

A curious story, but an entirely true one, is told, which shows the self-reliant character of Grant. Being one day in Washington during the latter part of April, 1864, the Lieutenant-General called on Secretary of War Stanton, purely as a matter of courtesy.

"Well, General, are you ready for a move?" asked Stanton, rubbing his spectacles.

"Yes, I think so. The roads will soon be dry enough for the wagons and artillery. Then the army will march," said General Grant.

"Of course, you have taken proper care that the defences of Washington are all right?" continued the Secretary.

"Oh, yes. There will be enough troops in the Alexandria forts to meet any emergency," replied Grant, quietly.

"That's right. You know we must have the forts completely garrisoned. That was why we organized those regiments of heavy artillery, so that they could not be taken from

the fortifications. It was my own idea. Our experience has been that that confounded rebel general, Lee, has generally contrived to threaten the national capital no matter how the Army of the Potomac moved against him."

"Well," replied Grant, very dryly, "when I once begin fighting Lee, he will have something else to think of. He will have no time to threaten Washington, so I have taken some of your heavy artillery to strengthen Meade."

"Have you?" exclaimed Stanton, thoroughly startled. "How many have you taken?"

"About thirty thousand up to the present time."

"Thirty thousand! Oh, see here, General Grant, this won't do. And I will not have it. We must feel perfectly safe while you are fighting in those Virginia woods beyond the Rapidan. I am Secretary of War, you know, and I shall insist on those heavy artillery regiments being sent back."

"I am very sorry," responded Grant, "but the men are needed, and they will stay where they are. As for the question of authority, I supposed when Congress made me a Lieutenant-General, to command all the United States armies, the rank carried some power. In fact, I rather think I outrank the Secretary of War when it comes to disposing of the troops."

"I don't want to quarrel with you, General," said Stanton ; "but this question must be settled at once. Let us go and see the President."

The Secretary and the General walked over to the White House together, very amicably, and, of course, were at once admitted to the presence of Mr. Lincoln. The President was surprised by the visit, for he read in the faces of these two distinguished men evidence of trouble.

"What has happened?" asked Mr. Lincoln, very gravely, and straight to the point.

"Well, Mr. President," replied Stanton, "the fact is, the Lieutenant-General has, without my sanction, taken away nearly all the garrisons from the Alexandria forts, and I have protested. You know we must protect Washington."

" Have you, indeed, taken the Alexandria garrisons?" inquired the President, turning to the heavy-bearded Lieutenant-General.

" Yes, Mr. President," replied Grant. "About half of them."

"And do you realize that this city may be in danger if not protected?" continued Mr. Lincoln in a surprised tone.

" I have already told the Secretary of War that when the Army of the Potomac begins hostilities the Confederates will not have any time to threaten Washington."

Mr. Lincoln remained silent for a minute or two, and then said:

" Well, Mr. Secretary of War, when the people of the United States selected Mr. Grant, as Mrs. Grant persists in calling the General, to take the chief command of all the United States armies, they and their Congress evidently intended that he should have

GEN INGALL'S AND OFFICERS, HEADQUARTERS ARMY OF POTOMAC.

some power. You and I have been trying for three years to run this war, and we don't seem to have made a very good job of it. Now, suppose we let the Lieutenant-General try his hand. He has to shoulder all the responsibility if he fails."

That settled it. The heavy artillery battalions remained in the Army of the Potomac, and right gallant service they did, too. In fact, when Grant subsequently ordered fifteen thousand more men to be sent him, Stanton made no objection.

General Burnside was marching toward the Rappahannock River from Centreville when Meade began assembling his three consolidated army corps, now under command of Major-Generals Winfield Scott Hancock, Gouverneur K. Warren, and John Sedgwick. General Sheridan was brought from the West to command the cavalry corps. Hancock had four divisions, under Generals Francis C. Barlow, John Gibbon, David B. Birney, and Gershom Mott: Warren had also four divisions, under Generals Charles Griffin, John C. Robinson, Samuel W. Crawford, and James S. Wadsworth. Sedgwick's three divisions were under Generals H. G. Wright, George W. Getty, and James B. Ricketts. Burnside's four divisions, under Generals T. G. Stevenson, Robert B. Potter, Orlando B. Willcox, and Edward Ferrero, whose troops were colored. Sheridan had three divisions, under Generals A. T. A. Torbert, D. McM. Gregg, and J. H. Wilson. The four brigades of reserve artillery were under General Henry J. Hunt. When the final orders were given to cross the Rapidan there were one hundred and sixteen thousand men under arms, with six thousand wagons, carrying twenty days' supplies of food and ammunition. No army was ever better equipped than this magnificent body of troops.

The several Federal columns crossed the Rapidan River on May 4, 1864. The day was warm and bright, and the atmosphere was burdened with the subtle perfumes of forest and field. Every tree and shrub was clothed in a tender garment of green ; the very earth seemed redolent of spring. Refreshed by their long winter's rest, and entirely refitted in clothing and military equipment, the troops were in splendid spirits.

The scenes at Germanna and Ely's Fords, where pontoon bridges had been constructed, were animated and exciting on that delightful May morning. The corps, division, and brigade banners floated lazily in the warm breeze as the several commands moved forward. With these fluttering ensigns were the regimental standards, their faded colors gaining new brilliance as the silken folds waved in tattered abandon amid the glitter of musket barrels and bayonets. Steadily marching in close ranks, the troops presented a solidity that betokened power and strength. With the long lines of infantry went heavy masses of artillery and cavalry, the sabres of these mounted men jingling musically as the well-fed horses trotted over the roads. While the troopers went swiftly to the front, and crossed the river in advance of the army, every road was occupied by the batteries of artillery, ponderous and grim. Each brigade had its quota of guns, and the corps of reserve numbered fully three hundred pieces, steel and brass, rifled and smooth-bore.

General Warren's corps was nominally the right wing of Meade's army, Sedgwick's the centre, and Hancock's the left. The Fifth and Sixth Corps crossed at Germanna Ford, the Second at Ely's, and so well timed was the entire movement that all the troops and two thousand wagons were over the stream inside of twenty-four hours. Warren, being in the advance, pushed on to Wilderness Tavern, where his corps went into bivouac during the night of May 4. Hancock crossed at six o'clock on Thursday morning, and halted at Chancellorsville. Sedgwick followed Warren, and massed his men on the bank of the river. Burnside had by that time reached Culpepper Court House, where he halted and awaited orders. There was no opposition to the Federal army while crossing the river, as the Confederate pickets quickly retired when the engineers began building their bridges.

Grant had now set all of his armies in motion. Sherman was moving from Chattanooga against Atlanta and Joe Johnston's army. Banks was to attack Mobile. Butler, with thirty-three thousand men in two corps, under Gillmore and W. F. Smith, was threatening Richmond by way of the James River. Sigel had eighteen thousand men, mostly cavalry, with which to advance up the Shenandoah Valley. The Confederacy was assailed on all points.

COUNCIL OF WAR AT MASSAPONAX CHURCH, MAY 21, 1864.

CHAPTER LVII.

THE FOREST BATTLE IN THE WILDERNESS.

The ground on which the Army of the Potomac now stood is well named The Wilderness, for it is covered·by a mass of oak and pine; the virgin parts of the forest being choked with dense undergrowth and a network of vines, while young pines on the abandoned cultivated land formed perfect screens to the movements of troops. The Wilderness was a *terra incognita* to the Federals, but the Confederates had a perfect knowledge of the labyrinth of roads and wagon paths intersecting the entire region. General Grant did not expect to fight so near the Rapidan, for he supposed that Lee would retire to some selected position before giving battle. The Federal commander, however, soon discovered that Lee was a great strategist and a desperate fighter, ready and quick in his movements.

Grant's aim was to first cut Lee off from Richmond. He, therefore, sent Sheridan with two cavalry divisions towards Hamilton's Crossing, near Fredericksburg, while Wilson, with the other division, moved towards Craig's Meeting House, on the Catharpin Road. Sheridan and Wilson were to seize and hold the several roads which might be available for the movement of the Confederates. Hancock was sent to Shady Grove Church, to connect with Warren at Parker's Store, the latter to draw his right towards Old Wilderness Tavern, where Sedgwick was to form his line. At sunrise of May 5 all the columns were in motion. As yet, there was no sign of opposition, but Lee had already divined Grant's plan, and decided to fall heavily on his flank. Ewell's Corps had been sent over the Orange Turnpike, and Hill's by the Orange Plank Road, and they were near Old Wilderness Tavern when Warren approached. Griffin's division touched Ewell, and Crawford struck Hill. A halt was made, the Federal movement being temporarily checked. Grant, however, imagined that Lee was retreating, and that Warren had struck the rear guard. He accordingly decided to crush it and seize Mine Run. At noon Warren advanced with Griffin's and Wadsworth's divisions and drove Ewell back. Johnson's division getting into temporary confusion, Rodes rushed forward and turned the tide, Griffin being overwhelmed and compelled to retire, after losing two pieces of artillery and several hundred prisoners. Wadsworth, in attempting to join Griffin, was confused by the forest and exposed his left flank, which, being attacked and crushed, the entire division fell back in disorder. McCandless' brigade, of Crawford's division, became isolated and was surrounded. The brigade fought with rare courage, and cut its way out to the main body, losing nearly all of two regiments. Warren having lost three thousand men in this brief but deadly encounter, formed a new line across the turnpike. The forest, amidst which the armies were now operating, was so dense that the Federal brigades maintained their for-

CAMP of MILITARY TELEGRAPH CORPS.

HEADQUARTERS OF GEN. D. B. BIRNEY.

PROVOST MARSHALL'S OFFICE.

CAP'T CLINTON'S QUARTERS.

HEADQUARTERS THIRD ARMY CORPS, ARMY OF THE POTOMAC.

mation with difficulty, while the vines and almost impenetrable undergrowth frequently prevented any movement except in single file.

Sedgwick assumed his assigned position in good time, but Hancock, who had gone by the Brock Road toward the point where it intersected the Plank Road, over which Hill was advancing, was delayed, so Sedgwick advanced Getty's division and occupied the Second Corps position. Scarcely had Getty formed line when Hill began pressing him, but the Federals stood fast. Hancock arrived at three o'clock, his men passing over the narrow wagon paths with remarkable rapidity, taking position along the Brock Road, the orders being to move forward and engage. Hancock sent Birney's and Mott's divisions on either side of Getty, but they failed to gain ground, as the Confederates were in strong force. Neither side could see the other, owing to the density of the forest, and the fighting was necessarily at close range. The brigades of Owen and Carroll, of Gibbon's division, then strengthened Hancock's line, but as they were facing Hill's entire corps, consisting of Anderson's, Willcox's, and Heth's divisions, the Federal charges were repelled. In one of their sallies the Confederates captured two guns of Rickett's

General View.

Camp of Sanitary Commission.

Pontoon Wharves.

Sanitary Commission Wagons.

Distant Views.

Camp of 2nd N.Y. & 1st Mass. Artillery.

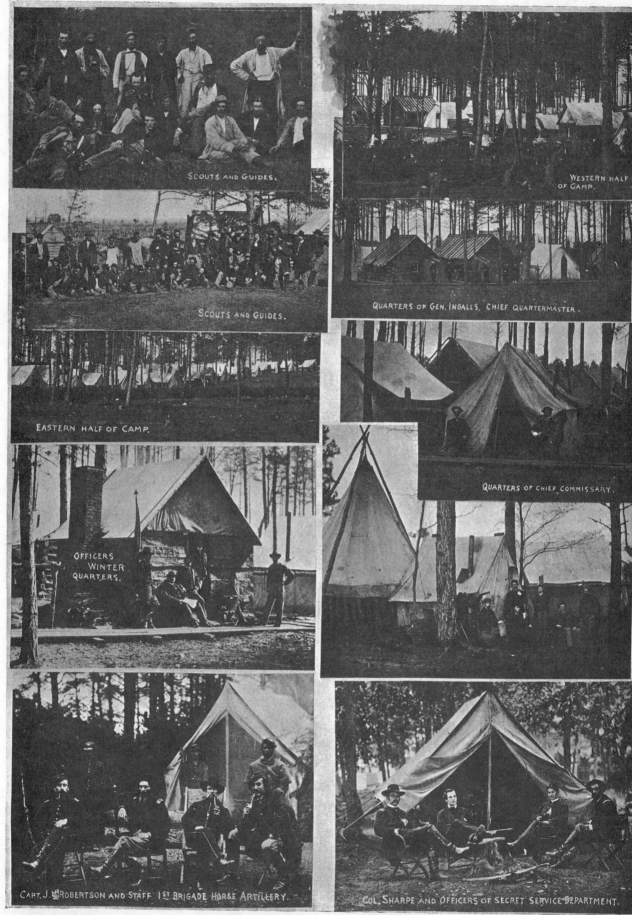

SCOUTS AND GUIDES.

WESTERN HALF OF CAMP.

SCOUTS AND GUIDES.

QUARTERS OF GEN. INGALLS, CHIEF QUARTERMASTER.

EASTERN HALF OF CAMP.

QUARTERS OF CHIEF COMMISSARY.

OFFICERS WINTER QUARTERS.

CAPT. J. M. ROBERTSON AND STAFF, 1ST BRIGADE HORSE ARTILLERY.

COL. SHARPE AND OFFICERS OF SECRET SERVICE DEPARTMENT.

SCENES AT HEADQUARTERS ARMY OF THE POTOMAC.

battery, killing nearly all the men and horses. Carroll's brigade recaptured the pieces, and Dow's Maine battery occupied the gap in the line. Mott's division then gave way, and General Alexander Hays was shot dead while reforming his brigade. Meade now sent Wadsworth with his division, and Baxter's brigade, from Robinson's division, to relieve Hancock, by moving southward through the woods, and strike Hill's flank and rear. But, owing to the density of the forest and his ignorance of the ground, Wadsworth did not reach his objective point until after dark, so halted and waited. Thus ended the first day of the battle, and Grant found himself in sudden peril. Hancock had failed to dislodge Hill, but held his own line. He was separated from Sedgwick and Warren by a deep ravine, which also ran between Ewell and Hill. Both of the opposing commanders had been unable to carry out their purpose, but the lines were well defined and so close

Cooking Tents.

Headquarters.

Store Rooms.

Sanitary Commission at Fredericksburg, Va.

Officers and Nurses.

View on the docks at City Point.

together that the men of both armies drew water from the same brook, but no shot was fired during that night.

General Burnside received orders to come up early on the morning of the 5th, and, though Culpepper Court House is over thirty miles from the Rapidan, his Ninth Corps was on the battlefield at daylight of the 6th, and took position between Hancock and Warren. Grant's line was now five miles long, being formed as follows: Sedgwick, with Wright's and Rickett's divisions, stood on the right; Warren came next, with Griffin's, Robinson's, and Crawford's divisions; Burnside stood on the left centre, with Stevenson's, Potter's, and Willcox's divisions, Ferrero's colored division having been left in the rear to guard the trains; Hancock had the extreme left with six divisions, under Barlow, Gibbon, Birney, Mott, Wadsworth, and Getty. Lee's right was held by Hill, his left by Ewell, and Longstreet's corps was hurrying up from Gordonsville to join Hill and assume the centre.

It was evident that the next day's engagement was to be a battle with bullets alone

BRIG.-GENERAL JAMES B. WADSWORTH, KILLED IN BATTLE OF THE
WILDERNESS.

BVT.-MAJOR-GENERAL ALEX. HAYS, KILLED IN BATTLE OF THE
WILDERNESS.

for not more than twenty pieces of artillery could be used by either army. In fact, the fighting all the way to the James gave little opportunity for the employment of field guns, and General Grant finally sent back over one hundred pieces, they not returning until the siege of Petersburg began.

Grant's plan for the following day was that Hancock should attack Hill on his flank and centre, Burnside engaging as soon as the Second Corps got fairly to work. Sedgwick and Warren were to make sufficient demonstration to prevent Early reinforcing Hill. If Burnside succeeded in breaking through Hill's line he was to swing round and envelop Early. General Sheridan was sent to connect with Hancock's left, and attack Stuart's cavalry, who were trying to reach the Rapidan and the Federal trains. Sheridan found his quarry at the intersection of the Furnace and the Brock Roads; also at Todd's Tavern, he defeating Stuart in three engagements. Hancock was misled by the cavalry carbine volleys, and supposed that a strong force of infantry was approaching, so detached a brigade to meet it. General Lee decided to fall upon Grant's left with two-thirds of his army and crush it, which would enable him to take the whole Federal line in flank. But Longstreet could not get up in time for an assault at daybreak, so Lee made a diversion on Sedgwick to gain time and conceal his real movements. Early, accordingly, opened a heavy musketry fire a few minutes before five o'clock, but Sedgwick's men clung to their position, and the feint failed.

Hancock sent forward Birney's and Getty's divisions, with Owen's and Carroll's brigades from Gibbon's command, along the Plank Road, while Wadsworth advanced on the right of the road to strike Hill's flank. The direct assault was a furious one, but was met by the Confederates with tolerable steadiness until Wadsworth's movement was developed, when Hill lost ground and was driven back over a mile, some of his men not stopping until they reached the trains and reserve artillery. The divisions of Heth and Willcox, of Hill's corps, were badly cut up, and the Federals captured over two thousand prisoners and five stands of colors. Had General Hancock been able to discern the full success of this movement he might have cut Lee's army in two, but the interminable forest concealed Hill's discomfiture. Birney, Getty, and Wadsworth paused, and General Hancock began getting his troops into better order. Burnside had sent him Stevenson's division, and he replaced Getty's division with Frank's and Webb's brigades, from Gibbon's and Barlow's divisions. It was not until nine o'clock that Hancock was ready and moved for-

Confederate Prisoners Captured from Johnson's Division

Allsop's House Near Spottsylvania Court House

Evacuation of Port Royal Rappahannock River.

Battery Wagons of Military Telegraph Corps.

Ruins of bridge at Germania Mills Rapidan River.

Wagons Crossing Rappahannock River on Pontoon bridges.

Troops Crossing Pontoon Bridges. Rapidan River.

ward, but to his surprise he found the Confederate line stronger than before, as Hill had brought up his reserve divisions, and Longstreet was with him. The latter had been marching towards Hancock's left flank, when Hill's sudden peril compelled Lee to recall him.

The battle now became a very deadly one. At times, single regiments fought each other among the trees and undergrowth as they became separated from the main line. For two hours this struggle in the forest continued, the Federals losing ground, General James S. Wadsworth being killed by a bullet through his brain. This incident so demoralized Wadsworth's division that they broke and ran. This shook Hancock's whole line, and the Confederates appeared to be carrying everything before them, when there was a sudden pause, and Hancock quickly reformed. For the second time these Southern troops were to pay the penalty for clinging to forest ground, for General Longstreet was

Confederate dead of Ewell's Corps on the field near Allsops House.

1 Mass. Artillery burying the dead at Allsops house.

shot and severely wounded by his own men, who mistook the group of horsemen for Federals. Longstreet had planned a decisive movement, which might have proved disastrous to Hancock, but when the mind that conceived it was no longer able to direct the details it could not be made. General Longstreet being carried from the field, General Lee assumed personal command of that part of his line.

Warren, Burnside, and Sedgwick had practically done nothing except hold the forces in front of them actively engaged, and the musketry died away throughout the Wilderness, until four o'clock in the afternoon, when Lee, having got all of Longstreet's and Hill's divisions together, hurled them on Hancock. The Confederates advanced, in four heavy columns, in utter silence, until they came within three hundred yards of the Federal line. Then they delivered a tremendous series of musketry volleys, but the Federals had thrown up breastworks, consequently the Confederate musketry made but little impression, while the Federal volleys were very effective. Still, the combat was a most destructive one, and it was rendered all the more demoniac by the dead leaves and branches catching fire. The wind drove the flames towards the Federal breastworks, which also became ignited. Amidst the hot flame and suffocating smoke Hancock's men clung to their rude defences until nearly exhausted. Then the Confederates charged and broke Hancock's line in several places. A panic ensued, and several brigades had already begun retreating toward Chancellorsville, when General Carroll's brigade rushed into the gap and drove Lee's men back. That ended the fighting on that part of the field.

Lee's strategy was shown later in the day, when he sent Early through the forest so secretly and securely that the one-legged general was able to completely surprise Sedgwick by suddenly striking him on his extreme right and part of his front. Early seized

LIEUTENANT-GENERAL U. S. GRANT.

over four thousand prisoners, of Rickett's division, among them Brigadier-Generals Shaler and Seymour. The movement was made at Lee's favorite hour, just before sunset, but Sedgwick quickly moved up his supports and repelled the attack in fine style. Then darkness enveloped the blood-stained forest, and the Battle of the Wilderness was over. The Federal loss in this battle was five thousand men killed, ten thousand wounded, and five thousand taken prisoners. The Confederates lost over four thousand killed, eight thousand wounded, and three thousand taken prisoners. Generals Hays, Webb, and Wadsworth were killed on the Federal side, while Generals Bartlett, Carroll, Getty, Gregg, Hancock and Owen were wounded. Confederate Generals Jenkins, Jones, and Stafford were killed, and Generals Hunter, Pegram, Pickett, and Longstreet wounded.

CHAPTER LVIII.

THE TWO DAYS' BATTLE AT SPOTTSYLVANIA COURT HOUSE.

While the battle of May 6 was in progress General Grant ordered all of the pontoon bridges, except the one at Germanna Ford, to be taken up. This was a stern announcement to his army that there would be no retreating, only wounded men being permitted to pass over the Rapidan. It was a new experience for the Army of the Potomac, but the soldiers were pleased with this evidence of their general's determination to fight it out, as he subsequently expressed it, " on that line, even if it took all summer."

On the morning of Saturday, May 7, both armies stood to arms in the Wilderness, but there was no fighting, beyond an occasional outburst on the skirmish lines. During the afternoon it was evident that Lee was falling back, and as Grant believed that the Confederate commander was endeavoring to reach his intrenchments at Mine Run, he resolved to make a flank movement on Lee's right, and, if possible, get between him and Richmond. The several corps were, therefore, put in motion as soon as darkness set in, and the entire army was marching towards Spottsylvania Court House, about thirteen miles southeast of the Wilderness. The Fifth Corps led the advance, over the Brock Road, followed by the Second. The Sixth and Ninth Corps marched by way of Chancellorsville. The intrepidity of Grant was shown by this movement, for it uncovered Germanna Ford and his line of communication, but he knew that Lee had something else to think about.

General Lee soon discovered the meaning of the Federal movement, and he directed General Anderson, who now commanded Longstreet's corps, to march for Spottsylvania Court House. Anderson had the shortest route, so he reached Spottsylvania first. It is a curious incident that Warren and Anderson were marching on parallel roads, unknown to each other, the natural consequence of manœuvering in a forest. General Sheridan had gone to Todd's Tavern to drive in Stuart's cavalry, which he succeeded in doing, but General Meade changed Merritt's orders, and the Confederates gained the bridge that had been held by the Federal cavalry. Thus, for the second time, an error in judgment gave Lee the advantage.

MAJOR-GENERAL J. SEDGWICK, KILLED.

About a mile south of the Wilderness Tavern four creeks run together. These creeks are known as the Mat, Ta, Po, and Ny, as they form the Mattapony River. A long ridge divides the Po and the Ny, Spottsylvania Court House occupying the crest of the ridge. Anderson's corps marched over the Catharpin Road, crossing the Po at Wooden Bridge. Warren and Hancock, being on the Brock Road, encountered none of the streams, but Sedgwick had to cross the Ny at Catharpin Furnace, while Burnside took the bridge at Gate's House, being compelled to fight for it, as the Confederates were extending their line in that direction. The movement of the Federal army was simply the elongation of its line, the right and centre passing behind the left, and the left following in turn until it reached the new position assigned it. Though the ground along the course of the Po and the Ny is somewhat difficult for campaign purposes, it was much more open than the Wilderness, yet better adapted for defensive than offensive operations.

Warren's orders were to march direct to Spottsylvania Court House, but he was delayed at Todd's Tavern, the road being blocked by Sheridan's cavalry, and he lost five hours. The road being also obstructed further on by felled trees, his progress was slow and difficult, and it was eight o'clock before Robinson's division reached Alsop's Farm, two miles from Spottsylvania. General Anderson had intended bivouacking, but the smoke from the fires in the forest compelled his men to keep moving all night, and they arrived at Alsop's Farm two hours before Warren, taking position on a wooded crest

BATTLE OF SPOTTSYLVANIA.

Copyright, 1887, by L. Prang & Co.

beside the Ny, on the other side of a wide clearing. Ignorant that he was facing Anderson's entire command, General Robinson led his division across the fields in two columns, which were saluted by a terrific artillery and musketry fire, which threw the command into temporary confusion. While reforming his line, Robinson was wounded in the knee, subsequent amputation removing him from active service. The loss of their General completed the discomfiture of the Second Division, but Warren assumed personal command, and was restoring order when Griffin's division arrived. The Confederates again opened fire, and Griffin's line was broken, as Crawford and Cutler, the latter now commanding Wadsworth's division, advanced, Crawford going to Griffin's left, Cutler to his right. Then the entire corps advanced in gallant style, and drove Anderson from the crest, the Confederates retiring to and taking possession of the Court House. This battle of Alsop's Farm, though brief, was a bloody one, for Warren had thirteen hundred men killed and wounded in less than two hours, the First Michigan Regiment losing one hundred and seventy-seven men out of the two hundred who had survived the carnage in the Wilderness. Grant's flank movement had failed.

It was not until the forenoon of Monday, May 9, that both armies faced each other in full force. Lee had established a semi-circular line which inclosed the town. His right was occupied by Anderson, his centre by Ewell, and his left by Early. Meade's right extended beyond the Brock Road, Warren covering all the converging roads in that direction. Sedgwick occupied the centre, and Burnside the left, Hancock being still at Todd's Tavern, expecting to meet Early. The latter, however, was recalled after the fight at Alsop's Farm, which being discovered by Grant, he ordered Hancock to leave Mott's division at the Tavern, and with the remainder of his corps take position on Warren's right. At the same time Sheridan started on a raid in the Confederate rear for the purpose of destroying Lee's railroad communication with Richmond. The Federal line now enveloped the Confederate one, and the day began with slight skirmishing. It was then that General John Sedgwick was killed. He was standing on the breastworks, on the right of his corps line, superintending the placing of some batteries, paying no attention to the bullets of the Confederate sharpshooters. When remonstrated with by members of his staff, Sedgwick laughed contemptuously. At that instant he fell dead, a bullet piercing his skull under the left eye. General Horatio G. Wright succeeded him in command of the Sixth Corps, and continued in that position until the close of the war.

General Sedgwick was a great soldier. He was very dear to the old Sixth Corps, as is evidenced by the statue erected to his memory at West Point by the rank and file of that organization before its disbandment. Sedgwick was fond of leaping from his saddle, during an engagement, for the purpose of advancing to the extreme front line and examining into affairs. It was this habit that led to his death. He always wore a regulation cavalry sabre, and it corresponded well with his massive figure. Sedgwick was a good deal like Thomas. He might be styled the "Old Reliable" of the Army of the Potomac, as was Thomas of the Western Army. He went into battle without haste or excitement, but when once fairly engaged he kept his lines intact. His death was a great loss to the Federal side, just as Jackson's crippled the efforts of Lee.

Monday wore away, but on Tuesday a tremendous battle occurred. Lee's right now rested on the Ny, his left on Glady Run, while his centre, being thrown forward, occupied a commanding position. Grant's line of battle was six miles long, his right extending across the Po, Hancock's position being nearly parallel with the Shady Grove Church Road. Warren held the right centre, on the east bank of the Po; Wright the left centre, facing the Court House; Burnside occupied the extreme left. Lee's troops were sheltered by a dense forest, and they had erected formidable barricades.

Grant decided to assault Laurel Hill, the apex of Lee's curved line, Hancock being ordered to send Birney's and Gibbon's divisions to strengthen the assaulting column. Anderson then fell upon Barlow, capturing a field gun, so Hancock was compelled to retire, leaving his wounded to perish in the woods, that had again caught fire.

Two attacks had been made on Laurel Hill, first by Carroll's and Webb's brigades, then by the divisions under Cutler and Crawford. Both failed. When Hancock joined Warren and Wright it was arranged that the Second, Fifth, and Sixth Corps were to make a combined assault. The advance of the Federal line was an imposing one, for the effort was similar to Pickett's charge at Gettysburg, except that the several columns had to climb a steep and densely wooded hill. Precisely at five oclock in the afternoon over thirty thousand infantry pushed forward, being met by a most destructive fire, the men being unable to effect a lodgment in the Confederate intrenchments, though one or two points were temporarily pierced. The loss was very severe, but at six o'clock the assault was renewed with the same dire results, for the Confederates drove back the Federals with tremendous slaughter. In ninety minutes six thousand men were killed or wounded, Generals James Clay Rice and Thomas G. Stevenson being among the Federal dead. While Warren was charging his front, Wright saw a chance, and, organizing a storming party consisting of twelve picked regiments, gave Colonel Emory Upton, of the One Hundred and Twenty-first New York, the command. Mott was to support Upton, but he utterly failed, and General Grant countermanded the movement, though Upton had already captured several guns and nearly one thousand prisoners. For his gallantry young Upton was made a Brigadier-General while the action was in progress, General Grant conferring the promotion while bending over the wounded Colonel. This ended the first day's battle at Spottsylvania. It might have been the last had General Burnside only known that he had really turned Lee's right flank. The Ninth Corps had met with little opposition in its advance,

MAJ. GEN. J. M. PALMER.

MAJ. GEN. G. M. DODGE.

BRIG. GEN. C. O. LOOMIS

BRIG. GEN. E. W. WHITTAKER

owing to the fact that Lee had temporarily weakened that part of his line, but the configuration of the ground and the density of the woods sheltering the Confederates rendered it impossible for Burnside to ascertain the exact strength of his opponents without destroying the continuity of the Federal line. At nightfall General Grant ordered Burnside to join Wright, and thus all the advantage was lost. In his memoirs Grant assumes all the blame for this oversight.

During this first day at Spottsylvania the Federals had lost fully ten thousand men, while the Confederate loss was very near nine thousand. The unburied bodies of three thousand men lay scattered along the slopes of the ridges or under the trees. Out of the two hundred thousand Federals and Confederates who had rushed into battle on May 5, forty-three thousand were either dead, wounded, or prisoners—a dreadful record for three days of fighting.

The morning of Wednesday, May 11, was a bright and sunny one. Having fought so desperately the day before, neither army was in spirit or condition for a speedy resumption of hostilities. The heavy skirmish lines were, however, in frequent collision, each endeavoring to conceal the movements of large bodies of troops behind them.

Grant had carefully surveyed Lee's lines and found that his centre formed a salient point near the Landrum House. Believing it to be vulnerable, he decided to make an attack, selecting the Second Corps to strike the blow. Hancock, therefore, withdrew from the front of A. P. Hill and, marching to the left of Meade's army line, took position between Wright and Burnside. As the assault was to have the support of the entire Federal forces, Wright extended his left, while Burnside and Warren prepared to move forward and engage the enemy on Hancock's right and left, in order to prevent a concentration against the Second Corps. Each corps expected to do some hard fighting, but the brunt was to fall on Hancock's. Rain began falling heavily during the afternoon, and continued through the night. Under cover of the intense darkness, Hancock withdrew his men from their intrenchments, and marching entirely by compass, moved past Warren and Wright, finally taking position only twelve hundred yards from the point to be attacked. Barlow's and Birney's divisions were in advance, having formed in two massed lines. Mott's division was supporting Birney's, while Gibbon's was in reserve, to move right or left, as necessity might demand. Thus the corps stood, waiting for dawn. At half-past four on the morning of Thursday, May 12, Hancock's men began moving, a heavy fog concealing their advance. Silently and steadily the lines stepped forward, Barlow's men finding themselves on comparatively open ground, while Birney's had to struggle through a thick wood. For seven hundred yards the two divisions advanced without firing a shot, but as they passed through the Confederate skirmish line a sudden cheer was given and the troops rushed forward like a mighty wave.

The charge was made so suddenly that the Federals were able to toss aside the rude *abatis* in front of the Confederate breastworks, and dash over the wall of logs and earth before Ewell's men could defend them. Inside these intrenchments a desperate hand-to-hand struggle ensued, but the Federals were victorious, capturing Generals Edward Johnson and George H. Stewart, with four thousand men. They also seized thirty cannon and as many battle flags. Then Ewell's line broke and retreated in confusion. Johnson's division being destroyed, Hancock advanced on Early's, and had the Second Corps been properly supported in this movement there is little doubt that Hancock would ultimately have cut Lee's army in two.

It was now half-past six o'clock, and as Wright took position on Hancock's right, the latter concentrated his force on the left of the Salient. General Lee then decided to crush Hancock and Wright, and massed nearly half of his army for that purpose. Again and again did the Confederates charge, each one weakening the Federal grasp on the position, when Cutler's and Griffin's divisions, of the Fifth Corps, were detached and hurried to the scene, though the entire line of both armies were fighting desperately. This reinforcement equalized matters, and though the conflict continued for a period of twenty consecutive hours, the Federals held their ground. No less than five charges were made by Lee, each being repulsed with terrible loss. The battle did not end until three o'clock on the morning of May 13, both sides resting on their arms during the day, Lee finally retreating to his second line of intrenchments. The Battle of Spottsylvania may be considered a Federal victory, though a very costly one, for Meade lost twelve thousand men, the Confederate loss being even greater. Masses of dead bodies were heaped up all along the disputed line, and the wounded were everywhere. The Army of the Potomac had now an effective strength of only eighty-seven thousand, nearly one-fourth of those who crossed the Rapidan River having been killed, wounded, or taken prisoner in the brief space of eight days. Lee had, however, lost as many more—truly an appalling record for a single week.

CHAPTER LIX

SHERIDAN'S RICHMOND RAID AND GRANT'S PASSAGE OF THE NORTH ANNA RIVER.

Rain had now fallen for nearly twenty-four hours. The earth was literally soaked, and the road a deep sea of mud. Consequently manœuvering of large bodies of men was very difficult, yet a severe engagement occurred on the 13th between Burnside and Hill. It had no result, however. For five days the relative position of the two armies continued unchanged, but Grant had kept throwing out his left until his army stood five miles

GENERALS OF THE CAVALRY CORPS—SHERIDAN, MERRITT, DAVIES, GREGG, TORBERT, AND WILSON.

northwest of Spottsylvania Court House, and on May 23 his left rested on Massaponax Church. On the 19th six thousand fresh troops from the defences around Washington and Alexandria arrived, the reinforcement of these heavy artillery regiments being received with cheers by the veterans of the Wilderness and Spottsylvania.

General Sheridan had started on a raid on May 9 with ten thousand sabres, and reaching the North Anna River, captured Beaver Dam Station, destroyed ten miles of railroad track, and three freight trains containing a million and a half of Confederate rations. Four hundred Federals taken prisoners at the Wilderness were also recaptured. Before leaving Beaver Dam Station, Sheridan was fiercely assaulted by "Jeb" Stuart, and the battle proved a savage one, the Federal loss being very heavy. But Sheridan coolly crossed the North Anna by Ground-Squirrel Bridge, and at daylight on May 11 captured Ashland Station, on the Fredericksburg Railroad. Destroying more property, he proceeded toward Richmond as far as Yellow Tavern, six miles from the Confederate capital, on the Brooktown pike. Here Stuart was found in strong force, he having reached that point by forced marches.

General Merritt was the first to discover the enemy, and moved forward to the

Canvas Pontoon Bridges,
across
North Anna River.

Corps Ammunition Train
Crossing Pontoon Bridge.

N.Y. Engineers Constructing
road on South bank of
North Anna River.

N.Y. Engineers Constructing
Road on south bank of
North Anna River.

Chesterfield Bridge
North Anna River.

attack. Wilson's division and one of Gregg's brigades were sent to his support. The Confederates had placed a battery in a position to enfilade the road, their guns doing considerable execution. But while Devin's and Gibbs' brigades stood fast, General Custer made a brilliant charge on Stuart's left, when two field guns were captured and Stuart's left turned, his right and centre being also driven in. General Stuart had never before suffered such a repulse, and grew so desperate in his efforts to reform his lines that he exposed himself and fell, being mortally wounded. He died in the City of Richmond on May 13. The fall of Stuart put an end to the battle of Yellow Tavern.

Sheridan had then the temerity to attempt a capture of the works around Richmond, Custer crossing the first line and seizing two pieces of artillery, with one hundred prisoners. The Confederate force was, however, too strong, so Sheridan and his troopers

Canvas pontoon bridges over Pamunkey River

Pontoon Bridge over Pamunkey River at Mrs. Nelsons.

Bethel Church, Headquarters of Gen. Burnside.

Ruins of Bridge.

retired toward the Chickahominy. While rebuilding Meadow Bridge he was attacked by Fitz Hugh Lee, who had succeeded Stuart, but the latter was handsomely repulsed. On May 14 Sheridan opened communication with General Butler on the York River, obtained rations, and gave his men and horses three days' rest. Then leisurely returning by way of Baltimore Store, White House, and Hanover Court House, the cavalry rejoined the Army of the Potomac on May 25.

Grant having successfully made his flanking movement, resolved to cross the North Anna River, setting his columns in motion at midnight of May 19. Lee was quick to discover the purport of this movement, and ordered Ewell to attack the Federal right wing. Ewell crossed the Ny during the afternoon, seized the Fredericksburg road and captured a Federal ammunition train. Ewell's troops then encountered the division of raw heavy artillery, under General R. O. Tyler, which fought gallantly and repulsed the Confederate veterans. Then the Fifth and Second Corps came up and continued the pursuit. This brief engagement for the possession of the North Anna delayed Grant in

Quarle's Mill. North Anna River.

Confederate Fortifications at Chesterfield Bridge.

Log Bridge across North Anna River at Quarles Mill.

Destroyed R.R. bridge across North Anna River.

Pontoon Bridges North Anna River.

crossing the Matapony River until the following night. His base of supplies was now at Fredericksburg, and he resolutely moved forward on his bloody campaign.

The Federal army began crossing the Matapony River, at Milford Bridge, on the morning of May 22, Warren pushing on to Harris' Store. Burnside and Wright had been left at Spottsylvania, confronting Hill, the corps under Ewell and Anderson having begun their race with Hancock and Warren for the North Anna. Then Burnside left Wright and moved to New Bethel Church, the Sixth Corps taking position at Guiney's Station. Here Hill made an attack, but was speedily repulsed by Wright, who finding that the Confederates were hastening to join their main body, also started to get in touch with Hancock. That night the Federal forces were reunited near the northern bank of the North Anna, Lee's entire army being strongly posted on the opposite side.

At sunrise of May 23 Warren marched for Jericho Ford, followed by Wright. The Fifth Corps reached the river at five o'clock in the afternoon, when a brigade waded

Burnett's House near Cold Harbor.

Collecting remains of the dead on the battlefield of Cold Harbor months after the battle.

Camp in the woods at Cold Harbor.

Old Church Hotel near Cold Harbor.

Photographer's Camp at Cold Harbor.

Part of Battlefield of Cold Harbor.

waist-high through the water, under cover of their sharpshooters, and captured the ford. Pontoons being laid, the corps crossed and formed line, Crawford's division being on Warren's left, next the river, with Griffin in the centre and Cutler on the right. Before the line was formed Hill's corps made an attack, but was repulsed, and Hill left behind five hundred men as prisoners, with his killed and wounded. By nightfall Wright crossed and strengthened Warren. Simultaneous with this movement, Hancock marched to a wooden bridge west of the Fredericksburg Railroad, arriving just after sunset. As the bridge was guarded, Egan's and Pierce's brigades charged and captured it. The Confederates retreated so rapidly over the structure that many men were pushed into the river and drowned. Hancock decided to wait for daylight before crossing. Burnside advanced to Ox Ford, midway between Telegraph Road and Jericho Ford, halting on the bank in the darkness.

At daylight of the 24th Hancock crossed without opposition and formed line, facing nearly west. He also destroyed part of the railroad. The remainder of Wright's corps joined Warren, extending his line on the right, south of the Virginia Central Railroad, which was also destroyed for a considerable distance. Burnside found the Confederates in great force at Ox Ford, and he was unable to cross. In the meantime Grant had ordered Hancock and Warren to each send a brigade to Ox Ford, but even with this increased force the passage was deemed hazardous. Another crossing being found, Burnside sent Crittenden's division over, and it connected with Crawford's left. Potter's division went over by the wooden bridge and joined Hancock. Crittenden lost heavily while crossing, being attacked by Hill. Burnside remained on the north bank with his remaining divisions.

The Federals were now straddling the North Anna. Lee, on the other hand, had a shorter line, and his army was all on one side of the river. He was also being heavily

reinforced, for Pickett's division had arrived from Richmond, and Hoke's brigade had come up from North Carolina. Breckenridge's command was also on the ground. The Federal base of supplies was now shifted to the White House, on the Pamunkey River, all of the wagon trains moving to that point, while transports passed down the Chesapeake Bay and up the York and Pamunkey Rivers, under guard of gunboats.

Sheridan's cavalry having arrived, Wilson's division moved south to Little River to give the impression that Lee's left flank was to be attacked, and the Confederates being deceived by this manœuvre, Grant's right wing was withdrawn to the north side of the river. Sheridan took Gregg's and Torbert's cavalry divisions, supported by Russell's division of infantry, to Hanover Ferry. The crossing was made on the morning of May 27, and a position south of the Pamunkey secured. On the morning of May 28 the entire Federal army crossed the Pamunkey, and were on McClellan's old ground. General Lee was completely deceived, and Grant had extricated himself.

DUTCH GAP CANAL.

CHAPTER LX.

THE SECOND BATTLE OF COLD HARBOR AND THE CROSSING OF THE JAMES RIVER.

The Army of the Potomac was now on the historic peninsula, and the veterans who had survived battle and skirmish during the Antietam, Rappahannock, Gettysburg, and Overland campaigns, pointed out to their younger comrades many familiar points and objects. General Butler having been "bottled up" at Bermuda Hundred, to use General Grant's expressive phrase, Beauregard found himself able to send Lee nearly two-thirds of his strength. Butler was ordered by Grant to send every man he could

spare, while additional troops came from every available point. In addition to Beauregard's reinforcement, Lee was joined by Breckenridge, who came from West Virginia with ten thousand men. Both armies being thus reinforced, they began manoeuvring for another battle.

On May 28 General Sheridan started on a reconnoissance over the Hanover Road, encountering the Confederate cavalry, under Wade Hampton and Fitz Hugh Lee, at Hawe's Store. A brisk battle ensued, when Lee and Hampton retired across the Tolopotomy Creek. Having thus se-

BERMUDA HUNDRED LANDING.

SIGNAL TOWER ON LEFT BERMUDA HUNDRED LINES NEAR APPOMATTOX RIVER.

ARMY BRIDGE ACROSS JAMES RIVER, NEAR VARINA LANDING.

DUTCH GAP CANAL.

VARINA LANDING JAMES RIVER.

SIGNAL TOWER ON LEFT BERMUDA HUNDRED LINES NEAR APPOMATTOX RIVER.

DUTCH GAP CANAL.

SIGNAL STATION, JAMES RIVER.

ARMY BRIDGE ACROSS JAMES RIVER NEAR VARINA LANDING.

AIKENS HOUSE. NEAR VARINA LANDING.

DUTCH GAP CANAL.

VIEWS ON JAMES RIVER NEAR DREWRY'S BLUFF.

CONFEDERATE OBSTRUCTIONS ON JAMES RIVER. NEAR DREWRY'S BLUFF.

CONFEDERATE OBSTRUCTIONS ON JAMES RIVER NEAR DREWRY'S BLUFF.

CONFEDERATE OBSTRUCTIONS ON JAMES RIVER NEAR DREWRY'S BLUFF.

FEDERAL OBSTRUCTIONS IN TREUT'S BEACH, JAMES RIVER.

CONFEDERATE GUNBOAT SUNK IN JAMES RIVER, ABOVE DUTCH GAP CANAL.

VIEWS ON JAMES RIVER NEAR DREWRY'S BLUFF.

VIEWS ON JAMES RIVER NEAR DREWRY'S BLUFF.

cured the roads, Grant ordered a reconnoissance in force. Hancock and Wright advanced on Hanover Court House by converging roads, while Warren moved toward Shady Grove Church. Burnside followed Hancock and Warren, as reserve.

General Wright arrived at Hanover Court House without serious opposition, but Hancock found the Confederates in strong force along the banks of the Tolopotomy, and he had to halt. Warren was also checked a mile or two from Shady Grove Church, at a point where the road crosses the Tolopotomy. Here Ewell was moving along the Mechanicsville turnpike in hopes of turning the Federal left. General Crawford, who now commanded the Pennsylvania Reserves, discovered the movement, and sent Colonel Hardin's brigade up the pike. Hardin got as far as Bethesada Church, where he met General Rodes, who made a furious attack and compelled the Reserves to retire to the Shady Grove Road. Here Crawford threw forward his remaining brigades, and by using several field guns, checked the Confederate advance, and extended his left to cover the Mechanicsville Road. General Meade now ordered Wright and Hancock to move forward and engage. The latter sent Barlow's division forward, which speedily broke the Confederate line.

Seeing the impossibility of forcing his way across the Chickahominy by an attack in front, Grant again adopted his old plan of turning Lee's right flank, and moved on Cold Harbor, as it commanded the White House and Richmond Roads. On May 31 General Torbert's cavalry division captured Cold Harbor and held it, despite the efforts of General Hoke, who made a determined attack on June 1. Being reinforced, Hoke pressed Torbert very hard, but could not dislodge him. General Wright had been marching his corps all night from the extreme right of Meade's line, and now advanced to Torbert's assistance. General W. F. Smith had left Bermuda Hundred on May 29 with the Eighteenth Corps and part of the Tenth, he having fully sixteen thousand men. His transports passed down the James and up the York and Pamunkey Rivers to White House in twenty-four hours. On landing, he marched to New Castle, but had to countermarch a distance of twelve miles in order to join Wright, which he did during the afternoon of June 1.

As the Federals, under Wright and Smith, began forming the Confederates threw up a line of rifle pits on the other side of a broad field, nearly a mile away, their main force being sheltered and hidden by a broad belt of woodland. Just before sunset Wright and Smith advanced, meeting a strong musketry fire, but their men rushed forward and captured the pits. A desperate struggle ensued at the second line of Confederate breastworks, the Federals being compelled to fall back to the first line, which they held and strengthened. Two thousand men fell in this brief engagement.

The 2d of June was Thursday, and both armies occupied the day and evening in massing for a general engagement, both Warren and Burnside being compelled to fight while the Federal lines were changing. Meade's line of battle that night extended from Tolopotomy Creek across the Cold Harbor Road to the Chickahominy River, while Sheridan's cavalry was guarding the right and the Chickahominy Fords down to White House. General Lee had strengthened his forest position by slashing timber all along its front, and digging rifle pits at every salient point. Longstreet occupied the Confederate centre, Ewell being on his left and A. P. Hill on his right. While making these dispositions of their troops Grant and Lee discovered that they were really on the old Gaines' Mills battlefield, but the positions were reversed, for the Federals occupied the ground previously held by Longstreet and Jackson, while the Confederates were manœuvering on McClellan's field of operations.

Rain began falling at midnight, and continued until long after sunrise. At daylight of June 3 Meade's entire army moved silently on the enemy. The result was the most deadly and desperate battle that occurred during the entire war. Not a shot was fired

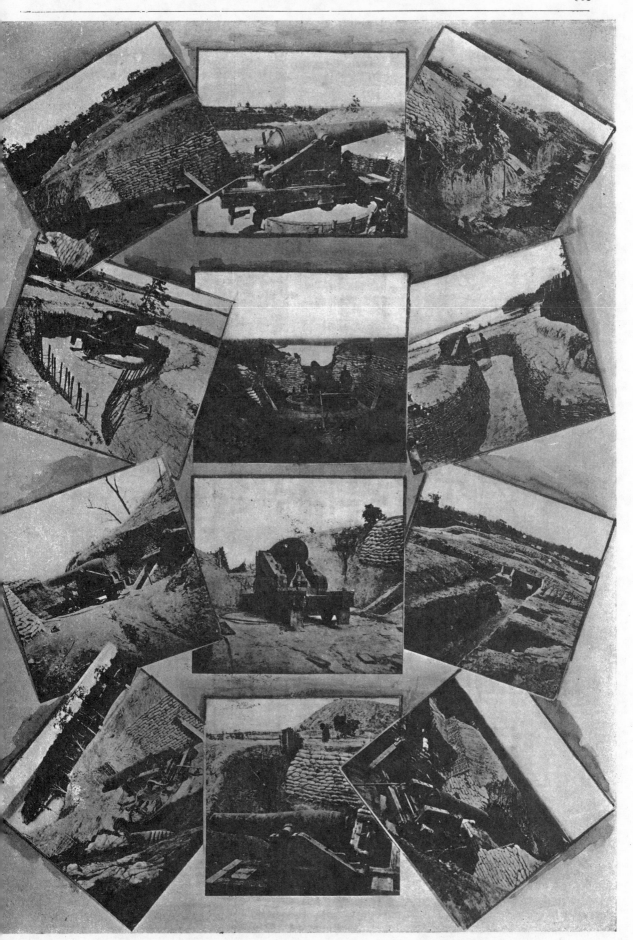

CONFEDERATE BATTERY AT HOWLETT HOUSE, TRENT'S REACH, JAMES RIVER.

FORT DARLING, DREWRY'S BLUFF, JAMES RIVER.

CONFEDERATE BATTERY ON JAMES RIVER, ABOVE DUTCH GAP.

until the Federals could see the faces of their antagonists in the drizzling rain, nor did the Confederates open until the last moment. The effect was terrific, for fully one hundred thousand muskets simultaneously began their murderous work at a range of from sixty to seventy yards. As the sullen crashes of musketry volleys broke on the misty air fully two hundred pieces of artillery added their thunder to the deafening uproar. The assault occupied a period of fifteen minutes, and the battle was over in less than an hour. The Federals were repulsed with a loss of thirteen thousand men. This engagement was really a series of battles, each corps operating separately. The desperate character of the fighting is proved by the fact that General Tyler was severely wounded, while Colonels McMahon, Haskell, McKeen, Morris, and Porter were killed. The loss of the Confederates was not more than three thousand men.

The two armies stood at Cold Harbor for ten days, working on their field intrench-

INTERIOR VIEW.

PARROTT GUN DISMOUNTED BY CONFEDERATE FIRE.

VIEW FROM COX'S LANDING

VIEW FROM NORTH SIDE JAMES RIVER.

INTERIOR VIEW

ments, fighting whenever either side grew too bold, or amicably exchanging coffee and tobacco under temporary truce. On June 7 the dead were buried and the wounded gathered up during an armistice of two hours. Grant then decided to cross the James. He had been unable to uncover Richmond, but Lee had suffered losses in men and material which he could not replace. General Sheridan began the movement toward the James by destroying the Richmond and Fredericksburg Railroad, at Chesterville Station, and the Virginia Central, at Trevillian Station. He went as far as Louisa Court House before meeting Wade Hampton's horsemen, and retired to Trevillian, where he was forced to fight for three hours, and then he cut around by Spottsylvania Court House back to Grant's lines. Sending all the ties and rails between White House to Despatch Station, Grant shipped them on barges to be taken up the James. On the night of June 12, Warren's corps, led by Wilson's cavalry, crossed the Chicahominy River at Long Bridge and assumed position on White Oak Swamp, in order to cover the

BATTERY ABBOTT.
INTERIOR VIEW.

FORT BURNHAM.
VIEW FROM EARTHWORKS

REDOUBT ZABRISKIE.
EXTERIOR VIEW.

FORT BURNHAM.
VIEW FROM EARTHWORKS.

REDOUBT ZABRISKIE.
EXTERIOR VIEW.

BOMB PROOF QUA...

INTERIOR VIEW.

FORT BURNHAM,
PREVIOUSLY CONFEDERATE
FORT HARRISON

FEDERAL EARTHWORKS
ON LEFT OF
BERMUDA HUNDRED LINE
NEAR POINT OF ROCKS.

BATTERY ABBOTT.
ON TRENTS BEACH, JAMES RIVER.

movement and mislead the enemy. Hancock's corps followed the Fifth, but marched straight to Wilcox Landing, on the James. Burnside and Wright crossed the Chickahominy at Jones' Bridge and moved to Charles City Court House. All the wagon trains went by Cole's Ferry. General Smith was sent to White House, where he disembarked, and once more made the grand tour by steamboat, reaching Bermuda Hundred before Grant's army was massed on the James River.

On ascertaining the scope of the Federal movements, Lee retired to Richmond, leaving Grant undisturbed. During the afternoon and night of June 14 the Federal engineers constructed a double pontoon bridge, two thousand feet long, at Douthard's Crossing, and the entire army, horse, foot, and artillery, had crossed the river by sunset of the 16th, carrying over all their supply trains and other impedimenta.

VIEW TAKEN NOV. 1864. VIEW TAKEN NOV. 1864. VIEW TAKEN APRIL 1865. VIEW TAKEN APRIL 1865. KEDGE BOAT SUNK BY CONFEDERATE SHELL

This Overland Campaign occupied a period of forty-three days. Six thousand five hundred and eighty-six men were killed in battle, with twenty-six thousand and forty-seven wounded, and six thousand six hundred and twenty-six reported as missing, an aggregate of thirty-nine thousand two hundred and fifty-nine. General Lee had eighty thousand men present in the Wilderness, and his reinforcements during the campaign amounted to thirty-eight thousand men. He lost five thousand three hundred and six men killed on the field; nineteen thousand one hundred and seventy-four wounded, and seven thousand four hundred and thirty-two missing, an aggregate of thirty-one thousand nine hundred and twelve. Hospital statistics show that out of the wounded and missing one-third are added to the list of dead within a very brief period, so that fully thirty thousand lives were sacrificed in these two armies during the forty-three days of battle and skirmish, while twenty thousand more were so maimed as to be unable to perform military duty. Such were the horrors of this dreadful Civil War.

ALLATOONA PASS.

CHAPTER LXI.

GENERAL SHERMAN'S MOVEMENT AGAINST ATLANTA.

When Major-General Sherman succeeded Lieutenant-General Grant in the command of the Military Division of the Mississippi, he assumed control of the Departments and the armies of Arkansas, Cumberland, Ohio, and Tennessee, commanded by Major-Generals Steele, Thomas, Schofield, and McPherson. Sherman thus had under his immediate control three separate armies, with a roster strength of three hundred and fifty-two thousand men, distributed in many garrisons over a wide expanse of territory. He therefore decided to mobilize one compact army of one hundred thousand men, which included seven thousand cavalry and two hundred and fifty pieces of artillery.

Opposed to General Sherman was Lieutenant-General Joseph E. Johnston, who commanded all the Confederate troops in the West, and held the City of Atlanta and the interior of Georgia. Johnston had gathered up the remnants of his own and Bragg's old army, and he had fully seventy thousand men in the field. His corps commanders were Generals Hood, Hardee, and Polk, General Wheeler commanding the ten thousand Confederate horsemen.

BREVET-MAJOR-GENERAL J. M. CORSE
("HOLD THE FORT.")

No. 7.   No. 8.   No. 9.

No. 10   No. 10   No. 11.

No. 11.   No. 12   No. 12.

No. 13.   No. 19.   No. 19.

FEDERAL FORTS.

Etowah River bridge, and its defences.

Chattachoocic River bridge, and its defences.

Buzzard's Roost, Ga.

View of Kingston, Ga.

Pine Mountain Ga.

The City of Atlanta was at that time of equal importance with Richmond, for it was a great railroad centre, and contained the Confederate depots, mills, foundries, and manufactories of military supplies. The city itself was strongly defended by formidable intrenchments, and all the approaches had been made difficult by obstructions of every conceivable character. Johnston's army was lying behind intrenchments at Dalton, thirty miles from Chattanooga, and he contemplated a defensive campaign.

General Grant had ordered Sherman to move simultaneously with the Army of the Potomac, and he started on May 6, the second day of the Battle of the Wilderness. A cavalry reconnoissance of the Confederate position at Dalton showed that it could not be carried by direct attack, even if Johnston was compelled to evacuate Tunnell Hill. South of the latter lies a valley bounded by Rocky Face Ridge, which is a steep and rugged mountain, heavily wooded, commanding all the approaches to Dalton. Midway between Tunnell Hill and Dalton is a narrow pass, known as Buzzard's Roost, it being the outlet to the valley, while through it runs the railroad. Johnston had rendered Buzzard's Roost impregnable by means of rifle pits, batteries, and *abatis*. This made him secure from attack on the northwest, while on the northeast he was protected by enormous works on Mile Creek.

General Sherman, therefore, decided to send General McPherson with his army on a rapid march southward from Gordon's Mills, through

BRIG.-GENERAL C. G. HARKER, KILLED.

Ship's Gap and Snake Creek Gap—the latter a pass in Rocky Face Ridge—toward Resaca, eighteen miles south of Dalton, on the Oostenaula River, where the railroad crosses. By this movement Sherman expected McPherson to capture and hold the railroad in Johnston's rear, and so compel the Confederates to evacuate Dalton. While McPherson was making this movement, both Thomas and Schofield advanced in strong force, ready to rush on Johnston should he leave Dalton.

On May 9 McPherson reported that he had found Resaca too strong for an attack, but he had possession of Snake Creek Gap, and was strongly fortifying himself. Thomas had, two days before, pushed forward from Ringgold to Tunnell Hill, and carried it, the Fourteenth Corps, under General Palmer, doing the work. Johnston then retired to Buzzard's Roost. On May 8 General Howard's corps succeeded in carrying Rocky Face Ridge. Schofield then took position on Thomas' left. McPherson's movement having failed,

Sherman started all of Thomas' army, except two of Howard's divisions, and also Schofield's army, toward the left of Buzzard's Roost. Resaca occupies a peninsula, formed by the junction of the Oostenaula and Conasauga Rivers. Across this neck of land the Confederates had erected a strong line of field works, further protected by rifle pits, which made it difficult of attack.

On May 13 Sherman's army passed through Snake Creek Gap, and took position in Sugar Valley. During this movement General Judson C. Kilpatrick, who commanded the cavalry, was severely wounded. The next day the Federal advance approached Resaca, the right, under McPherson, resting on the Oostenaula, the left, under Scholfield, extending to the Conasauga, while Thomas held the centre. Johnston now abandoned Dalton, and reached Resaca in advance of Sherman. About daybreak of May 14 skirmishing began, but there was no serious fighting, the Federals finally enveloping the town and threatening Calhoun Station. There was brisk, sharp fighting all along the lines during the 15th, several times almost rising to the dignity of a battle, but there was no result until the evening, when McPherson advanced his whole army line and took possession of a ridge overlooking the town. Planting several batteries, he shelled the railroad bridge across the Oostenaula River, when the Confederates then began what Sherman called very handsome fighting, but they were repulsed time and again.

Generals Sherman, Thomas, and McPherson were sitting in their saddles at a cross-roads when Hooker's note, announcing the capture of a four-gun battery, was brought by an aide. "Gentlemen," exclaimed Sherman, "we will advance on the enemy at all points at daylight." As he spoke a bright light appeared beyond the town of Resaca. "See," he continued, "that looks like a retreat!"

General Sherman's surmise was correct, for Johnston moved his army across the

BATTLE OF KENESHAW MOUNTAIN.

Copyright, 1887, by L. Prang & Co.

river during that night, setting fire to the bridges. At dawn of the 16th the Federals entered Resaca and began a vigorous pursuit, and on the evening of the 17th Newton's division, of Thomas' army, struck Johnston's rear guard at Adairsville. General Jefferson C. Davis reached Rome on the same day, at the confluence of the Oostenaula and Etowah, fifteen miles west of Kingston. On the 19th Davis had a sharp engagement, which resulted in his getting possession of the town and an immense quantity of stores, all of which were destroyed.

General Johnston retired to Allatoona Pass, five miles south of the Etowah River, and Sherman resumed his flanking movement. Leaving garrisons at Rome and Kingston, the Federal army cut loose from its railroad communications, and started, on May 23, for Dallas, fifteen miles south of Allatoona Pass. The route was difficult and the movement slow, but it compelled Johnston to move towards Dallas, in order to protect

View of Confederate Line.

View from Confederate Fort
on Peach Tree St.

View of
Confederate
Line
from
Fort E.

View from Confederate Fort, looking east.

View of Confederate Fort 'G'

View of Confederate Line.

View of Confederate Line.

View of
Confederate
Fort
'G'

Views from Parapet of Confederate Works.

CONFEDERATE FORTIFICATIONS AT ATLANTA, GA.

Marietta. A severe fight occurred on the 25th, near Pumpkin Vine Creek, between Hooker's corps and parts of Hood's and Hardee's commands. Johnston now concentrated his forces near New Hope Church, and attacked McPherson, but was driven back with heavy loss. Stoneman's and Garrard's cavalry then captured Allatoona Pass, and on June 4 Sherman marched away from Johnston, going to Big Shanty, General Blair joining the army with two divisions of the Seventeenth Corps and a cavalry brigade.

The Federal army was now marching through a mountainous country, the towering peaks of Lost Mountain, Kenesaw (or Twin Mountain), and Pine Mountain, forming a triangle. On all these heights the Confederates had signal stations, the outlying hills being occupied by batteries, while men were felling trees and preparing breastworks. Johnston had received fifteen thousand Georgia troops, which increased his force to

BATTLE OF ALLATOONA PASS.

Copyright, 1887, by L. Prang & Co.

seventy-eight thousand men, including fifteen thousand horsemen, who were hanging on Sherman's flanks or operating in his rear. Schofield was now on Sherman's right, facing Hood; Thomas remained in the centre, opposite Polk, while McPherson went to the left, confronting Hardee. McPherson moved towards Marietta, Thomas on Kenesaw and Pine Mountains, Schofield on Lost Mountain. Considerable manœuvering ensued, with desultory skirmishing, until June 15, General Polk being killed by an unexploded shell while a battery belonging to the Fourth Corps was cannonading Pine Mountain.

Rain began falling heavily, and the advance was necessarily slow and cautious. Sherman having learned that General Sturgis had been defeated by General Forrest, and driven into Memphis, he sent A. J. Smith after Forrest. This kept the Confederate general from entering Tennessee. Both Johnston's and Sherman's armies were cutting and slashing the timber, and erecting log breastworks at every new position, fully two hundred miles of log walls being built during a single week.   Clear sunshine greeted the troops on June 22, and the movement began at once, Pine Mountain having been abandoned by Johnston.   On the 22d Hooker and Schofield were attacked at the Kulp House, when Hooker suffered severely.   Sherman ordered an assault on Kenesaw Mountain on the 27th, but the effort failed, Generals Harker and Daniel McCook being among the Federal killed.   Sherman's troops had to climb the mountain slope, through tangled *abatis* and lines of rifle pits, in the face of a steady musketry and artillery fire.

Sherman's next movement was toward the Chattahoochee River, Schofield having crossed Olley's Creek, thus threatening Joe Johnston's rear.   The Federal army again left the railroad and depended on its wagons for supplies, the movement compelling Johnston to abandon Kenesaw Mountain on July 2 and assume temporary possession of a new position along the line of the Chattahoochee River.   This really ended the first stage of Sherman's campaign against Atlanta.   It had proved a very costly and bloody one to both Federals and Confederates.   Sherman's losses during May and June were over two thousand killed and thirteen thousand wounded.   Johnston lost during the same period twelve hundred men killed and nearly fourteen thousand wounded, the total for both armies during these fifty-four days being three thousand two hundred killed in battle and twenty-seven thousand wounded.   Of the latter fully nine thousand died in hospital.

SHERMAN AND HIS GENERALS.

CHAPTER LXII.

SHERMAN'S SIEGE AND CAPTURE OF ATLANTA.

On July 1, 1864, General Sherman began another flanking movement. While Schofield and Hooker marched two miles to the right, McPherson shifted his entire force from the extreme left to the right and pressed forward to Nickajack Creek, above its junction with the Chattahoochee. Garrard's cavalry division held McPherson's old ground, while Stoneman's horsemen moved on the extreme right flank, and struck Turner's Ferry, a few miles below the railroad bridge. Perched as he was on the top of Kenesaw Mountain, General Johnston detected the scope of the Federal movement, and promptly evacuated his stronghold, falling back to the Chattahoochee. When General Schofield's pickets discovered, on the morning of July 3, that the Confederate works had been abandoned, sunrise saw the Stars and Stripes fluttering on the crest of grim old Kenesaw.

VIEW OF THE SPOT AT WHICH GENERAL MCPHERSON WAS KILLED.

Thomas began marching in three columns to the line of the railroad, thence southward to the Chattahoochee. All of the Federal corps were in rapid motion, and Sherman entered Marietta as the Confederate cavalry were retiring before Logan's corps.
Schofield and McPherson were then ordered to cross Nickajack Creek and attack Johnston's flank and rear, in order to harass and confuse him while taking his army over the
Chattahoochee. The military sagacity of the Confederate commander had, however,
anticipated just such a movement, and he had thrown up a strong line of intrenchments
across the Smyrna Road, five miles from Marietta, his flanks being protected by Rotten-
wood and Nickajack Creeks.

On the 4th of July Sherman sent Thomas forward to engage, the fighting being of a
feeble and disjointed character, Sherman's aim being to keep Johnston occupied while
McPherson and Schofield swept round to the lower Chattahoochee crossings. At Vin-
ing's Station there is a high hill, from the top of which Sherman could distinguish the
houses in the City of Atlanta, only nine miles away. While personally reconnoitering
his own lines, General Sherman came near riding into a Confederate cavalry detachment.

Heavy skirmishing took place during the 5th, when Sherman discovered that the
only way to turn the Confederates' intrenched position would be to cross the river. The
Chattahoochee is a deep and rapid stream, the few fords being difficult and dangerous,
so the Federal movement was full of peril. Schofield crossed Soap Creek on July 7.
Rapidly constructing some bridges, the Army of the Ohio assumed a strong position on
the east bank. Garrard's cavalry were at Rosewell, destroying the Confederate cotton
and woollen mills that had been supplying Johnston's army. Thomas hurried forward
Newton's division to support Garrard and hold the fort until General Dodge's corps
arrived and crossed, followed by the remainder of the Army of the Tennessee. On the
9th Sherman was in possession of three crossing points above the Confederate position,
at Nickajack Creek, Power's Ferry, and the railroad bridge at Paice's Ferry. Johnston
was now again outmanœuvered and compelled to abandon his breastworks on the Chattahoochee, which had cost six weeks' labor of one thousand slaves. Burning his bridges
and concentrating his forces, Johnston abandoned all of the Chattahoochee country, east
and west, and retired behind the fortifications around Atlanta. Sherman then launched
an independent cavalry force, under General Rousseau. Starting from Decatur, Alabama, on July 10, Rousseau pushed across the Boosa River and destroyed several railroad bridges. Passing through Talladega, he broke up the tracks as far as Opelika, and
all the branches leading to Columbus and West Point.

General Johnston's withdrawal into Atlanta raised such a storm of indignation
throughout the Confederacy that this able Southern soldier threw up his command in
disgust, being succeeded by General J. B. Hood. On July 17 Sherman set his troops in
motion for Atlanta, Thomas crossing the turbid Chattahoochee at Power's and Paice's
Fords. McPherson moved toward Stone Mountain, Schofield going toward Cross Keys.
By a wheeling movement, the several corps faced to the right, Thomas forming line of
battle near Buckland, and fronting Peach-Tree Creek. McPherson stood on his right,
along the railroad between Stone Mountain and Decatur, Schofield being on the left.
On July 19 Sherman's troops were so near the coveted city, and had met with such
feeble resistance, that it was supposed that Hood was evacuating Atlanta. But Sherman
was soon undeceived, for on July 20 Hood fell upon Hooker. The Confederates poured
out of their intrenchments, and were pushing Hooker hard when Thomas hastened up
and placed several batteries on the north side of Peach-Tree Creek, which opened furiously on a mass of infantry that were passing round the Federal left. This changed the
complexion of affairs, the Confederates finally retiring, leaving their dead and wounded
on the field.

General Hood next resorted to stratagem, for he pretended to fall back, thus leading Sherman to advance only to find a stronger line of redoubts and curtains confronting him. Here the Federals sustained a grievous loss. General McPherson rode over to see Sherman on the morning of July 22, and reported having secured a position on a hill that overlooked the city. While they were conversing heavy firing broke out in the rear, and as it was evidently on McPherson's line, he rode off with his staff. Dispersing his aides as he galloped on various errands, the General unwittingly rode into a Confederate line, which, opening fire, he fell from his saddle a dead man. Ignorant of McPherson's fate, Sherman waited to hear from him, but it was nearly an hour before the truth was known. General Logan was placed in temporary command of the Army of the Tennessee, as the Confederates were attacking in three heavy columns, striking the Six-

SIEGE OF ATLANTA, GA.

Copyright, 1888, by L. Prang & Co.

teenth Corps. General Dodge's men met the assault in gallant style, but Hood's troops got in rear of the Seventeenth Corps, attacking Leggett's, Giles', and A. Smith's divisions in front and rear. The fighting became severe all along the line. Fuller's and Sweeney's divisions then advanced, though most of the men had exhausted their supply of cartridges, and drove back the Confederates at the point of the bayonet. The body of their dead General was found under some trees and sent to Sherman's headquarters.

At half-past four o'clock Hood sent in a heavy force, *en masse*, and assailed the Fifteenth Corps, now commanded by General M. L. Smith. The movement began auspiciously for the Confederates, as they drove back a part of the Federal line and captured two pieces of artillery. But Lightburn's brigade managed to check the movement. Then another column of Confederates came rushing through a deep cut of the Georgia Railroad, which carried them to Lightburn's rear, compelling him to retreat in considerable confusion, losing two batteries. The Fifteenth Corps now rallied, and receiving the support of Schofield, rushed back. A fearful fight ensued, the battle-maddened Southern and Northern soldiers clubbing their muskets as weapons in the hand-to-hand conflict. The Federal batteries next opened on the Confederate supports, which gave way, and the advance line fell back, followed by showers of grape and canister, which strewed the earth with more dead and dying men. The desperate and bloody character of this Battle of Decatur is shown by the terrible losses. There were three thousand two hundred and forty-six Confederate dead left on the field. Hood also lost three thousand men, taken prisoners. The Federal loss was three thousand seven hundred and twenty-two men. General Garrard returned from a raid around Covington while the two armies were burying their dead, having destroyed the bridges over the Ulcofauhatchee and Yel-

low Rivers, one or two trains of cars, several thousand bales of cotton, and the depots at Conger's Station and Covington.

The battle of Decatur compelled Hood to remain quiet, so Sherman started his cavalry on another and more extensive raid. Hitherto there had been four independent cavalry commands, under Generals Stoneman, Garrard, McCook, and Rousseau. These were now consolidated into two strong divisions, Stoneman's going to the left flank, while McCook took the right. Each was to move against the Macon Railroad, and meet at Lovejoy's, thirty miles south of Atlanta. General Stoneman had also been given permission to try and release the Federals imprisoned at Andersonville, but with the stipulation that Wheeler's Confederate cavalry must first be met and defeated. Stoneman, however, was so delighted with his own plan of rescue that he disobeyed orders by cutting his command in two.

Leaving Garrard at Flat Rock, Stoneman started for Macon to release the Federal

VIEWS ON MARIETTA ST.

THE SLAVE MARKET.

VIEWS ON WHITEHALL ST.

VIEWS ON WHITEHALL ST.

THE RAILROAD DEPOT

VIEWS ON WHITEHALL ST.

VIEW OF THE CITY HALL 2ND MASS. INFANTRY.

THE RAILROAD ROUNDHOUSE

STREET VIEWS.

VIEWS ON MARIETTA ST.

CITY OF ATLANTA, GA.

GEN. HOOD'S (CONFEDERATE) HEADQUARTERS, ATLANTA, GA.

prisoners, but found that they had been removed, and as he could not reach Andersonville, where Federals were suffering untold hardship and cruelty, Stoneman started back, but encountered General Wheeler, and was surrounded. One brigade was captured entire, but Colonel Adams carried his command back to Sherman in good order, while Colonel Capron's was dispersed and captured in detail. General McCook went to Rivertown, crossed the Chattahoochee on pontoons, and reaching Fayetteville, burned five hundred wagons, shot eight hundred mules, and took nearly one thousand prisoners. Arriving at Newman's Station on July 28, he met a strong force of Confederates, and being surrounded, had to cut his way through.

General Howard now assumed command of the Army of the Tennessee, General Stanley going to the head of the corps, and Hooker asked to be relieved, General Slocum coming up from Vicksburg to lead the Twentieth Corps. Hood seeing that Sherman was swinging round towards the Macon Railroad sent a large force over the Bell's Ferry Road, and then advanced against Logan's corps in a magnificent line of battle. The Federals saluted them with a steady volley of musketry, followed by swift discharges of grape and canister. So suddenly did the Confederate line begin to melt that the men broke in confusion and fled before the storm of lead and iron. Six times did their officers reform the assaulting line, but the continuity of the initial charge could not be sustained, and the effort ceased at four o'clock in the afternoon, the Confederates having lost fully five thousand men, Logan's being only six hundred. From that date the Confederates acted entirely on the defensive, meeting every southern extension of Sherman's by erecting new forts and curtains.

Though Hood's force was of inferior strength, the siege operations compelled Sherman to extend his line so much that he was unable to place a heavy force at any one point for an assault. Sherman therefore decided on pushing his right flank until it enveloped the Macon Railroad, which would enable him to starve Hood into surrender. The City of Atlanta was shelled and frequently set on fire, while traffic on the Macon Railroad was constantly interrupted.

General Sherman now ordered the Twentieth Corps, temporarily under General A. S. Williams, back to the intrenched depot at Chattahoochie Bridge, and General Kilpatrick, who had returned to the field, was given five thousand horsemen and sent to cut the railroads. Kilpatrick started on August 18, and reached both the Macon and West Point Railroads, but was unable to do much damage, owing to the presence of a large force of infantry and cavalry under General Ross. Then the Federal army stripped for its sweeping movement.

On the night of August 25 Howard's army moved from the extreme left toward Sandtown and across Camp Creek, Thomas marching south of Utoy Creek, leaving the Army of the Ohio in siege position. Then Howard struck the West Point Railroad, near Fairborn, Thomas being at Red Oak Station and Schofield going to Mount Gilead Church. These movements left Atlanta entirely uncovered, and Hood's first impression was that Sherman was retreating. On the 28th several miles of the West Point Railroad were destroyed, including Fairborn and Red Oak Stations. The next day Howard started for Jonesboro, Thomas marching to Shoal Creek Church, while Schofield moved to Morrow's Mills. General I. D. Lee's corps and General Hardee's were then sent by Hood to Jonesboro, but Thomas took position at Couch's, with Schofield at Rough and Ready, Howard succeeding after some opposition in passing Renfrew.

General Thomas sent Stanley's corps and one of Davis' divisions to connect with Schofield, who was advancing to seize the railroad. On August 31 Hardee and Lee attacked Howard, but were driven back with a loss of three thousand men and two batteries. Among their dead was Major-General Anderson. The result was that Schofield tore up the railroad, and General Sherman decided to move forward with his whole force. He met with very little opposition, and the work of destruction proceeded until, finally, it was ascertained that Hardee and Lee had disappeared. During the morning of September 1, sounds of what was supposed to be heavy cannonading were heard in the

VIEWS ON THE BATTLEFIELD AT ATLANTA, GA., JULY 22, 1864.

direction of Atlanta, and Sherman imagined that Slocum, who had arrived and relieved General Williams, had either been attacked or was obeying orders to feel the enemy left on his front. That evening Sherman received a letter from Slocum announcing the evacuation of Atlanta and his occupancy of the city.

General Hood, having decided to abandon Atlanta, loaded one hundred cars with ammunition, and when his rear guard had gone, set fire to the trains, depots, and storehouses. The explosions that ensued were the "cannonading" Sherman supposed was going on. The formal surrender was made by the Mayor on September 2, the pursuit of Hood and Hardee being abandoned. Then ensued a military measure which shows how cruel are the necessities of war. Every family having a member in the Confederate army was compelled to leave the city, over two thousand men, women, and children, with their servants, obeying the order. Atlanta thus became a military depot, governed only by military law. During this campaign of four months the Federals lost thirty-one thousand six hundred and eighty men. The losses of the Confederates footed up thirty-four thousand nine hundred and eighty-six.

ENGAGEMENT BETWEEN KEARSARGE AND ALABAMA.

Copyright, 1887, by L. Prang & Co.

CHAPTER LXIII.

OPERATIONS OF THE CONFEDERATE PRIVATEERS AND THE SINKING OF THE ALABAMA BY THE KEARSARGE.

For over two years the North had suffered severely by the operations of the Confederate privateers on the high seas in destroying Federal merchant shipping. The schooner Savannah was the first of these vessels of marque, but her career was brief, as she soon surrendered to the Perry. Then the Petrel, the Inda, the Nashville, and the Sumter appeared. The Petrel was blown to pieces off Charleston by the frigate St. Lawrence, the Inda was burned at Pensacola, and the Nashville was destroyed on the Ogeechee River, near Fort McAllister. The Sumter was commanded by Captain Raphael Semmes, who for months committed awful havoc among merchant vessels flying the Stars and Stripes. Semmes had been a distinguished officer in the United States navy before the war.

The frigate Tuscarora cruised after the Sumter, and finally forced Semmes to escape capture by taking refuge in the neutral waters of Gibraltar. Being blockaded there for weeks Semmes sold his privateer and proceeded overland with his officers to Calais, thence to Liverpool, where the famous Alabama was nearly ready for sea. British ship-yards turned out other vessels, among them the Oreto, which entered Mobile Bay as a blockade runner. Being armed and re-named the Florida, she cruised under the command of Captain Maffit, in West Indian waters. Reaching Brest in September, 1863, the Florida was detained for a time, and on being released, Captain Morris, who then commanded her, visited the coast of Brazil. The United States frigate Wachusett found her in the port of Bahia, and she was captured in neutral waters, contrary to international law. Being brought to Hampton Roads, pending legal proceedings for her release, the

CAPT., AFTER COM., JOHN A. WINSLOW, U. S. N.

CAPT. RAPHAEL SEMMES, C. S. .'.

Florida was "mysteriously" sunk one dark night, and that was the end of her. The Tallahassee, the Georgia, the Shenandoah, and the Chicamauga were also very destructive, the value of mercantile shipping burned by them at sea being many millions of dollars. Ultimately all four were driven into the harbor of Wilmington, where they were destroyed by the Confederates to avoid capture.

The Alabama was built by Laird, at Birkenhead, under the title of "The 290." Being ready for sea, she was taken to the Island of Terceira under British colors and a British captain, another British vessel carrying her armament. Semmes assumed command outside of port limits on August 26, 1862, and the "290" became the Alabama. Lowering the British ensign, Semmes hoisted the Confederate flag and started out on a cruise that lasted eighteen months, during which time he captured forty-seven Federal vessels, destroying all but three. The Alabama also fought the Federal blockader Hatteras, off Galveston, in January, 1863, sinking her opponent in less than twenty minutes. Cruising in the West Indies, along the coast of Brazil, and in the Malay Archipelago, Semmes finally entered the French harbor of Cherbourg, on June 11, 1864. Three days after her arrival, the United States frigate Kearsarge, Captain John A. Winslow, appeared off the mouth of the harbor and dropped anchor. Semmes coolly requested Winslow, through the United States Consul, to wait a few days, until he could put the privateer in fighting trim. This just suited Winslow. On Sunday morning, June 19, the Alabama steamed out of Cherbourg harbor in company with the French warship Caurronne. The latter drew off as the Confederate vessel left the limits of French waters, her duty being to see that the projected naval duel did not occur within the jurisdiction of France. The Alabama was also attended by Mr. Lancaster's English steam yacht Deerhound, on board of which were several personal friends of Captain Semmes. Their motive was subsequently explained.

As soon as he saw the Alabama coming out, Captain Winslow weighed anchor and steamed away to sea, a distance of seven miles from shore, in order that there could be no possible complication regarding neutral waters. Having reached his distance, Winslow put his vessel about and cleared decks for action. The Kearsarge's guns were pivotted to starboard as she bore down on the Alabama. When within a mile of his adversary Semmes let fly his guns, but received no reply, Winslow receiving three broadsides without firing a shot, the Confederate guns doing very little damage. Coming within one thousand yards' range, Winslow opened fire with his starboard battery, planting a solid shot in the Alabama's frame.

The battle then began in dead earnest, and the cannonading grew fast and furious during the next sixty minutes. The English gunners fired rapidly, but their aim was bad, while the Americans were more deliberate and took careful aim, consequently nearly every shot from the Kearsarge told. During this combat, both vessels were moving in a circle; the currents were, however, gradually drawing the vessels together until they came within five miles of the French coast.

At noon Captain Semmes discovered that his vessel was rapidly filling, she having been hit several times between wind and water. In hopes of saving the Alabama he started for shore, intending to beach her. The Kearsarge, though shattered in her upper works, was in excellent fighting trim, so Winslow ran across the Alabama's bows, raking the doomed vessel with all his heavy guns. Then the Confederate struck her colors and ran up a white flag in token of surrender. The Kearsarge immediately ceased firing, when, to the surprise of the Americans, the Alabama fired two guns, and Winslow angrily

OFFICERS ON DECK OF U. S. S. KEARSARGE, TAKEN ON RETURN TO UNITED STATES, AFTER DESTRUCTION OF THE ALABAMA.

resumed hostilities until an officer arrived from the Confederate privateer to make a formal surrender of the ship and crew.

At twenty minutes after twelve o'clock, while the Kearsarge was only a few hundred yards away, there was great commotion on board the Alabama, the crew leaping into the sea by scores. Then the vessel gave a sudden lurch, and the next instant her stern went under water, and the privateer swiftly disappeared in forty fathoms of water. The wrecked crew clung to boxes, spars, and other debris. Then two boats were sent from the Kearsarge to rescue the drowning men, being assisted by some French pilot boats. The yacht Deerhound picked up Captain Semmes and several of his officers, and steamed away, thus violating international law, as the Confederates were prisoners to the United States. Seventy men were picked up, and the Kearsarge proceeded to Cherbourg. The sinking of this famous Confederate privateer made a deep impression, for it was taken as another sign that the war could not last much longer. The frigate Kearsarge remained in the United States service until April, 1894, when she ran aground on Roncondor Reef, in the Bahamas, being totally destroyed—a sad fate for the gallant and historic ship.

GENERAL U. S. GRANT AND STAFF AT CITY POINT, VA., AUGUST, 1864.

CHAPTER LXIV.

BEGINNING OF THE SIEGE OF PETERSBURG AND THE MINE EXPLOSION.

The City of Petersburg, Virginia, is twenty-two miles from Richmond and ten miles southeast of the James River. It is the central point for five railroads, giving communication with the Carolinas and Southern Virginia. Its possession by Federal troops would cut off Richmond and necessitate the evacuation of the Confederate capital. The city, therefore, became the bonĕ of contention in the East, and when it fell the war ended. When Grant had crossed the James, Lee threw most of his forces into the intrenchments around Petersburg. It should be mentioned here that Generals Butler and Sigel had not succeeded in their movements up the James River, or through the Shenandoah, consequently Lee had not been enveloped as Grant had planned. Butler did get within striking distance of Richmond, but the effort failed through the activity of Beauregard, while Sigel was ignominiously driven back to the Potomac by Breckenridge.

On June 16 the new campaign began. The Second, Eighteenth and Ninth Corps formed line of battle, and advanced along the line of the Norfolk Railroad against some strong intrenchments. The engagement opened at six o'clock and lasted until nine with some severity. Barlow and Potter obtained a foothold, but were finally driven back with great loss. On the morning of the 17th Burnside made another effort, which proved successful, and the works were taken. The Fifth and Sixth Corps coming up, General Smith took his Eighteenth Corps across the Appomattox River pontoon bridge, and rejoined Butler at Bermuda Hundred. During the next four days several assaults were made by the Federal and Confederate troops, neither gaining anything, though ten

Officers Headquarters.

Camp Cooking Beans

Gen. Grant's Headquarters, officers hut.

Gen. Grant's Headquarters.

Hospital Wharf on Appomattox River.

Convalescent Soldiers at General Hospital.

General Hospital.

Camp of Provost Guard.

Hospital Wharf on Appomattox River.

Stairway & Slide of Commissary Building:

VIEWS AT CITY POINT, VA.

thousand men were killed or wounded on both sides. On June 21 and 23 efforts were made to seize the Weldon Railroad, but they failed, Meade, however, extending his line around Petersburg. During the remainder of June there was hot fighting every hour of the day, and frequently far into the night, for the two armies had now fought each other to a standstill. It would fatigue the reader to describe all the movements in detail, for they were monotonous in their similarity. A cavalry force under Generals Wilson and Kautz made an extensive raid, cutting the Weldon Railroad at Ream's Station, and the Lynchburg and Danville Road at Burkesville. Active work continued during July, the Federals gradually drawing their siege lines closer around the city. Secretary Stanton then relieved Butler from the command of the Army of the James, but Grant again

FORT MAHONE (CONFEDERATE FORT, CALLED BY THE SOLDIERS "FORT DAMNATION").

showed his authority by countermanding the order, and relieving Generals Smith and Gillmore, as chiefly responsible for Butler's failure.

The siege progressed until July 30, when a huge mine was exploded. Lieutenant Pleasant, of the Forty-eighth Pennsylvania, was a practical coal miner, and suggested running a sap through a ravine under a Confederate fort on Cemetery Hill, the key to Lee's lines. The sap was dug in thirty days and nights. When an enormous quantity of powder had been placed in the pockets, preparations were made for exploding it. By this time the Federal line of intrenchments was over twenty miles long. General Foster's division, of the Tenth Corps, occupied Deep Bottom, on the northern side of the James River, threatening the old ground at Malvern Hills. It also commanded three parallel roads leading to Richmond. While the Nineteenth Corps crossed the pontoon bridge in rear of Foster's position, the Second Corps moved from the extreme left of

Interior Views.

Exterior View.

Interiors Views.

Confederate Fortifications at Gracus Sauent

Interiors View.

View of Federal Line, from Right of Fort.

Ditch and Cheveux de frise in front of Fort.

Bomb-proof Quarters of Garrison.

Looking South from its Centre.

Ditch on West side of Fort.

FORT SEDGWICK (FEDERAL FORT, CALLED BY THE SOLDIERS "FORT HELL").

Meade's line, followed by Sheridan's cavalry. Both commands went over the bridge during the night of July 26, the sound of their passage being concealed by a thick covering of grass and hay. A line of battle was formed at daylight, on the New Market Road, Sheridan and Kautz holding the right with their horsemen. The Second Corps lay at Strawberry Plains, with the Nineteenth Corps connecting it with Foster. General Hancock's Gettysburg wound having broken out again, he was compelled to hand over his command to General Birney.

General Kershaw commanded the Confederate force in front of Birney, with a battery of heavy Parrott guns captured from Butler at Drury's Bluff. At daylight of the 27th Miles' brigade, of Barlow's division, got on the flank of Kershaw, and charged, compelling the Confederates to abandon their "Yankee" battery. During the 28th a further demonstration was made, when Sheridan pushed forward with all his sabres and drove back the Confederates, but they soon rallied and recovered their ground.

To further deceive Lee, four hundred empty wagons were ostentatiously sent across the pontoon bridge by daylight, to give the impression that a heavy force was advancing on Butler's right. In fact, twenty thousand men and four batteries had gone, and Lee became so alarmed that he detached several divisions and sent them to the Richmond side of the James. But during the night of the 29th most of the Federal forces recrossed the river, and prepared to support the columns that were massing in front of the mine.

The time set for exploding the mine was half-past three o'clock on the morning of July 30. The Ninth Corps had been selected to lead the assault, Leslie's division being the first line, with Ferrero's, Willcox's, and Potter's, as the second, third, and fourth. The Eighteenth and Second Corps were near at hand, so that they could move up on the left or right, as necessity might require.

Silently and steadily the several corps and divisions marched up and assumed their allotted positions. It was an impressive and thrilling scene. Every order was given in a whisper, and the silence grew oppressive. "Forward," ran the word along the line, then the whisper was "Halt." Again and again were these orders repeated, until the position of the several divisions had been reached.

As the light of dawn slowly appeared in the eastern sky every man nerved himself, for he knew the supreme moment was rapidly approaching. But the mine did not explode in time, for the fuse was imperfect. Two men volunteered to descend and apply the match to the break. At five o'clock the ground beneath the feet of the troops suddenly trembled, then there was an awful roar, and a mountain of earth rose in the air, accompanied by blinding flashes of light. Then pieces of timber, bodies, and shattered limbs of men fell in a dreadful shower. Two hundred Confederate soldiers were blown into eternity during those brief ten seconds.

As the reverberations rolled along the Federal lines one hundred heavy guns and mortars opened fire on one common centre. The mine did its work most effectually, for a huge gap had been made in Cemetery Ridge, and there was an open gate into the City of Petersburg. But for some unexplained reason the assaulting column did not move. Finally, General Leslie set his men in motion, when some mistaken order was given, and they were halted in the crater for nearly an hour. General Ferrero's colored troops were close behind, but they could not advance, though under fire. General Burnside was then ordered forward with his remaining divisions, when there was another delay. By this time the Confederates had recovered from their confusion, and assembled in heavy force on either side of the wide chasm. Relentless and maddened, they poured in an awful volley of musketry and grape, filling the deep crater with dead and dying Federals. There was no escape, no hope, and these men stood there like a flock of sheep until nearly all were killed outright or grievously wounded. General Bartlett, who led the charge, was taken prisoner, with most of his staff. The mine had failed, and five thousand men were lost. The next day was Sunday, and the Federals asked for a truce to care for their wounded, but it was not arranged until Monday morning, by which time most of the wounded were dead, and the corpses of white and black soldiers were alike in color. No man who witnessed these awful scenes can ever forget them.

General Butler had conceived a plan to change the course of the James River by cutting a canal at Dutch Gap. Thousands of colored laborers were thus employed for over two months, but the project failed. It, however, led to considerable fighting between the armies and the opposing ironclads. Then Grant made another effort to seize the Weldon Railroad. On the morning of August 13 the Second Corps marched to City Point, and with some display, embarked on board transports, which started down the river as if going to Washington. After nightfall the transports returned, and the corps landed at Deep Bottom, being joined by two divisions of the Tenth Corps, and Gregg's cavalry division. Advancing toward Strawberry Plains at daylight, the Confederates were driven back, and sharp skirmishing continued during that and the following day. On the 16th a hot, sharp fight occurred near Deep Run, on the Charles City Road, Gregg meeting a Confederate cavalry force under General Fitz Hugh Lee. A series of angry engagements followed until the 19th, when the movement was abandoned, after a total loss of five thousand men, the Confederates losing three thousand. Grant had now to look after a flank movement made by Lee, who sent Early with a tolerably large force into the Shenandoah Valley to cover the movement of gathering supplies.

PETERSBURG.

BATTLE OF MOBILE BAY.

CHAPTER LXV.

ADMIRAL FARRAGUT'S BRILLIANT NAVAL BATTLE IN MOBILE BAY.

For over a year the Federal Government had been anxious to gain possession of Mobile, Alabama. After the fall of Vicksburg, General Grant had planned a movement, but Rosecranz' defeat at Chickamauga prevented it. When Banks was relieved at New Orleans by Canby preparations for attacking Mobile were begun. The City of Mobile stands at the head of a large bay, thirty miles from the Gulf of Mexico, and it was an important Confederate naval station. Lying in the harbor were several powerful ironclads, the largest being the Tennessee, which resembled the famous Merrimac of Hampton Roads. She was over two hundred feet in length, her side armor being four inches thick, and her decks were covered with two inches of plate iron. She carried two heavy pivot guns and four broadside guns, throwing one hundred and ten pound and ninety-five pound projectiles. Farragut's fleet consisted of the wooden ships Brooklyn, Hartford, Richmond, Lackawanna, Monongahela, Ossipee, Oneida, Octorara, Metacomet, Port Royal, Seminole, Kennebec, Itasca, and Galena. To these were added the monitors Tecumseh, Winnebago, Manhattan, and Chickasaw.

Mobile Bay is land-locked by a narrow sandy peninsula, fifteen miles away, terminating in Mobile Point. It is also closed in on the west by Dauphin Island and a chain of sand banks, which divide Mississippi Sound from the Gulf. Dauphin Island is twelve miles long, and terminates on the south in Pelican Point. Grant's Pass, to the north of Little Dauphin Island, connects Mobile Bay with Mississippi Sound. The mouth of the bay lies between Mobile Point and the eastern end of Dauphin Island, being covered by

BATTLE OF MOBILE BAY.

Sand Island and a series of sand banks. The southwest entrance is called Middle Channel, the southeastern one being known as Swash Channel. On the western end of Mobile Point stood Fort Morgan, manning forty-eight guns, while Fort Gaines occupied the eastern end of Dauphin Island, with twenty-one guns. Both had been built before the war by the United States Government. Grant's Pass was guarded by Fort Powell. Rows of piles obstructed the channels, and the entire harbor was thickly planted with torpedoes.

At sunrise of August 5, 1864, General Granger's land force of twenty-five hundred men disembarked on Dauphin's Island, while Admiral Farragut's fleet moved forward, two abreast and lashed together. In the early sunlight, and under a cloudless sky, these eighteen Federal war vessels started through the entrance to Mobile Bay, a slight southwest breeze gracefully extending each ship's ensign. Moving at moderate speed, the imposing squadron reached the main channel, and at a quarter to seven o'clock the monitor Tecumseh fired the first shot,

MAJOR-GENERAL E. R. S. CANBY.

which was promptly responded to by Fort Morgan. Then the Brooklyn opened fire with her large guns, and the action became general, the monitor Tecumseh being suddenly sunk by a torpedo which tore a huge hole in her hull. Captain T. A. M. Craven and nearly all of his officers and crew went down with the vessel. Craven had been in the navy since 1829, and was a very brave officer.

The Brooklyn's torpedo machinery next became unmanageable, and she got a terrible pounding from the forts. For the moment it seemed as if the Brooklyn would foul the remainder of the fleet, but Farragut, who was perched half way up the rigging of the Hartford, ordered Captain Drayton to push the flagship forward, and signalled the fleet to follow. The movement was successful, for as the Hartford cleared the Middle Channel her broadside partially silenced the guns in Fort Morgan. By eight o'clock the fleet was sweeping past the fort, and the entrance to the Bay was assured. Admiral Franklin Buchanan (who had commanded the Merrimac), approached Farragut with the Tennessee. Avoiding the huge Ram, Farragut exchanged a furious broadside with his antagonist, and proceeded serenely up the Bay. Three Confederate gunboats, the Gaines, Selma, and Morgan kept ahead of the Hartford and delivered a destructive raking fire. Seeing the necessity for getting rid of these gunboats, Farragut signalled Captain Jouett, of the Metacomet, to start after them. In less than an hour the Selma was captured, with her officers and crew, while the Gaines and the Morgan were driven to the fort. Farragut then brought his ships to anchor, and the crews were piped to breakfast. While the men were enjoying their biscuits and hot cocoa, the Admiral, who was still in the Hartford shrouds, saw the Tennessee bearing down on the fleet at astonishing speed. Quickly answering their boatswains' whistles and tossing their cups of cocoa into the scuppers, the ships' crews prepared to meet their adversary. Admiral Buchanan believed his vessel could whip the entire Federal fleet, and he aimed at ramming each in turn and sinking them. Farragut ordered the three remaining monitors to move forward and use their rams, while the wooden vessels were to open fire.

The Monongahela was the first to strike the Tennessee, hitting her on the side, but losing her own prow and cut-water by the collision. Swinging round, the Monongahela delivered several eleven-inch shot at close range, which had no apparent effect.

The Lackawanna was the next to ram, but she had her stem crushed. Seeing the mistake of ramming at right angles, Farragut now took his flagship forward, and dealing the Tennessee a glancing blow, delivered his port broadside of nine-inch solid shot as the sides of the vessels rasped against each other. Yet the Tennessee did not seem to be injured, the huge balls flying off her armor at a tangent. The Federal fleet now adopted the Indian method of fighting, for the ships formed a circle, and moving round the huge Confederate ironclad, poured in a tremendous fire. Finally the monitor Manhattan placed a fifteen-inch solid shot under the stern of the Tennessee.

Farragut then tried to bring the Hartford into close quarters, but was delayed by coming in collision with the Lackawanna. Being disentangled, the flagship steamed toward the Tennessee. By this time the Tennessee's steering chains had been cut, and her port shutters so jammed they could not be opened, rendering the guns useless, and Buchanan had been severely wounded. Before the Hartford reached the Tennessee a white flag was run up, and her captain went on board the Hartford to surrender his own and his admiral's sword. That ended the naval part of the movement, and Mobile Bay was won. Farragut lost one hundred and sixty-five men killed and drowned, and one hundred wounded. Captain I. R. M. Mullany, of the Oneida, was killed. The Federal and Confederate wounded were sent to Pensacola, where Admiral Buchanan's leg was amputated. When the Tecumseh struck the submerged torpedo Captain Craven and his pilot were in the pilot house. Seeing that both could not escape, Craven said : "You first, pilot." The pilot got through the door, and was saved, but the gallant Craven went down with his ship.

General Granger had lost no time in investing Fort Gaines. Planting a battery of heavy Rodman guns, the fort was soon disabled, Anderson surrendering on the 6th. Granger then transferred his troops to the sandy peninsula behind Fort Morgan, which was speedily invested. Everything being ready, Farragut's fleet took convenient position in front of Fort Morgan during the night of August 21, and as the sun's red rays illumined Mobile Bay and threw into strong relief the wide stretches of dazzling white sand, the Federal land and naval forces opened fire. The scene was thrilling yet picturesque, for Farragut's battered vessels lay in a half moon, using every available gun. In twenty minutes a bank of hot, white smoke rested on the waters of the bay and partially hid the fleet, but through this sulphurous mist came vivid flashes of flame, as solid shot and loaded shell were launched against the granite walls of the grim. moss-grown fort. The narrow sand spit occupied by the troops was also covered with cannon smoke, while the cool morning air fairly trembled under the fierce and rapid concussions of the artillery.

The bombardment continued until late in the afternoon, General Page making a feeble reply. About four o'clock it was evident that the fort was on fire, and soon after sunset all of the naval and land guns ceased firing. When darkness fell the flames inside Fort Morgan cast a ruddy glare across the bay, but at nine o'clock the bombardment was renewed until nearly midnight, as the garrison was mastering the fire. At five o'clock the next morning every Federal gun again opened, the hail of iron falling for two hours, when an officer carrying a white flag emerged from the sally port, and Page made an unconditional surrender. The fort was a complete ruin. Page had thrown ninety thousand pounds of gunpowder into the cisterns, and spiked his guns. The City of Mobile and its magnificent bay fell into the possession of the National Government, and another blow was struck at blockade running.

SHERIDAN'S FINAL CHARGE AT WINCHESTER.

CHAPTER LXVI.

SHERIDAN'S SHENANDOAH CAMPAIGN AND THE BATTLE OF WINCHESTER.

It was General Jubal A. Early's division, of Ewell's corps, that compelled General David Hunter to retreat from Lynchburg, Virginia, during the latter part of May, 1864. Hunter had scarcely reached the Kanawha region when he found himself hampered by the contradictory orders of Secretary Stanton. The consequence was all of Hunter's plans were upset. When Early felt assured that Lynchburg and Lee's rear could not be again threatened by Hunter, he united to his own command the infantry division under General John C. Breckenridge and the cavalry brigades of Generals I. H. Vaughn, B. T. Johnson, John McCausland, and J. D. Imboden. With this imposing force Early entered the lower Shenandoah Valley. General Lee, growing restive under the galling fetters Grant was throwing around him at Petersburg, determined to make a diversion in hopes of loosening the chain, so he sent Early across the upper Potomac into Maryland and seriously threatened Washington. A rapid march enabled Early to reach Winchester on July 2, and he occupied Martinsburg on the 4th, driving Sigel out of the town on

BVT.-MAJOR-GENERAL DAVID A. RUSSELL, KILLED.

Sheridan and His Generals.

the same day that Hunter reached Charlestown. The Potomac River being thus open, the Confederate general crossed into Maryland, and moving over the old Antietam ground, passed through the South Mountain gaps to the banks of the Monocacy River. General Lew Wallace, in command at Baltimore, now found himself cut off from telegraphic communication with Washington by the operations of the Confederate cavalry, and Grant detached Wright's Sixth Corps and sent it to the relief of the National capital. Rickett's division reached Wallace at Baltimore in time to oppose Early at Monocacy Bridge, but the Federals had to retreat after a sharp engagement at Ellicott's Mills. The road to Washington being open, Early boldly marched thither, his audacity causing consternation among the bureaucrats. But Wright landed with two of his divisions and one from the Nineteenth Corps in time to move out to attack Early, who recrossed the Potomac near Berlin and proceeded to Leesburg. General Hunter was at Harper's Ferry, and Early reached Winchester, followed only by Crook. Early attacked Crook at Kernstown, driving him to Martinsburg and Harper's Ferry. The Confederates then again

BATTLE OF COLD HARBOR, VA.

crossed the upper Potomac and began gathering supplies of cattle and grain. General McCausland went to Chambersburg, where the cavalry raider summoned the inhabitants and demanded the sum of five hundred thousand dollars in cash. It being impossible to meet this requisition, McCausland laid the town in ashes, leaving over three thousand men, women, and children without food or shelter.

These depredations roused General Grant to decisive action. Uniting all the troops under Hunter, Sigel, Averill, and Crook, and reinforcing them with the Sixth Corps and Torbert's cavalry division, he selected General Sheridan to command the little army. Sheridan entered on his campaign with vigor, for on August 6 his troops were massing at Halltown, just beyond Harper's Ferry. Early was occupying Martinsburg, Williamsport, and Shepherdstown, raiding Maryland as far as Hagerstown. On learning that an increased Federal force was concentrating near the Ferry, Early recalled his raiding parties and prepared for defence. Sheridan had twenty-six thousand men for effective work, the Confederate force being about the same strength. Early retreated up the Valley, and Sheridan's troops made a leisurely promenade until August 13, when, learning that Early was being reinforced to the strength of forty thousand men, "Little Phil"

MAJOR-GENERAL C. CROOK.

fell back to the line of the Opequon Creek. Here he received Grover's division of the Nineteenth Corps and Wilson's cavalry division, which equalized matters. Grant then instructed Sheridan to drive Early out of the Valley at whatever cost, and strip the Shenandoah and Loudon region of crops, animals, and slaves—in fact, render these smiling valleys comparative wastes.

On September 16 Grant visited Sheridan, and as the latter had learned that Early's reinforcements were on their way back to Petersburg a vigorous offensive campaign was decided upon. The next day Sheridan's forty thousand men were in motion. The cavalry divisions advanced from Summit Point and over the Berryville Turnpike, thus threatening both of Early's flanks. The Sixth and Nineteenth Corps formed the left and centre of the main line, with Crooks' Eighth, or Kanawha Corps, on the right. General Averill had already driven General Gordon's infantry division out of Martinsburg, and Early's whole force now lay before Sheridan along an elevated line, two miles east of Winchester town, extending from Abraham's Creek, north, across the Berryville Turnpike to some heavy timber on Red Bud Run.

It was not until noon of September 19 that Sheridan got his troops in shape, the Nineteenth Corps being delayed by a confusion of orders. The divisions under Getty and Ricketts, accompanied by Wilson's horsemen, made some progress toward Winchester, on the Senseny Road, but the Confederates quickly assailed, smashing Colonel Keifer's small brigade. General David H. Russell's division, of Wright's corps, was then ordered forward to drive back Gordon and Rodes. The task was performed, but at heavy loss, General Russell being killed by a fragment of a shell shattering his head. This heroic officer had already received a bullet in his left breast, which would ultimately have proved mortal, but he gave no sign, and rode on to receive the shell and a quicker death.

Fighting now became obstinate all along the line, and the battle of Winchester assumed a desperate character. The ground occupied by the opposing armies was an ideal one for a general engagement. Wide stretches of wheat stubble gave ample scope for the movements of large bodies of men, a few scattered clumps of wood land and orchards lending picturesque diversity to the landscape. Wherever the eye turned it could clearly distinguish the formation of the antagonized lines, marked as they were by rolling clouds of smoke from musket and cannon. As Joaquin Miller wrote :

> "And here was the blue and there the gray,
> And a wide green valley rolled away
> Between where the battling armies lay,
> That sacred Sunday morning."

By three o'clock Crook's Kanawha Corps and Emory's Nineteenth, supported by Merritt's and Averill's cavalry, reached a desirable position on the Federal right. Though the day was now well advanced, Sheridan felt that he had succeeded in flanking Early's wings by the advance of his darling cavalry divisions. The sun was beginning to descend the sky when Sheridan rode up to a high sugar-loaf sort of hill in the centre of his assumed position. Scarcely had the staff ranged themselves behind the General than he began to execute a sort of dance in his saddle. Swinging to and fro like a Comanche, the General rapidly examined the field before him. Then a few hurried, excited orders were given, half a dozen aides started off in various directions at breakneck speed, after which Sheridan grew grave and silent. His beautiful horse arched its glossy neck and softly whinnied for recognition; but none came, for the soldier had made his last move on the field, and was now waiting for the result.

In less than twenty minutes the old Sixth Corps moved forward to charge on Early's centre. The movement had scarcely begun when the corps was met by a terrific series of musketry volleys, yet the men of the Roman Cross moved steadily over the ground, their path being marked by dead and wounded comrades. As soon as Wright's artillery opened fire Crook and Emory also moved forward in splendid style. For fully half an hour the hot sunshine was rent by the crash of musketry and the roar of artillery, and we could see that the Confederates were gradually giving way. At that moment there came to our ears the ringing notes of cavalry bugles, on the extreme right and left of Sheridan's army. Then the horsemen leaped into their saddles, and there was a sudden flash as thirteen thousand bright sabres kissed the September sunlight. More bugle notes broke on the clear, cool air, and the masses began deploying, until there were two distinct lines, and the brigade banners went to the front. Even at that distance the sight was an inspiring one, for we knew that an important movement was contemplated. Sheridan had discovered that both flanks of Jubal Early's line had been weakened to meet the threatened onslaught of the Sixth Corps, and he had ordered his cavalry to make a sweeping movement in order to push back the Confederate wings and force them on their centre.

Then there came to our ears a long, wild cheer as the horsemen began galloping over the wide fields, their bright swords still glittering in the sunshine as the weapons were waved overhead. On, on they went, the thunder of the horses' hoofs on the soft carpet of grass giving token of the tremendous blow about to be struck. On galloped Merritt and Averill, Custer and Wilson, until the cloud of horses and riders was hidden by intervening woods. Then the muskets of the Sixth Corps opened tongue, a vivid flash of light broke against the dense woods in which Early's men were gathered, and the air was rent by an awful, sustained crash of musketry, as thirty thousand men exchanged volleys. Pressing steadily forward, Wright's men continued to pour in a deadly fire, and the cheer that rose above the roar and racket of the battle told us that the Confederate centre had been pierced and was giving way before the terrible impact of the Federal line. Scarcely had the Sixth Corps divisions disappeared amid the trees, when the cavalry again appeared in sight, having executed a circular movement, which brought their leading squadrons fairly on the flanks of the enemy. Then there was another wild cheer, and the mounted brigades dashed forward and broke down all opposition. Seeing that his troops were carrying everything before them, Sheridan turned around in his saddle to his staff, and said in a mild tone:

"Gentlemen, I think we may now venture to ride forward."

The turmoil of battle had calmed Sheridan's explosive temper, and his words had the same significance as Napoleon's utterance, "The battle is won."

The Confederates now retreated in confusion, passing rapidly through Winchester to Fisher's Hill, three miles south of Strasburg, losing three thousand men as prisoners, five pieces of artillery, nine battle flags, and four thousand muskets. Three thousand Confederate wounded were found in Winchester, Early's total loss being over seven thousand, General Rodes being among his dead. Sheridan lost five thousand men. This battle gave the Federals full possession of the Shenandoah Valley, and they destroyed every atom of the garnered wheat and other supplies. This work done, Sheridan prepared to again attack Early, who still clung to Fisher's Hill.

CHAPTER LXVII.

THE BATTLE OF FISHER'S HILL.

"Having sent Early whirling through Winchester," as Sheridan so graphically expressed it in his despatch to Secretary Stanton, he gave orders for an active pursuit. The rear guard of the Confederate army cleared the streets of the old-fashioned town soon after sunset, with Sheridan's advance close on their heels. When night fell, the grass-grown cobblestone pavements of Winchester groaned under the weight of ponderous pieces of artillery, as they went rumbling through the irregular and picturesque main thoroughfare of the war-ravaged town. Every side street and lane was also filled with marching infantry columns, or the supply trains, so that from dark to dawn the next morning the inhabitants were kept awake by the rattle and rumble of wheels, the sharp crack of artillery whips, the angry oaths of excited teamsters, the murmur of many voices, and the muffled, mysterious tread of armed men. Accompanying all these strange and confused sounds there came to the ear the muttering of distant musketry, frequently punctuated by dull cannonading, while shrill bugle calls, rapidly repeated, told that the victorious army was closely pressing its foe. When the sun rose on the following morning the streets of Winchester contained only a few straggling Federal soldiers and wagons, the former being swept forward by the tireless provost guards.

General Torbert, who commanded Sheridan's cavalry, sent Averill's division along the Back Road leading to Cedar Creek, while Merritt's division moved up the Valley Turnpike toward Strasburg, Wilson's division advancing on Front Royal by way of Stevensburg. At daylight of September 20 the infantry pushed forward, the Sixth and Nineteenth Corps marching abreast in the open country to the right and left of the pike, Crook's Kanawha Corps following closely in their rear. Early's forces presented no opposition until Torbert's cavalry discovered them posted on Fisher's Hill, a position of great natural strength. Early's line extended in a westerly direction across the Strasburg Valley, his right resting on the North Fork of the Shenandoah River, while his left extended to Little North Mountain. Sheridan made no effort to dislodge Early, but after the Sixth Corps came up Wright went to the west of the Valley Pike, overlooking Strasburg, Emory taking position on his left, toward the Front Royal Road. Crook came up soon after sunset, and formed line in some heavy timber on the north bank of Cedar Creek.

The valley where Early now made his stand is only three and a half miles wide, for it is pinched just there by the Massanutten Range and Little North Mountain. The Confederate general had in August constructed a heavy line of earthworks all along the precipitous bluff which overhangs Tumbling Run, and his men were busily employed

GENERAL J. S. MOSBY.

in strengthening them when the Federals came in sight. So secure did Early consider himself that his ammunition chests were lifted from the caissons and placed behind the breastworks for convenience. General Wharton, who now commanded Breckenridge's division, held the right of the Confederate line, Gordon's division stood next, with Pegram, now commanding Ramseur's old division, on his left. General Ramseur had taken Rodes' division and occupied the left, with Lomax's cavalry acting as foot troops, extending the line to the Back Road. General Fitz Hugh Lee having been wounded at Winchester, the Confederate cavalry was now commanded by General Wickham, and he had gone to Milford to prevent Fisher's Hill from being turned through the Luray Valley. Both armies remained quiet during that night, though the pickets were tolerably active.

MAJOR-GENERAL R. RANSOM, C. S. A.

Knowing that a direct assault would entail terrible loss and be of doubtful result, Sheridan resolved to use a turning column against Early's left. On September 21, Crook being still concealed in the timber north of Cedar Creek, Wright and Emory moved up closer to the Confederate works, the Sixth Corps succeeding in gaining some high ground on the right of the Mannassas Gap Railroad and confronting the point where Early had massed most of his artillery. Then an elevated position on the north side of Tumbling Run was carried, Sheridan thus gaining commanding ground for his batteries. The Sixth Corps was now seven hundred yards from the Confederate lines. During that night Crook's corps crossed Cedar Creek and took position in some heavy woods behind Hupp's Hill. At daylight of the 22d Crook marched under cover of intervening ravines and woods beyond the right of the Sixth Corps, being again concealed by some timber not far from the Back Road. As soon as Crook had accomplished his task Ricketts' division was pushed out until it faced the extreme left of Early's infantry line.

This movement being discovered by the Confederate signal men posted on Three Top Mountain, Early prepared for an attack at that point. This was what Sheridan had been aiming at, and while Ricketts was occupying the attention of the Confederate left, Crook marched his men south in two parallel columns into the dense timber on the eastern face of Little North Mountain, until he gained the rear of Early's works, when, moving by the left flank, he led his command in an easterly direction down the mountain side. As Crook left the timber he was met by an artillery fire, but the Kanawha Corps rushed across the broken ground and threw the Confederate left into great confusion as Ricketts was swinging his division round, the whole force taking the works in reverse. Then Early's left gave way, and all of Sheridan's line swung round, the Confederates retreating in disorder, abandoning sixteen field pieces and all the ammunition in the works.

Early retreated through Woodstock, Sheridan's advance reaching the town during that night. Sheridan's pursuit was untiring, and he drove Early back day after day, through Newmarket and Harrisonburg. Early next fell back to Port Republic, thence to Brown's Gap, in the Blue Ridge, some fifteen miles southeast of Harrisonburg, and held the Gap, despite several attempts to dislodge him. Sheridan, finding Early so strongly intrenched at Brown's Gap, did not dare to advance on Lynchburg, for his own communications were in peril, and the guerillas, under Mosby and White, were cutting off Federal trains and stragglers all through the Shenandoah Valley. One of these bands murdered Lieutenant John Meigs, who was General Sheridan's chief engineer. For this act

Sheridan retaliated by burning every house within five miles of the scene of the tragedy. Every spy that was caught suffered death by order of a drum head court-martial. On October 6 Sheridan marched northward, destroying all the hay, grain, and forage that was not consumed by his own army. He put the torch to over two thousand barns, filled with grain, and seventy-five mills, capturing several thousand sheep and cattle. The Luray, Little Fork, and Shenandoah Valleys, from the Blue Ridge to the North Mountain, down to the Potomac River, were thus rendered untenable for a Confederate army. As Sheridan fell back toward Cedar Creek he was closely followed by Early. On October 15 General Sheridan was summoned to Washington for consultation. During his brief absence the entire success of his really brilliant campaign came near being overthrown.

BATTLE OF FISHER'S HILL.

SHERIDAN'S RIDE.

CHAPTER LXVIII.

THE BATTLE OF CEDAR CREEK AND SHERIDAN'S FAMOUS RIDE.

While Fisher's Hill was a good position for resisting an army moving up the Valley, it presented no advantage to Sheridan, now that Early was following him in the opposite direction. He therefore placed his army on rolling and rising ground along the eastern bank of Cedar Creek, the Sixth Corps occupying the right; the Nineteenth the centre, and the Eighth Federal the left. The line was five miles long, and Sheridan considered it strongly placed, as Crook's left rested on the North Fork of the Shenandoah River, and Wright held the Middle Road and some high ridges. Having made the customary provisions for protecting his flanks and rear, General Sheridan obeyed Halleck's summons, leaving General Wright in temporary command. While passing through the mountains Sheridan received from Wright a copy of a message from Longstreet to Early, telling him to be ready to smash the Federal forces when their two corps got together.

The conference between Stanton, Halleck, and Sheridan was very brief, the latter upsetting the paper plans of the bureau general. Being nervous concerning the position of his army, Sheridan asked for a special train for Martinsburg, on the upper Potomac. Leaving Martinsburg on the morning of October 18, Sheridan rode over the Valley Pike to Winchester, a distance of twenty-eight miles. There he received word that all was quiet on the front, and that one of Grover's brigades was to make a reconnoissance the next morning. So the General went to his bed, being exhausted by his three days' journey. Irregular firing was reported on October 19, but Sheridan supposed that it was

Grover's reconnoissance, and he did not start until after nine o'clock.   In the meantime Early had planned a most brilliant movement.   Sending his light artillery and cavalry to make a demonstration against the Federal right, he formed his infantry into five columns, three of which, under Generals Ramseur, Pegram, and Gordon, were sent to place themselves on the left rear of Sheridan's army.   The other two columns, under Kershaw and Wharton, were to get in front of Crook.   The flanking columns had to pass through a gorge at the foot of Massanutten Mountain, ford the North Fork of the Shenandoah River, and pass round Crook's line.   Starting at sunset of October 18, Gordon, Ramseur, and Pegram accomplished their task, and at daybreak of the 19th their line stood within six hundred yards of the Federal camps.   Before the cool autumnal mists were dispersed by the rising sun, Kershaw made an assault on Crook, which was a complete surprise, the flanking line also advancing.   General Crook lost some eight or ten guns and eight hundred men in fifteen minutes, and the Nineteenth Corps was next threatened.   Though enveloped by the attacking force, General Emory held his ground for an hour, when he was compelled to give way with the loss of more artillery and men.   The Sixth Corps, under temporary command of General Ricketts, now crossed to the left, and checked the Confederate movement, giving opportunity for Crook and Emory to reform their lines. The battle was resumed at nine o'clock, General Wright trying to regain his old positions, but he was gradually forced back nearly three miles, to the village of Middletown, having lost his camps and earthworks, eighteen hundred men, and twenty-four cannon.

All this time Sheridan was riding toward the battlefield.   Before he was an hour on the road he learned that a disaster had occurred, but it was not until he reached Newtown that the full extent of the repulse was realized.   The roads were choked with wagons, as the teamsters applied their whips to avoid capture, while a line of wounded men streaming to the rear attested the severity of the engagement.   Sheridan found Getty's division about a mile north of Middletown, under command of General Louis A. Grant, General Getty having taken charge of the Sixth Corps, General Ricketts being badly wounded.   Among the officers in this division was Colonel Rutherford B. Hayes, acting as a brigade commander.   He became President of the United States in 1877. General Wright then came up, his uniform coat saturated with blood that flowed from a wound in his chin where a musket ball had cut it.

Sending Wright to resume command of his corps and ordering Getty to his division, Sheridan began forming a new line, the news of his arrival restoring confidence, and the men voluntarily began returning to their commands.

It is only just to General Wright to say that he had restored order before Sheridan arrived, and as one of the disinterested spectators of this memorable battle, the writer has no hesitation in expressing the belief that Wright would have gained a victory over Early without Sheridan. This fact, however, does not detract anything from Sheridan's fame.

The line being formed, Sheridan rode along it, being received with cheers by his troops.   At three o'clock Sheridan gave the following order: "The entire line will advance.   The Nineteenth Corps will move in connection with the Sixth.   The right of the Nineteenth will swing to the left, so as to drive the enemy upon the pike."

This order was obeyed with promptness, the whole line moving forward in perfect unison and splendid shape.   The charge was led by Getty's division, with Custer's and

COLONEL RUTHERFORD B. HAYES.

Merritt's cavalry covering the flanks. Scarcely had the imposing movement begun, when the Confederates opened a terrific artillery and musketry fire, which temporarily checked the Sixth Corps. Then Emory swung his line round and made two distinct and successful charges, which disordered Early's lines and threw them back. At the same time Torbert's cavalry division struck the Confederate flank and doubled it up. The tide was now turning, but Early's troops fought with desperation, the battle assuming a sanguinary character.

Pushing steadily forward, Generals Wright, Crook, Emory, and Torbert pressed back the Confederate line, until it finally broke in confusion, when the Federal movement grew into a pursuit. All of the captured cannon were recovered, and Early was not able to halt until he had passed through Strasburg and reached Fisher's Hill. That night the Federal corps rested in their old camps, leaving the cavalry to harass Early, who continued his retreat southward during October 20 and 21, abandoning all further effort to regain the Valley. During his entire Shenandoah campaign Sheridan lost sixteen thousand men. Early's loss was ten thousand men killed and wounded, and thirteen thousand taken prisoners. General Ramseur was mortally wounded at the battle of Cedar Creek, and died the following day at Sheridan's headquarters. As a reward for his gallantry and success, Sheridan was made a Major-General in the Regular Army. Colonels Hayes and Hamblin became Brigadiers of Volunteers. The Sixth Corps was subsequently transferred to Petersburg, and Sheridan's forces went into winter quarters.

MAJOR-GENERAL A. D. McCOOK AND STAFF.

GENERAL U. S. GRANT AND STAFF IN FRONT OF WINTER QUARTERS HUT AT CITY POINT, MARCH, 1865.

CHAPTER LXIX.

GRANT'S ACTIVE OPERATIONS IN FRONT OF RICHMOND AND PETERSBURG.

When news of Sheridan's victory at Winchester reached General Grant at City Point, he at once set the Armies of the Potomac and the James at work, in order to prevent General Lee sending reinforcements to Early. At daylight of September 21 every cannon and mortar in the Federal lines opened a furious and rapid fire. From Deep Bottom, north of the James River, to the Jerusalem Plank Road, in front of Petersburg, a distance of twenty-one miles, there were over three hundred Dahlgren, Rodman, and Parrott rifled cannon engaged. With these were one hundred brass field guns and nearly as many wide-mouthed mortars. From early dawn until sunset was this terrible bombardment maintained, and all of the larger guns were kept busy during the entire night. Lee's gunners made a vigorous response,

GENERAL U. S. GRANT, WIFE, AND CHILD IN FRONT OF WINTER QUARTERS HUT
AT CITY POINT, MARCH, 1865.

so that during these terrible twenty-four hours there were nearly eight hundred pieces of artillery engaged. The detonations were so rapid and so deafening that it seemed as if fifty thunderstorms had come together. A hot, white mist clung to the war-scarred fields. Through the dense masses of smoke bright flashes sprung forth, followed by sullen roars. During that night scarcely a man slept more than an hour, for the concussions filled the air and shook the ground. Fresh men were ordered forward the next morning to relieve the exhausted artillerists, and the fusilade was maintained with the same vigor and fury for another day and night. During these forty-eight hours over fifty-seven thousand shells were delivered, while the Confederates threw fully thirty-five thousand.

Long before daylight of September 22 the Second and Fifth Corps were moving to

SIEGE OF PETERSBURG, VA.

the extreme left of Meade's intrenched line, their path being illuminated by the cannon flashes and bursting shells. So swiftly did these corps move that at daylight they struck the Weldon Road. The assault was so sudden that the Confederate fortifications were taken after one volley, and the coveted railroad was in Federal possession, Meade extending his line of circumvallation nearly three miles to the left. Butler's army also succeeded in extending its investing lines.

On September 15 General Wade Hampton's four brigades of cavalry and two light batteries had marched rapidly around Meade's left, and seized a large herd of cattle at Sycamore Church, near Coggin's Point, on the James. It was a brilliant exploit and revictualed the Confederate army. On September 28, the Tenth and Eighteenth Army Corps moved from the right of Butler's line to Aiken's Landing, advancing over the Varina

FORT RIEL
INTERIOR VIEW.

RIFLE PITS
FEDERAL PICKETT
LINE

CHEVEUX DE FRISE,
CONFEDERATE FORTIFICATIONS

RIFLE PITS
FEDERAL PICKETT
LINE

REMOVING
CAPTURED
ARTILLERY.

CHEVEUX DE FRISE,
CONFEDERATE FORTIFICATIONS.

CONFEDERATE
FORTIFICATIONS.

LARGE GUN IN
CONFEDERATE
WORKS

CONFEDERATE
FORTIFICATIONS.

TRESTLE BRIDGE
ON SOUTHERN RAILWAY.

SIEGE OF PETERSBURG, VA.

Road. At Chapin's Farm the Federals found a fort flanked by well-constructed curtains. The Eighteenth Corps dashed forward and succeeded in capturing Fort Harrison with sixteen large guns and two hundred prisoners. The Confederate gunboats and the forts on the opposite side of the James made the position untenable, and it was abandoned. Meanwhile the Tenth Corps crossed Four Mile Creek and attacked the Confederates at New Market Heights, Paine's colored division making a charge. The Federals were, however, handsomely repulsed, with a loss of fifteen hundred men, chiefly negroes. General Birney then marched toward Richmond, reaching Laurel Hill, where Fort Gilmer stood. Here another sharp fight occurred, but the Federals were compelled to retreat, General Kautz' cavalry succeeding, however, in getting within sight of the spires of Richmond. On September 30 a large force of Confederates attacked Ord and

VIEWS ON APPOMATTOX RIVER.

Birney, when a fierce engagement ensued, lasting from two o'clock to sundown. The burden of loss fell on Lee's troops.

These movements having drawn a large force from Lee's right, the Second Corps and two divisions each from the Fifth and Ninth Corps were sent, on September 30, under command of General Warren, across the Weldon Railroad, at Four Mile Station. Griffin's, Ayres', Willcox's, and Potter's divisions moved toward Poplar Grove, on the South Side Railroad, striking the Squirrel Level Road, and reached Peeble's Farm, four miles southwest of Petersburg. A general engagement followed, as the Confederates poured out of Petersburg to resist this movement. They succeeded in breaking through the Federal line between the Fifth and Ninth Corps, sweeping up fifteen hundred prisoners from Potter's division. Warren held his ground, however, and sent Mott's division toward the Boydton Plank Road, which was used as a wagon supply route by Lee. Mott found it amply protected, and retired.

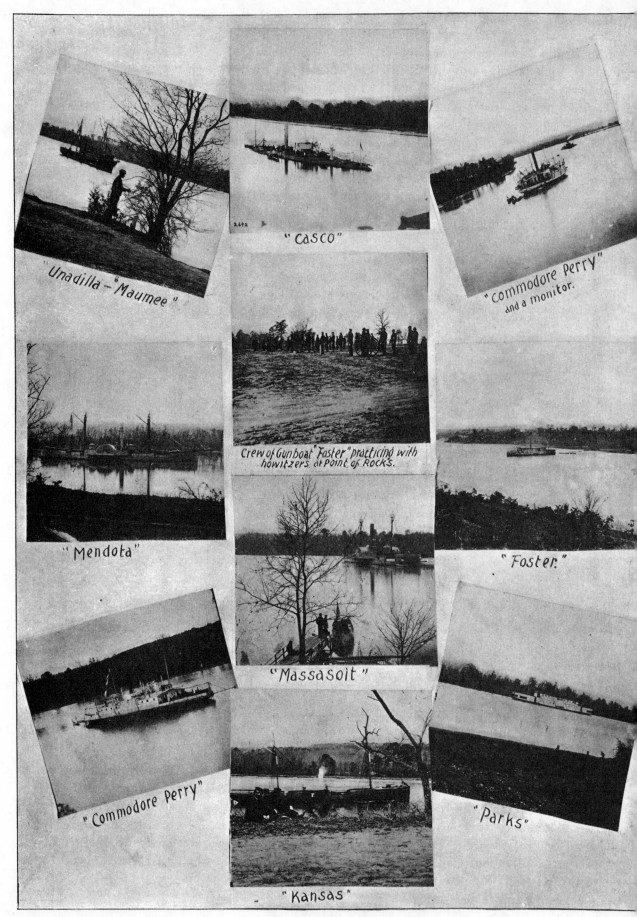

Unadilla - "Maumee"

"Casco"

"Commodore Perry" and a monitor.

"Mendota"

Crew of Gunboat "Foster" practicing with howitzers at Point of Rocks.

"Foster."

"Massasoit"

"Commodore Perry"

"Kansas"

"Parks"

U. S. GUNBOATS IN JAMES RIVER.

The untiring energy of Grant caused another movement by Butler on October 1, when Terry's division and Kautz' cavalry made a reconnoissance along the Darbytown and Charles City Roads, but there was no other profitable result. On October 7 the Confederate cavalry struck Kautz' brigades, under Spear and West, on the Charles City Road, five miles from Richmond, and made so sudden an attack that the Federal horsemen were routed, losing all their batteries. Fighting then began all along the lines, the Confederate infantry being finally driven back. Having kept Lee so busy, Grant gave his troops a resting spell.

Receiving news of Sheridan's victory at Cedar Creek, Grant gave secret orders for a general movement, which he hoped would lead to the capture of Petersburg and the fall of Richmond. Every horse was re-shod, the interior corduroy roads across swamps

PONTOON BRIDGE ACROSS APPOMATTOX RIVER.

EXCHANGED CONFEDERATE PRISONERS ON THEIR WAY TO COX'S LANDING.

COX'S LANDING, JAMES RIVER.

JAMES RIVER, NEAR VARINA LANDING

JAMES RIVER, NEAR VARINA LANDING.

COX'S LANDING, JAMES RIVER.

mended, and all the batteries and infantry received fresh ammunition, the army being stripped of impedimenta. At two o'clock in the morning of October 27 the entire army began its march. Hancock and Gregg were to make a wide detour toward Reams' Station and get on the Boydton Plank Road, a feat they succeeded in accomplishing. Warren went over the Squirrel Level Road, while Parkes led his Ninth Corps toward Hatcher's Run. The Fifth and Ninth Corps were to attack the Hatcher's Run fortifications and form connection with the Second. Hancock's corps, accompanied by Gregg's cavalry, reached the Boydton Plank Road at noon, finding the Confederates waiting behind formidable intrenchments. Sharp fighting ensued, but it was not until Warren's guns were heard that Hancock prepared for serious work. Before Warren could come up, Mahone's division managed to get between him and Hancock, when the Confederate General swept round Hancock's right. A prolonged battle followed, Mahone being finally compelled to withdraw. The movement, as a whole, was a failure, though Meade's permanent line was a mile longer. The return of the Federal troops to their intrench-ments was made during the day and night of October 28, over muddy roads and in a heavy storm of rain, leaving nearly all their wounded behind for lack of transportation.

This ended the manœuvres of both the Army of the Potomac and the Army of the James for nearly two months, though the work of the siege was maintained with unceas-ing severity and duration. Week after week, during every hour of the day and night, the air was filled with shells from siege cannon and mortars, the roar of the opposing guns deafening the ear, while the rattle of musketry formed the monotone of the mighty orchestra of war. Grant's line was twenty-five miles long, but the forts, curtains, approaches, and parallels multiplied this line to over ninety miles of intrenchments.

VIEWS IN AND ABOUT CONFEDERATE FORT MAHONE (CALLED BY THE SOLDIERS "FORT DAMNATION").

Fort Hell and Fort Damnation, as the soldiers called them, on either side of the Jerusa-lem Plank Road, were the nearest to the City of Petersburg. From their casements the movements of Confederate soldiers in the streets of the beleaguered city were distinctly visible. The guns of these two advanced forts were never silent, the garrisons being constantly changed, in order that the men might endure the fatigue. Even along the curtains that connected the principal forts there were cannon and huge, wide-mouthed mortars, while little barking coehorns lay concealed in convenient pits. The pickets went in every evening with one hundred and fifty rounds of ball cartridges, and few men returned, on being relieved at the end of twenty-four hours, with more than a dozen car-tridges in their pouches. So deadly was the fire that these Federal and Confederate marksmen discharged their pieces from narrow openings in the breastworks, which were so filled with lead that whenever a truce happened the soldiers used to dig them out with their fingers.

Siege duty is both tiresome and exacting, for the troops have to dwell in bomb-proof or deep ditches, and these are unhealthy and depressing. To sleep in burrows at night, with the boom of cannon constantly assailing the dormant ear, and pass the daylight hours listening to the sudden crashes of musketry, the roar of huge siege guns, the shriek of rifled shells, and watch for the occasional plunge of mortar bombs in the parallels and approaches, is very exciting at first, but these sights and sounds become wearisome in their monotony. Men can endure this sort of this thing for a week or two, but then they must be relieved, for human nature can no longer stand the strain. It is this fact that explains why beleaguered armies are usually conquered; for to them there is no relief from the exposure from solid shot, shells, and bombs. Then, too, their lines of outer communication are constantly being cut, which decreases the supplies of food and ammunition, so that the men grow weary, disheartened, and often mutinous.

But while Meade and Butler were thus simply clinging to Lee's throat and exhausting his effective strength, General Sherman was busy in the State of Georgia.

GENERAL SHERMAN AT SAVANNAH, GA.

CHAPTER LXX.

GENERAL SHERMAN'S MARCH TO THE SEA.

The combined armies under General Sherman lay in and around Atlanta until October, 1864, many of the regiments returning home, as their term of service had expired. The remaining troops were consolidated and reorganized, equipped and clothed, for another campaign. The effective strength of Sherman's army was then reduced to about sixty thousand men.

General Hood was retained in the command of the Confederate troops, and he reorganized his army until he mustered forty thousand men. It was then decided that Hood should march north of Atlanta, tear up the railroad between Chattanooga and the Chattahoochee River, and on reaching Bridgeport, destroy the huge bridge over the Tennessee River. This would sever the communications between Atlanta and Chattanooga, and cut off Chattanooga from Nashville. Forrest's cavalry was already at work in Tennessee, and committing considerable havoc. Hood's three corps were commanded by Generals Cheatham, S. D. Lee, and Stewart, with General Wheeler at the head of an increased cavalry force. Moving westward toward the Chattahoochee, the Confederates faced Sherman, covering the West Point Railroad near Palmetto Station. Throwing a pontoon bridge across the Chattahoochee, Hood sent cavalry to Carrollton and Powder Springs, his entire force crossing the river on October 2, and marching toward Dallas, thus threatening Kingston and Rome, and all the Federal fortified positions on the railroad. Hood captured Big Shanty and Ackworth Stations, destroying the railroad and telegraph. General S. D. French's division then started for Allatoona Pass, where Lieutenant-Colonel Tourtellotte, one of Sherman's aides, was guarding the railroad and two millions of Federal rations with three regiments.

General Sherman was prompt in moving against Hood, his main body crossing the Chattahoochee River on October 4, and reached Marietta and Kenesaw the following day. General John M. Corse was ordered to march from Rome to Tourtellotte's assistance, and he reached Allatoona Pass in time to repulse French, being himself badly wounded in the head. Sherman stood on the top of Kenesaw Mountain, and saw the smoke of the battle in the Pass. The fight was a severe one, for Colonel Redfield, of the Thirty-ninth Iowa, was killed, and Colonel Tourtellotte received a ball through his hips. French was finally repulsed, losing nearly two thousand men.

Discovering that Hood was still moving westward, Sherman pushed on to Kingston, going through Allatoona Pass, reaching the town on October 10. Hood had gone beyond Rome, and was crossing the Coosa River. Sherman then sent General Cox with the Twenty-third Corps and Garrard's cavalry division across the Oostenaula River to threaten Hood's flank. On October 12 Hood appeared before Resaca with Stewart's corps, and demanded Colonel Weaver's unconditional surrender, promising the garrison

VIEW ON BATTLEFIELD OF RESACA, GA.

VIEW ON BATTLEFIELD OF RESACA, GA.

VIEW OF RESACA, GA.

VIEW ON BATTLEFIELD OF RESACA, GA.

VIEW ON BATTLEFIELD OF RESACA, GA.

of six hundred immediate parole, adding that if he was compelled to make an assault he would kill every man. Colonel Weaver had only three cannon, but his reply to Hood was, "If you want Resaca, come and take it." The Confederates skirmished for a day, and then marched on as far as Tunnel Hill.

No decided engagement occurred during the remainder of October, Hood retreating into northern Alabama, where he came under the direction of General Beauregard, who was commanding the Confederate Military Division of the West. Then, for the first time, General Sherman announced his purpose of marching through Georgia to the seacoast, a movement General Grant had finally approved of. On October 19 Sherman telegraphed to Halleck that he intended to push into the heart of Georgia and come out at Savannah, destroying all the railroads of the State.

The Confederates were now at Decatur, Alabama, and Sherman realized that Hood had really escaped from him, so he decided to leave General Thomas, then at Nashville,

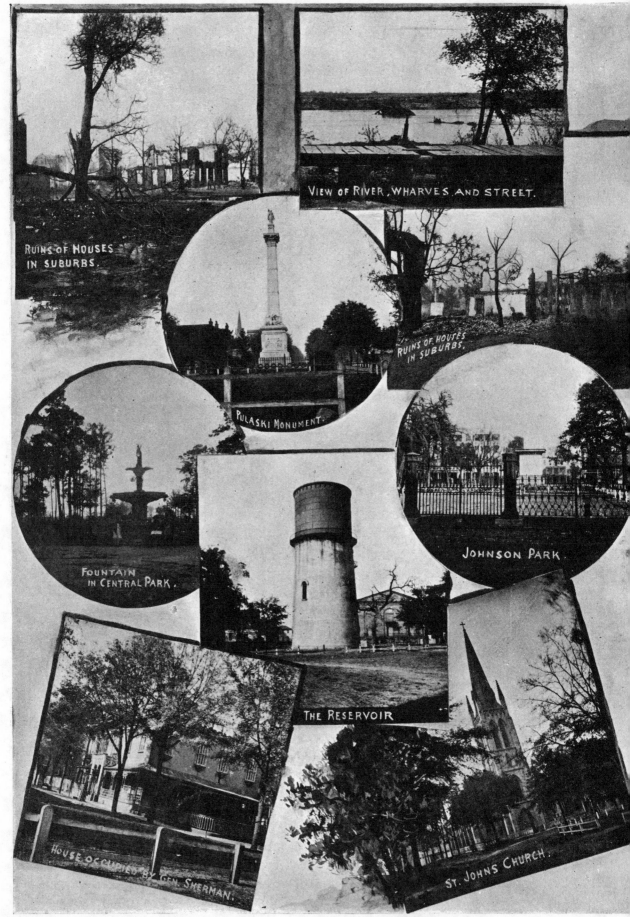

RUINS OF HOUSES IN SUBURBS.

VIEW OF RIVER, WHARVES, AND STREET.

PULASKI MONUMENT.

RUINS OF HOUSES IN SUBURBS.

FOUNTAIN IN CENTRAL PARK.

JOHNSON PARK.

THE RESERVOIR

HOUSE OCCUPIED BY GEN SHERMAN.

ST. JOHNS CHURCH.

to fight Hood, and sent him General Schofield's Twenty-third Corps, and General Stanley's Fourth Corps. Thomas had now forty-five thousand men and an independent command, while Sherman prepared for his darling project.

On November 2 Sherman's forces consisted of the Fourteenth, Fifteenth, Seventeenth, and Twentieth Army Corps, with one division of cavalry. Having repaired the railroads and telegraph lines, he sent his sick and wounded by rail to Chattanooga, packed all his wagons, and deliberately prepared for the march to Savannah, three hundred miles from Atlanta. All extra supplies, stores, and machinery accumulated at Atlanta were sent to Chattanooga, and General Corse was ordered to destroy all the foundries, shops, mills, warehouses, and bridges at Rome, and join the army. The last train left Atlanta during the night of November 11, and on the 12th Sherman telegraphed

CITY OF COLUMBIA, S. C.

three words to Thomas : "All is well." Then the wires were cut and Sherman's concentrated army stood alone, all its lines of communication being severed. None but men in full health remained, the official reports showing an aggregate of fifty-five thousand three hundred and twenty-nine infantry, five thousand and sixty-three cavalry, and eighteen hundred and twelve artillery—in all, sixty-two thousand two hundred and four officers and men. Only sixty-five pieces of artillery were taken, and the smallest possible number of wagons (twenty-five hundred), the horses and mules being carefully selected.

At that time General Hood was occupying both banks of the Tennessee River, collecting ammunition and supplies from Mobile, Selma, and Montgomery for his projected invasion of the State of Tennessee. Beauregard was at Corinth. Thomas remained at Nashville, watching Hood. Sherman's march did not begin until November 15, the right wing going toward Jonesboro, the left marching eastward toward Madison, via Decatur and Stone Mountain, thus threatening both Augusta and Macon. As the columns left Atlanta the Federal engineers applied their torches to the depot, round-house, and machine shops of the Georgia Railroad. A large quantity of Confederate ammunition in one of the shops exploded, and the flames were extended to the business part of the city. Stores, warehouses, hotels, mills, and factories were thus consumed in rapid succession, with many private dwellings, so that in all over two thousand buildings were destroyed, the aggregate value of the sacrificed property amounting to more than three millions of dollars. It was amid the fierce heat and roar of the uncontrolled flames, and listening to the terrific fusilade of bursting shells among the heaped up ammunition, that Sherman and his rear guard rode out of the fair but doomed City of Atlanta on the afternoon of November 16. Behind the General was a thick, ominous cloud, in front his entire army was march-

SHERMAN AND HIS GENERALS.

ing, they knew not where. The most curious feature of this strange movement was the absolute secrecy maintained regarding its ultimate destination. As they trotted over the soft dirt roads Sherman's men believed that they were going to Richmond.

Sherman's rear guard consisted of the Fourteenth Corps, and it marched as far as Lithonia, near Stone Mountain, a mighty mass of granite, where the command bivouacked for the night. The sky was lighted up by the fires of Howard's men as they destroyed the railroads, and for several weeks the army's path was marked by flames at night and black clouds of smoke in the daytime. The following day Sherman passed through Covington, the Fourteenth Corps marching in solid column, with unfurled colors, to the music of the bands, bivouacking on the banks of the picturesque Ulcofauhachee River. Turning to the right, Sherman guided his own column to Milledgeville, via Shady Dale. General Slocum was ahead at Madison, the Twentieth Corps having torn up the railroad, and General Geary's division had marched to the Oconee River and burned all the bridges. General Howard's Fifteenth Corps encountered Iverson's Confederate cavalry at Jonesboro, but they were soon dispersed by Kilpatrick's horsemen, when the columns moved eastward through McDonough and Jackson to the Ocmulgee River, crossing at Planter's Mills, and passing southward through Monticello and Hillsboro, finally striking the Georgia Central Railroad at Gordon, twenty miles east of Macon. Kilpatrick then swept round on the right, through Griffin and Forsyth, towards Macon, finding Wheeler there with a small body of cavalry and several brigades of militia.

On November 20 two of Kilpatrick's regiments and a light battery made a feint on East Macon, driving the Confederates inside their breastworks, the Federal cavalry withdrawing to Griswoldville, after destroying the railroad east of Walnut Creek, a similar work being performed by the Fifteenth and Seventeenth Corps as far as Gordon. Then a severe engagement took place. Walcott's brigade, with part of a battery, and a few squadrons of cavalry, was covering the right flank of the Fifteenth Corps, arriving at Griswoldville on November 22. Burning the principal buildings in the town, Walcott posted his men in a wood behind a swamp and threw up a breastwork. General Anderson, with five thousand men, moved out of Macon, and charged Walcott's line six times, being repulsed with fearful slaughter, for the Confederates had to flounder through a swamp, exposed to a heavy fire. Anderson was severely wounded, and the Confederates left three hundred men dead on the field. So far Wheeler had supposed that the capture of Macon was Sherman's principal object, but as all the railroad connections had been destroyed the Federal troops marched to the right and left, leaving Wheeler to his own devices.

The Georgia Legislature was in session in Milledgeville, but on Sherman's approach the members fled to Augusta. A part of a brigade entered the State capital and proceeded to destroy the magazines, depots, arsenals, factories, and storehouses, with other government property, including two thousand bales of cotton. Two or three hundred Federal prisoners were released from the penitentiary, and three thousand muskets captured. While Slocum's wing was resting near Milledgeville, Howard advanced eastward along the Georgia Central Railroad, destroying it as far as Tennills Station. Seeing that Macon was not threatened, Wheeler crossed the Oconee River, and prepared to resist the Federal passage. On November 23 Howard struck General Wayne's militia, and entered into a skirmish, while his main force moved eight miles down the river, and crossed on a pontoon bridge. Wayne then retreated, and Howard's command continued its work of destroying the railroad.

One of the features of Sherman's movement was the celerity displayed in collecting supplies. Each brigade commander detailed a force of fifty men under a commissioned officer, and these parties visited every plantation within five miles of the route of march. Procuring a wagon or a family carriage, these men would gather up bacon, chickens, corn, meal, turkeys, ducks, hams—in fact, anything in the shape of food, besides ample supplies of forage for the cavalry.

For so extended and rapid a march as Sherman contemplated pontoon trains were absolutely necessary. These pontoons were of the skeleton pattern, covered with cotton canvas, each boat with its balks and chesses filling a wagon. Two sections would furnish a bridge eighteen hundred feet long, but the advanced brigades frequently constructed timber bridges before the pontoons could come to the front.

Pressing forward, Howard and Slocum reached Sandersville on November 25, their progress being delayed by finding the bridges across Buffalo Creek all destroyed, for Wheeler had now grasped the scope of the Federal movement, and his active cavalry were doing all they could to impede Sherman. Finding that the Confederate General was proving himself a serious obstacle, Sherman directed Kilpatrick to leave his wagons with Slocum and advance on Augusta, and accommodate Wheeler with the battle he evidently desired. Taking Baird's division of the Fourteenth Corps, General Kilpatrick proceeded with his entire mounted force to Waynesboro, arriving there on December 3. Wheeler's force was found at Thomas' Station, and driven headlong through Waynesboro and across Brier Creek, the Federals burning the bridges. Two days after Kilpatrick rejoined Slocum at Jacksonboro, twenty miles east of Millen.

The Fourteenth Corps crossed the Ogeechee River at Fenn's Bridge on November 20, and, marching along its northern bank, entered Louisville. Turning eastward at Buckhead Creek, the corps proceeded to Lumpkin's Station, on the Augusta and Millen Railroad, which was destroyed with several miles of track. The Fifteenth and Seventeenth Corps passed along the south side of the railroad, while the Twentieth destroyed railroads and public property as far as Davisboro Station. The Ogeechee having been left behind, the Federal columns were now headed for Savannah, the feint against Augusta leading the Confederates to mass their troops there, thus leaving Savannah unprotected. But, though their feeble army had been outmanœuvred, the citizens of Georgia turned out, and skilled axemen felled trees across all the roads at difficult points, and burned all the bridges. The necessity for removing or overcoming these obstructions delayed Sherman's army, but did not change its projected route, and the vicinity of Savannah was reached on December 7.

While Sherman's men were thus advancing overland, General Foster and Admiral Dahlgren were operating against Savannah from Hilton Head. The city was defended by fifteen thousand men, under General Hardie, his principal work being Fort McAllister, mounting twenty-three large guns. The Federal army invested Savannah, but made no assault until December 13, when General Hazen's division attacked Fort McAllister and captured it after a brief struggle. General Hardie declined to surrender, but when Kilpatrick destroyed the Gulf Railroad, and Dahlgren dispersed the Confederate fleet, he withdrew with his garrison to Charleston on December 20. General Sherman entered Savannah the next day, coming into possession of one thousand prisoners, one hundred and fifty pieces of artillery, thirteen locomotives, two hundred cars, four steamboats, and thirty-three thousand bales of cotton, besides vast quantities of military stores. General Geary was appointed military commander of the city, and order was at once restored.

BATTLEFIELD OF NEW HOPE CHURCH, GA.

Thus ended the famous March to the Sea. During five consecutive weeks sixty-two thousand men and twenty thousand horses and mules marched three hundred miles, their path being from twenty to sixty miles in width. The army captured twenty million pounds of corn and fodder, three million rations of bread and meat, one million rations of coffee and sugar. Three hundred and fifty miles of railroad track were destroyed, thus annihilating the Confederate army communications, while the aggregate value of property destroyed is estimated by General Sherman, at over one hundred millions of dollars. The Federal losses during the campaign were sixty-three men killed on the field, two hundred and forty-five wounded, and two hundred and fifty-nine missing. The Confederacy was now cut fairly into two, and another step toward ending the Civil War had been taken.

CHAPTER LXXI.

THE ANNIHILATION OF HOOD'S ARMY BY GENERAL THOMAS.

Events occurred in rapid succession in the Southwest during the closing months of 1864. While Sherman was cutting loose from Atlanta, General Forrest made a raid along the Tennessee River, capturing Athens and its garrison. Forrest committed much havoc, despite the efforts of the Federal cavalry, Generals Rousseau, Washburne, Granger, and Morgan. Thomas, learning that Hood aimed at invading Middle Tennessee, started out to meet him. Another large force of Confederate troops, under General Price, moved toward Missouri, reaching Pilot Knob on September 23. General Hugh S. Ewing was in command of the garrison, having fourteen heavy guns. Price was driven back on the 27th after a most desperate assault, losing one thousand men. But the Confederates gained complete possession of Shepherd Mountain, which compelled Ewing to evacuate Pilot Knob. General Rosecranz, who was at St. Louis, prepared to meet Price by throwing forward various commands, under Generals Pleasanton, A. J. Smith, Brown, O'Neil, Sanborn, and Fisk, which prevented Price approaching the city, so he contented himself with destroying all property that came in his way. There were several battles, the most important being at Westport, near the Big Blue River, when Pleasonton and Curtis captured Price's camp and nearly all of his plunder, the Confederates escaping into Western Arkansas. Price made a stand at Fayetteville, but he was ignominiously defeated and his force scattered. He had destroyed property valued at three millions of dollars and seized a vast quantity of supplies, but in his retreat from Newtonia five thousand men deserted him, and he lost nearly all his artillery and wagons. Soon after this General Morgan, the famous Confederate commander of irregular cavalry, was surprised by General Gillem in East Tennessee, and killed. Breckenridge attacked Gillem on November 13, near Knoxville, the result being that the Federals were routed and lost six guns, seventy wagons, eighteen colors, many men and supplies, the remnant finding shelter in Knoxville. General Stoneman was then ordered into East Tennessee by Thomas. With Gillem's and Burbridge's commands he drove Breckenridge helter-skelter through Bristol, across the north fork of the Holston River. During his movement Stoneman captured twenty field guns, one thousand prisoners, ten thousand head of cattle and hogs, with hundreds of wagons and mule teams. He also destroyed the extensive lead works at Wytheville, and the Confederate salt machinery at Saltville, and other property valued at over four millions of dollars. Had the war lasted much longer the Confederate territory would have become a barren waste.

Hood now sent Forrest from Corinth, with nine thousand horses and ten mounted batteries, to the Tennessee River. On November 2 Forrest appeared before Fort Heiman, where he captured a Federal gunboat and four steamers. Forrest then retired before Schofield, who was advancing. Hood and Thomas were now fairly confronted. The Confederate general had sixty thousand men, while Thomas could only mus-

MAJOR-GENERAL J. H. THOMAS.

ter thirty thousand. It was not until November 19 that Hood crossed the Tennessee River, Thomas meanwhile gathering up ten thousand additional men. General Schofield then fell back on Columbia, Thomas' other corps moving to the Duck River crossings. On November 25 the Confederates threatened the crossings, and there was considerable fighting. Hood made a bold attack on Schofield at Franklin, his troops moving forward in long massive lines. As Cheatham's and Stewart's corps advanced they encountered a steady and merciless artillery and musketry fire, but though the lines were shattered, they were not checked. Cheatham and Stewart finally succeeded, after a bloody battle, in capturing the Federal breastworks. General Stanley made a counter-charge with

VIEWS FROM THE CAPITOL, NASHVILLE, TAKEN DURING THE BATTLE OF DECEMBER 15, 1864, SHOWING CIVILIANS AND SOLDIERS WATCHING THE FIGHT.

Opdyke's brigade, which broke the Confederate line and drove it back, the Federals recapturing their works and lost cannon. Three times did Hood renew the fight, but he was repulsed over and over again, until night put a stop to the struggle. Generals Stanley and Bradley were wounded, and General Opdyke was the hero of the battle. Hood lost six thousand men; Schofield twenty-three hundred. Hood had thirteen generals killed, wounded, or captured.

Thomas now concentrated his army at Nashville, having fifty-six thousand men at his command. Hood appeared on December 4, but no fighting occurred for ten days, though some of Thomas' communications were cut. Grant became alarmed at the apparent delay, and gave Thomas positive orders to fight Hood at once. But George H. Thomas would never move until he was ready, being of stubborn mind. Aiming to strike Hood heavily on the right, with a strong feint on his left, Thomas sent his several cavalry divisions, under Steadman, Wilson, Wheeler, and Johnson, during the night of December 14, over the Nolensville, Hillsboro and Harding Turnpikes, Johnson riding down to engage the fort at Ball's Landing, on the Cumberland River. Wilson's division opened the battle at daylight, driving the Confederates across Richland Creek and capturing a redoubt, when Schofield's corps became the right wing, Wood's Fourth Corps being the left. These dispositions occupied the forenoon, but at one o'clock, the Fourth Corps assaulted Montgomery Hill, carrying it in fine style, capturing eight pieces of artillery and two battle flags. The Confederates, however, clung to the base of the Harpeth Hills, protecting the Granny White and Franklin Turnpikes. Schofield and Smith then engaged, and Hood was forced back at every point, losing during the day sixteen cannon, his loss in killed, wounded, and missing being very heavy.

CITY OF NASHVILLE, TENN.

At nightfall Thomas ordered his troops to bivouack in line of battle, and at six o'clock of the 16th all of his corps pressed forward. Wood seized the Franklin Turnpike and advanced as far as Overton's Hill. Holding Schofield fast, Thomas then moved Smith in between the Twenty-third and Fourth Corps, which gave him an advantageous front toward the South. The assault on Overton's Hill was met by a strong force drawn from Hood's left and centre. Wood's corps pushed up the hill in face of a terrific fire of musketry, grape, and canister, until near the crest, when the Confederate reserves ran forward and delivered so destructive a volley that the Fourth Corps was broken and retired, leaving their dead and wounded. While Wood was reforming Schofield and Smith charged on their respective fronts, capturing all of the Confederate artillery and two thousand prisoners, among them four generals. At the same time Wilson seized the Granny White Turnpike, thus closing one of Hood's lines of retreat. Wood's infantry and Steedman's horsemen again assaulted Overton's Hill, carrying it so suddenly that the Confederates lost all of their artillery, over two thousand men becoming prisoners. Wood pursued the flying columns to Brentwood Pass, halting at dark. Hatch's and Knipe's cavalry divisions scattered Chalmer's horsemen on the Granny White Turnpike, taking many prisoners, among them General Rucker. During these two days Thomas took forty-five hundred men as prisoners, of whom nearly three hundred were officers, fifty-three field guns, and over six thousand muskets. Hood left three thousand dead and wounded on the ground. The Federal loss was three thousand.

Thomas took up the pursuit at daylight, his advance finding Hood's rear guard at Hollow Tree Gap, four miles north of Franklin. The Confederates fell back on Franklin, only to meet Johnson's cavalry coming up on the south side of the Harpeth River, which compelled Hood to retire toward Columbia. During the night of December 17 Hood escaped across the Harpeth, and was on the other side of Duck River by the 22d. The weather was very cold, but Thomas maintained his pursuit most relentlessly. Hood's men were disheartened, ragged, and barefooted, the conscripts deserting or surrendering. Thomas chased Hood to the Tennessee River, finding cannon, caissons, wagons, and small arms scattered along the roads, and thirteen thousand men were taken prisoners. Hood's army was practically annihilated, and on December 30 Thomas went into winter quarters. Hood took his shattered army to Tupelo, Mississippi, and was relieved by his own request, retiring from active service minus the arm he lost at Gettysburg and the leg he left at Chickamauga.

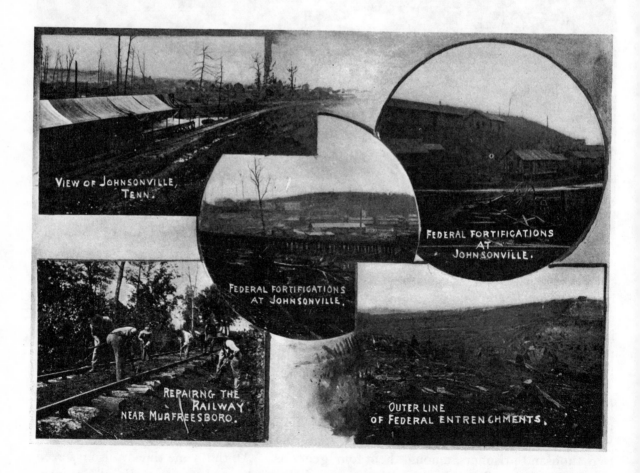

VIEW OF JOHNSONVILLE, TENN.

FEDERAL FORTIFICATIONS AT JOHNSONVILLE.

FEDERAL FORTIFICATIONS AT JOHNSONVILLE.

REPAIRNG THE RAILWAY NEAR MURFREESBORO.

OUTER LINE OF FEDERAL ENTRENCHMENTS.

FLEET OF FORT FISHER EXPEDITION IN HAMPTON ROADS, DECEMBER, 1864.

CHAPTER LXXII.

CAPTURE OF SOUTHERN SEAPORTS AND THE FALL OF FORT FISHER.

January, 1865, found Sherman still at Savannah, Grant at Petersburg, and Thomas on the Tennessee River. Sherman began overrunning the Carolinas, sending Howard by sea from Savannah to Beaufort, when he seized the Charleston Railroad at Pocotaligo. Engagements occurred on the line of the Salkahatchie, Congaree, and Edisto Rivers, Howard and Slocum marching to Columbia, on the Saluda River. Wade Hampton had already destroyed ten thousand bales of cotton by setting them on fire in the streets, the consequence being the destruction of the business part of the city, despite the efforts of the Federals to save it. The fall of Columbia occurred on February 12, Charleston being surrendered the following day, Hardee destroying the railroad buildings and an immense quantity of rice before evacuating. While the women and children were gathering the rice, two hundred kegs of gunpowder caught fire and exploded, killing two hundred persons, nearly one thousand more being injured. The city was in ruins, and the population had fallen to ten thousand. Taking possession on February 18, General Gillmore secured nearly five hundred cannon and considerable railroad property. The surrender took place exactly four years after the inauguration of Jefferson Davis as the Confederate President. They had been four years of suffering and horror for the entire country. The tattered flag lowered by Major Robert Anderson in 1861 was hoisted by the General on the fourth anniversary of his humiliation.

General Sherman went on marching through the Carolinas, destroying railroads, bridges, and public property. Flame and smoke marked every step of his army along the Broad, Catawba, Cheraw, Wateree, Pedee, and Cape Fear Rivers. There was constant fighting, but no pitched battles until March 14, when Hardee crossed the Cape

Fear on his way to join Johnston's army with the Columbia and Charleston garrisons and Cheatham's corps. The fight that ensued was sharp and decisive, the Confederates being compelled to retreat, only to be attacked the following day at Averysboro, when they were again driven back. Another engagement occurred at Bentonville, on the Goldsboro Road, when Joe Johnston made a desperate effort to win a decided victory. The Confederates made six desperate charges with their whole force, but as they had very little artillery, the defeat was a crushing one. This battle placed Sherman finally on the line of communication between Richmond and the Carolinas.

During Sherman's movements a successful attack was made on Fort Fisher, which commanded the northwest channel of the Cape Fear River and the approach to Wilmington, the haven of blockade runners. In December, 1864, Admiral Porter and General Butler made an attempt, but owing to a hurricane which scattered the Federal

ADMIRAL PORTER AND STAFF ON BOARD FLAGSHIP MALVERN, NORFOLK, VA., DECEMBER, 1864.

fleet and a disagreement between the naval and army commanders it failed. General Alfred H. Terry was then placed in command of the troops, and a new effort was made. Arriving off New Inlet on January 12, Terry landed with eight thousand men, behind Fort Fisher, cutting it off from reinforcement, Porter's fleet raining fifty thousand shells on the fort, making several breaches. Fleet Captain K. R. Breeze landed on the beach with fifteen hundred sailors and marines, while Ames' division was to attack on the land side.

The combined assault occurred during the afternoon of January 15. Breeze's force was beaten back, and Ames had to pause after a hand-to-hand fight of two hours, but secured a permanent hold at nightfall, the battle only ending at nine o'clock. General Whitney was severely wounded before he surrendered, and on the Federal side General Bell was killed, Generals Curtis and Pennybacker being wounded. The Confederates destroyed their other forts, and the approaches to Wilmington were free. General Schofield's corps was then transferred from Tennessee to the sea coast by steamboat and rail, via Washington and Alexandria, arriving on February 9. After some severe fighting, Terry and Schofield captured Wilmington on the 22d.

The end of the war had now become only a question of weeks. The Confederate armies in the South and Southwest were broken or dispersed, while Grant's grasp on Lee's lines could not be shaken off. Desertion grew epidemic, supplies were exhausted, and the Confederacy was crumbling to pieces. At Petersburg the siege operations were conducted with vigor, several engagements taking place, each one weakening Lee's brave army. The Dutch Gap Canal was a failure, but the Confederate gunboats could do nothing. Hancock assumed command in the Shenandoah, leaving Sheridan free to make a raid around Richmond and join Grant in the siege lines. The cavalry General started on February 27, and arrived at Petersburg on March 24, having destroyed everything in his path.

CAPTURE OF FORT FISHER.

Lee having determined to abandon Richmond and Petersburg and attempt a junction with Joe Johnston, who was elbowing his way northward, a diversion was made on Meade's line at Fort Steadman. The movement took place at dawn of March 25, and though of a desperate character, it failed in its purpose. The day proved a memorable one, for while flags of truce were flying on Meade's right for the removal of the Confederate dead, President Lincoln was reviewing the Fifth Corps in the centre, and the Second Corps was briskly fighting on the left. Thus the strange spectacle was presented of a truce, a review, and a battle in the lines of one army. General Sherman arrived at City Point on March 27, when President Lincoln urged him and Grant to put an end to the terrible sacrifice of human life. The two Generals told Lincoln that one more battle would close the war, but neither knew whether it would occur in Virginia or the Carolinas. Sherman returned to his army the following day.

CITY OF RICHMOND, VA.—RUINS OF STATE ARSENAL AND VIEW DOWN JAMES RIVER.

CHAPTER LXXIII.

BATTLE OF FIVE FORKS, AND THE FALL OF RICHMOND AND PETERSBURG.

Grant now set his columns in motion to intercept Lee. General Ord, who had succeeded Butler in command of the Army of the James, crossed the James during the night of March 27 with one division of the Twenty-fifth Corps, two divisions of the Twenty-fourth Corps, and a division of cavalry, to occupy the left of Meade's line. Thus relieved, the Second and Fifth Corps started, on March 29, across Rowanty Creek and Hatcher's Run, striking the Confederates on the White Oak Road and quickly driving them back. Sheridan's entire cavalry corps had meanwhile reached Dinwiddie Court House, so that Grant's army line then extended from Dinwiddie to the Appomattox River, a distance of thirty-five miles. Ignorant that Grant's right was very weak, Lee prepared to meet the expected blow on his own right.

Considerable fighting occurred during the next two days, the Confederates being unable to break the Federal line, though they inflicted a heavy blow on the Fifth Corps. Sheridan had seized Five Forks, but Lee sent Pickett and Bushrod Johnson against him. They soon drove the Federal cavalry in confusion to Dinwiddie Court House, but were, after another severe fight, compelled to retreat in turn. Grant sent Warren to Sheridan's assistance, but the Fifth Corps was delayed at Gravelly Run by being compelled to rebuild the bridge, so it was long after midnight when Ayres, who had the advance, could cross and march for Dinwiddie. At daylight of April 1 Sheridan moved his entire force toward Five Forks, having been joined by Warren with his remaining divisions. By four o'clock in the afternoon the Fifth Corps was ready, the second and third divisions forming the front line, with the first in reserve. They were posted on the White

Oak Road and faced a strong line of Confederate breastworks concealed by a dense mass of young pines. Both Ayres and Crawford met a severe musketry fire, as their men pushed forward through the dense undergrowth, which cut down the leading ranks in a terrible way. Crawford obliqued to his right to gain a ridge, which movement created a gap between him and Ayres. Seeing this, Griffin rushed forward with the first division, and the entire corps made a headlong charge, seizing the salient point of the Confederate breastworks and capturing three thousand prisoners. As soon as Warren's artillery opened, the cavalry advanced, but met with a vigorous resistance, which temporarily threw them into confusion.

The engagement now became a general one, all along the opposing lines, Lee's men fighting with bitter and despairing courage. Warren rode to the front and gallantly led his men in a brilliant, heroic charge. The onslaught proved too much for the Confederates, for their line shook, and the Federals carried the works and captured fully one-half of Picketts' and Johnson's divisions. Warren had his horse shot under him, and escaped probably a fatal wound by the devotion of Colonel Richardson, who covered him, being severely wounded in the act. The Confederates, retreating in confusion, were pursued by Merritt's and McKenzie's horsemen, until they reached Lee's main line. The Confederates lost one thousand men killed and wounded, besides five thousand more who became prisoners. The Federals also captured eight pieces of artillery and fifteen regimental colors, losing less than one thousand men.

The battle being won, General Sheridan committed an act which has tarnished his reputation, for he relieved General Warren on the field and placed General George Griffin in command of the corps. His excuse was that Warren had been dilatory in his movement toward Dinwiddie. The records of history, however, show that General Warren did his whole duty.

The disaster at Five Forks was an awful blow to General Lee, for his right flank had been turned, placing a large force of Federal infantry in his rear. He saw that a retreat was the only course left open. Lee had about forty-five thousand men when Gordon made his despairing assault on Fort Steadman in March, the losses attending that desperate movement and at Five Forks reducing his strength to about thirty-eight thousand. Defeat and annihilation stared him in the face.

News of Sheridan's victory reached Grant at eight o'clock on the evening of April 1, and in less than an hour the entire artillery force in the trenches before Petersburg opened a tremendous cannonading, which continued until dawn of the following morning, Sunday. As the guns slackened in the rosy sunrise, the Ninth and Sixth Corps rushed forward. Parke carried the outer line before Petersburg, Wright swept over the Boydton Plank Road intrenchments, and Ord captured the Hatcher's Run breastworks, while Humphreys, Sheridan, and Griffin seized the South Side Railroad. On the other side of the James, Gibbons endeavored to take Forts Gregg and Alexander, but was repulsed by Longstreet with heavy loss. But the entire movement had so tightened the investing line around Petersburg that its evacuation could not be delayed any longer.

General Longstreet now joined Lee, and the Confederate army was massed. Sending Heth's division of A. P. Hill's corps to retake a part of the line captured by Parke's corps, a desperate battle took place, Parke succeeding in holding his position with the aid of the City Point garrison, which hurried up in the nick of time. During this movement General Ambrose Powell Hill rode forward, accompanied by an orderly. In a ravine he encountered a few Federal soldiers who fired, and Hill dropped dead from his saddle.

After Heth's repulse Lee telegraphed to Jefferson **Davis** that his lines were broken in three places, and suggested the evacuation of Richmond. The Confederate President

CITY OF PETERSBURG—VIEWS TAKEN APRIL, 1865, IMMEDIATELY AFTER CAPTURE.

received the message in church, and the minister announced from the pulpit that General Ewell desired the troops to assemble at three o'clock that afternoon. The President and his Cabinet, the members of the Confederate Congress, and the State Legislature had departed by nine o'clock that night, with many of the citizens. A dreadful scene of confusion ensued, the City Council ordered all spirituous liquors to be poured into the gutters, and a mob took possession of the city. At three o'clock on Monday morning General Ewell ordered all the warehouses to be set on fire, the flames soon leaping beyond control, until thirty squares were ablaze, consuming over one thousand buildings. The drunken mob liberated the penitentiary prisoners and set fire to the prison. A magazine that had been overlooked exploded with a fearful concussion, which increased the destruction and appalled the inhabitants, the air being rent soon after when two ironclads were blown up just below Richmond. After four long and weary years of bloody war the beautiful city of Richmond lay in ruins. General Weitzel took possession soon after sunrise with part of the Twenty-fourth Corps, and restored order, the Federal soldiers extinguishing the flames. One thousand prisoners, five thousand sick and wounded, five hundred siege and field guns, thirty locomotives, and three hundred railroad cars fell into the hands of the Federals.

At daylight of that memorable Monday morning Lee evacuated Petersburg, General Parke entering the city about nine o'clock, finding the streets almost deserted, for most of the inhabitants had moved away during the long and exhausting siege.

VIEW IN BURNT DISTRICT.

RUINS OF SHOT AND SHELL IN ARSENAL YARD.

RUINS OF MAYO'S BRIDGE.

RUINS OF GALLEGO FLOUR MILLS.

RUINS OF MAYO'S BRIDGE.

CITY OF RICHMOND, VA., AFTER CAPITULATION, APRIL, 1865.

CASTLE THUNDER

VIEWS ON JAMES RIVER.

VIEW FROM LIBBY HILL

GOVERNORS MANSION

LIBBY PRISON.

RESIDENCE OF JEFFERSON DAVIS.

VIEW OF JAMES RIVER FROM LIBBY HILL, LOOKING WEST.

VIEW FROM GAMBLE HILL.

RESIDENCE OF GEN. ROBERT E. LEE.

PONTOON BRIDGE ACROSS JAMES RIVER.

SURRENDER OF GENERAL LEE, 1865.

CHAPTER LXXIV.

THE FINAL SURRENDER OF THE CONFEDERATE ARMIES.

On leaving Petersburg Lee concentrated his shattered columns at Chesterfield Court House, and then marched to the west, intending to reach Burkesville, fifty-two miles from Petersburg. There he hoped to gain the Danville Railroad, burn the bridges, and join Joe Johnston. The General had ordered a quarter of a million of rations to be forwarded from Danville to Amelia Court House. When his army arrived there it was learned that the supply train had been ordered to Richmond, the officer in command obeying without unloading his supplies. This cruel blow, inflicted as it was by the Confederate government, was all the harder to bear, for it decided the fate of the Army of Northern Virginia.

The Federal pursuit was relentless. Sheridan's cavalry went to Jettersville, on the Danville Railroad, which placed him on Lee's line of retreat. The Second and Sixth Corps reached Jettersville on the morning of April 5, while General Ord moved on to Wilson's Station, and the Twenty-fourth Corps went to Burkesville. At Paine's Crossing General Davies' cavalry brigade captured and destroyed two hundred wagons, after defeating a body of Confederate horse and seizing their artillery.

General Meade returned the Fifth Corps to his army, leaving Sheridan to look after his cavalry corps. Meade was very ill at the time, but he remained at the head of his troops to prevent Sheridan being given the chief command. It would weary the reader to describe in detail the movements that followed, but mention must be made of an affair at Farmville, as it shows that the fighting was hard and bitter to the very end.

Desirous of destroying the bridges across the Appomattox River, General Ord sent forward two regiments and a cavalry squadron under General Thomas Read. Before he reached Farmville Read struck the advance of Lee's army, and was at once overwhelmed. Read's men fought desperately until their General was killed in a personal combat with General Dearing, when they broke in confusion. Dearing saved the bridges, and was intrenched when Ord came up with his corps.

Sheridan caught a Confederate supply train at Sailor's Creek, and, after a hot fight, captured four hundred wagons, sixteen cannon, and most of the guard. By this movement General Ewell's corps and a part of Pickett's division was separated from Lee's main force. The Sixth Corps arrived in time to see the burning wagons and Sheridan's troopers charging all around Ewell. The Confederates found themselves hemmed in, but for two hours this heroic remnant of a heroic army fought with the energy of despair, giving blow for blow, and tearing wide rents in General Wright's line. Finally the contest became so unequal that further resistance was madness, and six thousand men threw down their muskets and surrendered. General Ewell and four of his division and brigade commanders shared the fate of their men. The Federals lost one thousand men, killed and wounded; the Confederates nearly fifteen hundred.

General Humphreys and the Second Corps also captured a supply train and some artillery, following Lee's rear guard so closely as it crossed the Appomattox that the Confederates could not destroy the wagon bridge. The sufferings of the Army of Northern Virginia had now reached a stage when further endurance was impossible. Lee's generals consulted during the night of April 7, and advised their commander to surrender. The next day a correspondence was opened between Generals Grant and Lee.

Wherever the Federals struck the Confederate lines a fight occurred. General Barlow destroyed over one hundred wagons beyond Farmville, and Humphreys gave battle soon after. Miles' division made a bold attack, but was driven back, General Smyth being among the Federal killed. On the 8th of April Lee was completely surrounded, every avenue of escape being covered and guarded. Out of forty-five thousand men who were under arms in March, Lee now had about twenty-eight thousand left, his brave dead lying in heaps along the route of his awful retreat. Finally hemmed in at Appomattox Court House, Lee made one last effort, for he ordered Gordon to cut his way through the Federal cavalry. Weak as was Gordon's line, it was gaining ground when Ord came up and settled the question. Just as Sheridan's bugles were beginning their clamor for a charge General Gordon sent a flag of truce to General Custer, asking for an armistice. The two historic armies never more exchanged another shot.

In a heavy fog General Lee left his camp fire, where he had passed the night with Longstreet and Mahone. By preconcerted arrangement the Confederate general was met and conducted to the McLean house, in Appomattox Court House. Here he found General Grant awaiting him. The terms of surrender were that all officers and men were to be paroled, the officers retaining their swords and baggage. When the actual surrender took place, on April 12, there were only eight thousand men to pass through the painful ceremony of laying down their arms, the remaining eleven thousand having avoided the humiliation by throwing aside their muskets during the last hours of the retreat. Having signed the terms, General Lee returned to his men and bade them farewell. The scene that ensued was a most painful one. Thronging around the officer who had led them through so many campaigns, these Confederate veterans wept like children as they tried to reach his hand. Lee finally broke down, and saying, "Men, we have fought through the war together, I have done the best I could for you," he rode away a broken-hearted man.

On the night of April 14 President Lincoln was assassinated in Ford's Theatre,

Washington, by John Wilkes Booth, an actor and a Secessionist. The dreadful crime was a terrible ending to a terrible war, and though it was intended to avenge the South, Lincoln's murder roused so much sectional and political passion that the South suffered additional indignity. Booth was shot dead in a barn, twenty miles from Fredericksburg, and several persons, among them a woman—Mrs. Surratt—were executed as conspirators in the plot to kill Vice-President Johnson and Secretary Seward.

The news of Lee's surrender and Lincoln's assasination reached Sherman while his army was marching to join Grant. After some correspondence, General Joe Johnston surrendered on April 26, near Durham's Station, with thirty-five thousand men. The terms granted by Sherman were considered unwise, for it was not a formal surrender, and the National government refused to sanction the memorandum. Finally the terms

THE ASSASSINATION OF PRESIDENT LINCOLN.

were modified to conform with those formulated by Grant at Appomattox Court House. Wade Hampton escaped with his cavalry, but his command finally fell to pieces. General Taylor surrendered his Mississippi command at Citronella, Alabama, on May 4, and Admiral Thatcher surrendered his naval vessels in the Tombigbee River at the same time. President Davis was captured on May 10, and was kept a prisoner for some time at Fortress Monroe on the charge of treason, but was finally released without trial. Vice-President Stephens was also made prisoner, and passed several months in confinement at Fort Warren, Boston Harbor. On May 11 General Jefferson Thompson surrendered, with nearly eight thousand men, at Chalk Bluff, in Arkansas, but General Kirby Smith held out in Texas. A battle occurred on the Rio Grande, near Brazoo Santiago, on May 13, between a Federal force commanded by Colonel Theodore H. Barrett, and a strong body of Confederates under General Slaughter. It ended in a Federal victory, and then Kirby Smith abandoned his troops and escaped, leaving General Buckner to assume the command and surrender, as he had done at Fort Donelson when deserted by Floyd. The war finally ended on May 26, having lasted four years and forty-two days.

The statistics of this tremendous Civil War are both colossal and astounding. During the entire period of hostilities there were mustered into the service of the United States, as soldiers and sailors, of all ranks, two million eight hundred and ninety-six thousand five hundred and thirty-seven men; the Confederacy had one million six hundred and thirteen thousand two hundred and thirty-four—an aggregate of four million five hundred and nine thousand seven hundred and seventy-one combatants. There were killed in action seventy-three thousand four hundred and eighty-six Federals, and

FUNERAL CAR.

FUNERAL PROCESSION, PENNSYLVANIA AVE. WASHINGTON.

FUNERAL PROCESSION PENNSYLVANIA AVE. WASHINGTON.

FUNERAL PROCESSION PENNSYLVANIA AVE. WASHINGTON.

THE ASSASSINATION OF PRESIDENT LINCOLN.

fifty-nine thousand eight hundred and seventy-two Confederates. There were also forty-one thousand seven hundred and ninety-four Federals mortally wounded, who died within a few days after battle; the Confederates lost in the same way forty-two thousand seven hundred and eighteen men. Another item in the death-roll is eight thousand one hundred and eighteen Federals who lost their lives by accident on land and sea; the Confederate total from the same cause being six thousand and forty-one. On the Federal side there were fifteen thousand two hundred and seven men reported as missing who were never after accounted for, and must be reckoned among the killed; the Confederate loss in this way was sixteen thousand one hundred and eighty-four men. Appalling as are these figures, they are exceeded by the deaths from disease, induced by exposure, fatigue, and privation; for the Federals lost one hundred and eighty thousand three hundred and twenty-four men; the Confederates one hundred and thirty-eight thousand five hundred and sixteen. It will thus be seen that the distracted country sacrificed during forty-nine months five hundred and eighty-six thousand two hundred and sixty human

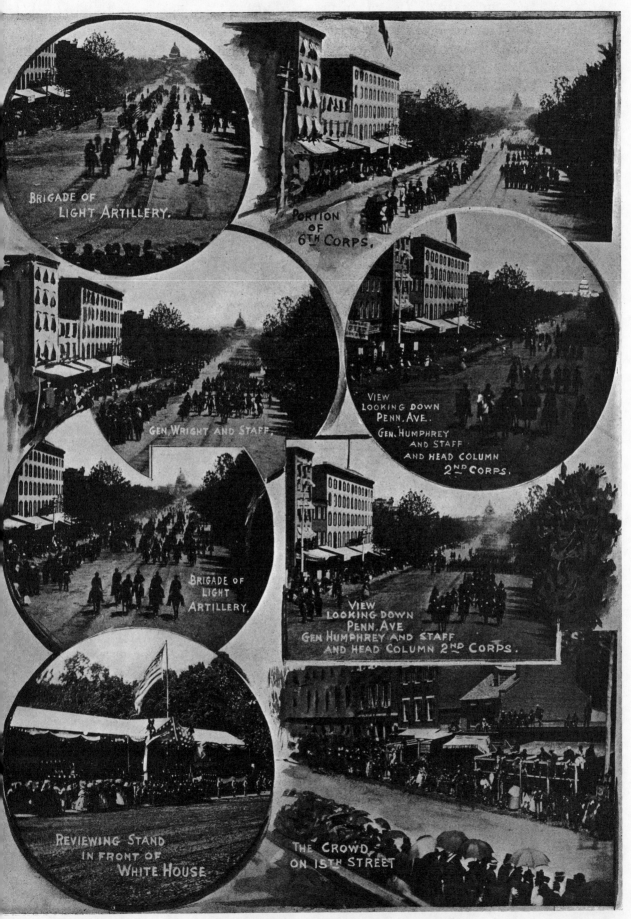

BRIGADE OF LIGHT ARTILLERY.

PORTION OF 6TH CORPS.

GEN. WRIGHT AND STAFF.

VIEW LOOKING DOWN PENN. AVE. GEN. HUMPHREY AND STAFF AND HEAD COLUMN 2ND CORPS.

BRIGADE OF LIGHT ARTILLERY.

VIEW LOOKING DOWN PENN. AVE GEN HUMPHREY AND STAFF AND HEAD COLUMN 2ND CORPS.

REVIEWING STAND IN FRONT OF WHITE HOUSE

THE CROWD ON 15TH STREET

GRAND REVIEW OF THE ARMY IN WASHINGTON, D. C., MAY, 1865.

lives, and there were fully six hundred thousand other men who were so badly crippled that they were unfit for the usual occupations of life.

The financial losses can be only approximately estimated. The expenses of the Federal government during the war were one million and a half of dollars a day, making a total of twenty-two hundred and twenty-five millions of dollars. Taking the Confederacy expenditures in equal ratio, and adding the value of public and private property

GRAND REVIEW OF THE ARMY IN WASHINGTON, D. C., MAY, 1865.

destroyed by the opposing armies, it is within bounds to say that the actual cost and losses of the war was over three thousand millions of dollars.

On May 22 and 23, 1865, the troops under Meade and Sherman marched through Washington and were reviewed by President Johnson. By November of that year only a few thousand of the State Volunteer soldiers remained in service, the rest quietly re-entering the pursuits of peace. The war being finally at an end, and the institution of slavery forever abolished, the nation entered on an era of such prosperity as has since made it the wonder of the civilized world.

THE END.

INDEX.